The Hound of Conscience

A HISTORY OF THE

NO-CONSCRIPTION

FELLOWSHIP

1914–1919

THOMAS C. KENNEDY

THE UNIVERSITY OF
ARKANSAS PRESS
FAYETTEVILLE, 1981

Library of Congress Cataloging in Publication Data

Kennedy, Thomas Cummins, 1937–
The Hound of Conscience.

    Bibliography: p. 303
    Includes index.
    1. No-Conscription Fellowship—History.
2. Military service, Compulsory—Great Britain—
History—20th century. 3. European War, 1914–1918—
Conscientious objectors—Great Britain. I. Title.
UB342.G7K46   355.2′24′06041   80-39677
ISBN 0-938626-01-9   AACR1

Jacket photograph reprinted by permission of the British Library.

Bertrand Russell's letter to Edith Ellis (11 September 1917), quoted in Chapter 10 and other unpublished material from the Bertrand Russell Archives © Res-Lib 1981.

Materials from the Public Record Office are under Crown Copyright.

Materials from the House of Lords Record Office reproduced by permission of the Clerk of the Records.

Quotation from the Haldane Papers reprinted by permission of The Trustees of the National Library of Scotland.

Parts of this book have previously appeared in *Russell*, the *Journal of British Studies*, and *Quaker History* and are used here with permission.

For the two
great women in my life,
Mary Adlyn and Mary Lynn

Preface

Over twenty years ago Lord Blake, in his biography of Andrew Bonar Law, *The Unknown Prime Minister,* noted that the "question of conscription would indeed be a tedious topic to pursue through all its ramifications. The endless discussions, the attitudes taken by public men at various times, the compromises, the disputes, constitute a chapter in English history to which no doubt in years to come dull history professors will direct their duller research students." What follows is a study of one aspect of the conscription question that I have pursued, tediously perhaps, for over a decade. I must confess that throughout that time I have found the subject fascinating not only because of the individuals involved but also because it seemed to encompass so much that is of significance to the British experience in the twentieth century. If what I have finally produced is indeed dull or, worse, mistaken in accuracy or judgment, then I must bear sole responsibility. I had been warned.

In fact, many other studies of the ramifications of conscription during the Great War have preceded this one, the first being John W. Graham's *Conscription and Conscience* (1922), the latest Keith Robbins's *The Abolition of War* (1976), and the best John Rae's *Conscience and Politics* (1970). None of these, however, does justice to the largest and most effective antiwar–anticonscription movement in modern British history, the No-Conscription Fellowship (NCF). "It is still difficult to separate facts about the N.-C.F. from fiction; legend and propaganda from brutal truths; or to assess what the organization actually achieved."[1] This study of the NCF is, first and foremost, concerned with the question of dissent and liberty of conscience in a liberal society at war, both in the sense of the war resisters' conception of what should be permitted and of the government's view of what could be tolerated. The British peace movement during the First World War was a product of diverse elements—Liberal, Radical, Christian, socialist—that the NCF attempted to blend into a united anticonscription–antiwar movement.

1. Ronald W. Clark, *The Life of Bertrand Russell* (New York, 1976), p. 273.

The organization that emerged somehow survived public hostility, official harassment, and, perhaps most damaging of all, hair-splitting factionalism; and, though gravely weakened by its wartime struggle, the NCF continued into the postwar period long enough to point up both the possibilities and difficulties that faced pacifists and peace advocates in the 1920s and 1930s.

For whatever has emerged from the time I have spent in research and writing, I am deeply indebted to a very large number of people and to the institutions that some of them represent. The late Lady Marjory Allen, widow of Clifford Allen, and Martin Gilbert, fellow of Merton College, Oxford, encouraged the project when I first undertook it and offered numerous helpful suggestions as did Benjamin Sacks. Charles Coolidge, Richard Rempel, Gordon McNeil, and Cameron Hazlehurst have read the manuscript at various stages of its development; each has given invaluable advice and saved me from many embarrassing errors. Those that remain are of my own making.

The staff of the University of South Carolina libraries was unfailingly helpful. Kenneth Blackwell, archivist of the Bertrand Russell Archives, offered his knowledge, his cooperation, and his friendship, all of which were (and are) invaluable. I am also most grateful for the quiet, patient expertise of Edward Milligan, Malcolm Thomas, and the entire staff of the Friends House Library who surely reflect the best tradition of the Quaker spirit as does Ms. Ardith Emmons, former curator of the Swarthmore College Peace Collection. Another good and generous Friend is Jo Vellacott of Acadia University, Wolfville, Nova Scotia, who opened her home to me, shared much of what she knew on the subject, allowed me to see her microfilm copies of the Catherine E. Marshall Papers, and, in the meantime, became an esteemed and inspiring friend and colleague to whom I shall always be indebted. (Her work cited herein was published under the name Jo V. Newberry.) Finally, I must thank Horace G. Alexander, an original member of the Friends Service Committee, who has provided me with valuable information and has also shown a generous tolerance, even when he disagreed with my interpretations.

Others whose aid I must acknowledge, however briefly, include James S. Chase, Timothy P. Donovan, and Willard

B. Gatewood, Jr., chairmen and colleagues at Arkansas who never flagged in supporting my work; Richard Reed and Joan Roberts of Mullins Library at the University of Arkansas; Robert Ochs, Brian O'Farrell, Ashley Brown, and John Rae, headmaster, Westminster School, have provided aid on both sides of the Atlantic. William Igo of the Beaverbrook Library, Peter Boyden of the National Army Museum, the keeper of Western MSS., Bodleian Library, and the staffs of the British Museum, Imperial War Museum, National Library of Scotland, and the Public Record Office have all contributed to this study.

Suzanne Stoner-Williams coordinated the final, frenzied production of the manuscript and proofread the finished product. Kathy Bundy typed the last draft with amazing speed and accuracy; Jamie Freeman-Lax aided in a variety of ways. I am grateful to each of them for their patience and good humor despite the problems that inevitably arose. Miller Williams also remained undaunted in a sea of troubles, and his calm professionalism made him an invaluable editor.

Finally, I must give special thanks to some very special friends who helped me in a variety of ways: to Ellen Shipley, who proofread the manuscript; to Jim Whitehead, whose passion for good prose inspired me; and, most of all, to my wife who corrected, proofread, and typed the manuscript at least four times; encouraged me when I was despondent; and always waited up for me after those long nights at the library.

T. C. K.
Fayetteville, Arkansas
September 1980

Contents

Abbreviations

BRA — Bertrand Russell Archives, Mills Memorial Library, McMaster University, Hamilton, Ontario

CAB — Cabinet Papers, with series numbers, Public Record Office, London

CAP — Clifford Allen Papers, McKissick Memorial Library, University of South Carolina, Columbia, South Carolina

CEMP — Catherine E. Marshall Papers, Cumberland County Record Office, the Castle, Carlisle

COIB — Conscientious Objectors Information Bureau

FHL — Friends House Library, Friends House, London

FOR — Fellowship of Reconciliation

FSC — Friends Service Committee

HO — Home Office Papers, Public Record Office, London

LGB — Local Government Board Papers

MH — Ministry of Health Papers, Public Record Office, London

NCF — No-Conscription Fellowship

NIA — *The Nation in Arms*

NSJ — *The National Service Journal*

NSL — National Service League

PRO — Public Record Office, London

SCPC — Swarthmore College Peace Collection, Swarthmore, Pennsylvania

Trib. — *The Tribunal*

UDC — Union of Democratic Control

WO — War Office Papers, Public Record Office, London

Parliamentary Debates have been abbreviated as follows: series, House of Commons (H.C.) or House of Lords (H.L.), volume, column, and date; for example, 5 H.C., 86:716, 13 December 1915.

1

The Roots of Resistance

Press Gang or Patriotism

When Sir John Simon rose in the House of Commons on 5 January 1916 to speak against a newly proposed conscription bill, he pictured voluntary service as the "real heritage of the English people."[1] No doubt Simon saw compulsory military service as a threat to those precious liberties that had raised British citizens to a higher moral plane than that occupied by their less-fortunate Continental neighbors. But, however accurately Simon's remarks reflected the tenets of nineteenth-century liberalism, they stood on shaky historical ground.

Britain's rejection of enforced military service was manifestly Victorian in origin. Recent scholarship has confirmed the assertion of older historians such as William Stubbs and Frederic Maitland that English citizens from the Anglo-Saxon period through the Middle Ages had frequently been compelled to serve. By shrieval summon, commission of array, mustering statute, militia ballot, and impressment, Englishmen of all ages and classes had been called—willingly or otherwise—to fight for king and country at home and abroad.[2] The victories at Crécy, Poitiers, and Agincourt were all won with the aid of longbowmen forced into service. During the English Civil War a substantial portion of the parliamentary forces, including over half of Oliver Cromwell's New Model Army, was made up of men impressed by county committees. Impressment for the army was abolished after the Restoration, but the enforced enlistment of vagrants remained legal for another century and a half.[3]

1. 5 H.C., 87:974, 5 January 1916.
2. For example, see William Stubbs, *Constitutional History of England*, 3 vols. (Oxford, 1889), 3:286n.
3. For useful recent discussions of enforced military service from the medieval period to the early nineteenth century, see Michael Powicke, *Mili-*

1

2 / **The Hound of Conscience**

Under the Militia Ballot Act of 1757 and under numerous other related statutes passed during the Napoleonic Wars, counties and parishes were made liable for providing recruits. Quotas were generally drawn by lot from among the able-bodied men in the county, and service was obligatory. Substitutes could be purchased, however, and most often these substitutes actually served in the ranks. A survey of the 43,492 men raised by ballot in 1803 indicated that nearly 95 percent of them were substitutes.[4] Thus, while it is technically true that conscripted men helped to hold the squares at Waterloo and that impressed sailors had handled Nelson's guns at the battle of Trafalgar, such compulsion was neither an impartial nor an efficient means of raising men.[5]

During the century after Waterloo, the only hint of compulsion was a militia ballot held in 1831 as a panicky response to the disorders springing from the agitation for parliamentary reform. The ballot was not used during the Crimean War, and in 1865 Parliament removed the last lingering dregs of compulsion with a law suspending the militia ballot altogether. This suspensory act was renewed yearly until the outbreak of World War I.[6] The rejection of enforced military service in the nineteenth century was certainly in keeping with the tenor of the times. Free trade and individual liberty, "the pacifist prophecies of the Manchester School," set the tone for an era of strong feelings against conscription.[7] The novelist Anthony Trollope caught the

tary Obligations in Medieval England (Oxford, 1962); Stephen J. Stearns, "Conscription and English Society in the 1620's," Journal of British Studies 11 (May 1972):1–23; and J. R. Western, The English Militia in the Eighteenth Century (London, 1965). Works written early in the twentieth century that support proconscriptionist views by citing historical precedents include G. G. Coulton, The Case for Compulsory Military Service (London, 1917), and George F. Shee, The Briton's First Duty: The Case for Conscription (London, 1901).

4. Coulton, Compulsory Service, p. 107; F. C. Hearnshaw, "Compulsory Military Service in England," Quarterly Review 225 (April 1916):429–30; Joseph A. Rice, If Conscription Comes (Dublin, 1914), p. 6; and Elie Halévy, England in 1815 (London, 1960), pp. 52, 69–70.

5. Shee, Briton's First Duty, p. 98, and Coulton, Compulsory Service, pp. 107, 125.

6. Rice, If Conscription Comes, pp. 7–8, 11–12; Denis Hayes, Conscription Conflict (London, 1949), p. 170; and Coulton, Compulsory Service, p. 125.

7. See Peter Brock, Twentieth-Century Pacifism (New York, 1970), p. 9;

prevailing mood in a letter to an American friend during the American Civil War:

> This conscription is very bad. Was it absolutely necessary? My feeling is that a man should die rather than be a soldier against his will. One's country has no right to demand everything. There is much that is higher and better and greater than one's country.... If a country cannot get along without a military conscription, it had better give up—and let its children seek other ties.[8]

Trollope and the great majority of his fellow Victorians saw such anticonscription views as a glory of triumphant liberalism.[9] They were not pacifists; they were libertarians. They were not opposed to war but to the idea of being compelled to fight in one. There were pacifist elements that rejected war completely, but they were a distinct minority. Most Englishmen were not averse to a good scrap. Though the regular army was not well thought of in peacetime, recent scholarship has revealed that the volunteer force, created in 1859, enjoyed wide popularity.[10]

The vast majority of England's nineteenth-century wars, especially those after 1870, were made to order for a public that did not have to fight them. They were characterized by the elements of romantic heroism, the stuff of Kipling, Henty, and Rider Haggard: exciting adventures in faraway lands, dashing cavalry charges against savage hordes, and mercifully short casualty lists, chiefly confined to the lowest

---

Willis H. Hall, *Quaker International Work in Europe since 1914* (Savoy, 1938), p. 47; and George Bernard Shaw, *What I Really Wrote about the War* (London, 1931), p. 213.

8. Trollope to Kate Field, 23 August 1862, in Bradford A. Booth, ed., *The Letters of Anthony Trollope* (London, 1951), pp. 117–18. Also see Michael Sadleir, *Trollope, a Commentary* (London, 1947), pp. 227–28.

9. Negative attitudes toward conscription were not universal among Victorians; see Matthew Arnold, *Culture and Anarchy* (Cambridge, 1963), pp. 75–76, and Hugh Elliot, ed., *Letters of J. S. Mill*, 2 vols. (London, 1910), 2:267, 291, 303–4. Also see John Stuart Mill, *On Liberty* (London, 1859), p. 24.

10. Hugh Cunningham, *The Volunteer Force: A Social and Political History, 1859–1908* (Hamden, Conn., 1975), chap. 5. Also see Anne Summers, "Militarism in Britain before the Great War," *History Workshop* 2 (Autumn 1976):106–7, and Olive Anderson, "The Growth of Christian Militarism in Mid-Victorian Britain," *The English Historical Review* 86 (January 1971):46–72.

classes of society. If an occasional disaster like the massacre at Isandhlwana or the fall of Khartoum marred a slate of consistent victories, there was always Wolseley or Buller or "Bobs" to avenge the fallen martyrs and to continue the illustrious spectacle of bringing civilization to the benighted savage. For the average nobody, for Mr. Pooter and his neighbors,[11] the chief expression of imperialism was sharing in the reflected glory of countless small campaigns against Zulus, dervishes, and Afghans. A good war was not unlike a good football match—something to be enjoyed, briefly discussed, and then forgotten until it could be compared to the next one. Then, in the last year of the nineteenth century, Britain faced a challenge not only to Victorian complacency but to the voluntary principle as well. By any criterion, the war in South Africa was a sobering and humiliating experience. After the shattering defeats of "Black Week," no one could ignore the British army's inadequacy against a well-armed European foe.[12] The national trauma created by this military insufficiency was made even more acute by the worldwide condemnation of "John Bully's" blundering attempts to subdue the tiny Boer republics. As one peer noted in the House of Lords on 27 July 1900: "Never was there so unfriendly a feeling all over Europe towards this country as there is now." Others pointed with alarm to alleged German feints toward forming a "continental league" against the temporarily defenseless British Empire.[13]

The exigencies of war thus caused a number of politicians to make somber connections between Britain's military weakness and her "splendid isolation" and to conclude that one of the most significant factors isolating Britain was its dependence on a volunteer army.[14] Some cabinet ministers

---

11. See George and W. Grossmith, *The Diary of a Nobody* (London, 1965).

12. Arthur Balfour admitted to the House of Commons that for a brief time in early 1900 only thirty-three hundred rounds of small-arms ammunition were available for the home forces; 4 H.C., 94:382–83, 16 May 1901. Also see 4 H.C., 146:67–68, 11 May 1905.

13. 4 H.L., 86:1476–77, 27 July 1900. For the "continental league," see A. J. P. Taylor, *The Struggle for the Mastery of Europe* (Oxford, 1954), pp. 385–90, 401–2; Ulrich Kroll, *Die Internationale Bureau-Agitation, 1899–1902* (Münster, 1973), deals with international attacks on British policy in South Africa.

14. 4 H.L., 78:31, 30 January 1900. Also see Christopher Howard, *Splendid Isolation* (London, 1967), p. 72.

apparently gave serious, if very brief, consideration to ending this deficiency. During the debate on army estimates in 1901, St. John Brodrick, the secretary of state for war, announced: "My adhesion to the Voluntary principle... is strictly limited to our ability to obtain under it a force with which our military authorities can satisfy the Government that they have sufficient force to resist invasion."[15] Such pronouncements apparently aroused anticonscriptionist suspicions to the point that Lord Lansdowne found it expedient to state that the government did not "contemplate compulsion for service beyond the seas as a possible solution of our recruiting difficulties."[16] But Lansdowne's denial had been preceded by a spate of proconscription articles in leading journals.[17] The opening round of the debate on compulsory military service closely coincided with the beginning of the new century, to which French historian Hippolyte Taine had already issued a sinister warning: "Universal conscript military service, with its twin brother universal suffrage, has mastered all Continental Europe—with what promises of massacre and bankruptcy for the 20th century."[18]

Militarism and Antimilitarism in Edwardian Britain

The beginning of the Edwardian age found Britain recovering from the shock of the Boer War. Although the nation could relinquish its distaste for the Boers rapidly enough to

15. 4 H.C., 90:1060, 9 March 1901. Also see Brodrick to Salisbury, 20 January 1901, cited by Lowell J. Satre, "St. John Brodrick and Army Reform, 1901–1902," *Journal of British Studies* 15/2 (Spring 1976):129.
16. 4 H.L., 96:215, 28 June 1901. Lansdowne was responding to a speech by Lord Monkswell, 202–8.
17. For articles in favor of the militia ballot, see Sidney Low, "The Military Weakness of England and the Militia Ballot," *Nineteenth Century* 47 (March 1900):365–77; Henry Birchenough, "Our Last Effort for a Voluntary Army," *Nineteenth Century* 49 (April 1901):545–55; Sir George Sydenham Clarke, "The Defense of the Empire and the Militia Ballot," *Nineteenth Century* 47 (January 1900):2–13; and "Home Defense," *Blackwood's Magazine* 173 (June 1903):257–66.
18. From *Les origines de la France contemporaine*, quoted by Bernard Semmel, *Imperialism and Social Reform: English Social-Imperial Thought, 1895–1914* (London, 1960), p. 208. Also see V. G. Kiernan, "Conscription and Society in Europe before the War of 1914–1918," in *War and Society*, ed. M. R. D. Foot (New York, 1973), pp. 141–58.

hand them back effective control of South Africa in less than a decade, some consequences of the unsavory conflict lingered on. Certainly the Boer War had a decisive influence on the public's view of the military, as well as on the attitudes of soldiers and strategists. Historians of the period have called attention to a "tremendous upsurge of interest in things military" and to an increasing "tolerance for military values."[19] This phenomenon was not, as Richard Price has illustrated,[20] an aspect of working-class jingoism. Rather, it arose from a predominantly middle-class and lower-middle-class sense of menace about external threats and internal decay. The former endangered the security of the empire and perhaps even that of the home islands, while the latter weakened the moral and physical fiber of the nation and invited exploitation by revolutionary socialists, often of foreign extraction.[21]

This uncharacteristic support for the military establishment did not go unchallenged. Increased tolerance for military ideals was met by antimilitarist oppositon that was larger than ever before. The conflict between these differing visions of how to bring stability and security to an uncertain society is an important aspect of the turbulent years before 1914. Although the debate about the efficacy of military values and military solutions took place largely outside regular government and party channels, it was prominently featured in the printed media and was widely discussed in public gatherings and other popular forums. Sometimes the contest became so spirited that the government was reluctantly drawn in, either to defend its military policy or to repudiate charges made by its critics who, at one time or another, included both proconscriptionists and an-

19. Summers, "Militarism in Britain," p. 111, and John Springhall, *Youth, Empire and Society: British Youth Movements, 1883-1940* (London, 1977), p. 18; Zara S. Steiner, *Britain and the Origins of the First World War* (New York, 1977), p. 155, makes the same point. The theme of militarism in Edwardian society was introduced by Caroline E. Playne, *The Pre-War Mind in Britain* (London, 1929).

20. *An Imperial War and the British Working Class* (London, 1972), pp. 233-41. Also see Price's essay, "Society Status and Jingoism: The Social Roots of Lower Middle Class Patriotism, 1870-1900," in *The Lower Middle Class in Britain,* ed. Geoffrey Crossick (New York, 1977), pp. 89-112.

21. Springhall, *Youth, Empire and Society*, pp. 14-18, and Summers, "Militarism in Britain," pp. 111-12.

timilitarists. Thus, it seems fitting to outline briefly the major developments in official military policy during the period.

In the aftermath of the Boer War, the pressure of public criticism forced the Unionist government of Prime Minister Arthur Balfour to appoint a number of royal commissions to investigate the reasons for past failures and to recommend measures for future improvement. The results of this process were a series of unflattering reports about the condition of the British army and some politically unpalatable suggestions about remedies for it. For example, one commission, headed by Lord Elgin, that studied preparations for the war and for its conduct recommended the development of a more comprehensive reserve army for home defense that could also be counted on, in an emergency, to support imperial commitments. The report hinted that this reserve force could only be created by compulsory means.[22] The duke of Norfolk chaired a second commission that investigated the volunteer and militia forces that comprised Britain's reserve army. This committee was more plainspoken, concluding that even a semblance of military equality with Britain's Continental neighbors depended on the building of a home defense army whose size could only be attained on the basis of conscription.[23]

What the Balfour government had expected to hear from these royal commissions is not fully clear, but it is obvious that what they did hear did not please them. The idea of compulsory military service, especially in peacetime, was politically unthinkable even for a Conservative administration. Therefore, Unionist military reforms proceeded along more modest and tactful lines. But while Balfour's government was partially successful in reorganizing and revitalizing the military bureaucracy in accordance with the recommendations of the Esher committee, attempts to restructure

---

22. Report of the Royal [Elgin] Commission to inquire into the military preparations and other matters connected with the war in South Africa (Cd. 1789, 1903) 40, 1904. *The Times*, 26 August 1903, contains a convenient summary of the Elgin commission report.

23. Report of the Royal [Norfolk] Commission on the militia and volunteers (Cd. 2061, 1904) 30, and *The Times*, 29 May 1904. For ministerial reactions to this report, see "Remarks on Report of R. C. on Militia and Volunteers," 30 May 1904, CAB 37/71/73.

the army itself faltered badly under two secretaries of state for war, Brodrick and H. O. Arnold-Forster.[24]

The first workable scheme for army reform was introduced by Richard Burdon Haldane, Liberal war minister from 1906 to 1910. Besides assigning the bulk of the regular British army to a highly mobile expeditionary force to be used as needed overseas, Haldane's reform plan created an enlarged reserve army through the consolidation and expansion of existing militia and volunteer units. By the provisions of the Territorial and Reserve Forces Act of 1907, young men eighteen to twenty-four were encouraged—not compelled—to join the so-called territorial force and to undergo annual training periods of about two weeks for four years. Haldane thus hoped to build a large, partially trained reserve force without involving Great Britain in the expense and controversy of compulsory service.[25] The plan was successful to the extent that it created a larger, better-organized, better-administered reserve, but historians have begun to question whether Haldane deserves all the credit he has traditionally received for his accomplishments at the War Office.[26]

After 1907 the territorial force was increasingly troubled by questions about its mission in Britain's defense scheme. Originally the primary objective of the territorials was to provide support—with six months' training *after* the onset of an emergency—for the overseas commitments of the regular army. In the years before 1914, however, political necessity forced the government to deemphasize this role and to picture the territorial force chiefly as a home defense army. But, as critics were quick to point out, if the "Terries"

24. Report of the [Esher] Committee on the reconstitution of the War Office (Cd. 1932, 1904), 8. The Brodrick and Arnold-Forster schemes are well presented by Satre, "St. John Brodrick and Army Reforms," pp. 117–39, and Albert Tucker, "The Issue of Army Reform in the Unionist Government, 1903–05," *Historical Journal* 9 (1966):90–100. Also see W. S. Hamer, *The British Army: Civil-Military Relations, 1885–1905* (Oxford, 1970), chaps. 6 and 7.

25. Haldane discusses his scheme in *An Autobiography* (New York, 1929), pp. 192–208, and *Before the War* (New York, 1920), pp. 156ff. Also see Michael Howard's analysis of the territorial army in *Studies in War and Peace* (New York, 1971), pp. 83–98, and Elie Halévy, *The Rule of Democracy, 1905–1914* (New York, 1961), pp. 148–86.

26. See Cunningham, *Volunteer Force*, pp. 140–49.

needed six months' training before engaging an enemy, they were scarcely competent to defend Britain's shores from invasion.

The public debate over the role of the territorial force reflected the importance that military matters had attained in Edwardian society. Less apparent but even more significant was the controversy within the political and military establishment concerning the disposition of the expeditionary force. During the nineteenth century, the regular army had been used chiefly to bolster the defenses of a far-flung empire, especially in India, while the navy—the more important and influential service—protected trade routes and guarded the home islands. In the period following the Boer War, however, there was a virtual revolution in British military thinking that was acquiesced in by the leaders of both major political parties.[27] After 1905 strategic planning was dominated by men who conceived of intervention on behalf of France in a Continental war against Germany as the major function of the British regular army. The Continentalists and Germanophobes won a signal victory over the navalists of the "Blue Water" school; the new breed of "thinking" soldiers vastly increased their influence at the expense of the Admiralty. Of course, as long as Britain maintained only its small professional volunteer army, their ideas could only be carried out by subordinating British actions to French needs. Most soldiers were willing to pay this price in exchange for independence from the navy, but the ultimate dream of many of them was some form of conscription that was, in the words of the most ambitious, intriguing, and ubiquitous soldier of all, Henry Wilson, the only thing "of any *real* use" in the "saving of the Empire."[28]

Wilson and his allies did not get conscription before 1914,

27. See Michael Howard, *The Continental Commitment* (London, 1972), chap. 2; John McDermott, "The Revolution in British Military Thinking from the Boer War to the Moroccan Crisis," *Canadian Journal of History* 9 (August 1974):159–77; and J. E. Tyler, *The British Army and the Continent, 1904–1914* (London, 1938).

28. Diary entries, 15 September and 10 October 1905, 5 March 1906, 3 November 1909, 15 and 29 May and 3 June 1912, Henry Wilson Papers, Imperial War Museum, London. Nicholas d'Ombrain, *War Machinery and High Policy: Defense Administration in Peacetime Britain, 1902–1914* (London, 1973), pp. 141–51, provides an excellent analysis of the post–Boer War "thinking" army.

for which they blamed politicians, especially Liberal politicians, most severely. It is perhaps in the nature of things for military leaders to be perpetually dissatisfied with political decisions involving military affairs because such decisions are based on more than simply military considerations. An ironic aspect of civil-military relations during the Edwardian period was the fact that, while British soldiers were more successful than ever before at implementing their desires, they were even less satisfied with the results.

In any case, military matters, though not of course the nature of Britain's commitment to France, came more and more to the fore in Edwardian society. As they did so, the single most important unofficial manifestation of militarist ideals was the campaign on behalf of compulsory military training conducted by the National Service League (NSL).

In February 1902 Lord Newton and a few friends, humiliated and outraged by the South African debacle, formed the NSL and called on the government "to abandon make-shifts and to face the duty of national defence seriously, manfully and honestly" by creating a nation in arms.[29] The original inspiration for the league was a small book, *The Briton's First Duty* (1901), in which George F. Shee, a self-styled liberal imperialist, had presented the case for universal military training for home defense. Shee was enlisted as secretary and editor of the league's newspaper, the *National Service Journal,* and the NSL began to solicit memberships. Early results were not encouraging. Despite a number of prominent recruits, including Adm. Lord Charles Beresford; the bishop of Exeter; the dukes of Argyll, Westminster, and Wellington; the poet laureate (Alfred Austin); and Rudyard Kipling, the league failed to elicit significant public response and by the end of 1904 had fewer than two thousand members.[30]

During the next year, the NSL was rescued from this slough of despond by Alfred Lord Milner, lately returned from his South African consulship. Milner not only gave the NSL the benefit of his administrative talent, which, accord-

29. Statement issued by the duke of Wellington, first president of the NSL, quoted in *NIA,* n.s., 2 (May 1907):122. Also see *The Times,* 6 March 1902; Lord Newton, *Retrospection* (London, 1941), pp. 115–16; and Hayes, *Conscription Conflict,* pp. 36–39. Hayes provides the most complete study of the NSL to date.

30. Membership figures from *NSJ* 1 (October 1904):212.

ing to Alfred Gollin, "saved the organisation of the League on more than one occasion,"[31] but he also played John the Baptist to the NSL's messiah, Field Marshal Frederick Sleigh Roberts, earl of Kandahar, hero of the Boer War, and a recent convert to the cause of universal military service. Lord Roberts resigned from the Committee of Imperial Defense when it refused to consider his personal plan for compulsory training and, at age seventy-three, devoted the last decade of his life to the NSL's cause. As president of the NSL, "Bobs" brought with him the popularity befitting a great war hero as well as a reputation for selflessness and sincerity of purpose. Under his leadership the league prospered famously, more than doubling its membership in four successive years. By December 1909 the NSL claimed forty-three thousand regular members in addition to seventy thousand "adherents" in more than fifty branches throughout the country.[32]

The NSL's followers were largely middle- and lower-middle-class, satisfied, or upwardly mobile people to whom concepts like patriotism and empire were truly meaningful. League efforts to recruit workers by offering reduced membership fees or by sponsoring prize contests for "genuine" working-class people bore little fruit.[33] This lack of success has been ascribed to "the persistent British working class tradition of resistance to any form of organized militarism" or to the fact that imperialism and its results were largely irrelevant to working-class life.[34] But even though the NSL was never a mass movement, it was a popular, dynamic, and effective body that, it has been asserted, "permeated the social life of England" to a greater extent than any other Edwardian pressure group.[35]

Undoubtedly one important reason for the league's popu-

31. Alfred Gollin, *Proconsul in Politics: A Study of Lord Milner in Opposition and in Power* (New York, 1964), pp. 188–89.

32. Figures quoted in *NIA*, n.s., 5 (January 1910):1.

33. For example, see *NSJ* 1 (February 1904):64.

34. J. O. Springhall, "The Boy Scouts, Class and Militarism in Relation to British Youth Movements, 1908–1930," *International Review of Social History* 16 (1971–pt. 2):141, and Price, *Imperial War*, pp. 239–41. Also see Steiner, *Origins of the First World War*, pp. 161–62, and Stephen Reynolds, *Seems So: A Working Class View of Politics* (London, 1911).

35. Playne, *Pre-War Mind*, p. 147. Springhall apparently accepts this view for he reproduces it nearly word for word in "Boy Scouts, Class and Militarism," p. 156n.

This poster was part of the National Service League's campaign for universal military training. (Courtesy National Army Museum)

larity was the apparent moderation of its proposals. Roberts had assumed the presidency of the NSL with the express understanding that the league would disavow conscription of the Continental variety. What he wanted, Roberts said, was "national service" under a system of compulsory training for home defense. The league offered, at various times, a somewhat dizzying array of plans concerning the structure, training, and length of service for its projected "nation in arms," but above all it retained the Swiss militia as a model for fear of antagonizing would-be supporters with anything less democratic. Roberts consistently maintained that the league's program implied only that every able-bodied man had sufficient patriotism to help defend his country from invasion and enough common sense to realize that patriotism had need of discipline.[36]

Despite such advertisements of moderation, the NSL represented more than middle-class patriotic enthusiasm. Its most influential, if not most popular, leaders—Milner, Wilson, Leopold Amery, Leo Maxse, and F. S. Oliver[37]—were the embodiment of what Paul Guinn has called "the new dynamic imperialist view of an authoritarian Empire administered with impartial efficiency by an *elite* military service and civil bureaucracy."[38] For the league's true believers, compulsory military service was not just a means of defending Britain's shores but a genuine panacea. Its adoption, they believed, would symbolize a determination to begin dealing with that host of national ills to which the failures of liberalism had left the nation heir. From the deterioration of the national physique that brought on moral slackness and industrial inefficiency to the rottenness of urban society that robbed an ignorant democracy of decent homes, decent schools, and a decent respect, and from the selfishness of

36. See *Lord Roberts' Message to the Nation* (London, 1912), pp. 3, 3n, and his remarks to the NSL annual dinner as reported in *The Times,* 25 June 1908. Also see Summers, "Militarism in Britain," pp. 114–15.

37. As a serving officer Wilson could not publicly advocate the NSL's cause, but his diaries reveal his key role as an adviser to Lord Roberts and as a confidant of Milner and later even of Conservative leader Andrew Bonar Law.

38. Paul Guinn, *British Strategy and Politics, 1914–18* (Oxford, 1965), p. 2. Also see Max Beloff, *Imperial Sunset,* vol. 1, *Britain's Liberal Empire, 1897–1921* (New York, 1970), pp. 130–31, and Robert J. Scally, *The Origins of the Lloyd George Coalition* (Princeton, 1975), pp. 132, 136.

laissez-faire that weakened the national spirit, to the foolishness of party politics that enfeebled the national defense, the NSL excoriated every complacent, optimistic assumption that sirenlike beckoned the British Empire toward moral disintegration and race suicide.

For public consumption, the NSL fixed on the possibility of foreign invasion of the British Isles as the most persuasive rationale for the immediate introduction of compulsion.[39] In 1908, to illustrate the danger of invasion, Roberts and a group of associates, including Charles à Court Repington, military correspondent of *The Times,* persuaded the Liberal government to appoint a subcommittee to the Committee of Imperial Defense to investigate the possibilities for a successful seaborne invasion of the British Isles. Roberts and his friends claimed to have evidence showing that past assessments of the improbability of invasion (the last of which had been completed under Roberts's own direction in 1903) were dangerously obsolete, given the emergence of German sea power. After months of hearings, however, this subcommittee concluded that large-scale foreign invasion was highly unlikely and that, even in the absence of the expeditionary force, smaller raids could easily be handled by the remaining regular army in conjunction with the territorial force.[40]

Although this conclusion disappointed and angered NSL leaders, they might have claimed partial success: there is no doubt the league's invasion propaganda made a significant

39. L. S. Amery, *My Political Life,* , vol. 1, *England before the Storm, 1896–1914* (London, 1953), p. 215, notes that the NSL had to settle for a Swiss-type system in public propaganda and thus was "obliged to put in the forefront of our campaign the need for home defence against invasion." Also see Summers, "Militarism in Britain," pp. 114–15.

40. "INVASION: Report of a Sub-Committee appointed by the Prime Minister to Reconsider the Question of Overseas Attack," 102d meeting of Committee of Imperial Defense, 22 October 1908, CAB 38/14/44A. The report also provides background information on how Roberts's scheme on the feasibility of invasion came into the committee's hands. This story is presented in some detail by one of the members of the invasion subcommittee; see M. V. Brett, ed., *Journals and Letters of Reginald Viscount Esher,* 4 vols. (London, 1934), 2:97–118, 263–317 passim. For Repington's low estimate of Roberts's opinions, see Repington to Marker, 15 October 1905 and 29 June and 5 July 1906, Marker Papers, Add. Ms. 52277, British Library, British Museum, London.

contribution to the naval panic of 1908–1909. Public hysteria arising from this chimera helped to sell thousands of books recounting dozens of fictional invasions, to make a roaring success of a silly play called *An Englishman's Home,* and to sustain the myth of a vast network of German spies.[41] The naval panic was, as Lord Esher said, "the mill of God which grinds . . . a Navy of Dreadnoughts,"[42] and it probably benefited the NSL's membership drive as well.

In mid-1909, while the naval scare was still raging, NSL spokesmen in the House of Lords introduced a bill that would have made training with the territorial force compulsory for all males not serving in the regular forces. The measure was defeated by a surprisingly narrow margin (123–103) when Unionist leader Lord Lansdowne refused to commit his party on the grounds that public opinion was "not yet ripe for a compulsory system."[43] But while Lansdowne was correct in assuming that peacetime compulsory service was never a serious possibility, the ideals of the NSL did receive increasing support not only from the Germanophobic right-wing press and the tariff-reform faction of the Unionist party but also from maverick socialist Robert Blatchford of the *Clarion* and even from the leading Radical cabinet minister, David Lloyd George.[44]

During the summer of 1910, in the midst of the constitutional conferences among party leaders following the death of King Edward VII, Lloyd George produced an extraordinary memorandum listing a twelve-point program as the

41. For late-Victorian and Edwardian invasion literature, see I. F. Clarke, *Voices Prophesying War, 1763–1914* (London, 1966), pp. 64–162. Also see David French's essay, "Spy Fever in Britain, 1900–1915," *Historical Journal* 21/2 (1978):355–70. For examples of the sort of nonsense that was apparently taken seriously by military intelligence, see correspondence between Lord Roberts and Judge Hans Hamilton, June–July 1909, Roberts Papers, WO/105/45, PRO.

42. Quoted by Arthur J. Marder, *Fear God and Dread Nought: The Correspondence of Admiral of the Fleet, Lord Fisher of Kilverstone,* vol. 2, *Years of Power* (London, 1956), p. 144n. Also see Ruddock F. MacKay, *Fisher of Kilverstone* (Oxford, 1973), pp. 381–94.

43. For the debate on this measure, see 5 H.L., 1:255–470, 13 July 1909.

44. Blatchford later repudiated the NSL and compulsory service because of the government's use of army troops as "blacklegs" in industrial disputes; the ruling classes, Blatchford said, could "not be trusted"; Blatchford to Lady Roberts, 29 March 1912, and Henry Wilson to Roberts, 9 April 1912, Roberts Papers, 7101–23, 47/85, National Army Museum, London.

basis for a coalition government of all the Talents. The second item under Lloyd George's heading of "National Reorganisation" was a proposal for compulsory military training on the model of the Swiss militia, a proposition that would have warmed the hearts of all but the most extreme devotees of the NSL.[45] In the end nothing came of the plan, but thereafter Lloyd George—later joined by Winston Churchill—continued, quietly to be sure, to adhere to the conscriptionist view.[46]

After the first parliamentary elections of 1910, the NSL consistently claimed the support of more than 150 members of the House of Commons.[47] Indeed, the league's growing political influence was causing considerable concern among supporters of the voluntary system, one of whom warned that "the danger threatening our national institutions through the propaganda of the National Service League is far more serious than the general public realises."[48] At the War Office, Haldane was receiving reports from, among others, Sir John French, inspector general of the forces, that NSL propaganda critical of the territorial force was having seriously adverse effects on recruitment.[49] In an attempt to counter the league's assault, Haldane commissioned Gen. Sir Ian Hamilton, a member of the Army Council, to prepare a memorandum presenting the War Office view. Hamilton who, with Douglas Haig, was one of the few top soldiers who

45. The memorandum is printed in Kenneth O. Morgan, ed., *The Age of Lloyd George: The Liberal Party and British Politics, 1890-1929* (London, 1971), pp. 150-55. Also see Don M. Cregier, *Bounder from Wales: Lloyd George's Career before the First World War* (Columbia, Mo., 1976), pp. 150-62 passim, and Lord Riddell, *More Pages from My Diary, 1909-1914* (London, 1934), p. 140.

46. See diary entry, 5 November 1912, Wilson Papers, where Wilson noted that both Lloyd George and Churchill had privately voiced their support for conscription as a nonpartisan issue. Also see Roberts to Churchill, 21 January 1912, and Churchill to Roberts, 23 January 1912, Roberts Papers, 7101-23, 125/2 and 22/6. Roberts's letter was drafted by Wilson; see his diary entry, 21 January 1912, Wilson Papers.

47. *NIA*, n.s., 5 (June 1910):263, sets the number at 160. Summers, "Militarism in Britain," p. 113, says that the NSL claimed the support of 177 M.P.s in 1911 but that only 80 of those could be identified as dues-paying members. Also see Roberts Papers, 7101-23, 130/2, pp. 105-7.

48. Col. F. N. Maude, "Voluntary versus Compulsory Service," *Contemporary Review* 100 (July 1911):31.

49. See Haldane's "Memorandum on Events, 1906-1915," pp. 133-39, Haldane Papers, 5919, National Library of Scotland, Edinburgh.

remained loyal to the "Terries"[50] responded with a long paper that was quickly published as *Compulsory Service: A Study of the Question in the Light of Experience* (London, 1912). Haldane himself added a complimentary introduction.

The substance of Hamilton's case against the NSL was that its plan for compulsory service for home defense was practically useless since in any conceivable future war the navy would protect the home islands while the army would be required for overseas service. Hamilton did not oppose compulsion on principle, noting that conscription for overseas service might become necessary in some future conflict, but since the British people would not accept such a scheme in peacetime, the territorial force was the best means for repelling would-be raiders from the coasts and for providing a body of partially trained men who could be prepared for service abroad.[51]

Haldane's use of a military subordinate to defend government policy was severely criticized by the Unionist opposition in Parliament,[52] and Lord Roberts's biographer notes that, except for the death of his son, Hamilton's book was the "most cruel personal blow that Roberts ever suffered."[53] Injured feelings, however, did not prevent the NSL's president from collaborating with Prof. J. A. Cramb, Amery, and ghost-writer Wilson in a response to Hamilton's "preposterous" and "ridiculous" arguments.[54] The result, an overlong and somewhat ponderous effort entitled *Facts and Fallacies: An Answer to "Compulsory Service"* (London, 1911) was widely reviewed,[55] and if it did not, as Gen. Sir Henry Rawlinson

50. Haig to Haldane, 5 January 1911, Haldane Papers, 5909. Also see Cunningham, *Volunteer Force*, pp. 147–48.

51. For a summary of Hamilton's arguments, see Hayes, *Conscription Conflict*, pp. 99–106.

52. See statement by Arthur Balfour, 5 H.C., 22:1972–74, 13 March 1911, and Haldane's reply, 5 H.C., 22:2073, 14 March 1911.

53. David James, *Lord Roberts* (London, 1954), p. 449. Also see undated holograph notes by Roberts commenting on Hamilton's action; Roberts Papers, 7101–23, 122/29.

54. For references to this collaborative effort, see diary entries, 11 and 22 January 1911, Wilson Papers; Milner to Roberts, 17 January 1911, Roberts Papers, 7101–23, 45/121; and Milner's *Diaries*, Milner Papers, 274, Bodleian Library, Oxford.

55. The Roberts Papers contain a 130-page scrapbook collection of over one hundred reviews of *Facts and Fallacies*, three-fourths of which are favorable; Roberts Papers, 7101–23, 129.

claimed with partisan enthusiasm, deal a "crushing blow" to Hamilton and Haldane, it did keep the question very much alive.[56]

Even though *Facts and Fallacies* indignantly rejected the Haldane–Hamilton claim that the NSL was hampering recruitment for the territorial force, league literature increasingly concentrated on the inadequacies of the "Terries," while the private correspondence of NSL leaders reveals their view that "smashing the Territorial Army" was a necessary first step toward compulsory service. Indeed, the attacks on the territorial force caused dissension in NSL ranks because some league members were also enthusiastic territorials who resented slurs on what they considered a noble band of patriotic volunteers.[57]

After 1910 the league attempted to carry its message to a larger audience by organizing a great series of public meetings throughout the country. The largest of these were addressed by Lord Roberts, whose public utterances became less and less restrained. He made over a dozen major speeches between June 1912 and June 1913, some of them written by Wilson. Roberts's most controversial presentation was in Manchester on 22 October 1912 when he warned that compulsory training for the entire male population was essential because the Germans would attack Britain the moment they had established overall military superiority. This moment, Roberts implied, was near at hand, and yet petty politicians continued to deny the people the "right to be taught to defend your country—the right . . . to defend your honour as Britons and your liberties as citizens of this Empire."[58]

56. Rawlinson to Roberts, 8 April 1911, Roberts Papers, 7101–23, 61/ 138. Also see *The Times* correspondence columns, 15, 17, and 21 April 1911, for a continuation of the debate.

57. Diary entries, 28 November and 8 December 1912, 28 November and 21 December 1913, Wilson Papers. Also see memoranda, speeches, and letters by Roberts attacking the territorial force in Roberts Papers, 7101–23, 125/2; Repington to Haldane, 27 November 1912, Haldane Papers, 5909; and Haldane to his mother, 28 November 1912, Haldane Papers, 5988. Also see correspondence of December 1911–January 1912 between Roberts and Lord Derby indicating that Derby had resigned from the NSL because of its attacks on the territorial force; Roberts Papers, 7101–23, 125/1, 125/2.

58. See Roberts Papers, 7101–23, 125/2, for a printed copy of the Manchester speech. Also see *The Times,* 23 October 1912.

The Times was much impressed and solemnly announced that if the nation would follow the lead of Lord Roberts it could still throw off "the hard and narrow commercialism bequeathed to us by the Manchester School" and could find its salvation in the "educative force" of universal military training. Liberal opinion was outraged. The *Manchester Guardian* and *Daily News* both accused Roberts and the NSL of planning to use their conscript armies for a preemptive invasion of German territory. *The Nation* called the speech "diabolical" and branded Roberts "a mere Jingo in opinion and character" who disrupted the affairs of the nation by giving hysterical voice to "the crude lusts and fears which haunt the unimaginative soldier's brain."[59]

The storm of indignation that greeted Lord Roberts's Germanophobic pronouncements at Manchester reflected a strong undercurrent of antimilitarism, but while such opinions could be temporarily loud, they were also scattered and, among liberals at least, rather complacent. When dealing with groups such as the NSL, the most widely read and influential radical journalists—Gardiner, Massingham, Hirst, Hobhouse, and Hobson—tended to be condescending in their attitudes, sweeping in their criticisms, and ill informed about the facts. They made no great impact because they spoke only to a narrow, mainly middle-class, and nonconformist audience; because they thought so little of those they attacked; and because, in the final analysis, they never could believe that the worst might happen and leave them dangling precariously between the two peaks of popular patriotism and anathematized war resistance.[60]

There were more persistent, if ultimately no more successful, representatives of antimilitarism. The glowing embers of the "old" nineteenth-century pacifism were kept alive by organizations such as the Peace Society and the Interna-

59. *The Times*, 23 October and 20 December 1912; *Manchester Guardian*, 28 October 1912; *Daily News*, 30 October 1912; and *The Nation*, 26 October 1912.

60. For critical discussions of the decline of radicalism, see A. J. A. Morris's introduction to *Edwardian Radicalism, 1900-1914* (London, 1974), pp. 2-6, and Steiner, *Origins of the First World War*, pp. 144-54. Also see Clive Trebilcock, "Radicalism and the Armament Trust," in Morris, ed., *Edwardian Radicalism*, pp. 180-201, and "Legends of the British Armaments Industry, 1890-1914: A Revision," *Journal of Contemporary History* 5/4 (1970).

tional Arbitration League, but these groups had lost much of their fervor and most of their membership.[61] The exception among the old-pacifist groups was the Society of Friends. In the course of the so-called Quaker Renaissance of the 1890s and early 1900s, the society vigorously revived the peace testimony that had all but drowned in the swells of evangelicalism that had engulfed Friends in the early nineteenth century. The Boer War stimulated Quaker journals and organizations to establish an advanced and vigilant posture in the fight against militarism.[62] A good example of Quaker watchfulness is Edward Grubb, theologian, teacher, social reformer, and editor of *The British Friend* from 1902 to 1913.[63] In 1909 Grubb, ever mindful of the special dangers of militarism wrapped up in the alluring package of idealism and righteousness, published an earnest and forceful reply to *A New Way of Life* (1909) by J. St. Loe Strachey, editor of *The Spectator* and ardent devotee of the NSL. Strachey's book, a collection of editorial essays from *The Spectator,* voiced his fear that self-indulgence, complacency, and "swinish equanimity" were dragging Britain down to ruin. The effective cure for this national malaise, Strachey insisted, was universal military training, which would teach the citizen to recognize his duty to the state and community and would restrain him from indulging in any vice or frivolity that might hinder him from serving the nation in time of crisis.[64]

In his response, entitled *The True Way of Life,* Grubb ex-

61. Keith Robbins provides a brief discussion of such organizations in *The Abolition of War: The "Peace Movement" in Britain, 1914–1919* (Cardiff, 1976), pp. 7–26.

62. The best discussion of the Quaker Renaissance is in R. A. Rempel's unpublished paper, "Edward Grubb and the Quaker Renaissance in Britain, 1880–1914" (McMaster University, Hamilton, Ontario). For Quaker response to the Boer War, see Rempel's "British Quakers and the South African War," *Quaker History* 64 (1975):75–95.

63. For Grubb, see James Dudley, *The Life of Edward Grubb, 1854–1939: A Spiritual Pilgrimage* (London, 1946). Rempel and I are currently collaborating on a new study of Grubb, his impact on the Society of Friends, and the place of the Friends in early twentieth-century British society.

64. The profits from *A New Way of Life* (London, 1909) were to be donated to the NSL, but the league probably gained little from it since sales for the book were, in Strachey's words, "very disappointing indeed." Strachey to Lord Northcliffe, 12 July 1909, J. St. Loe Strachey Papers, S 11/4/23, House of Lords Record Office, London.

pressed his horror at Strachey's view that the citizen had no more exhalted purpose than surrendering his will to the state in order to be made into an efficient killer. Sloth, greed, and vice, Grubb said, would not be rooted out by preparing young people to slaughter their fellow men in the interests of the state but rather by teaching them to heal the ills of the nation in the interests of common humanity and Christian civilization.[65]

With spokesmen such as Grubb, the Society of Friends was an articulate and persistent foe of militarism, but the audience for its public pronouncements was extremely narrow. A more broadly based "pacifist" organization was the Independent Labour Party (ILP). Although the ILP's membership rolls (sixteen thousand in 1908) were no larger than those of the Society of Friends, one might suppose that the ILP spoke for a much larger working-class constituency. Recent studies, however, seem to indicate that the party's staunch and outspoken commitment to international peace was never embraced by more than a miniscule portion of the laboring classes. Keir Hardie or George Lansbury might rage in evangelical eloquence against the exploitation of working people by the avaricious minions of capitalism who everywhere supported preparations for slaughter and destruction, but the great majority of British workers were as sullen and cynical about universal peace as they were about universal military training for war.[66]

However limited their appeal, groups such as the Society of Friends and the ILP were generally well organized and close-knit. The one really popular and influential antimilitarist movement in Edwardian Britain was scarcely organized at all. It was made up of a loosely associated welter of groups and societies that existed to spread the message of Norman Angell's famous book, *The Great Illusion* (1910). Perhaps Angell's views were so popular because they were so well tuned to the pitch of Edwardian "progressive" thought—

65. Grubb, *The True Way of Life* (London, [1909]), pp. 44–45, 48–49, 56, 63–64.

66. Standish Meacham in *A Life Apart: The English Working Class, 1890–1914* (Cambridge, Mass., 1977), reaffirms Price's view of the working class as alienated, withdrawn, sullen, and generally outside the mainstream of national life as viewed by the more politically involved; see Price, *Imperial War*, pp. 233–42. Also see Steiner, *Origins of the First World War*, pp. 134–35.

practical, materialistic, logical, and, most of all, filled with optimism. Angell argued that war among advanced industrial states was irrational folly; the economic interdependence of the would-be belligerents made the victors as well as the vanquished subject to wrenching economic dislocations that would spell disaster for all. Angell never said war was impossible; he only said that rational human beings who were aware of its consequences might successfully strive to secure a stable and peaceful world order. For a time "Norman Angellism" or the "new pacifism" was quite the rage, enlisting conservative statesmen and wealthy industrialists as well as young idealists. But the great majority of these summertime soldiers for peace abandoned Angell and his doctrine once World War I began.[67]

The overwhelming popular support for the war in August 1914 was a terrible and inexplicable blow not only to the optimistic supporters of the new pacifism but to all those antimilitarists who had assumed that humankind was, however gradually, moving toward more rational, less-destructive means of resolving its conflicts. But there were ominous signs that even the most blissfully buoyant could have seen. As Elie Halévy later noted, "pacifist opinion, though often more vocal was also more superficial and . . . the militarization of the nation . . . if more silent, was more profound."[68]

Social historians of the Edwardian period have called attention to the means by which the agents of militarization endeavored to take control of the social and moral education of British youth. The work of John Springhall[69] is particularly illuminating on the manner in which youth movements were manipulated and directed by conservative middle-class gentlemen, many of whom were retired military officers. Their objectives were to instill the sort of patriotism and military spirit that would inspire young boys not only to fight

67. The best brief discussion of Norman Angellism in Edwardian Britain is Howard Weinroth, "Norman Angell and *The Great Illusion:* An Episode in Pre-1914 Pacifism," *Historical Journal* 27/3 (1974):551–74.
68. Halévy, *The Rule of Democracy,* p. 186.
69. See Springhall, *Youth, Empire and Society,* pp. 14–18, and "The Boy Scouts, Class and Militarism," pp. 125–27, 155–58. Also see Steiner, *Origins of the First World War,* pp. 157–60, and Summers, "Militarism in Britain," passim.

for the protection of the physical empire but also for the social order on which that empire was founded. This process of militarization was in considerable measure associated with Christian churches and with the late Victorian tendency to relate manliness to godliness and virtue to love of country. Army life in particular was idealized as the highest and purest calling to which the Christian citizen could aspire.[70]

The earliest and, for a long time, the most successful manifestation of the militarization of British youth was the Boys' Brigade, founded in 1883 by William Smith, an officer in the First Lanarkshire Rifle Volunteers and a Sunday-school teacher at the North Woodside Mission in Glasgow. The brigade was originally conceived as a means for controlling and directing ill-disciplined boys from the slums surrounding the mission.[71] Smith's movement, generously aided by contributions from wealthy patrons and chiefly led by Bible-class teachers, incorporated concepts of Christian manliness and intense patriotism with military uniforms and drill. The brigade was such a success, especially in Scotland, that within a few years it was complimented by the appearance of numerous imitators including the Catholic Boys' Brigade, the Jewish Lads' Brigade, and, most prominently, the Anglican Church Lads' Brigade, which came to rival the pioneer group in size and influence.[72] The members of these organizations were not primarily slum children of poorer working-class families, but the sons of respectable and upwardly mobile working- or lower-middle-class parents.[73]

The rapid growth of a semimilitarized Christian youth movement naturally became a source of grave anxiety to

70. The NSL stressed the fact that national duty was intimately related to religious duty and that one was not complete without the other; see *NIA* 2/13 (May 1907):115, and NSL Leaflet L, "Religious Thought and National Service." Also see Summers, "Militarism in Britain," pp. 118–20.

71. Springhall, *Youth, Empire and Society*, pp. 22–36; Benjamin F. True-blood, *The Boys' Brigade: Its Character and Tendencies*, pamphlet published by the Peace Society (London, n.d.); and Samuel Milliken, *Christian Soldiers*, pamphlet published by the International Arbitration League (London, n.d.). Also see issues of *The British Friend*, 1887–1889, for early attacks on the Boys' Brigades.

72. Each of these groups is briefly sketched by Springhall, *Youth, Empire and Society*, pp. 37–52.

73. Ibid., p. 25.

Edwardian youth prepare to defend the empire. (Courtesy National Army Museum)

Christian antimilitarists who felt that it undermined the fundamental qualities of Christian manhood by replacing them with a spirit that was "essentially military."[74] Such concern could only deepen when the movement broke free from the confines of religious connection. Lord Meath's Lads' Drill Association (LDA), founded in 1899, was probably the first to have no religious pretenses and to profess its frank devotion to instilling patriotism and a military spirit in the nation's youth. The LDA, which merged with the NSL in 1906, was never a great success, but Lt. Gen. Robert S. S. Baden-Powell, another hero of the Boer War, managed to combine patriotic enthusiasm, paramilitary organization, and woodcraft skills into the most successful youth movement of all, the Boy Scouts. By 1912 the Scouts were larger than the Boys' Brigade and Church Lads' Brigade combined.[75]

One fascinating aspect of the prewar youth movement was the NSL's attempt to take control of the Boy Scouts as a part of the league's campaign for compulsory military training. This effort, which appeared to justify the most paranoid imaginings of antimilitarists, became a public issue of some importance in 1910 when Sir Francis Vane, former Scout commissioner for London, exposed the infiltration of important NSL leaders into the executive committee of the Boy Scouts' governing council.[76] Vane, who had himself seen active service, used the *Westminster Gazette* to publicly attack the "military direction" in which the Scouts were being led by the proponents of compulsion. After Baden-Powell dismissed Vane from his post, Sir Francis, with strong support from London Scout leaders, founded a rival organization, the British Boy Scouts or National Peace Scouts, which expunged all hint of militarism from its activities. Among those on the Governing Council of the British Boy Scouts were Quaker leaders George Cadbury and T. E. Harvey, M.P., as well as two representatives from the National Peace Council. But the Peace Scouts, like the peace movement generally,

74. Trueblood, *The Boys' Brigade*, pp. 3-4.
75. Springhall, *Youth, Empire and Society*, pp. 53-70, 127, and app. 5, and "Boy Scouts, Class and Militarism," passim.
76. Springhall, "Boy Scouts, Class and Militarism," pp. 137-38, 148, 156-58.

enlisted too few recruits to affect the prevailing mood in youth organizations.[77]

The Boy Scouts were not the only youth group honeycombed with conscriptionists. Indeed, NSL leaders formed part of an interlocking directorate within the British youth movement.[78] In 1910 the attempt to use youth groups for military purposes became more overt when the War Office tried to pressure all youth organizations into becoming officially recognized cadet corps connected with and supplying recruits for local Territorial Force Associations. While Smith of the Boys' Brigade and Baden-Powell both managed to steer their organizations clear of any official relations with the military, the executive committee of the Church Lads' Brigade voted to accept War Office recognition and thus affiliation with the territorial force.[79]

Whether or not they were officially connected with the War Office, ex-members of various paramilitary youth groups made a considerable contribution to the war effort of 1914–1918. Probably no definitive statement can be made about why the British nation and particularly British youth greeted World War I with such unbounded enthusiasm, but one may legitimately speculate that the growing tolerance for military methods and the military spirit as well as the continued picturing of war as a romantic, larger-than-life adventure helped to ensure "that the propaganda of the National Service League and others like it . . . did not fall entirely on fallow ground."[80]

In the House of Commons during April 1913 representatives of each of the leading antimilitarist factions—Radical Liberals, Labourites, and religious pacifists—took part in the debate on a bill sponsored by the NSL that would have re-

77. See Sir Francis Vane, "A Danger in the Boy Scout Movement," *Westminster Gazette*, 1 March 1910. Also see C. Brightwen Rowntree, "The Adult School and the Boy Scout," *Friends' Quarterly Examiner* 44 (1910):324–31, and Irene Midgley, "Scouting for Boys," *Friends' Quarterly Examiner* 46 (1912):449–52.

78. Springhall, *Youth, Empire and Society*, p. 48, n. 12, and Steiner, *Origins of the First World War*, pp. 159–61.

79. Springhall, *Youth, Empire and Society*, pp. 29–30, and "Boy Scouts, Class and Militarism," pp. 144–47, 157.

80. Springhall, "Boy Scouts, Class and Militarism," p. 158. Also see Clarke, *Voices Prophesying War*, p. 131, and Playne, *Pre-War Mind*, p. 162.

quired compulsory training for the territorial force.[81] The most significant speeches against the bill were by Hardie of the ILP and by Arnold Rowntree, a Liberal M.P. and a Quaker. Hardie said that, as an international socialist, he did not "believe in war or preparations for war" and that any act that advanced militarism weakened the power and threatened the liberty of the working class.[82] After expressing the most widely held fear of trade unionists—that an enlarged conscript army might become a strikebreaking tool of the ruling class—Rowntree went on to explain his own strongest objection to conscription, that it would "force men against their conscience to take service."

> Rightly or wrongly [he continued], there are large numbers of people in this country, with a profound regard for the sanctity of human life, who believe that in every human personality there is something of the divine, and that for Parliament to force men against their will to train to kill one another is a function that it has no right to perform.[83]

The measure under consideration was easily defeated, but agitation for compulsion continued right up to the summer of 1914 and grew progressively stronger after the first few months of the war. Once the war began, the "large numbers of people" of whom Rowntree had spoken generally failed to materialize. Those who opposed the war and who continued to fight against conscription were relatively few and were manifestly unpopular, though it may be argued that their depth of conviction compensated for their lack of influence. What follows is the story of an organization that incorporated a considerable number of that despised minority—those who would not follow the dogs of war but were instead pursued by the hound of conscience.

81. The National Service (Territorial Force) Bill was moved by G. J. Sandys. For the debate, see 5 H.C., 51:1517–94, 11 April 1913.
82. Ibid., 1591–93.
83. Ibid., 1564–65.

2

"We Think You Ought to Go"

The Dogs of War

The jubilant exhilaration that prevailed among the English bank-holiday crowds awaiting the news that their country had gone to war was not unique to the British Isles. A significant portion of the population in every belligerent country greeted the declaration of war as the beginning of a grand adventure. Some still find this phenomenon as frightening and inexplicable as it was to Bertrand Russell when he stalked the streets of central London on the evening of 3 August seeking a rational man.[1] Students of the period have attributed this mood to a variety of causes, some simple, others sinister and all-embracing. Were the heedless Britons who, with Rupert Brooke, thanked God for matching them with His hour too innocent of war to imagine the horror into which they and their country had stumbled?[2] Or did they see the conflict as a means of blessed release from the stifling stodginess of middle-class society or from the drab awfulness of a working-class slum? Perhaps the Boys' Brigades, Boy Scouts, and similar groups did help to create an atmosphere in which joyous celebration of and massive volunteering for the war seemed the only right, the only honorable, the only "sporting" thing to do.[3] Michael Howard has said that the war was welcomed because it was

1. Bertrand Russell, *The Autobiography of Bertrand Russell*, 3 vols. (London, 1967–1969), 2:16–18. A good account of the general reaction is H. Stuart Hughes, *Consciousness and Society* (New York, 1958), pp. 336–91.
2. Paul Fussell, *The Great War and Modern Memory* (London, 1975), pp. 18–29, discusses the theme of innocence with great insight, humor, and sympathy.
3. The work on this topic by John Springhall, Anne Summers, Caroline E. Playne, and others has been mentioned in the notes to Chap. 1. Also see H. J. Hanham, "Religion and Nationality in the Mid-Victorian Army," in *War and Society*, ed. M. R. D. Foot (New York, 1973), pp. 173–74.

"exactly that trial of patriotism, manliness and endurance for which the nations of Europe had been preparing themselves for an entire generation."[4]

In the beginning, then, little proselytizing was needed to convince the long lines of prideful young men that they would be fighting in a just and holy cause; they volunteered by the thousands.[5] By December 1914, however, the torrent of volunteers had been reduced to a slowly diminishing stream of less than thirty thousand a week. Although Kitchener still felt this was a "satisfactory level" of recruitment, other officials believed that the growing reluctance of young men to volunteer necessitated continued pressure on the civilian populace. Of course, unofficial recruiters had swung into action rapidly. By early September, newspapers were carrying stories of militant suffragettes handing out white feathers to young men in civilian clothes. Music halls were also prominent recruiting platforms; popular entertainers like Leo Dryden, Charles Colburn, and Harry Lauder had an inexhaustible supply of patriotic songs. The newly reopened London Opera House staged *England Expects,* which featured songbird Phyllis Dare twittering "Oh, we don't want to lose you but we think you ought to go." Not to be outdone, the Empire Theatre donated its stage to Horatio Bottomley of *John Bull* for fifteen minutes each night so that he could present his famous (and lucrative) appeal for recruits and reform.[6]

4. Michael Howard, "Lest We Forget: 'Oh What an Unlovely War . . . ,'" *Encounter* 22 (January 1964):64. Also see Arno J. Meyer, "Domestic Causes of the First World War," in *The Responsibility of Power: Historical Essays in Honor of Hajo Holborn,* ed. Leonard Krieger and Fritz Stern (New York, 1967), p. 292, and A. J. P. Taylor, "Fritz Fischer and His School," *Journal of Modern History* 47 (March 1975):123.

5. See *Statistics of the Military Effort of the British Empire during the Great War, 1914–1920* (London, 1922), p. 364. Such diverse individuals as Lord Haldane, Spencer Wilkinson, Lord Roberts, and Lord Milner severely criticized Kitchener's refusal to make use of the existing territorial organization as the basis for building a new army. See Haldane, *An Autobiography* (New York, 1929), pp. 297–98; Wilkinson's memoranda to the prime minister, 24 August and 22 and 27 September 1914, Spencer Wilkinson Papers, OPT 13/36/1–6, Army Museums Ogilvy Trust, London; Lady Roberts's remembrances, Roberts Papers, 7101–23, 205, National Army Museum, London; and Lord Midleton to Arthur Balfour, 6 November 1914, Balfour Papers, Add. Ms. 49721, British Library, British Museum, London.

6. Roy Douglas, "Voluntary Enlistment in the First World War and the

Government efforts to enlist volunteers were somewhat less chaotic. Atrocity propaganda no doubt played some part in arousing a sense of indignation in decent post-Victorians,[7] but most official recruiting was organized and directed by the Parliamentary Recruiting Committee (PRC). The PRC was responsible for the famous Kitchener poster as well as for others encouraging young men to "Join the brave throng that goes marching along" and warning slackers "Don't Lag! Follow your flag!" Another recruiting technique developed by the PRC was the so-called householders' return, a form signed by the leaders of the three political parties and sent to every householder in England, asking all eligible men from nineteen to thirty-eight to indicate their willingness to enlist.[8]

By such diverse methods, a reasonably steady flow of volunteers continued through the first months of 1915. The problem, however, was not simply one of men. More emphatically it was a question of "which men?" The army was insufficiently housed and equipped, but the manufacture of essential war material was being seriously disrupted because from one-sixth to one-quarter of the men in nearly every vital war industry had left their civilian jobs to take the colors. Thus, the government not only had to build a sufficiently large army but also had to keep enough skilled workers at their posts to equip that army. Lloyd George later noted that this nearly hopeless endeavor resulted in a "deplorable waste and mismanagement of our available manpower."[9] A major portion of the blame for this grave state of

Work of the Parliamentary Recruiting Committee," *Journal of Modern History* 42 (December 1970):566, 566n, 571, 577, and *The Times*, 4 August 1914 and 15 and 20 January 1915. Also see Sylvia Pankhurst, *The Home Front* (London, 1931), p. 217; A. J. P. Taylor, *English History, 1914–1945* (Oxford, 1965), pp. 20–21; and Alfred E. Havighurst, *Twentieth-Century Britain* (New York, 1966), p. 132.

7. For atrocity stories in the First World War, see James M. Read, *Atrocity Propaganda, 1914–1919* (New Haven, 1941), and Arthur Ponsonby, *Falsehood in Wartimes* (New York, 1929).

8. Douglas, "Voluntary Recruiting," pp. 568–75 passim. Members of the PRC are listed in 5 H.C., 70:1432, 10 March 1915. The text of the householders' return was published in *The Times*, 11 November 1914.

9. David Lloyd George, *War Memoirs*, 6 vols. (London, 1933), 2:711–12, 716. The figures given here are based on Hubert Wolfe, *Labour Supply and*

affairs was rightly traced to the haphazard voluntary recruiting system that one critic called "neither truly voluntary nor much of a system."[10]

Actually, the question of compulsory service was raised in both the cabinet and the House of Commons within three weeks after the war began. On 25 August Churchill bored his cabinet colleagues with a long diatribe on the necessity for conscription, but on the following day Asquith told questioners in Commons that the government was not considering the imposition of compulsory military service.[11] The question was not debated in Parliament throughout the remainder of 1914, largely, no doubt, because opposition leader Andrew Bonar Law did not believe it should be. Some prominent Unionists, however, privately urged Lord Kitchener to speak out for compulsion.[12] On 8 January 1915 several peers, including Selborne and Curzon, asked for a reexamination of Britain's commitment to a voluntary army. Though he defended the superior quality of volunteer forces, Haldane, as lord chancellor, noted that since it was the obligation of every male citizen under common law to aid his sovereign in preserving the realm, compulsory service was "not foreign to the Constitution of this country." Lord Crewe, speaking for the government, attempted to lay the matter to rest by announcing that conscription "was not presently within the landscape."[13] It was, however, in the air and in the weeks that followed references to the necessity for

---

Regulation (Oxford, 1923), p. 14. Also see R. J. Q. Adams, "Delivering the Goods: Reappraising the Ministry of Munitions, 1915–1916," *Albion* 7 (Fall 1975):238–50, and Andrew Bonar Law to F. S. Oliver, 18 December 1914, Bonar Law Papers, 37/4/39, House of Lords Record Office, London.

10. John Buchan, *A History of the Great War*, 4 vols. (New York, 1922), 2:149.

11. 5 H.C., 66:43, 26 August 1914. Asquith's questioners were two back-bench Conservatives, A. St. G. Hamersley and H. Terrell. For reactions to Churchill's harangue, see Cameron Hazlehurst, *Politicians at War* (New York, 1971), p. 301, and Martin Gilbert, *Winston S. Churchill*, vol. 2, *1914–1916* (London, 1971), p. 57, who follows Hazlehurst but gives the date as 26 August.

12. Bonar Law to F. S. Oliver, 18 December 1914, Bonar Law Papers, 37/4/39; Walter Long to Kitchener, 2 December 1914, Kitchener Papers, 30/57/73 WS/16, PRO; and Lord Derby to Kitchener, 23 December 1914, Kitchener Papers, 30/57/73 W/17.

13. For the debate, see 5 H.L., 19:365–98, 8 January 1915.

or danger from compulsory service appeared with increasing frequency in the papers of prominent political figures on both sides.

Indeed, these constant references to compulsion have recently given rise to a considerable debate among historians over the importance of the conscription question to the political crisis of May 1915, which was only resolved by the formation of a coalition government. Following A. J. P. Taylor, Alfred Gollin has pictured the conflict over compulsory service as central to the larger debate over how the war should be fought—by retaining a measure of traditional freedom or by imposing wide-ranging state controls. This view has been challenged by Cameron Hazlehurst who asserts that "it was the political crisis [of May 1915] which precipitated discussion of conscription," not vice versa.[14]

The controversy continues,[15] but it must suffice here to give the story only in the barest outline. Asquith did have an old-fashioned view of how the war should be conducted and of how the nation should be organized to support the military effort. His chief objective was not the prevention of conscription or any other form of government control but the maintenance of national unity, a circumstance that he believed would best be ensured by his retaining national leadership. Of course, Asquith was widely informed by people whose judgment he had every reason to trust that compulsion would be dangerous and perhaps even catastrophic if it was introduced before the failure of the voluntary system had been clearly demonstrated.[16] One historian has estimated that as many as three-quarters of the Liberals

14. See Alfred Gollin, *Proconsul in Politics: A Study of Lord Milner in Opposition and in Power* (New York, 1964), pp. 223-87 passim; and "The Unmaking of a Prime Minister," *Spectator* 214 (28 May 1965):686; A. J. P. Taylor, *Politics in Wartime and Other Essays* (London, 1964), pp. 13-21; and Hazlehurst, *Politicians at War*, pp. 266 and 264-69 passim.

15. See Alfred Gollin, "Freedom or Control in the First World War (the Great Crisis of May 1915)," *Historical Reflections* 2 (Winter 1975):135-55, and Martin D. Pugh, "Asquith, Bonar Law and the First Coalition," *Historical Journal* 17 (1974):813-36. The latter scarcely mentions conscription as a consideration.

16. Earl of Oxford and Asquith, *Memories and Reflections*, 2 vols. (Boston, 1928), 2:131, 150, and Trevor Wilson, *The Downfall of the Liberal Party* (Ithaca, N.Y., 1966), pp. 70-73.

in Commons would not have supported the introduction of conscription in the summer of 1915.[17]

On the other hand, the overwhelming majority of Tory members strongly supported compulsory measures for both the military and vital industries. By insisting on the necessity of continuing the party truce, Bonar Law had been able to keep demands for compulsion outside the political arena, but as the crisis of May 1915 began to unfold, conscriptionist elements came increasingly to the fore. On 16 May, for example, Walter Long enjoined the party leader to press for a thoroughgoing system of compulsion that would direct every man into the place where he could best support the war effort. High-ranking military supporters of the Conservative party believed that the immediate institution of compulsory service should be the sine qua non for Tory participation in any coalition government.[18]

None of this came to pass, however, because when the Conservatives were brought into the government, they came in on Asquith's terms rather than on their own. For example, two days after the formation of the coalition, Lord Selborne, the new president of the Board of Agriculture, circulated a note demanding that "men . . . from 17 years upward be made subject to military law,"[19] but the prime minister easily turned this thrust aside. With the support of such strongly anticonscriptionist Liberals as Walter Runciman, Louis Harcourt, Reginald McKenna, and Sir John Simon, Asquith could not be stampeded by the Tories. The single

---

17. John Rae, *Conscience and Politics: The British Government and the Conscientious Objector to Military Service, 1916–1919* (London, 1970), p. 9. Other prominent Liberals were receiving similar warnings. See Ellis Davies, M.P., to David Lloyd George, 31 August 1915: "I gather . . . that there is almost unanimous objection to compulsion"; Lloyd George Papers, D/20/2/73, House of Lords Record Office, London.

18. Long to Bonar Law, 16 May 1915, Bonar Law Papers, 37/2/32, and Col. T. Bridges to Bonar Law, 18 May 1915, Bonar Law Papers, 37/2/39. Also see diary entry, 19 May 1915, Henry Wilson Papers, Imperial War Museum, London.

19. Cited by Peter Fraser, "The Impact of the War of 1914–1918 on the British Political System," in Foot, ed., *War and Society*, p. 128. Also see Walter Long to Bonar Law, 1 June 1915: "It seems to me that the adoption by the Cabinet of some form of compulsion . . . is not only absolutely necessary but most pressing"; Bonar Law Papers, 50/4/5.

most important Liberal minister, Lloyd George, so often pictured as a plotting intriguer and ardent compulsionist, seems not to have been converted to the necessity for conscription until August 1915, though from March on he did favor some form of industrial compulsion to ensure the more rational organization of key industries like munitions.[20]

On the other hand, Asquith was perfectly willing to prepare the groundwork for conscription if it became a necessity. One of his first acts after the formation of the coalition was to set Long to work drafting a bill for the establishment of a national register that could provide a complete record of available sources of manpower for the army as well as for the munitions plants. Such a proposal caused little concern among liberal opinion and was positively alluring to those favoring conscription.[21] On 29 June Long presented a bill that proposed compulsory registration of all men between the ages of fifteen and sixty-five. While he denied that the measure was in any way connected with compulsory service, some M.P.s attacked it as the thin end of the wedge for military conscription.[22]

Probably the most significant opposition to any expansion of government controls was centered in the trade-union movement. While almost all labor and trade-union leaders supported the war, they were convinced that it would be a small step from military conscription to the sort of industrial control that would strike a death blow at the entire trade-union movement. Lloyd George's pronouncements as minister of munitions did little to assuage labor's fears. In a speech at Bristol on 12 June 1915 he indicated that the need to organize labor in the workshop was even more pressing than the need to organize soldiers for the battlefield. Many people interpreted this statement as a thinly veiled threat of full-scale industrial conscription.[23]

20. On Lloyd George's position, see Lord Riddell's *War Diary, 1914–1918* (London, 1933), p. 117; *Lloyd George: A Diary by Frances Stevenson*, ed. A. J. P. Taylor (New York, 1971), pp. 55–57; and Hazlehurst, *Politicians at War*, pp. 302–3.

21. The *Manchester Guardian* editorially endorsed a national register on 29 May 1915. Also see memo by Long, "Registration for War Purposes," 11 June 1915, CAB 37/129/35.

22. 5 H.C., 72:1651–55, 29 June 1915, and 73:20–161, 5 July 1915.

23. See *Manchester Guardian*, 14 June 1915, for the speech and editorial

The answer of the Trades Union Congress (TUC) when it met in Bristol in early September was a resolution that emphatically rejected any type of conscription. Two days later Lloyd George delivered a speech to the congress and, while he did not directly threaten conscription, he skillfully put the workers on the defensive by illustrating in great detail the ways in which labor knowingly or otherwise was holding back the war effort.[24]

Stung by Lloyd George's rejoinder, Labour and trade-union leaders, though they remained solidly opposed to compulsion, felt the need to give substantial proof that they were not slacking. By late September the national advisory council of the TUC had agreed to assist in the dilution of labor in the munitions industry. In addition, Labour party leaders both in and out of Parliament cooperated in the establishment of a special labor recruiting committee. The rationale for these actions was to prevent the necessity for conscription, but they were bitterly denounced by the Independent Labour Party (ILP) and others on the Labour left who saw the trade-union movement being rendered impotent through the machinations of Lloyd George and the treason of its own leaders.[25] As one socialist writer later recounted: "The division of the spoils by the Parliamentary Recruiting Committee filled the pockets of Labour recruiting orators. The rank and file were duped and cajoled by all the well-known arts of well-paid recruiting sergeants; but the sergeants were their own trusted officials."[26]

Labour's active participation in recruiting activities reflected the growing intensity of the struggle over conscription. During the summer of 1915 Leopold Amery and

comment on it. On the question of Lloyd George's relations with trade-union leaders during this period, see Chris Wrigley, *David Lloyd George and the British Labour Movement: Peace and War* (Hassocks, 1976), pp. 81–163 passim.

24. See Wrigley, *Lloyd George and British Labour*, pp. 137–39, and Stevenson, *Lloyd George Diary*, p. 60.

25. See Douglas, "Voluntary Recruiting," p. 576; Wrigley, *Lloyd George and British Labour*, pp. 139–40; J. R. Clynes, *Memoir, 1869–1924*, 2 vols. (London, 1937), 1:190; and Philip Snowden, *Autobiography*, 2 vols. (London, 1934), 1:389–90.

26. C. H. Norman, *A Searchlight on the European War* (London, 1924), pp. 101–2. Also see A. Fenner Brockway, *Socialism after Sixty Years* (London, 1946), pp. 139–40.

Churchill's cousin Frederick Guest led a bipartisan group of serving M.P.s who returned from France to argue the case for compulsory service in the House of Commons.[27] In early August the Northcliffe press intensified its campaign against the voluntary system and shortly thereafter, Lord Milner, as president of the National Service League (NSL), called on NSL members to end their year of self-imposed silence and to throw all their resources into the renewed struggle for conscription.[28]

Asquith's response to such pressure was to keep one step ahead of his adversaries while balancing the conflicting opinions within his cabinet against each other. In August 1915 he appointed a cabinet committee under Lord Crewe to investigate the question of compulsion.[29] By early September this committee had reported that the voluntary system was keeping Great Britain from making a military effort commensurate with its resources, but Asquith was still unwilling to act on the sense of their recommendations. Apparently the prime minister was convinced by dire predictions of industrial unrest. For example, in August 1915 J. H. Thomas asserted, "without fear of contradiction that any attempt to impose Conscription will be most bitterly opposed."[30] On 18

27. There were four separate debates on compulsory military service: 5 H.C., 73:2395–2457, 28 July 1915; 5 H.C., 74:51–127, 15 September 1915; 5 H.C., 74:171–291, 16 September 1915; and H.C., 74:766–864, 28 September 1915. See L. S. Amery, *My Political Life*, vol. 2, *War and Peace, 1914–1929* (London, 1953), p. 63, and Riddell, *War Diary*, pp. 119–20.

28. See National Service League, "Occasional Notes," September 1915, Milner Papers, 137, Bodleian Library, Oxford, and J. O. Stubbs, "Lord Milner and Patriotic Labour, 1914–1918," *English Historical Review* 87 (October 1972):708–27. Some proconscriptionists believed that Northcliffe and Milner would injure the chances for compulsion. Lord Cromer noted: "Their advocacy would spoil almost any cause"; Cromer to Lord Mersey, 2 September 1915, Cromer Papers, FO 633/24, PRO. Haldane felt that "Northcliffe and the N. Service League . . . have ruined the chances of national service"; Haldane to Esher (copy), 10 September 1915, Haldane Papers, 5912, National Library of Scotland, Edinburgh.

29. In a strongly worded note, Bonar Law protested his exclusion from this "most important Committee" to be formed under the coalition government but subsequently refused the prime minister's invitation to join. Bonar Law to Asquith (copy), 12 August 1915, Bonar Law Papers, 53/6/38–39.

30. J. H. Thomas to Asquith, 20 August 1915, Asquith Papers, 14, f. 157, Bodleian Library, Oxford. Also see Asquith, *Memories and Reflections*, 2:131, 150.

September Asquith wrote a long letter to Arthur Balfour, the Unionist minister he found most congenial to his point of view, noting that in the past few days he had received communication from "the most trusted and representative men" of the Liberal party indicating their own vehement opposition to conscription as well as that of organized labor and the Irish Nationalists. Balfour responded by circulating a memorandum to the cabinet in which he questioned whether compulsory service would actually improve the efficiency of Britain's war machine.[31]

Asquith might congratulate himself on having secured a valuable ally, but proconscriptionists were not overly concerned with Balfour. The key to the success of their cause was Lord Kitchener. Though widely accounted a failure as war minister, Kitchener was still felt to have sufficient authority to single-handedly carry the cabinet, the Parliament, and the nation for compulsory service. Up to this time the secretary of state for war had accepted the prime minister's judgment, but by mid-September 1915 Kitchener seemed to be weakening. Sensing victory, Unionist leaders circulated a "possible scheme of Compulsory Military Service" drawn up by Amery. At the same time, Selborne increased the pressure on Kitchener, warning that if he delayed too long in introducing conscription, there would be "a serious revulsion" against him within the army.[32]

On 8 October Kitchener outflanked his tormentors by presenting a completely new recruiting scheme to the cabinet. This proposal was a kind of modified militia ballot; the country was divided into districts, and each district was assigned a quota of recruits based on returns from the national register. This plan was apparently defended by Lloyd George and seems to have temporarily shocked the conscriptionist faction into silence.[33] In the end, however, the Kitch-

31. Asquith to Balfour (most secret), 18 September 1915, Balfour Papers, Add. Ms., 49692, and CAB 37/134/25, 19 September 1915.

32. Curzon to Lloyd George, 15 September 1915, Lloyd George Papers, D/16/10/4, and Selborne to Kitchener, 17 and 21 September 1915, Kitchener Papers, 30/57/80, WV5 and 7. There is a copy of Amery's sixteen-page plan dated 15 September 1915 in Milner Papers, 137.

33. See CAB 37/135/15, 8 October 1915. Also see Christopher Addison, *Politics from Within, 1911–1918*, 2 vols. (London, 1924), 1:171; Stevenson, *Lloyd George Diary*, p. 68; and Riddell, *War Diary*, p. 119. Selborne later

ener scheme was dropped as too clumsy and complex, and both sides were left poised on the horns of an unyielding dilemma.

At this juncture, Asquith masterfully played his last trumps, first by convincing Kitchener to accept one final test of the voluntary system, and then by securing the appointment of Lord Derby as director general of recruiting. Derby, a popular figure and an enthusiastic recruiter, had long been an advocate of conscription; he accepted the position only after receiving assurances from Asquith and Kitchener that, if his efforts failed to obtain sufficient men, conscription would inevitably follow.[34]

On 11 October Lord Derby assumed his post as director general and ten days later introduced his program for raising the necessary men. The plan, universally dubbed "the Derby scheme," was a complicated and somewhat disingenuous compromise. Its first major feature was a personal canvass of every male between the ages of eighteen and forty-one based on information taken from the national register. The appeal included a special message from the king and a letter from Lord Derby emphasizing that the voluntary system was receiving its final chance. Second, all eligible men were divided into forty-six groups, twenty-three for married men and twenty-three for those who were single. The idea was that each eligible man not working in some "starred" (exempted) occupation would "attest" to his willingness to answer the nation's call if and when his group was summoned to the colors. Since all twenty-three groups of single men were to be called before any of the married

---

noted that, but for Kitchener's intervention at this critical juncture, the "Unionists in the Cabinet would have forced compulsory service in September or October 1915"; quoted by Fraser, "The Impact of War," in Foot, ed., *War and Society,* p. 128.

34. Lord Beaverbrook, *Politicians and the War, 1914–16* (London, 1928), pp. 246–48; Philip Magnus, *Kitchener: Portrait of an Imperialist* (London, 1958), p. 153; Randolph Churchill, *Lord Derby: King of Lancashire* (New York, 1960), pp. 187, 191–92; Lord Hankey, *The Supreme Command, 1914–1918,* 2 vols. (London, 1961), 1:427; and Douglas, "Voluntary Recruiting," pp. 578–79. For Derby's assessment of the recruiting situation and Asquith's leadership, see Derby to Cromer, 25 September 1915, Cromer Papers, FO 633/24, and Derby to Kitchener, 8 October 1915, Kitchener Papers, 30/57/73, WS/31.

groups, further inducement was given for the attestation of married men, many of whom perhaps felt that they could perform their patriotic duty and attest with little danger of actually being taken into the forces.[35] To give added assurance to married men and to guarantee that bachelors would not be derelict in their duty, Asquith told the House of Commons that no attested married man would be called in unless and until all the single men had been dealt with. He also noted that if single men did not attest voluntarily, some form of legal obligation might be fixed upon them.[36]

The Derby scheme was a great political stroke for the prime minister since it undercut and thus effectively silenced conscriptionist criticism within the cabinet. There were the inevitable protests, but even the staunchest pro-conscriptionists agreed that "Derby and his plan must have a . . . trial," hoping that its failure would ensure "compulsion almost by unanimous consent."[37] In the meantime, Asquith had regained the initiative, and on 16 October he circulated a secret note to his cabinet colleagues stressing that "the special appeal now being made for recruits should not suffer by controversies about compulsion."[38] For the next two months, while the Derby scheme operated, no formal papers were circulated in the cabinet concerning the question of compulsory service.

Finally, these events allowed Asquith to reconstitute and strengthen his line of communication with the politically innocent Kitchener. On 17 October he sent Kitchener a "most secret" note warning of a conspiracy

35. For a good discussion of the Derby scheme, see Wolfe, *Labour Supply and Regulation,* pp. 34–37. The king's message was written by Lord Esher; see Peter Fraser, *Lord Esher* (London, 1973), p. 294. There is a copy of Derby's form letter in the Sydney R. Turner Papers, SCPC.

36. 5 H.C., 75:524, 2 November 1915. This statement was apparently made to comply with Conservative demands that Asquith publicly announce that compulsion would be adopted if the voluntary system was shown to have failed. Memorandum to the prime minister (copy), 16 October 1915, Kitchener Papers, 30/57/73, WS/36.

37. Walter Long to Law, 12 October 1915, Bonar Law Papers, 51/4/7. Also see Edmund Talbot to Law, 16 October 1915, Bonar Law Papers, 51/4/16. Curzon circulated two protesting memoranda to the cabinet; CAB 37/135/24, 12 October 1915, and CAB 37/136/7, 13 October 1915.

38. Copies in Lloyd George Papers, D/24/10/40, and Kitchener Papers, 30/57/73, WS/30.

being engineered by men (Curzon and Lloyd George and some others) whose real objective is to oust you. They know that I give no countenance to their project and consequently they have conceived the idea of using you against me. . . . It is essential that you and I should stand together and that the intrigue which has for its main object . . . to divide and to discredit us both, should be frustrated.[39]

As one historian has said, the Derby scheme may have been a "shot-gun wedding . . . between the fair maid of Liberal idealism and the ogre of Tory militarism."[40] Certainly, it had the unfortunate result of pitting married and unmarried men against each other. But whatever else might be said about it, the Derby scheme did provide Asquith with time to demonstrate the government's willingness to give the voluntary system every possible chance. If such an all-out effort failed to produce sufficient men for the army, then the prime minister could introduce some form of compulsory service with the nearly unanimous support of the cabinet and the civilian population. Those who would still deny the necessity for conscription even after so clear a demonstration of need, and in the face of their country's mortal danger of military defeat, could surely be dismissed as perverse, ignorant, or cowardly. Or so it seemed.

The Hound of Conscience

Because the war descended on Europe so swiftly, opposition to British involvement was scattered and ineffective.[41] In the last frenzied days before war was declared, two desperate campaigns were launched to prevent Britain's being

---

39. Asquith to Kitchener, 17 October 1915, Kitchener Papers, 30/57/76, WR/25.
40. Arthur Marwick, *The Deluge: British Society and the First World War* (Boston, 1965), p. 77.
41. The best discussions of the brief neutrality campaign are Marvin Swartz, "A Study in Futility: The British Radicals at the Outbreak of the First World War," in *Edwardian Radicalism, 1900–1914*, ed. A. J. A. Morris (London, 1974), pp. 246–61, and Morris, *Radicalism against War, 1906–1914: The Advocacy of Peace and Retrenchment* (London, 1972), pp. 403–20. Also see Keith Robbins, *The Abolition of War: The "Peace Movement" in Britain, 1914–1919* (Cardiff, 1976), pp. 27–31.

drawn in: the British Neutrality Committee organized by Graham Wallas, J. A. Hobson, Charles Trevelyan, and others; and Norman Angell's British Neutrality League with a less-prestigious membership but a more ambitious program of activities.[42] Representatives of these two groups met but were unable to resolve their differences, which was an ominous portent for those disparate elements that continued to oppose the war. Official Labour party attempts to evoke the antiwar spirit culminated on 2 August in a large and impressive demonstration in Trafalgar Square addressed by Arthur Henderson, Keir Hardie, and others. In Parliament, Arthur Ponsonby led a small group of Radical members protesting British intervention in Continental affairs, and there were even waverers in the cabinet.[43] But after the invasion of Belgium, when hostilities became imminent, the neutrality campaigns, the Labour party, most of the Radicals, and all of the cabinet (except for John Morley and John Burns) succumbed to war fever. As Ramsay MacDonald said, the nation linked arms with Mars "as the saviour of society and the herald of peace."[44]

Some dissenters, of course, remained steadfast in their opposition to the war, or at least to the way that it had originated and was being conducted. Roughly speaking, antiwar elements can be divided into three groups. Religious pacifists, especially as represented by the Society of Friends, maintained their traditional stand against violence, though with less unanimity than is generally thought since around one-third of all Quakers of military age joined the armed forces.[45] The second dissident group was the radical liberals whose opposition was most coherently represented by the Union of Democratic Control (UDC) founded on 5 August

42. Angell's group spent over twelve hundred pounds in trying to stop the war, while the neutrality committee spent less than twenty; Swartz, "Study in Futility," p. 257. Also see Neutrality League manifestos in the *Manchester Guardian*, 3 and 4 August 1914.

43. See Hazlehurst, *Politicians at War*, pp. 33–65.

44. J. Ramsay MacDonald, *National Defence: A Study of Militarism* (London, 1917), p. 12. Also see Iconoclast [Mary Agnes Hamilton], *J. Ramsay MacDonald* (New York, 1925), p. 28.

45. See *Extracts from the Minutes and Proceedings of the London Yearly Meeting of Friends* (London, 1923), pp. 231–32. Many who served were birthright Quakers not active in the religious Society of Friends.

1914. Although MacDonald was a cofounder of the UDC and the union generally cooperated with the ILP, its chief architects and builders were middle-class radicals like E. D. Morel, Trevelyan, and Ponsonby, who with Angell, were the union's other cofounders. The UDC was not a stop-the-war movement. Instead, it attempted to define the means by which international peace could be established and maintained once the war ended. Its basic tenets included national self-determination; parliamentary, and therefore democratic, control of British foreign policy; open diplomacy through the aegis of some international council; and postwar disarmament.[46] While bourgeois radicals and some middle-class socialists found a home in the UDC, the bulk of the third antiwar group, chiefly represented by the rank and file of the antimilitarist ILP, could not be satisfied with the UDC's essentially moderate policies. On 13 August 1914 the ILP had issued a manifesto condemning the war, and five ILP members of Parliament upheld the party's antiwar stand. Many of the party's younger pacifists, however, felt the need to engage in more energetic and purposeful antiwar activities.[47]

One of the younger socialists who was disappointed by the apparent lack of vigor in the ILP's antiwar posture was Archibald Fenner Brockway. The son of an Indian missionary, Brockway had abandoned organized Christianity and nonconformist politics to follow a career as a left-wing journalist and socialist organizer. He had served on the staff of the *Examiner* and the *Christian Commonwealth* before moving on to the official ILP organ *Labour Leader* whose editor he became in 1912 at the age of twenty-three. When the war began Brockway, a staunch pacifist, had thrown his entire

46. On the UDC, see Marvin Swartz, *The Union of Democratic Control in British Politics during the First World War* (Oxford, 1971), which supersedes previous accounts by Helena W. Swanwick, *Builders of Peace* (London, 1924), and A. J. P. Taylor, *The Troublemakers: Dissent over Foreign Policy, 1792–1939* (Bloomington, Ind., 1958), pp. 132–38. Robbins, *Abolition of War*, pp. 55–69, provides an interesting brief account of the early development of the UDC. For the relationship between the UDC and the ILP, see Robert E. Dowse, *Left in the Centre: The Independent Labour Party, 1893–1940* (London, 1966), pp. 24–26.

47. G. D. H. Cole, *History of the Labour Party from 1914* (London, 1948), pp. 19–21; Dowse, *Left in the Centre*, pp. 20–27; and A. Fenner Brockway, *Inside the Left* (London, 1942), pp. 48–55 passim.

weight and that of the *Labour Leader* into the antiwar struggle, but, like many other socialists, he found it exceedingly difficult to fix a specific course of action for the war-resistance movement. When Brockway's wife Lilla suggested that he place a letter in the *Labour Leader* calling on all men of military age who would resist conscription if it became law to enroll themselves in an anticonscription organization, Brockway accepted the idea, probably more as an outlet for frustrated energy than from any hope of significant results.[48] However, his letter, which appeared on 12 November and again on 19 November 1914, drew an eager response. Within six days, he had collected over 150 names. As Brockway later recalled, the replies to his inquiry were so earnest and enthusiastic "that it at once became clear that there was need for a Fellowship in which the prospective resisters might unite."[49]

Even after this first wave of enthusiasm, Brockway scarcely envisaged anything more than an informal group of like-minded men.[50] But as the responses continued to flow into the Brockways' cottage in Marple, Derbyshire, and Lilla was kept busy with a nearly full-time job of arranging and answering this correspondence, Brockway concluded that he had accidentally discovered a significant vehicle for carrying forward the principles of the pacifist left in Great Britain. These were the origins of the No-Conscription Fellowship (NCF).

One of the first to answer Brockway's call was Reginald Clifford Allen, secretary and business manager of the official Labour party newspaper, *The Daily Citizen*. Allen had embraced socialism while an undergraduate at Peterhouse College, Cambridge. After earning his B.A. in 1911, he had devoted himself to Labour journalism and to building up the University Socialist Federation (USF), an association dedicated to converting university undergraduates to socialism.

48. Brockway, *Inside the Left*, pp. 34, 43–49, 66; William J. Chamberlain, *Fighting for Peace* (London, [1928]), p. 27; and *Trib.*, 8 January 1920.

49. [A. Fenner Brockway], ed., *The No-Conscription Fellowship: A Souvenir of Its Work during the years, 1914–1919* (London, 1919), p. 22. Hereafter cited as *NCF Souvenir*, this booklet was republished in 1940 by the Central Board of Conscientious Objectors as *Troublesome People*.

50. *The No-Conscription Fellowship: A Summary of Its Activities* (London, n.d.), p. 4, and *Trib.*, 8 March 1917.

He also became, with G. D. H. Cole, the youngest member of the Fabian executive committee. Like Brockway, Allen was a great admirer of Hardie and strongly devoted to the doctrine of socialist internationalism. Before the war, when there was talk of instituting compulsory military training for Cambridge undergraduates, he had written an anonymous anticonscription article in the *University Socialist,* the official organ of the USF.[51] From the beginning of the conflict, he had consistently held that Labour should stand fast for peace and brotherhood in order "to save the self-respect and the reputation of the Socialist Movement." A contemporary, Mary Agnes Hamilton, remembered him as "by far the ablest and most convincing exponent of . . . total pacifism."[52] But Beatrice Webb, who was acquainted with Allen through the Fabian Society, called him "a fanatical antiwar, pro-German advocate who distorts every fact to prove his country wrong."[53] Indeed, one of Allen's antiwar speeches had been published under the title *Is Germany Right and Britain Wrong?*[54] These circumstances very early established him as one of the leading "peace cranks" in the country.

Although Brockway found "C. A." (as his friends called him)—with his perfect manners and impeccable dress—vastly different from those ILP'ers with whom he usually associated, he recognized Allen as "an exceptional man" with great potential as a leader. Allen dominated his associates not only because of his obvious intellectual ability but also through an immense personal charm that nearly always silenced or reconciled those who disagreed with him.[55]

The other member of what was to become the first trium-

---

51. B. A. [Clifford Allen], "Cambridge and Conscription," *University Socialist* 1 (Michaelmas Term, 1913):104–7. There are two studies of Allen: Arthur Marwick, *Clifford Allen: The Open Conspirator* (Edinburgh, 1964), a brief, competent summary, and Martin Gilbert, ed., *Plough My Own Furrow* (London, 1965), which is a compilation of some of the more interesting material from Allen's private papers (CAP).

52. See Allen to *Daily Citizen,* 27 August 1914, and Mary Agnes Hamilton, *Remembering My Good Friends* (London, 1944), p. 116.

53. Beatrice Webb, *Diaries, 1912–1924,* ed. Margaret I. Cole (London, 1952), p. 33.

54. This pamphlet was used as part of a German propaganda booklet published in the United States called *England on the Witness Stand* (New York, 1915), pp. 63–71.

55. Brockway, *Inside the Left,* pp. 66, 141.

Clifford Allen (ca. 1911). (Courtesy Friends House Library)

virate of the NCF was C. H. (Clarence Henry) Norman, a London shorthand writer and socialist. By the autumn of 1914, Norman had already made a considerable splash in antiwar circles through his work with Scott Duckers, a London solicitor, in organizing an abortive stop-the-war committee. Norman had also published a series of muckraking articles on the "hidden scandals behind the war." A courageous but unmelting skeptic, Norman proved to be a difficult colleague, and he figured prominently in nearly every dispute that later troubled the NCF.[56]

In late November 1914 Brockway, Norman, and Allen met with Walter H. Ayles and James H. Hudson, two future Labour M.P.s, and the Reverend Leyton Richards, a Congregational minister and later general secretary of the Fellowship of Reconciliation (FOR). Together these six planned the formation of an anticonscription organization. As a result of this meeting, another letter appeared in the *Labour Leader* on 3 December advertising the formation of a "No-Conscription Fellowship" that offered membership to all men of military age "who are not prepared to take a combatant's part, whatever the penalty for refusing." Headquarters was moved from Derbyshire to London, with offices at Merton House, Salisbury Court, Fleet Street. Allen became responsible for central operations.[57]

Early in February 1915 a membership list of nearly 350 names was published, but, as an attached financial statement listing a total subscription of £4 19s. 4d. illustrated, the NCF was not as yet a particularly substantial organization. Its founders were nonetheless convinced that their fellowship could become a significant national movement. To provide

56. C. H. Norman, *Britain and the War* (London, 1914). Part of this booklet also appeared in the German-American propaganda effort *England on the Witness Stand*, pp. 28–44. The Home Office kept a close watch on Norman's antiwar activities; for example, see HO 45/10782/27853/18a. In a letter to Miles Malleson, H. G. Wells said of Norman that he had never heard him "speak lovingly of any human being. [His] . . . normal attitude has always been one of opposition—to anything"; quoted in Russell, *Autobiography*, 2:72.

57. Clifford Allen, "Pacifism: Then and Now," in *We Did Not Fight*, ed. Julian Bell (London, 1935), p. 27; Brockway, *Inside the Left*, p. 67; and *NCF Souvenir*, pp. 22–23. Also see NCF circular letter, 25 September 1915, CAP. There are incomplete files of these letters to NCF members in CAP, SCPC, and BRA.

the organization with a formal structure, the membership was asked to nominate and elect regular officers and a national committee.[58] Allen was chosen as chairman and Brockway became national secretary; Norman, Hudson, and Richards were elected to the national committee. These men, most of whom were in their mid-twenties, formed the first "headquarters staff" of the antiwar–anticonscription forces in Great Britain.[59]

By the spring of 1915 the NCF had elected leaders, enrolled some hundreds of members, established a national headquarters in London, and set up branches in Birmingham, Glasgow, Sheffield, and Manchester. But much remained to be done. As Allen later recalled:

> In one year between March 1915 and March 1916 we had to create our organisation and its branches; equip them with machinery more complex than that of any ordinary propaganda or political organisation . . . [in order to] make it impossible for even a war government to suppress it . . . and last but not least, shape a common philosophy upon which we could agree.[60]

This last objective proved to be the most difficult to achieve. What was to be the organization's primary purpose? What principles should bind the members to each other and to the fellowship they had created? How should these principles be conveyed to the government and to the public to ensure that they were properly understood? There seemed to be no simple answers to these questions. Allen noted that when the war began, pacifists were placed in "a very special psychological situation . . . which made it exceedingly hard for them to satisfy themselves as to their attitude, far less to convince the public."[61] They might say—as indeed they did say on the letterhead of the NCF's first publications—that they were men of enlistment age who were "not prepared to

58. The No-Conscription Fellowship, list of members and circular letter, 2 February 1915, NCF File, SCPC.

59. NCF circular letter, 24 May 1915, NCF File, SCPC, and *The No-Conscription Fellowship: A Record of Its Activities* (London, 1916), p. 3.

60. Quote is from Clifford Allen's unpublished manuscript (hereafter referred to as Allen ms.) on conscription and conscientious objectors, chap. 1, pp. 4–5, CAP. Also see NCF circular letter, 24 May 1915, NCF File, SCPC.

61. Allen ms., chap. 1, p. 8, CAP.

take up arms in case of Conscription." But this statement would hardly suffice as a credo for a broad national movement. In truth, it seemed very like saying: "We oppose conscription because it is inconvenient and might cause a number of us to be killed who would not otherwise be killed!" Obviously their stand had to encompass more if they were to convince the world that they were not merely cowards and shirkers.

The name, No-Conscription Fellowship, implied opposition to the government's right to impose military conscription even in wartime. This view was essentially a libertarian stand, and the fellowship did have members who were civil libertarians rather than pacifists, but, for most men in the NCF, libertarianism alone did not adequately represent their objection to conscription and to the war. Some members, for example, saw their pacifism as a way of life that governed all their personal decisions and all their relationships with other human beings.[62] One pacifist writer recalled his belief as "something spiritually flaming"; another believed pacifism to be "something far deeper, far more real than the mere negation of war. It is that Divine Force which must, when it dominates the hearts of men, dominate the world." War resisters might be "freethinkers," followers of the pacifist philosophy of Count Tolstoy, Quakers, or members of some lesser-known religious sect whose doctrine forbade combatant service.[63]

Although Quakers were not the largest single body of religious objectors in Britain, they were the predominant religious body within the NCF in numbers as well as influence.[64]

---

62. Allen made this point twenty years after the events he was recalling. It does not, in fact, accurately represent his viewpoint during the war; see Allen, "Pacifism: Then and Now," pp. 27-28.

63. Gilbert O. Thomas, *Autobiography: 1891-1941* (London, 1946), pp. 128-32, and Howard Marten [in prison] to friends, 5 May 1917, BRA. A good brief discussion of religious objectors is Rae, *Conscience and Politics*, pp. 72-81.

64. There were 1,716 Christadelphian objectors but few, if any, joined the NCF; Quaker objectors numbered 750 according to the Report of the Pelham Committee, Schedule 4, T. E. Harvey Papers, FHL. For the Christadelphian experience, see F. G. Jannaway, *Without the Camp* (London, 1917); the Quaker view is presented by Edward Grubb, "Why the Quakers Object" (London, n.d.), and by Henry T. Hodgkin, *A Quaker View of War* (Leeds, n.d.).

In 1915 the Friends' witness against war, though widely misinterpreted, was so well established that there was every reason to believe that they would be specifically excluded from any future conscription law. Yet the conviction had been long growing, especially among younger Friends, that passively stepping aside while others served would not suffice to soothe the true Christian conscience. No longer satisfied with using their probable immunity to military service as a means of escaping sacrifice, many Quakers of military age saw as their duty to the nation, to their fellow men, and to God, the joining together in sympathy and brotherhood with all who genuinely opposed war and militarism. Moved by this spirit, in 1915 the London Yearly Meeting of the Society of Friends recommended that, if conscription became law, "no exemption be given to members of the Society of Friends, which is not equally applicable to those outside it."[65]

Besides representing a clear break with the traditional social passivism of British Friends, this new attitude greatly aided the NCF in accommodating its principles to both Friends and non-Friends. As one socialist and agnostic NCF pioneer, A. M. (Arthur Maxwell) Sanders, recalled forty years later, "the glorious attitude of the Quakers who scorned to take advantage of the offer their previous stand entitled them to" prevented socialist objectors from being completely "isolated and despised."[66]

In the beginning, the decision of antiwar Quakers to make common cause with the other antiwar and anticonscription groups provided a considerable boost to NCF morale and, eventually, to its financial situation. But it also meant that, in defining the fellowship's principles and objectives, the Quaker–Christian view had to be reconciled not only with

65. *London Yearly Meeting of Friends*, Minute 31. Also see FSC, *Minutes, Records of Work and Documents Issued* (hereafter referred to as FSC *Minutes*) 1 (June 1915–June 1916):7, FHL.

66. A. M. Sanders, "My Experiences as a Conscientious Objector and the Life That Led up to Them," unpublished ms., p. 4, CAP. Also see Allen ms., chap. 2, pp. 10–11, CAP. Arthur Maxwell Sanders (1892–) was a rank-and-file member of the NCF from Brighton. He was imprisoned for his stand during the First World War and refused to act as an air warden in the second. In 1957 he contacted Lady Marjory Allen, widow of Clifford Allen, and on her request sent a typescript recounting his experiences. Lady Allen deposited this typescript in her late husband's papers.

libertarian individualism but also with the ideals of a wide range of socialist war resisters who accounted for 75 to 80 percent of the NCF's membership. In many cases, this presented no difficulty. Some socialists opposed the war primarily on the ethical grounds that violence and killing were morally repulsive, a position not markedly different from that of Christian objectors. Others resisted the war because they saw it as an extension of the essentially evil capitalist system and as another means of destroying the international solidarity of the working classes. Socialists often combined the ethical and anticapitalist arguments as was the case, for example, with both Allen and Brockway.[67] Still another socialist faction, generally militant Marxists, did not reject violence; they would be ready to fight and kill for the overthrow of the capitalist system, but they resisted what they saw as a capitalist war aimed at exploiting the masses. At first this group was neither large nor loud, though it became more important and considerably more vocal as the war dragged on.[68] In the early stages of the NCF's development, the question for most socialist objectors was, as Sanders put it: "Should I fight with arms for capitalism, perhaps die a soldier's death possibly with glory, or should I fight without arms for socialism, perhaps die a traitor's death, certainly without glory?"[69]

Faced with such an ideological tangle, leaders of the NCF had to consider as many viewpoints as possible and attempt to bind them all together with some force as meaningful as the patriotism, idealism, and fear that made the overwhelming majority of British citizens ardent supporters of the war. In mid-1915, before the objectors' resolve was tested by the

67. For example, see Clifford Allen, "Alternative Service," *Ploughshare* 1 (May 1916): 101–4; Allen ms., chap. 2, p. 5, CAP; Dr. Alfred Salter, "The Religion of a C.O.," *NCF Souvenir*, pp. 14–16; and *The Position of the Conscientious Objector*, NCF pamphlet (London, n.d.), pp. 1–2.

68. See Dowse, *Left in the Centre*, pp. 21–22, and *NCF Souvenir*, pp. 10–13. Also see Chap. 11. In his book on conscientious objectors in the First World War, David Boulton says that "only a minority [of socialist objectors] were out-and-out pacifists whose objection was to violence itself, irrespective of the justice of its cause"; *Objection Overruled* (London, 1967), p. 12. Such a statement might have some validity if Boulton is speaking of the socialist objectors in 1918 or 1919, after they had been punished for their resistance to conscription. In 1915, however, nonviolence was the accepted view of a majority of NCF members, socialist and nonsocialist alike.

69. Sanders, "My Experiences," p. 3, CAP.

realities of compulsory military service, the national committee of the NCF felt they had discovered a single, central
principle that could give unity and direction to their cause.
They found this principle not so much in the dissection of
their own views as in the recognition by democratic states of
the singular quality of actions and events involving the taking of human life. This acknowledgment of the sanctity of
human life, even by those intimately involved in destroying
lives, became the central pivot on which the NCF turned to
face a hostile nation. As Allen later noted: "This matter of
giving your life and taking other people's is so different from
almost everything else in the world, the killing of a man is so
irreparable . . . that here at any rate the State, whatever
other powers it may possess, must not step in. It must not
make men kill by compulsion."[70] As early as November of
1914 Allen had recognized the strength of this appeal when
he said, "the sacredness of human life is the mainspring of
all our [ILP] propaganda."[71]

In the spring of 1915 the NCF issued a statement of principles that was meant to be the fundamental article of the
conscientious objectors' faith.

> The No-Conscription Fellowship is an organisation of men
> likely to be called upon to undertake military service in the
> event of Conscription who will refuse from conscientious
> motives to bear arms, because they consider human life to be
> sacred and cannot, therefore, assume the responsibility of in-
> flicting death. They deny the right of governments to say "you
> *shall* bear arms," and will oppose every effort to introduce
> compulsory military service into Great Britain. Should such
> efforts be successful, they will, whatever the consequences may
> be, obey their conscientious convictions, rather than the com-
> mands of Governments.[72]

By issuing a statement based on the principle of the sanctity of human life, the NCF was, in effect, setting itself in a
mold that would be difficult to remodel. Certainly, most

70. Allen ms., chap. 3a, p. 7, CAP, and Allen, "Pacifism: Then and
Now," pp. 29-30. Compare with a passage written by Samuel in 1902:
"Universal service cannot fail to do much to destroy that respect for the
sanctity of human life, to have established which in the modern world is one
of the noblest results of the triumph of Christianity"; Herbert Samuel,
Liberalism (London, 1902), p. 372.

71. Quoted by Gilbert, ed., *Plough My Own Furrow*, p. 38.

72. NCF, *Statement of Principles*, leaflet, CAP. Also see *NCF Souvenir*, p. 8.

liberal and Christian pacifists could accept such a definition of their beliefs, and, in 1915 at least, most socialists were willing to accommodate themselves to the statement. But, as time passed, many socialist objectors, wrung by the frustration and despair of imprisonment and public hostility, would attempt to break away from the mold and even, if possible, to smash it to pieces. To a considerable extent, they succeeded.

In retrospect, it is easy to detect basic flaws in the original statement of principles. First, it implied that the NCF primarily objected to the act of killing. Thus, later, when the government offered to release conscientious objectors from the burden of taking life, it could point to the NCF's stated principles and say "we have done what you asked us to do." When NCF members refused to accept even noncombatant military service, the government could feel justified in classifying them as perverse impossibilitists who deserved to be punished.[73] Second, and even more significant, the statement on the face of it virtually eliminated the political objector from consideration. Could a man who did not invariably and in all circumstances accept the sanctity of human life still have a truly conscientious objection to war? The NCF seemed to be saying no, he could not. This limitation would regularly return to haunt the fellowship. After the war, Allen recalled that the statement of principles had been adopted on the spur of the moment by men who were still ignorant of how a conscription system would operate. In the end, the establishment of dogma constricted the base of the NCF and caused innumerable problems within the organization.[74] Yet, in spite of the difficulties and controversies that arose later, the NCF succeeded not only in providing thousands of young war resisters with aid, comfort, and camaraderie but also in severely testing the limits of dissent in a liberal society at war. There was no equivalent organization in any other belligerent country from 1914 to 1918, and

73. In November 1915 the NCF did try to clarify this problem by adding a clause to the statement of principles that condemned "compulsory alternatives to military service involving a change of occupation."
74. Allen ms., chap. 2, pp. 7–8, CAP, and *NCF Souvenir*, p. 8. Norman was one NCF leader who condemned the "dogma of the sanctity of human life" from the beginning; see extracts of letter from C. H. Norman to A. Fenner Brockway, [October 1916], in the unsorted FSC Files, FHL.

there has been none since. Thus, if organized resistance to total war has any meaning or message, it must be found in the No-Conscription Fellowship's struggle against the Great War.[75]

75. In asserting the uniqueness of the NCF, I do not intend to imply that it is the only peace group that has accomplished anything. During World War II antiwar organizations in both Great Britain and the United States carried out many of the functions that the NCF had earlier performed. Certainly, the protests against American involvement in Vietnam during the 1960s had a profound political effect. My point is that only with the NCF is there coherent, large-scale, long-standing, and nationwide resistance against a total war that is strongly supported, or at least accepted as necessary, by an overwhelming majority of the population.

3

The NCF before Conscription

The Fellowship Comes of Age

After an initial rush to the pacifist colors, the NCF's growth was not spectacular, a fact that probably reflects general quiescence about the conscription question during the early months of 1915. Some war resisters no doubt saw the fellowship as a shaft of light in the stygian darkness of a world gone mad. It gave them something to cling to while those about them embraced the national cause. Though dissenters believed that cause insufficient or wrong, it was difficult to remain apart from it, especially when all the "right" people pictured it as something necessary, good, and even sacred.[1] In a sense, the slow growth of the NCF in its early stages only reemphasized the isolation of those who did join. As one early member put it: "my hopes did not run very high when upon enquiry of the local branch of the ILP I learned that only two others had sent up their names."[2]

Lacking the emergency atmosphere so necessary to the dynamic growth of a minority cause, the fellowship's leaders had to be content with a rather plodding membership campaign, although they still believed that thousands of others shared their convictions and their resolve to resist war service. Growth was, to some degree, impeded by the restrictions that the NCF imposed on itself. To avoid the unnecessary alienation of public opinion, the national committee

1. See Allen's reflections on this difficulty in Allen ms., chap. 4, pp. 3–4, 6–8, CAP. In May 1915 Bertrand Russell wrote to Ottoline Morrell: "I find it unspeakably painful being thought a traitor. Every casual meeting . . . makes me quiver with sensitive apprehension"; Russell to O. Morrell, 27 May 1915, quoted in Bertrand Russell, *The Autobiography of Bertrand Russell*, 3 vols. (London, 1967–1969), 2:17–18.

2. A. M. Sanders, "My Experience as a Conscientious Objector and the Life That Led up to Them," unpublished ms., p. 3, CAP.

decided that the NCF's propaganda efforts should be limited to passing out literature among likely prospects. They even frowned on writing letters to local newspapers to explain the fellowship's aims and policies.[3] Members were reminded that the NCF's purpose was "not to urge upon men that they should not bear arms, but to unite for common counsel and action those who have already made up their minds that they cannot do so." Similarly, NCF publications reiterated that the fellowship did not intend to disparage patriotism or to sit in moral judgment over those who supported the war. Rather, conscientious objectors should "let the example of those who have gone out at great sacrifice in response to what they felt to be their highest duty, inspire us to follow the call of conscience . . . with the same enthusiasm and devotion."[4]

The magnanimity in these pronouncements, made before the fight for conscience was well underway, unfortunately, though not unnaturally, began to fade as the contest between war and peace advocates grew more intense. It was, indeed, rather like the fraternization of German and Allied troops on the first Christmas of the war in the days before what was still only a bad dream had become an enduring nightmare.

In July 1915 the passage of the National Registration Act, which many war resisters saw as the first step toward organizing British society for conscription, provided the stimulus for a rapid expansion of NCF operations. Clifford Allen once claimed that during this period the NCF launched a "campaign of organization which has probably not been equaled in any similar controversy."[5]

In May 1915 the NCF had five branches with a membership in the hundreds; by October over fifty branches had

3. NCF circular letter, July 1915, CAP. Previously, the NCF had encouraged members to write to the press; see NCF circular letter, 24 May 1915, NCF File, SCPC.

4. *Why We Object*, NCF pamphlet (London, n.d.), p. 1. Also see *Activities of the Fellowship* (London, n.d.), CAP, and Sylvia Pankhurst, *The Home Front* (London, 1932), p. 260.

5. Clifford Allen, "The Conscientious Objector's Struggle: A History of the No-Conscription Fellowship," *Labour Leader*, 20 July 1916. *NCF Souvenir*, p. 23, and Allen ms., chap. 1, pp. 4-5, CAP.

been formed, claiming a membership of over five thousand.[6] These local associations attempted to draw together antiwar elements in one locale for discussion and encouragement. Such groups might also make a larger, more effective protest against the increasing victimization of those who refused to enlist. Members were still enjoined against overt propaganda outside their branches, lest the group be accused of organizing opinion or creating "artificial consciences."[7]

In the beginning, NCF membership was open only to male British subjects of military age, but a considerable number of people ineligible for military service because of age or sex were also interested in joining the struggle against conscription. At the suggestion of the fellowship's Birmingham branch, the national committee agreed to accept women and older men as associate members.[8] The decision to admit associate members seemed almost incidental at the time, but eventually it proved to be momentous. By 1917, when nearly all the regular members were in some sort of custody, associate members kept the NCF operating under far more difficult circumstances than the early leaders of the organization had had to face.

As the NCF expanded and solidified its organizational structure, the social and semifraternal aspects of its program were most immediately apparent. But the NCF represented more than a group of individuals with tender consciences leaning on one another in a time of trial. It also became a highly organized political pressure group using every legal device provided by a liberal society to protect the interests of a numerically insignificant minority. With relatively little money and almost no popular support, the fellowship attracted a remarkably able band of social activists and political organizers. Together these men and women shaped an organization that caused the government more grief than any other body of dissenters against the war.

6. William J. Chamberlain, *Fighting for Peace* (London, [1928]), p. 28. Compare with NCF circular letter, 24 May 1915, NCF File, SCPC.
7. Clifford Allen, "C.O.'s Struggle"; NCF circular letter, July 1915, and untitled NCF pamphlet, CAP.
8. NCF circular letter, 24 May 1915, NCF File, SCPC; also see NCF circular letter, July 1915, asking non-British subjects to withdraw from the fellowship.

Most NCF leaders came from the Independent Labour Party (ILP). Besides Fenner Brockway, Allen, and C. H. Norman, the ILP provided James H. Hudson, a Lancashire schoolmaster who was later elected to Parliament and became Philip Snowden's parliamentary private secretary. In South Wales, Councillor Morgan Jones was the NCF standard-bearer. After the war, Jones became the first former conscientious objector to sit in the House of Commons and was a junior minister in the second Labour government. Another important socialist recruit was William J. Chamberlain, one of Allen's co-workers on the *Daily Citizen,* whose great energy and organizational ability more than compensated for his rather embarrassing lack of silence and humility. Chamberlain became the NCF's national organizer and the first editor of the fellowship's newspaper, *The Tribunal.* For a time, James Maxton of Glasgow, a rising star on the extreme left, served as Scottish member of the national committee. But Maxton's pacifism was of a most militant variety and, as Brockway has noted, "he was not at home with us. . . . We were too far removed from the class fight."[9]

When the original NCF national treasurer resigned his post in July 1915, Edward Grubb, a sixty-year-old Quaker who had figured prominently in the prewar debate over conscription, was asked to replace him. Grubb's appointment was somewhat unusual. He had had no previous connection with the NCF, but, since the fellowship was recommended to him by fellow Quakers, he accepted the position in order to "do his bit" for the pacifist cause. It was fortunate for the NCF that he did. Few men contributed more to the organization's growth and survival, and Grubb came to be regarded, in Brockway's words, as "the father of the movement."[10] Certainly, Grubb was a good provider who did yeoman work in raising the money that allowed the group to carry on its propaganda and maintenance activities. His chief sources of supply were wealthy members of the Society

9. A. Fenner Brockway, *Inside the Left* (London, 1942), p. 68. Also see Robert E. Dowse, *Left in the Centre: The Independent Labour Party, 1893–1940* (London, 1966), p. 22, and Chamberlain, *Fighting for Peace,* p. 22.

10. NCF circular letter, July 1915, CAP, and Brockway, *Inside the Left,* p. 64. Also see Edward Grubb, "War Resistance," in *We Did Not Fight,* ed. Julian Bell (London, 1935), p. 143, and James Dudley, *The Life of Edward Grubb, 1854–1939: A Spiritual Pilgrimage* (London, 1946), pp. 104–6.

Edward Grubb (ca. 1920). (Courtesy Quaker Collection, Haverford College)

of Friends, some of whom donated as much as five hundred pounds a year.[11]

Grubb's service on the NCF national committee brought him into close contact with the fellowship's young leaders, and he later referred to them as "among the noblest spirits, morally and intellectually, that I have ever been privileged to meet . . . united in single-minded devotion to what they sincerely believe to be the good of their country and of humanity. . . . They not only talk about Peace, they live it."[12] He added that he could recall only one occasion when a committee member lost his temper[13]—surely a significant advertisement for pacifism. This was a considerable achievement; despite the diversity of its members' backgrounds as well as of their political and religious views, the NCF national committee never entirely succumbed to the kind of self-indulgent factionalism that has immobilized so many minority movements.

Close observers of the NCF give most credit for the group's public unity, even in the face of enormous pressure, to Allen's uncommon leadership qualities. Bertrand Russell called him "a man of genius—not at all simple, with a curious combination of gifts. . . . I have never seen anyone comparable to him as a Chairman." In Brockway's words: "Allen was . . . the best chairman I have known, either in committee or conference, and the most efficient administrator, seeing everything through to the last detail." Years afterward, Corder Catchpool, a leading Quaker objector, recalled Allen's "intense activity and ability. . . . Though I admired him immensely it used to give me rather an inferiority complex." Another committee member, Francis Meynell, said that Allen's leadership was "magnificently impartial and evocative and controlling. . . . I have sat under many . . . chairmen but I never met his like." And finally, Grubb again: "On nearly every question of prime importance . . . the committee was found to be equally divided in opinion; and only a chairman of consummate ability and character could have kept the organization together. Such was Clifford Allen. . . . No

11. Dudley, *Edward Grubb*, p. 108, and Grubb, "War Resistance," p. 148.
12. Edward Grubb to the editor of *The Friend* 56(14 July 1916):551.
13. Grubb, "War Resistance," p. 146. Also see Dudley, *Edward Grubb*, p. 107, and Mary E. Pumphrey, *Edward Grubb, a Brief Memoir* (London, 1940), p. 14.

cause, I think, ever had a more inspiring leader. . . . He was a statesman as well as a prophet."[14]

The adroitness of Allen's leadership, as well as the intensely emotional atmosphere in which the NCF operated, helps to explain the unusual respect in which he was held by rank-and-file members. Mary Agnes Hamilton has provided a graphic description of Allen as he looked then, with his "strikingly handsome head . . . its mass of wavy auburn hair above a high forehead, which topped his tall willowy, attenuated figure; . . . C. A. . . . looked like a saint; but he was a saint of the militant Jesuit type; there was a powerful brain and a will of iron behind his apparent fragility."[15]

At the same time that the NCF was attempting to develop a coherent program and structure, it was also establishing close liaison with other antiwar organizations. One of the first peace groups formed during the war was the Fellowship of Reconciliation (FOR). Founded at Cambridge in late December 1914 after a conference of Quaker and other religious leaders, the FOR was a nonsectarian Christian body "open to all . . . who wished to promote a spirit of Christian Reconciliation in the world at war."[16] Even more significant, though limited to Quakers, was the Friends Service Committee (FSC), the anticonscription arm of the Friends Yearly Meeting. Appointed by the yearly meeting in May 1915, the FSC's goal was "to strengthen the Peace testimony among Friends of military age."[17]

In July 1915 the FSC took the initiative by inviting leaders of the NCF and the FOR to a conference from whence emerged a Joint Advisory Council (JAC) of antiwar organi-

14. Russell to Ottoline Morrell, 10 April 1916, quoted by Ronald W. Clark, *The Life of Bertrand Russell* (New York, 1976), pp. 276–77; Brockway, *Inside the Left,* p. 141; Catchpool's remarks are from a typewritten statement in CAP; Meynell is quoted in Martin Gilbert, ed., *Plough My Own Furrow* (London, 1965), pp. 56–57, and Grubb in Dudley, *Edward Grubb,* p. 107.

15. Mary Agnes Hamilton, *Remembering My Good Friends* (London, 1944), p. 116. Compare with Pankhurst, *The Home Front,* p. 297.

16. Quoted by Dudley, *Edward Grubb,* pp. 105–6. For the FOR, see Vera Brittain, *The Rebel Passion* (London, 1964), and *First Annual Report of the Fellowship of Reconciliation* (London, [1916]).

17. The FSC manifesto and a list of original members are in FSC *Minutes,* 1:78, FHL. Also see T. Corder Catchpool, *On Two Fronts* (London, 1918), p. 104n, and John W. Graham, *Conscription and Conscience* (London, 1922), pp. 160–62.

zations. Although the NCF appeared to be the dominant partner—Allen was the JAC's first chairman and Brockway its secretary—each of the participating groups retained its individual character and leadership. The JAC operated throughout the war and later took the lead in arranging for the rehabilitation of conscientious objectors released from prison. Local joint committees modeled on the national council were also organized in many areas to avoid overlapping propaganda and to increase the general efficiency of the struggle against conscription.[18]

At about the same time that the JAC was being formed, Barry (A. Barratt) Brown and John P. Fletcher, two of the FSC's most influential leaders, took seats on the NCF national committee. Many starry-eyed youngsters who joined the NCF in the early stages of the war were still probing the depths of their commitment to pacifism; they must have been impressed by articulate Friends like Brown and Fletcher who seemed so sure of their pacifist principles and so dedicated to carrying them out. Brown, Allen's boyhood friend and schoolmate, was extremely influential among younger Friends. Brockway remembered him chiefly for his "boyish mischievousness." Both Brown and Fletcher—who had already served two prison terms for agitation against conscription in Australia and New Zealand—advocated a brand of pacifism that less spiritually minded members eventually found puzzling and ultimately found impossible. Later both men were major figures in a series of disputes that troubled the fellowship and, for a time, threatened to destroy the united pacifist front. But those differences would arise only after conscription had been imposed. In the earlier, halcyon days, fellow feeling, mutual admiration, and undiluted idealism were the most obvious characteristics of the pacifist alliance.

The passage of the National Registration Act in July 1915 gave war resisters their first opportunity for joint action. Conflicting opinions on the NCF national committee made it

18. See "Resume of Proceedings of the Friends Service Committee," 2 July 1916, FSC *Minutes,* 1:11, FHL, appointing Roderic K. Clark and Robert O. Mennell as FSC representatives on the JAC, and Hubert Peet to Friends, 14 December 1915, FSC *Minutes,* 1:34, FHL. Also Allen ms., chap. 2, p. 9, CAP; Allen, "C.O.'s Struggle"; and NCF circular letters, July 1915 and 9 September 1915, CAP.

necessary to poll the entire membership to ascertain whether the fellowship should recognize state authority to the point of signing the national register. The question was resolved when the national committee, following the FSC's lead, recommended that members register in compliance with the law, but when listing the voluntary service, if any, they would be willing to perform, they should add the following statement:

> Whilst registering as a citizen in conformity with the Government demand, I could not, for reasons of conscience, take part in military service; in any employment necessitating the taking of the military oath; or in the production of materials the purpose of which is the taking of human life.[19]

After the institution of the national register, the national committee decided to issue a general manifesto that would broaden and clarify the fellowship's position and would prevent the government and the public from misinterpreting its objectives. This manifesto, published in September 1915, emphasized that the fellowship's stand was in no way meant to reflect on the courage and patriotism of Britain's soldiers and sought only to establish that conscientious objectors were ready "to sacrifice as much in the cause of the World's peace as our fellows are sacrificing in the cause of the nation's war." It also stressed the principle of the sacredness of human life, noting that, while opposition to conscription arose from many sources,

> first and foremost our decision rests on the ground of the serious violation of moral and religious convictions which a system of compulsion must invoke. . . .
> We believe the real inspiration that prompts all efforts towards progress is a desire that human life may become of more account. This ideal we cannot renounce; its claim is absolute.[20]

19. See "Memorandum on National Service," undated, signed by Allen as NCF chairman, CAP; NCF circular letter, July 1915, CAP; and minutes of FSC meeting, 2 July 1915, FSC *Minutes,* 1:8, FHL. On 20 September 1915 *The Times* reported that Stanley Adams of Croydon, a conscientious objector, was fined five pounds or one month for refusing to sign the national register.

20. "Manifesto Issued by the No-Conscription Fellowship," signed by officers and members of the national committee, September 1915, CAP. The civil authorities duly noted the issuance of the manifesto; see HO 45/10786/297549/10.

For those already converted to the cause, the London office produced a steady stream of printed material dealing with the policies and fortunes of the movement. One provincial member recalled that during the early days of the war he had "only one life line to cling to . . . the circular letters that arrived from time to time from our head office, informing me how the movement was progressing."[21] These letters outlined the current thinking of the national committee and recommended action on the local level. They also revealed that, for a group advocating individual liberty of thought and expression, the NCF seemed to be a somewhat autocratic organization. Concerned about the possibility that the fellowship might splinter into the ideological fragments from whence it came or might run afoul of the law, the national committee instituted tight administrative and financial controls over local branch activities.[22]

When this imperious approach elicited criticism from individual members and caused restlessness in some branches, the committee defended its position by stressing the NCF's extreme vulnerability, especially if the leadership did not retain control of propaganda and recruiting activities. Most members seemed ready to follow the national committee's lead, for there is no evidence of wholesale defection. In any case, the head office always paid lip service, at least, to the idea of freedom of conscience and invited all those who could not accept its advice to retain their membership with the proviso that their actions would "not command the official support of the Fellowship."[23]

During the late summer and early autumn of 1915, besides enrolling new members, the fellowship's chief activity was establishing the machinery for a nationwide organization. Where possible, each member was placed in a local branch, and each branch was assigned to a geographical district or division. Chamberlain became the chief coordinator of this national structure. Members were asked to aid in distributing NCF literature to sympathetic people in their own localities, but, as always, they were enjoined not to "argue men into the organisation." Ample dissemination of

21. Sanders, "My Experiences," p. 4, CAP.
22. See NCF circular letters, July 1915 and 25 September 1915, CAP.
23. Ibid.

printed material would suffice to make the fellowship's existence and objectives known to the "thousands of men who intend to make a stand against Conscription . . . [but] have never heard of our organisation."[24]

The NCF's increasing size and the growing scope of its activities brought it face to face with a new problem: the possibility of police action against the organization or its members. When Brockway noted in his memoirs that police surveillance of prominent NCF leaders did not begin until September 1915,[25] he either confused his dates or was genuinely unaware of how early the careful watching of dissident elements had begun. Home Office files indicate that as early as July 1915 Brockway himself was the subject of a memorandum commenting on speeches that were "influencing" munitions workers at the Vickers and Maxim plants in Barrow. The note does not specify how Brockway was influencing the men, but apparently not all the workers were influenced in the way he intended: A subsequent Home Office file contains a newspaper account of 30 July 1915 describing how a mob bent on violence broke up a pacifist meeting that Brockway was addressing in Marple.[26] Another file includes a memorandum for the attorney general stating that the 5 August 1915 issue of the *Labour Leader* had printed the NCF's statement for the national register, as well as information on NCF membership that "contained a direct incitement not to obey the Munitions of War Act, 1915 . . . the mischief of which was gravely enhanced by the success which was announced as having attended Mr. Clifford Allen's proselytising efforts in South Wales."[27]

Even before these incidents, police officers had visited the rooms of the London branch secretary, collected his papers, and taken him to Scotland Yard for questioning. A few days later, policemen interrogated Allen in his London office. Allen, who had arranged for a lawyer and a shorthand writer to be present, assured the officers of the NCF's intention to be completely cooperative and law-abiding. Nothing significant developed out of this particular interview and,

24. NCF circular letters, 25 September and 12 November 1915, CAP.
25. Brockway, *Inside the Left*, p. 71.
26. HO 45/10741/26375/61 and 74.
27. HO 45/10786/297549/10.

indeed, Home Office records seem to indicate that, while exceedingly watchful, the government was at that time more interested in, or at least receiving more information about, various stop-the-war committees. During July 1915 the NCF was simply listed without comment as one of over a hundred pacifist organizations.[28] As time passed, however, members of the NCF national committee grew increasingly suspicious of some far-reaching official plot against the fellowship. Members were warned against volunteering information to the police, and anyone approached by police officers was cautioned to make it clear that he could not officially interpret the NCF's policy and indeed knew "nothing more about the Fellowship than what [had] already appeared in printed documents."[29]

With growing conviction that the government intended to crush their "perfectly legitimate organization," the national committee set out to thwart the state by developing a complex and clandestine infrastructure. Special means of communication were devised linking the entire network of divisions, branches, and single members into a grid system through which messages and instructions could pass rapidly and safely. Even more important and elaborate was the distribution of responsibility throughout the country to the point where theoretically hundreds of people would have to be arrested simultaneously before the group's administrative machinery could be brought to a halt. This organization was chiefly accomplished by means of a "shadow" system—an arrangement already used by suffragists and later widely developed and extended by Sinn Fein.[30] Every responsible officer, from national chairman to branch secretary, had a shadow or replacement who would automatically assume his

28. NCF circular letter, July 1915, CAP, and HO 45/10742/263275/47, 50, 51, 61, and 73. This same series of reports includes an authorization for stopping and opening mail thought to contain pacifist or stop-the-war pamphlets, including three written by Norman and one each by Allen and Brockway; see HO 45/10742/263275/166.

29. NCF circular letter, July 1915, CAP.

30. See Allen ms., chap. 2, pp. 11–12, CAP, and Allen, "C.O.'s Struggle." The idea of duplicate administrative machinery was unquestionably copied from the suffragist movement. The NCF had no direct contact with Sinn Fein, though obviously the Irish learned from the C.O. and suffragist examples. Compare Graham, *Conscription and Conscience*, p. 175, and Arthur Marwick, *Clifford Allen: The Open Conspirator* (Edinburgh, 1964), p. 26.

position should he be arrested or otherwise neutralized. Whenever possible, this shadow official was an associate member unlikely to be subject to any future conscription law. This contingency plan seems to have worked reasonably well since the activities of the fellowship were maintained and even broadened after most of the original leaders were arrested and imprisoned.[31]

Detailed instructions for the nationwide establishment of the duplicate organization were sent out from the head office immediately following the NCF's first national convention in November 1915.[32] By this time, fear of pressure from the police and of the threat of conscription had markedly increased. Each branch was advised to set up a committee of "six energetic and able" associate members who would henceforth meet with the regular branch committee to become fully acquainted with the branch's activities and ready to take them over at any time. In case of emergency, but not until then, these committees would deal directly with the national associates' committee headed by Dr. Alfred Salter of Bermondsey, London, the shadow chairman.[33]

As a final safeguard against the threat of suppression, manifold copies of all the fellowship's important records and documents were made and widely distributed throughout the country. Chamberlain, relishing his days of conspiratorial magnificence, later recalled that "in various secret places, buried in an orchard in Surrey, or locked in an unsuspecting city merchant's safe, or at the back of the bookshelf in the house of a remote sympathizer . . . were duplicates of every document likely to be seized."[34]

At first glance, there seems to be something wildly ludi-

31. *NCF Souvenir*, p. 23; Brockway, *Inside the Left*, p. 70; and *Bermondsey Story* (London, 1949), p. 66.

32. See this chapter for a discussion of the first national convention.

33. NCF circular letter, 7 December 1915, CAP, and Brockway, *Bermondsey Story*, p. 66. Alfred Salter (1873–1945), socialist, pacifist, and convert to the Society of Friends, had been resident obstetric physician in Guy's Hospital and a bacteriologist for the British Institute of Preventive Medicine. In 1900 he abandoned his promising medical career to work among the poor in Bermondsey. He was elected as a Labour M.P. in 1922–1923 and in 1924–1925.

34. Chamberlain, *Fighting for Peace*, p. 68. Also see Allen ms., chap. 2, p. 18, CAP, and Pumphrey, *Edward Grubb*, p. 14.

crous about grown men flitting across the country hiding documents, holding secret meetings, and issuing coded messages like prankish adolescents. But if mature men did find pleasure and excitement in trying to fool the authorities, were they any more remarkable than the millions who happily rushed to arms as a refreshing escape from normality or responsibility? Leaders of the NCF have overestimated the government's interest in their activities prior to the imposition of conscription, but they were serious and earnest men for all of that. They believed in the rightness and necessity of what they were doing. The ordinary member, sincerely convinced of the wickedness of the war, could always look back, as A. M. Sanders did, with honest pride at his part in building the fellowship "from obscurity to a movement with ramifications so vast and complex that we continually had the authorities guessing as to what our activities really were. . . . It was to me, and always will be, the grandest of all movements."[35]

In the Shadow of the Sword

By the time the Derby scheme was announced, the NCF's activities had already been brought to the attention of the House of Commons several times,[36] though this notoriety and the public hostility that accompanied it took a surprisingly long time to develop. As late as May 1915 Russell had written to an American friend acknowledging a "comparative calm" in British society; at about the same time, Beatrice Webb noted the absence of any "Jingo mob" or "popular anti-pacifist feeling."[37] But as public frustration over the war mounted, so did public distaste for those who would not support it. The last months of 1915 were trying and anxious times for war resisters. One example was the by-election for Keir Hardie's seat in Merthyr Tydfill. Two months after Hardie's death in September 1915, his seat was won by C. B.

35. Sanders, "My Experiences," p. 4, CAP.
36. See 5 H.C., 74:1468, 1777, 1998, 14, 20, and 21 October 1915.
37. Bertrand Russell to Lucy Donnely, 7 May 1915, BRA, and Beatrice Webb, *Diaries, 1912-1924,* ed. Margaret I. Cole (London, 1952), p. 35.

Stanton, a strongly prowar Labour candidate, who defeated the anticonscriptionist supported by the ILP by a three-to-two margin.[38] During the same month, at the urging of newspapers like the *Daily Sketch* and *Daily Express,* a meeting of the Union of Democratic Control (UDC) was forcibly broken up in London.[39]

Amid growing anxiety over public attitudes and the heightening threat of some form of compulsion, NCF leaders decided to bring their scattered followers together to show the organization's strength and solidarity and to plan its future policy. Branches were instructed to prepare for a national convention on 27 November by drawing up resolutions dealing generally with NCF principles and policies and specifically with the continuing crisis over conscription.[40] The first national convention of the NCF gathered at Memorial Hall in London in the midst of increasingly abusive attacks in the proconscriptionist press. Epithets like "pasty-faces," "won't fight funks," "save-their-skin brigade," and "conchies" were becoming widely known and used. Such an atmosphere had its effect on the delegates, many of whom were convinced that their organization headed the list of societies that the government would stop at nothing to destroy. One of these recalled Allen's telling the assemblage to carry on even if the meeting were raided and the chairman arrested.[41] Some delegates may have been sorely disappointed when the raids never came.

In the long address opening the afternoon session,[42] Allen traced the history of the movement and noted that the NCF

38. The poll was C. B. Stanton (Independent Labour), 10,286; J. Winston (Labour), 6,080; see J. Vincent and M. Stenton, eds., *McCalmont's Parliamentary Poll Book, 1832–1918* (Brighton, 1971), pt. 3, p. 93. Also see G. D. H. Cole, *History of the Labour Party from 1914* (London, 1948), p. 29, and Pankhurst, *The Home Front,* p. 278.

39. See *The Attack upon Freedom of Speech* (London, [1915]). Also see Marvin Swartz, *The Union of Democratic Control in British Politics during the First World War* (Oxford, 1971), pp. 110–11, and HO 45/10742/263275/10.

40. NCF circular letters, 25 September and 12 November 1915, CAP.

41. See Brockway, *Inside the Left,* p. 67; Sydney R. Turner, "For Faith and Freedom: Being the Story of My Personal Adventures during the First Three Years of the Persecution," p. 3, handwritten manuscript in Sydney R. Turner Papers, SCPC; and *Daily Express,* 25–29 November 1915.

42. Allen's speech was reprinted by the NCF as *Conscription and Conscience* (London, 1916).

The NCF Convention, November 1915. *From left to right:* Aylmer
Rose (hand on chin), Clifford Allen (standing), A. Fenner Brock-
way (with glasses), and C. H. Norman. Edward Grubb is behind
Norman, and John P. Fletcher is on Grubb's left. (Courtesy Friends
House Library)

opposed conscription not only because of the threat it represented to individual liberty and the trade-union movement,
but more fundamentally because of a sincere belief in the
sanctity of human life. Its opposition, therefore, was not
"mere political objection" but was based on moral and religious beliefs with which the state had no right to interfere.
He went on to claim that the NCF had had more to do with
preventing conscription "than any other influence at work in
our country."[43] Furthermore, he warned that while the fellowship had heretofore limited its anticonscription campaign to a restricted audience, it had prepared the machinery for full-scale resistance. "If now the majority in the
State through their Government . . . decides to impose a sys-

43. Ibid., p. 9. Allen's was an idle, if rhetorically effective, boast. There is
no evidence that any important government official was influenced by the
NCF's anticonscription drive in 1915. It may be, of course, that some officials connected the NCF with labor opposition to conscription, which was a
factor of some weight.

tem which violates men's deepest religious convictions, we are not going to play at opposition." Concluding on a note of high idealism and expectation, the chairman pictured the fellowship's greatest difficulty as its inability to share the sacrifices of the men in the trenches and to render national service for the good of humanity. But he promised that the day would come when the objective of the community would be to build human life rather than to destroy it and to glorify humanity rather than to degrade it. On that future day, the service of those presently considered pariahs might "bring into human existence as much joy as there is now grief burdening the hearts of men." Allen ended his performance with a masterful application of mass psychology, asking all the delegates to stand in silent reaffirmation of their intention to remain true to the NCF's principles and to resist conscription regardless of the cost.[44]

The convention was obviously moved by Allen's stirring presentation, which was one more example of his talent for saying and doing the right thing at the right time. This ability allowed him to maintain his saintly image among the rank and file while keeping tight control of the fellowship's administrative machinery. This control had been well illustrated in the morning session of the convention when all the resolutions introduced or sponsored by the national committee were adopted without significant opposition. One rather disquieting motion, however, was introduced during a discussion on amending the statement of principles. In direct opposition to the entire basis of the fellowship as it was then constituted, the Glasgow branch, chiefly composed of militant Clydeside socialists, introduced an amendment calling for "the omission from the Statement of Faith of the words 'because they consider human life to be sacred, and cannot therefore assume the responsibility of inflicting death.' "[45]

---

44. Ibid., pp. 11–15 passim.

45. *Agenda for National Convention at Memorial Hall, 27 November 1915* (London, [1915]), p. 4, CAP. A Quaker in Glasgow wrote to the FSC's London office to report that many of the 225 NCF members in Glasgow were munitions workers who joined the NCF "before . . . the official basis of the fellowship was published, and that a number of the members joined more on the political ground of opposition to conscription than from an objection to war"; Richard H. Field to Hubert W. Peet, 2 February 1916, Hubert W. Peet Papers, FSC Files, FHL.

The Glasgow resolution was easily defeated, but it brought into the open a question that would arise again and again, and that the NCF could never satisfactorily dispose of: Could a man be a sincere opponent of conscription, war, and militarism, if under certain conditions, for example, overthrow of the capitalist system, he would be willing to engage in violence and even kill? The national committee did show its willingness to go beyond the NCF's original stance when it recommended that the following clause be added to the statement of principles:

> The members of the Fellowship refuse to engage in any employment which necessitates taking the military oath. Whilst leaving the decision open to the individual judgment of each member, the Fellowship will support members who conscientiously resist compulsory alternatives to military service involving a change of occupation.[46]

With this resolution, the NCF gave notice of its intention to oppose conscription as a means of organizing the nation for war rather than simply to resist the imposition of compulsory military service.

In other important business, the convention accepted the national committee's suggestion for the establishment of a system whereby members and their families who were, or might become, victims of persecution could be maintained with some degree of dignity. Finally, it was decided that the NCF should begin active and open propaganda in opposition to the introduction of a conscription bill, but only "with the approval of and in cooperation with the National Committee."[47]

The NCF's first convention served every purpose that the national committee had hoped it would. A feeling of group solidarity was greatly enhanced by the growing threat of conscription and by the emotional impact of the meeting itself. NCF leaders were confident that they had the support of the rank and file since the new policies they had devised had been almost unanimously approved in a democratic poll of delegates. Finally, the convention produced a substantial bonus as well. For among the observers sent by sympathetic

46. Quoted in NCF circular letter, 9 December 1915, CAP. Also see Allen ms., chap. 2, pp. 13–14, CAP.
47. *Agenda for National Convention*, p. 6, CAP.

organizations was Catherine E. Marshall, representing the
Women's International League. Impressed by the fellowship's spirit and inspired by Allen's magnetism, Marshall
began almost immediately to immerse herself in NCF work.
Bringing with her a fund of knowledge on political organization and methods of dealing with the authorities garnered
from years of experience in the suffragist movement, C. E.
M., as she was called, was a skilled and dedicated worker
willing to devote her seemingly unlimited resources of time,
energy, and ingenuity to a cause that she embraced with as
much passion as she had formerly fought for women's
rights. During 1916 and 1917 little transpired in the NCF
that Marshall's hands did not in some way direct, influence,
or inspire.[48]

Its resolve strengthened by the emotional impact of the
national convention, the NCF set out to translate the convention's decisions into concrete action. The fellowship freed its
propaganda campaign from its previous restraints, and a
considerable volume of leaflets and pamphlets began to be
distributed throughout the country. In addition, members
were issued detailed instructions on how to conduct the
campaign against conscription and were urged to prevail on
every group to which they might belong, especially labor and
church organizations, to pass anticonscription resolutions
and to convey these to the press and the government. Public
protest meetings were also organized but only with the approval of the still cautious national committee.[49] The central
theme of the NCF's propaganda message was that all "lovers
of liberty should work to prevent freedom of conscience—
the symbol of British spiritual values—from being sub-
merged by military necessity."[50]

A final touch to the NCF's postconvention campaign was

48. Catherine E. Marshall's papers (CEMP) are housed in the Cumberland County Record Office, the Castle, Carlisle. There are also microfilm
copies in the possession of Jo Vellacott, Acadia University, Wolfville, Nova
Scotia. Future citations refer to those copies that Vellacott, who is presently
engaged in writing a biography of Marshall, has graciously allowed me to
see.

49. NCF circular letter, 9 December 1915, CAP. See 5 H.C., 74:1468 and
1998, 14 and 21 October 1915, and 5 H.C., 75:1332-33, 11 November
1915, for attempts by military authorities to prevent the NCF from holding
anticonscription meetings.

50. Quote is from NCF leaflet, *Shall Britons Be Conscripts*, NCF File,
SCPC. Since May 1915 the NCF had published detailed instructions on

the implementation of the maintenance program to provide for those victimized by any future conscription act. Since the regular members of branch committees would almost certainly be liable for arrest under a system of military compulsion, it was decided to operate the maintenance program through the associates' committees. Five members of each branch's associates' committee were each assigned one aspect of the maintenance program in his or her own branch. For this purpose, a questionnaire was mailed to each member containing five detachable sections, each section covering a specific phase of the project. Thus, one associate committeeman was to handle all requests for assistance, another all offers to provide assistance, a third was made responsible for member's requests for employment, and the fourth for all offers of employment. The fifth committeeman received and distributed all contributions sent into the maintenance fund. Requests for and offers of employment were sent on to a central labor bureau at the head office whose task was to redistribute them on the basis of need. Hospitality and relief work for C.O.s was to be controlled locally, but at least 20 percent of all funds collected at the local level were to be forwarded to headquarters so that the branches in greatest need or members not connected with a branch could be aided. A sixth member of each associates' committee was charged with the task of keeping up agitation against a conscription bill and finding local people who would agree to stand bail for arrested members of the fellowship.[51]

All NCF members of military age were promised legal assistance in the event of any conscription law, and each was cautioned to arrange to have a friend inform the local and national committees of his arrest. These committees were responsible for providing legal aid and also for drawing public attention to any arrests for conscience' sake.[52] Thus every member could rest secure in the knowledge that he would not be abandoned, forgotten, or carried away unaware, even by a military machine supported by the entire power of the state.

---

steps to be taken in the event that a conscription bill came before Parliament; see NCF circular letters of 24 May 1915, NCF File, SCPC; 12 November and 9 December 1915, CAP.

51. NCF circular letter, 9 December 1915, CAP.
52. Ibid.

By the end of 1915, the NCF claimed to have mobilized nearly two hundred branches in the fight against conscription.[53] But even if each of these passed dozens of anticonscription resolutions, wrote hundreds of letters to their M.P.s, and distributed thousands of anticonscription leaflets, their activities were trifling compared with the rising demands in press and Parliament for some sort of enforced military service. NCF members were no doubt encouraged and inspired by the impressive coordination of war resistance that the fellowship had supervised, but the larger the NCF grew in absolute numbers, the more isolated it became from society in general.

Public exasperation with young men who were "skrimshanking"[54] at home while others died in their defense became more and more pronounced and belligerent, especially toward those who actually organized to oppose the national cause. The NCF and its leaders came under increasingly abusive attack after the publicity aroused by its national convention. On 1 December 1915, for example, the *Daily Sketch* printed a vulgar, insulting article on Allen's educational shortcomings. Two days later, a correspondent to one provincial paper said of Allen: "like Lord Haldane, your spiritual home is in Germhuny [*sic*] and I wish you would go there." On the NCF he added: "Like the vast majority of men in the street I have come to believe that it is to pacifist cranks and international faddists that we owe this war. By their sickly sentimentality and peace at any price prattle, they encouraged the Arch Hun in his scheme and presented a broken front to his machinations."[55] Such examples may have been interesting illustrations of wartime mass psychology or patriotic frustration, but, for the would-be conscientious objector, they were still personally innocuous. As long as Britain depended on the voluntary system of recruitment, neither the dissenter's resolve nor the public's patience would be pushed to the sticking point. But the testing time was at hand.

53. See Allen, "C.O.'s Struggle."
54. This word was used by David Lloyd George, *War Memoirs*, 6 vols. (London, 1933), 2:712, though evidently he borrowed it from another source.
55. T. Anderson to *Nelson Leader*, 3 December 1915.

4

The Politics of Conscience

The Sword Falls

While the NCF was preparing itself for a showdown battle against conscription, the Derby scheme's canvass of eligible young men continued. Because of unproductive results in its early stages, the canvass was extended for two weeks beyond its original termination date of 30 November. As the scheme drew to a close on 11 December, great queues began building up at recruiting stations throughout the country. Obviously, hundreds of thousands of men were attesting their willingness to serve. Some anticonscriptionists felt certain that the campaign had saved the voluntary system, but they had forgotten that, because of the prime minister's pledge, the success or failure of the scheme depended not on the total number of men who attested but on the percentage of single men who came forward. On 15 December Lord Derby gave a hint of what was to come when he asked the House of Lords to support the position that no married men would be taken unless and until the country was assured that single men had come forward in sufficient numbers.[1]

On the same day Derby gave a preliminary report to the cabinet that indicated that 651,160 single men had either refused to attest or were otherwise unaccounted for. The corrected results of the scheme, later published in a white paper, clearly revealed its failure.[2] Asquith now had a clear case for the imposition of some type of compulsory enlist-

1. 5 H.L., 20:641–42, 15 December 1915, and Derby to Kitchener, 14 December 1915, Kitchener Papers, 30/57/73, WS/39–40, PRO. Also see Ray Douglas, "Voluntary Enlistment in the First World War and the Work of the Parliamentary Recruiting Committee," *Journal of Modern History* 42 (December 1970):581, and Randolph Churchill, *Lord Derby: King of Lancashire* (New York, 1960), p. 201.

2. For Derby's original report, see CAB 37/139/26; the corrections are given in CAB 37/140/1. Also see *Report on Recruiting, Parliamentary Papers, 1914–1916*, 39:8149, and Douglas, "Voluntary Enlistment," p. 582.

ment if only to fulfill his pledge to attested married men. On 15 December the prime minister appointed a cabinet committee chaired by Walter Long to work out the form for "any amendment to the law in the direction of compulsion."[3]

It may be, as John Rae has asserted,[4] that in view of the military situation, Asquith had already decided to embrace full-scale conscription. If so, he managed to keep this fact well hidden from his cabinet colleagues. Indeed, Lloyd George was so upset with the prime minister's apparent indecision about conscription that on 27 December he presented Asquith with an ultimatum to the effect that unless the prime minister kept his pledge to married men, Lloyd George would resign. Whether Lloyd George's ultimatum or an implied Tory threat to block any extension of the existing Parliament in the House of Lords, thereby forcing a general election on the question of compulsion, finally moved Asquith to action, on 28 December he agreed to a draft bill presented by Long's committee that called for the conscription of single men who had not attested under the Derby scheme.[5]

As always, the main thrust of Asquith's efforts was to keep his government from being shattered by the resignation of his anticonscriptionist colleagues. Of these, only the home secretary, Sir John Simon, was opposed on the basis of pre-war Liberal principles. Others, especially Walter Runciman and Reginald McKenna, rejected military conscription because they believed it involved commitments of resources that Britain could not spare without damaging its chances to survive the war.[6] The prime minister accepted Simon's loss

3. CAB 41/36/55 and Cabinet Letters, 1915–1916, 15 December 1915, p. 122, Asquith Papers, Bodleian Library, Oxford.

4. John Rae, *Conscience and Politics: The British Government and the Conscientious Objector to Military Service, 1916–1919* (London, 1970), pp. 20–21.

5. Churchill to Lloyd George, 27 December 1915, Lloyd George Papers, D/16/8/2, House of Lords Record Office, London. Also see Christopher Addison, *Four and a Half Years: A Personal Diary from June 1914 to January 1919*, 2 vols. (London, 1934), 1:156–59; Trevor Wilson, ed., *The Political Diaries of C. P. Scott, 1911–28* (Ithaca, N.Y., 1970), pp. 147, 166, 168; and *Downfall of the Liberal Party* (Ithaca, N.Y., 1966), pp. 71–75.

6. See CAB 37/130/17, CAB 37/134/2, and CAB 41/36/48 for examples of these objections. Also see Alfred Gollin, "Freedom or Control in the First World War (the Great Crisis of May 1915)," *Historical Reflections* 2 (Winter

as inevitable and concentrated on convincing the others that their economic objections to compulsion did not warrant the destruction of the government. He succeeded and, by denying the possibility of industrial conscription, even managed to keep Arthur Henderson and the other Labour ministers in the cabinet.[7]

Certainly, an important reason why Asquith was able to maintain the integrity of his government through this political crisis was the moderate nature of the conscription measure that he presented to the Commons on 5 January 1916. In essence, this bill treated all unexempted single men and childless widowers between the ages of eighteen and forty-one as if they had attested under the Derby scheme and "deemed" them to have enlisted in His Majesty's forces for the duration of the war.[8] The prime minister could claim not only to have fulfilled his pledge to attested married men, but to have done so without abolishing the voluntary system that continued to operate side by side with partially applied compulsion.

Critics in the Liberal and Labour press declared that the government was dangerously and unnecessarily chopping away at one of Britain's most cherished liberties. The *Manchester Guardian* was incensed that the prime minister had called the voluntary system a failure "in the very hour of its most startling success" and asked why he was attempting to foist onto the public "an incomplete and botched piece of work."[9] George Lansbury's *Herald* began the new year by issuing a special "Smash Conscription" supplement, fol-

1975):147, and Barry McGill, "Asquith's Predicament, 1914–1918," *Journal of Modern History* 39 (September 1967):290.

7. Cabinet Letters, 1915–1916, 11 January 1916, p. 122, Asquith Papers. Also see Roy Jenkins, *Asquith: Portrait of a Man and an Era* (London, 1965), pp. 388–90, and Wilson, ed., *C. P. Scott's Political Diaries,* pp. 165–66.

8. See Asquith's introduction of the bill, 5 H.C., 77:949–62, 5 January 1916. For detailed discussion of the Military Service (No. 2) Act from an anticonscriptionist view, see Philip Snowden, *The Military Service Act* (London, 1916).

9. *Nation,* 15 January 1916, and *Manchester Guardian,* 5 and 6 January 1916. A few days earlier *Guardian* editor C. P. Scott told Bonar Law: "I can imagine no adequate reason for pressing for an immediate decision"; 2 January 191[6], Bonar Law Papers, 52/2/8, House of Lords Record Office, London.

lowed one week later on 8 January with a full-page cartoon showing the prime minister wielding a knife labeled "Asquith Pledge" toward the throat of Freedom who was lashed to the stake. The caption read: "Protesting, Madam Freedom! Would you have an English Prime Minister break his pledge?" Calling conscription a giant step toward "the enslavement of the masses to a small gang of rich and powerful men," the *Herald* held out hope that labor would unite to smash this attempt to coerce the working classes. The ILP's *Labour Leader* was even more explicit. An article on 13 January noted that if the government continued "its foolish attempts to impose military servitude upon the people of this country, it will meet with a resistance which may easily develop into revolution."

Labor did indeed protest. At a special London conference convened on 6 January by the Labour party and the Trades Union Congress (TUC), delegates voted overwhelmingly against conscription and urged Labour M.P.s to fight its adoption. The *Labour Leader* called the meeting "the most momentous conference in the history of the Labour movement" and felt that its defiant attitude would prevent the yoke of conscription from being placed on the necks of the working classes.[10] In the end, however, the sound and fury came to nothing. As already noted, the Labour ministers remained in the cabinet, and the trade-union leadership and the official Labour party ultimately accepted the government's assurances that industrial conscription would never occur and offered only token opposition.[11]

In the meantime, the NCF, united as labor could not be, mustered its forces for an all-out struggle against the long-dreaded conscription bill. NCF members were urged to put everything else aside and to give all their time and energy to working against the bill. Vast quantities of posters and leaf-

10. *Labour Leader*, 6 January 1916. M. I. Thomis, "The Labor Movement in Great Britain and Compulsory Military Service, 1914–1916" (M.A. thesis, London University, 1966), is a detailed consideration of trade-union and Labour party reactions to conscription.

11. The Labour Party Conference meeting at Bristol in late January made a nominal protest against conscription but did not actively oppose it. See G. D. H. Cole, *History of the Labour Party from 1914* (London, 1948), pp. 27–28, and Chris Wrigley, *David Lloyd George and the British Labour Movement: Peace and War* (Hassocks, 1976), p. 167.

lets were distributed, hundreds of protest meetings were held, and thousands of anticonscriptionists followed the national committee's instructions "to bombard the Prime Minister, Mr. Lloyd George and Sir John Simon... with suitable letters." The fellowship's literature insisted that the conscription bill "need never become operative," if every member were "sincere, active and courageous in working to defeat it." Brockway later boasted that it was "doubtful whether any organisation ever carried on... keener or more extensive propaganda than did the NCF during these weeks."[12]

Throughout this period, the Friends Service Committee (FSC) worked "in the closest conjunction" with the NCF and took pains to inform the government "that Friends were concerned not so much with their own traditional right as for the liberty of the individual conscience."[13] The FSC fully agreed with the NCF's emphasis on defeating the entire bill and not merely gaining special exemption or privileged status for conscientious objectors. FSC honorary secretary Robert O. Mennell felt that if anticonscriptionists openly worked for exemption, "we should bargain away our right to continue opposition to the Act... [once] we were exempted."[14] But at the same time that leaders of the NCF and the FSC were publicly vowing not to compromise with the monstrous evil of conscription, some of them were privately laying plans to ensure that any conscription measure that passed through Parliament would contain an exemption clause for conscientious objectors.

On 3 November the FSC agreed to join with the NCF in sending representatives to a deputation that would interview certain members of Parliament on the subject of an exemption clause. The invitation made it clear that, while the fellowship did not intend to publicly advocate such a clause, they believed it right "to lay their opinion before those who

12. *NCF Souvenir*, pp. 23–24, and NCF circular letter, 9 January 1916, CAP.

13. H. W. Peet to FSC members, 13 December 1915, FSC *Minutes*, 1:33, FHL, and "Draft Report of the Friends Service Committee to the Friends Yearly Meeting [1916]," n.d., FSC *Minutes*, 2:1, FHL.

14. R. O. Mennell to A. Barratt Brown, 22 November 1915, Robert O. Mennell Papers, FSC Files, FHL; and NCF circular letter, 9 January 1916, CAP.

may care to advance it in Parliament." To this end, Clifford Allen produced a detailed memorandum on a possible conscience clause that included everything from suggested wording to advice on what types of political pressure should be exerted and upon whom.[15] At this point, the FSC executive committee balked, obviously concerned about the inconsistency of war resisters working behind the scenes to secure a policy they would not publicly recommend. In the report of a joint meeting of the FSC and a conscription committee appointed by the Meeting for Sufferings, it was decided not to join in any deputation to Parliament in connection with the exemption clause proposed by the NCF. At the same time, the report expressed the hope that delegates could meet privately with M.P.s and "lay before them the strength of the feeling against conscription in any form." On the next day, when the Joint Advisory Council (JAC) accepted the view presented in the FSC report, it seemed to be saying that potential conscientious objectors should not work for exemption themselves, but they should make sure somebody did.[16] Clearly, the only way for C.O. organizations to extricate themselves from this dilemma was to form yet another group whose object, in addition to fighting conscription, would be to work for the inclusion of a conscience clause in any future conscription law.

Such was the tangled background to the emergence of the National Council against Conscription (NCAC). When the conscription bill was about to be introduced to Parliament, the JAC invited previously selected individuals who opposed compulsory military service "on general as distinct from ethical grounds" to join a deputation waiting upon anticonscriptionist M.P.s. This body of some fifty people, most of whom were prominent in labor or civil-libertarian circles, formed the nucleus of the NCAC (which changed its name

15. Proceedings of the FSC meeting at Devonshire House, 3 November 1915, FSC *Minutes*, 1:21; R. O. Mennell to Clifford Allen, 10 November 1915, Mennell Papers; and Clifford Allen, "Memorandum Re. 'Conscience Clause,'" 18 November 1915, FSC *Minutes*, 1:22, FHL.

16. Report of joint session on 18 November [1915] of FSC and Committee appointed by Meeting for Sufferings to watch conscription, FSC *Minutes*, 1:23–24, FHL. Also see Horace G. Alexander and Roger Clark to *The Friend* (26 November 1915):880, and Notes of Recent Meetings, 21 December 1925, FSC *Minutes*, 1:38, FHL.

to the National Council for Civil Liberties after conscription became a reality). Robert Smilie, leader of the Miners' Federation, was selected as the NCAC's first president, and F. W. Pethick-Lawrence, a prominent prewar suffragist, served as honorary treasurer. E. D. Morel's top aide in the UDC, B. N. Langdon-Davies, resigned in order to become the NCAC's secretary. Allen was also elected to the executive board.[17]

The government marked the NCAC down as a dangerously subversive organization as soon as it was formed. A Home Office memorandum pointed out "that the real aims of the organisers are . . . directed against the war and in opposition to measures undertaken for its successful prosecution . . . most of those who form its council are active opponents of the war who have not raised a finger to help their country in her hour of need."[18] This view was used to justify frequent raids on NCAC offices, but police action did not deter the group from cooperating closely with the NCF in fulfilling its self-appointed role as protector of all citizens subjected to overzealous enforcement of wartime laws such as the Military Service and Defense of the Realm (DORA) acts.

None of the multitudinous and sometimes frenzied activities of the allied anticonscription bodies had any noticeable effect on the Military Service Act's swift passage through Parliament. Asquith had been as astute in eliminating parliamentary opposition to the bill as he had been in preparing the groundwork for its public acceptance.[19] The Irish, who formed the bulk of the opposition on the first reading (59 of 105), abstained when Ireland was excluded from the provisions of the act, and no doubt many wavering Liberals

17. See HO 45/10801/307402/75 for copy of a letter dated 4 January 1916 from R. O. Mennell (FSC), Richard Roberts (FOR), and Clifford Allen (NCF) inviting recipients to join a deputation to anticonscription M.P.s, and "The Crisis," notes to local correspondents of the FSC from R. O. Mennell and H. W. Peet, 11 January 1916, FSC *Minutes*, 1:42–43, FHL. Also see Allen ms., chap. 2, p. 16, CAP.

18. HO 45/10801/307402/75. This same file contains over seventy antiwar–anticonscription leaflets and pamphlets seized at NCAC headquarters.

19. See Rae, *Conscience and Politics*, pp. 14–38 passim, for an informative and perceptive analysis of Asquith's maneuvering on the conscription issue.

were reassured by the inclusion of a "conscience clause" that recognized moral as well as religious objections. Opponents from the Labour party dwindled to a few ILP diehards who, with a handful of Radicals and Quakers, fought the bill to the end. They provided some extremely lively debate, but when the measure received a third reading on 24 January, they could muster only thirty-six negative votes.[20]

Conscription and Conscience: Provisions for Conscientious Objection

When Asquith, in introducing the military-service bill, presented the fourth and last ground for exemption—"conscientious objection to undertaking combatant service"—he was interrupted by a considerable volume of groans, catcalls, and laughter.[21] The prime minister reacted to this demonstration by noting that William Pitt had exempted Quakers from the Militia Acts during the French War (1792–1802) and, citing recent precedent, that both South African and Australian conscription laws had allowed for conscientious objection, "and with the best results."[22]

In his study of the development of government policy with regard to conscientious objectors, Rae maintains that Asquith's defense of exemption for C.O.s was a "blend of history and deception, of bogus precedent and heroic tradition." Because the section exempting conscientious objectors was added only after Simon's resignation, Rae surmises that its inclusion was chiefly a political ploy to mollify Liberal opinion.[23] Thus, however much the NCF or other an-

20. Division lists for the second and third readings are 5 H.C., 77:1251–56, 10 January 1916, and 5 H.C., 78:1037–42, 24 January 1916. Christopher Addison noted that the debate over the Military Service Act reminded him of the great debates on home rule and the Parliament bill; *Four and a Half Years*, 1:160.

21. The other grounds were performance of civilian work in the national interest, grave hardship (when a man's enlistment would deprive helpless persons of maintenance), and serious ill-health or infirmity; 5 H.C., 77:956, 5 January 1916.

22. Ibid.

23. Rae, *Conscience and Politics*, pp. 27–35 passim. Rae's analysis of the factors and personalities involved in the drafting and development of the conscience clause has caused me to substantially alter my view of these proceedings. I must acknowledge a considerable debt to him.

ticonscription groups might take credit for the legal recognition of conscientious objectors,[24] the government's decision seems to have been based largely on political rather than ideological or ethical considerations.

In any case, when the clause was included in the bill, some Tory back-benchers considered it to be nothing less than a "slacker's charter." In outraged indignation, William Joynson-Hicks presented an amendment that would have limited conscientious objection to members of religious bodies traditionally opposed to war. In rejecting this amendment for the government, Bonar Law put on record the view that moral or intellectual grounds were as valid as religious beliefs in establishing a conscientious objection.[25] Not only back-bench Tories were upset by the government's apparent flexibility in this regard. Most high-ranking military officials also invariably linked conscience with Christianity and therefore felt that objections based on other than religious grounds were "political." But when military leaders, including Brig. Gen. Wyndham Childs, director of personal services, attempted to argue for the elimination of nonreligious exemption, Asquith stood his ground.[26] It is perhaps of some interest that the first British conscription law was more liberal in treating conscientious objectors than any written stipulation of draft laws in the United States until the landmark cases of *U.S.* v. *Seeger* (1965) and *Welsh* v. *U.S.* (1970). In its decisions in these two cases, particularly the latter, the U.S. Supreme Court broadened the legal grounds for conscientious objection to a point approximating those established in Great Britain in 1916.[27]

Recognizing the existence of the conscientious objector is of course very different from meeting the objection that he

24. For example, see *Trib.*, 17 March 1917, and Arthur Marwick, *The Deluge: British Society and the First World War* (Boston, 1965), pp. 80–81.

25. For debate on this amendment, see 5 H.C., 78:422–31, 19 January 1916.

26. See Sir Wyndham Childs, *Episodes and Reflections* (London, 1930), p. 148.

27. *U.S.* v. *Seeger*, 380 US, 163 (1965), and *Welsh* v. *U.S.* (1970). For brief discussion, see Arlo Tatum, ed., *Handbook for Conscientious Objectors*, 11th ed. (Philadelphia, 1971), pp. 39–42. For reflections on this point by a parliamentary defender of C.O.s, see T. E. Harvey, "Records of Conscience," *Friends' Quarterly Examiner* 66 (1922): 187. Excepting Great Britain and the United States, no major belligerent nation made any provisions for conscientious objection.

claims. In this regard, there are obviously two fundamental questions: How do you separate the legitimate objector from the shirker? And, what kind or degree of exemption should be provided for those accepted as genuine objectors?

With regard to the first question, anticonscriptionists in Parliament offered the precedent provided by an amending act of 1907 to the Vaccination Act of 1898. This amending act—passed by a Liberal government with specific reference to freedom of the individual conscience—allowed parents to avoid compulsory vaccination of their children by making a statutory declaration under oath before two justices of their conscientious objection to such vaccination.[28] The NCF itself had long advocated such a procedure in the event of conscription.[29]

In answering for the government, Long, president of the Local Government Board, noted that, based on his and other magistrates' experiences in petty session courts, the acceptance of such a declaration would likely provide a sheltering place for more unconscientious shirkers than honest objectors. Long believed that a far more scrupulous and efficient test of the sincerity of all claims for exemption would be a board or tribunal composed of responsible local citizens. There was, he said, every reason to believe that such bodies would perform their duties "with single-mindedness, honesty and integrity."[30] Long's arguments won the day, and local tribunals were handed the unenviable task of separating honest men from dishonest cowards. If they often failed to live up to Long's expectations, the fault was not entirely of their own making.[31]

The prime minister seemed to be dealing with the second question—the sort of exemption to be given to genuine conscientious objectors—when he emphasized that objectors would be excused from combatant duties involved in the taking of human life, but not from military service altogether. (Certainly, this degree of exemption would seem

28. This precedent was offered by R. L. Outhwaite, Radical M.P., 5 H.C., 78:462–65, 19 January 1916. The 1898 act had provided for exemption if parents could convince two justices that they believed vaccination to be harmful; see Rae, *Conscience and Politics*, pp. 28–29, 43–44.

29. See NCF circular letter, 24 May 1915, NCF File, SCPC, and Allen, "Memorandum Re. 'Conscience Clause,'" p. 22.

30. See 5 H.C., 78:465, 19 January 1916, and 738–45, 20 January 1916.

31. See Chap. 5.

to meet the terms of the original NCF statement of principles regarding the sanctity of human life.) During the course of the debate on the bill, the government agreed to modify this rather rigid interpretation by accepting an amendment offered by two Quaker members, T. E. Harvey and Arnold Rowntree, that specified that conscientious objectors who refused any military service might still be exempted if they agreed to perform or to keep performing some work of "national importance."[32] Apparently, the government felt that these types of exemptions would meet every or nearly every case. This was a considerable, though perhaps understandable, miscalculation.

The government's original scheme of providing noncombatant military service for those who refused to kill was partially based on the precedent established by the Friends Ambulance Unit (FAU). The FAU was a strictly unofficial nursing corps that, with the support and encouragement of the Friends Yearly Meeting, enlisted the services of younger Friends and non-Quaker volunteers.[33] In the beginning, military officials tended to be skeptical, but the FAU proved its mettle and performed yeoman service. Indeed, the army thought so well of the unit that ultimately it succeeded in turning the FAU into a quasi-military organization. With the passing of the conscription acts, the unit became closed to all but Quakers, and this restriction caused it to be disowned by the FSC. Not many C.O.s came into the FAU after March 1916, and, in fact, some of its pioneer members like T. Corder Catchpool resigned from ambulance work and returned to England to fight against conscription.[34]

Government officials were, however, apparently con-

32. For Asquith's statement, see 5 H.C., 77:957–58, 5 January 1916; the amendment is stated in 5 H.C., 78:430–31, 19 January 1916.

33. See FSC *Minutes*, 1:5, FHL, for an extract from minute 3 of the Yearly Meeting of 1915, which reads: "We are warmly in sympathy with the proposal to help by advice and financial assistance young Friends to train for non-combatant service." A history of the FAU is Meaburn Tatham and James E. Miles, *The Friends' Ambulance Unit, 1914–1919* (London, [1919]). Also see T. Corder Catchpool, *On Two Fronts* (London, 1918), pp. 9–92, for an eyewitness account of the work done by the FAU prior to 1916. After 1916 the FAU was the source of considerable bitterness among Friends who felt that it had become too cosy with military authorities.

34. See Catchpool, *On Two Fronts*, pp. 104–8; Jean C. Greaves, *Corder Catchpool* (London, 1953), p. 12; and *Trib.*, 30 March 1916. For military praise of the FAU, see Childs, *Episodes and Reflections*, p. 150.

vinced that, using the FAU as a model, they could create a special kind of military body that would simultaneously satisfy the objection of most C.O.s and provide useful services for the army. In early March, the formation of the Non-Combatant Corps (NCC) was announced. Ideally, this unit was to perform transport, supply, and construction duties that would not only be vital to the army but would also release thousands of other men for combat duty. Conscientious objectors who accepted induction into the NCC were often members of religious sects such as the Plymouth Brethren and Seventh-Day Adventists who had not joined any anticonscriptionist organization.[35] Most members of the NCF, however, found the concept of a noncombatant corps entirely repugnant. Their opposition, as stated in a joint NCF–FSC letter to the prime minister, was "one of fundamental objection to war on religious or moral grounds . . . no plea of necessity or of policy can justify us in participating in its prosecution." As Allen noted: "It is not fighting in particular which revolts us, it is war itself that we will not assist."[36]

The NCC not only failed to satisfy the NCF and its allies; its entire history was marked by frustration and futility. Its numbers never rose above three thousand, and its effect on the prosecution of the war was negligible. In addition, many men who did enter the NCC discovered to their chagrin that it was a more thoroughly military organization than they had been led to believe. Some of these unsuspecting noncombatants were to suffer gross brutalities for their refusal to knuckle under to military discipline, and eventually all were discriminated against because of official disillusionment with their organization.[37]

Though members of the NCC suffered a good deal from ridicule and discrimination, there was never any question that NCC service required considerable personal inconve-

35. See Childs, *Episodes and Reflections*, pp. 149–50; *The Times*, 13 March 1916; Allen ms., chap. 2, p. 9, CAP; and Rae, *Conscience and Politics*, pp. 191–94.

36. Printed copy of FSC–NCF letter to Asquith, 14 March 1916, CAP. Reprinted in *Trib.*, 15 March 1916, as was a letter to Walter Long. Also see Allen ms., chap. 2, p. 23a, CAP.

37. For examples of discrimination and brutal practices against members of the NCC, see Rae, *Conscience and Politics*, pp. 192–95, 235–36.

nience. This sort of sacrifice was not so clearly demonstrable among those C.O.s who refused to serve under military control while alleging their willingness to undertake or to continue civilian work of national importance. Although deciding whether an applicant should be granted conditional exemption on conscientious grounds because he was doing or would be willing to do work of national importance was left to the local tribunals, in their first weeks of operation the tribunals were not even provided with lists of occupations considered to be of national importance.[38] As a result, overzealous tribunals, waving the banner of patriotism and shouting the battle cry "equality of sacrifice," often gave only noncombatant exemption or none at all to men who would not accept any type of military service but were perfectly willing to do useful civilian work. Usually this kind of decision simply created more difficulties for the army and the government as well as for the C.O.s.

Eventually, in late March 1916, the government created a committee on work of national importance to cope with this problem. Supervised by the Board of Trade, the so-called Pelham committee (for its original chairman, the Honorable T. W. H. Pelham, an assistant secretary on the Board of Trade) was charged with finding suitable employment for conscientious objectors. The committee seems to have done its work reasonably well. Drawing on a comprehensive list of essential occupations that C.O.s might take in lieu of military service, it handled, in all, about four thousand cases.[39] But since the Pelham committee was without statutory power to enforce its decisions, the tribunals could use or ignore its findings as they saw fit.[40] Despite this weakness, the Pelham committee must be judged the most successful of the schemes devised by the government, though neither it nor the NCC

38. R. 4, LGB Instructions to Local Tribunals, 19 November 1915, listed starred or exempted occupations, but most individuals in these trades would have been exempted without having to claim conscientious objection.

39. The Pelham Committee Papers are included among the T. E. Harvey Papers, FHL; Harvey, Charles Fenwick, M.P., and G. S. Spicer were the other members of the committee. When T. H. W. Pelham died in December 1916, he was succeeded as chairman by Col. Sir Hildred Carlisle, M.P. The best discussion of the committee's work is Rae, *Conscience and Politics*, pp. 125–28, 195–99, and apps. H and I.

40. See Graham, *Conscription and Conscience*, pp. 99–101.

could satisfy the scruples of nearly six thousand conscientious objectors, the vast majority of whom were members of the NCF, and all of whom were eventually subjected to military or civil imprisonment or some lesser degree of detention.

In summary, it may be said that Britain's provisions for dealing with conscientious objectors were generous in intent but that good intentions were often frustrated by the actions of local bodies that were generally ill informed or highly prejudiced. As a result, administrative burdens were created that were far out of proportion to the numbers of men involved. Only one-third of one percent of all men recruited or conscripted during the war invoked the exemption for conscientious objectors, but these 16,500 men proved to be a continuing and at times a major distraction for an already overburdened government. More than any other organization, the NCF was responsible for the state's protracted difficulties in dealing with conscientious objectors. From the first, the NCF's leaders saw all government plans for military or civilian service as a subterfuge for quietly disposing of troublesome people and for ensuring the success of the conscription system and refused to acquiesce in any of them. Allen counseled members not to accept alternative service that would aid in organizing the country for war "and thereby help to fasten upon the nation that very militarism against which our consciences rebel." Instead, all members were advised to apply for absolute exemption since by doing so they could "advance our real objective and make our testimony effective in the country."[41] Many objectors seemed to believe that they would be granted total exemption, a contingency that the government had anticipated and was apparently prepared to grant. The chief barrier that stood across their paths was the system of tribunals established by the acts to deal with claims for exemption. Although neither the C.O.s nor the government realized it, no more formidable barricade could have been erected.

41. NCF circular letter, 6 February 1916, CAP; *Trib.*, 30 March 1916; *The Position of the Conscientious Objector*, NCF pamphlet (London, n.d.), p. 4; and W. E. Wilson, "The Conscientious Objector and Non-Combatant Duty," CAP.

5

The Tribunal System

The Tribunals and the NCF

In order to deal with the flood of claims for exemption that would inevitably follow the imposition of conscription, the government chose to utilize existing machinery rather than to create an entirely new system. Under the Derby scheme, local tribunals were appointed in each registration district established by the National Registration Act to consider exemptions for attested men. A central tribunal was also created to act as an appellate body. Under the Military Service Act, these tribunals were for the most part kept intact and simply given statutory power. To fill out the tribunal structure, appeal tribunals were set up in each county area. Claimants had an absolute right to petition their county appeal tribunals, but cases were not intended to come before the central tribunal unless they involved some important question of principle. For this reason, applicants had to secure leave from their appeal tribunal to present their case to the highest authority. In all, over two thousand local tribunals and seventy appeal tribunals were formed,[1] but even this vast improvised network was inadequate to cope with the hundreds of thousands of exemption claims.

Town councils, metropolitan borough councils, and urban and rural district councils were responsible for establishing local tribunals that were to have from five to twenty-five members, though generally no more than five heard any one case. The only statutory requirement concerning the membership of local tribunals—one not always followed—

---

1. Those figures were given by Lord Lansdowne, 5 H.L., 21:926; also see Statutory Rules and Orders, 1916, 53, 3 February 1916, for guidelines on setting up tribunals and regulating their hearings. The most thorough discussion of the operation of these various tribunals is John S. Hughes, "The Legal Implications of Conscientious Objection" (Master of Law thesis, Victoria University of Manchester, 1973), pp. 6–45.

was that labor be adequately represented.[2] Beyond this, local authorities were free to choose the members of local tribunals according to their own lights. Not surprisingly, these bodies were dominated by the same groups that dominated local politics. There were exceptions, but most tribunal members were middle-class, middle-aged, without judicial experience, and notable for their zealous support of the war. Indeed, many men owed their seats on the Derby tribunals to their prominence in local recruiting activities.[3] In addition to its regular members, each tribunal had a full-time clerk and at least one military representative, appointed by the War Office, who attended all its hearings. This military representative, who was in a sense an army counsel, almost invariably opposed applicants for exemption, especially conscientious objectors, and also had the right of appeal to the central tribunal. The adversary role of the military representatives and the intimacy of the relationship between them and tribunal members were strongly attacked by critics of the tribunal system,[4] but the conduct of the military representatives must be considered in light of the fact that they were in a real sense competing for men to fill the ranks. The army did not receive its men from a civilian board of manpower allocation and had to get them however it could. All in all, the tribunal system was not only inefficient; it also made the problem of dealing with conscientious objectors much more difficult.[5]

Local tribunals began to discharge their duties in early

2. See Long's argument for including a labor representative; 5 H.C., 78:745–46, 20 January 1916. Also see John Rae, *Conscience and Politics: The British Government and the Conscientious Objector to Military Service, 1916–1919* (London, 1970), pp. 56–57, and Adrian Stephen, "The Tribunals," in *We Did Not Fight*, ed. Julian Bell (London, 1935), p. 377.

3. For a contemporaneous analysis of tribunals, see William Grist Hawtin, *The Law and Practice of Military Conscription under the Military Service Acts*, 2 vols. (London, 1917–1918), 1:56–57. Also see *The Times*, 15 March 1916, for an account of Councillor Ling who "invariably supported application for exemption," and *Manchester Guardian*, 22 November 1916, which reported on a tribunal member who was himself a conscientious objector.

4. See especially Philip Snowden's attack on the activities of military representatives; 5 H.C., 81:268–69, 22 March 1916. Also see the remarks of W. M. K. Pringle, 5 H.C., 81:309–10, 22 March 1916.

5. Hughes, "Legal Implications," pp. 40–45, and Rae, *Conscience and Politics*, pp. 66–67, 103.

February 1916. Thousands of men (as well as a few women) served on these tribunals without pay for over three years. Considering the years of service, the volume of work, and the personal sacrifice freely given by tribunal members, one might anticipate that, in retrospect, one would hear at least some faint praise for them. Instead, nearly everywhere one turns, there is a loud chorus of abuse. Eventually, government ministers joined with anticonscriptionists in Parliament in condemning the tribunals, and military men as well as conscientious objectors maligned their efforts.[6] From the mock trial in *Alice in Wonderland* to Judge Jefferys's Bloody Assizes, every sort of opprobrious historical and literary analogy was used to illustrate the inadequacy and injustice of the tribunals. Popular literature invariably represents them as one of the great travesties of modern British legal history.[7]

This picture is not fully true. The tribunals were victims of inadequate preparation, of ill-defined jurisdiction, and of a skillful propaganda campaign. Certainly one important reason for the general disillusionment with the tribunals was the manner in which the NCF seized on their weaknesses and paraded them before the nation.

Actually, the immediate result of the tribunals' establishment was the first really serious internal crisis within the NCF. The national committee was faced with two alternatives: Should the fellowship accept the state's challenge and send its members before the tribunals to claim absolute exemption, or should it refuse to recognize the state's right to judge an individual conscience? The national committee debated these points for three days. One faction led by Barry Brown and C. H. Norman argued for noncoopera-

6. For example, see the criticisms of Lords Derby and Milner, CAB 23/4/246 (I) (a–b), and those of General Childs on the "ineptitude of the tribunals," CAB 24/23/1799. Hughes, "Legal Implications," p. 45, notes that the real weakness of the system was that government officials of different departments "took advantage of the fragmented administrative structure to avoid responsibility, rather than to modify the structure as soon as its faults became clear."

7. See A. J. Cronin, *The Stars Look Down* (New York, 1935), pp. 311–31; Stephens, "The Tribunals," p. 392; and "Casey," *Labour Leader*, 30 March 1916. One book that presents the case from the viewpoint of a tribunal member is Sir Harry Cartnell, *For Remembrance* (Preston, 1919).

tion. They felt that pleading before the tribunals would compromise the C.O.'s position because it would involve a tacit recognition of the validity of the Military Service Act and would also create the impression that objectors were merely attempting to escape the rigors of military life.[8]

On the other hand, more moderate voices argued that extreme noncooperation would make C.O.s look like cowardly obstructionists. They wanted objectors to demonstrate their courage and idealism: "When members cannot accept the decisions of Tribunals, and have to suffer, we shall have an unanswerable case to advance. We can show how our men faced every ordeal, and how those who failed to convince the Tribunals with words are now proving their sincerity by deeds."[9]

As usual, Norman was the most vociferous of the extremists, and, when the committee split its vote six to six, he demanded a national referendum of the membership. Clifford Allen, fearful that such a poll might split the fellowship at a time when unity was essential, ended the debate by voting with the moderates. Once the chairman's vote had been cast, the other committee members, except for Norman, agreed to join in urging the rank and file to follow the course decided on. In reporting its narrow verdict to the membership, the national committee noted Norman's refusal to endorse its action, but the majority's position was enhanced when both the Friends Service Committee (FSC) and the national administrative council of the Independent Labour Party (ILP) took essentially the same course.[10] In any case, only a small minority of NCF members chose to follow Norman's example and refused to appear before their local tribunal.[11]

Norman did not withdraw from the national committee,

8. NCF circular letter, 31 January 1916, CAP; C.H. Norman, *A Searchlight on the European War* (London, 1924), pp. 92–94; and Scott Duckers, *Handed Over* (London, [1917]), pp. 23–25.

9. NCF circular letter, 31 January 1916, CAP.

10. Ibid.; FSC circular letter No. 10, 15 February 1916, CAP; *Extracts from the Minutes and Proceedings of the London Yearly Meeting of Friends,* 28–30 January 1916, Minutes 157 and 158; Norman, *Searchlight on the European War,* p. 92.

11. In its circular letter of 23 March 1916, CAP, the NCF offered some possible arguments for those who did not intend to appear before the tribunals.

but its decision rankled him sorely and he never ceased to denounce it. He believed that the appearance of conscientious objectors before the tribunals not only helped to ease the administration of the acts but also made objectors mere supplicants to the government, putting them at a great moral and psychological disadvantage. Had the "overconfident leaders" of the NCF allowed the rank and file to vote on the matter, Norman said, his advice would almost certainly have been followed and the NCF vastly strengthened.[12]

Having determined to fight conscription on the government's battleground, the NCF's leaders wanted to ensure that there would be tactical unity among their scattered forces. A circular letter reminded members that the fellowship's "supreme object" was "to demonstrate the curse of militarism and cause the removal of Conscription from the life of this country of free tradition." The best way to secure these objectives, said the letter, was to claim absolute exemption while expounding one's beliefs about the evils of war. Such action would serve the dual purpose of spreading peace propaganda and of notifying the government that NCF members could not be mollified by the offer of safe alternative service. Clearly, the fellowship's goal was to break down the act's machinery by waging a great campaign to show the injustice of any measure interfering with liberty of conscience and by raising "the whole moral issue from one end of the country to the other. . . . [We] shall stir the conscience of the nation, whilst all the time showing ourselves willing to accept any challenge to explain our belief."[13]

In order to give further witness to the fact that the NCF was not acting out of pure self-interest or attempting to "manufacture" conscience, the national committee temporarily closed down the enlistment of new members when it learned in late January that fear of imminent conscription had brought a number of insincere men into the organization.[14] Thus only those dedicated slackers who had the pres-

12. Norman, *Searchlight on the European War,* pp. 93–94; "The Future of the NCF," *Trib.,* 8 May 1916; Clara Gilbert Cole, *The Objectors to Conscription and War* (Manchester, 1936), p. 7; and Allen ms., chap. 3a, pp. 12–14, CAP.

13. NCF circular letter, 31 January 1916, CAP.

14. See S. Rowland Pierce, Secretary, London Branch of the NCF, to members, 22 February 1916, CEMP (microfilm). Also see Edward Grubb, "The No-Conscription Fellowship," *The Friend* 56 (14 July 1916): 551.

ence of mind to join early managed to get into the NCF. In March the national committee took a final step by recommending that any member who received anything short of absolute exemption should return the certificate stating that it would be dishonorable to take an exemption whose provisions he could not fulfill.[15]

Members were advised that prior to appearing before the tribunals they should think out their views about the war, write them down, and discuss them with other C.O.s in order to accustom themselves to presenting their ideas in a clear and reasonable manner. If a man had any lingering doubts about his stand or about offers of noncombatant or other conditional exemption, he should clear them up before appearing at the tribunal. Finally, to reduce the possibility of provoking or alienating the tribunal, applicants were cautioned to "state their case with restraint and simplicity, avoiding all appearances of lecturing," while at the same time making it clear that they could not be frightened or bullied into abandoning their convictions.[16]

The detailed instructions given to NCF members and the mock hearings held by some branches to prepare men for their appearances before the tribunals inevitably led to the accusation that the fellowship was manufacturing conscientious objectors in order to sabotage the act. Actually, nothing the fellowship did in this regard went beyond the law. Legally, the applicant could present any evidence that he felt would help his claim. What the NCF did do was to warn its members that if articulate and well-known objectors were to produce vast quantities of evidence, it might well work to the disadvantage of less-forceful or less-famous men. An overabundance of material evidence could cause tribunals to define conscience entirely in those terms. Therefore, individuals were cautioned against doing anything that might reflect badly on their comrades, and branches were asked to ensure that less-articulate members received as much documentary support as possible. In spite of these attempts to ensure that each conscientious objector presented a strong case for his

15. NCF circular letter, 23 March 1916, CAP. The FSC made the same recommendation to its members; see FSC, "Third Communication Regarding the Military Service Act, 1916," 23 March 1916, FSC Files, FHL.

16. NCF circular letters, 31 January and 6 February 1916, CAP.

claim, many applicants, as Norman had warned, were badly muddled and were unable to give a clear expression of their beliefs. "So many people," said a Manchester C.O. to the national secretary of the FSC, "can't express their thoughts at all."[17] Such performances tended to exasperate tribunals and to confirm their preconceived notions about the insincerity of most conscientious objectors.

If the head office could not ensure that every member gave a reasonable presentation of his case, it could try to ensure that no individual would be forgotten. This task was undertaken by the NCF records department under the direction of Catherine E. Marshall. In order for the central headquarters to keep an accurate record of each conscientious objector who appeared before the tribunals, every NCF member was supposed to receive a printed form with six perforated sections. At each stage of his progress through the tribunal system, the member was asked to fill in the appropriate section and mail it to his branch secretary or to national headquarters. If the membership complied with instructions, the NCF would have the type of claim made by each member, the date of his hearing, the results of his appearance before both local and appeal tribunals, and knowledge of any further action by the authorities.[18] But accuracy was only one goal of this system. The fellowship also wanted to provide every member with the security of knowing that he could not simply be gobbled up by the military machine. For a time the procedure worked reasonably well, but it had to be revised later when it became obvious that many objectors would not or could not send in the necessary reports.

As the young men of the NCF prepared to meet the tribunals, their colleagues in the branch associates' committees were planning the best means of overseeing the actions of the tribunals and of protesting any decisions they considered to be unfair. One particularly active associates' committee was located in Croydon and numbered Edward Grubb among its members. The minute book for this committee

17. J. H. Crosland to Hubert W. Peet, 5 February 1916, Hubert W. Peet Papers, FSC Files, FHL. Also see NCF circular letters, 19 February and 23 March 1916, CAP; Norman, *Searchlight on the European War*, pp. 92-93; and Rae, *Conscience and Politics*, pp. 111-12.

18. NCF circular letter, 6 February 1916, CAP.

has been preserved[19] and gives a fascinating, if somewhat sketchy, picture of the work that was done. Following the instructions of the national committee, the Croydon associates set up a system of watchers to hear every case presented to the local tribunal and to record any procedural irregularities or ill-treatment of the applicants. In this manner, they managed to compile a permanent record of most cases in their branch area.[20] There were dozens of similar committees that, taken together, help to explain the NCF's ability to maintain contact with thousands of otherwise isolated young men. To a great extent, these watchdog committees and others simultaneously created by the Society of Friends accounted for the enormous waves of negative publicity that battered the tribunals in the spring of 1916.

The Tribunals in Operation

As soon as they began their deliberations, local tribunals were nearly deluged by applicants for exemption (750,000 men filed for exemption between January and June 1916).[21] Because of the pressure of work, no individual was likely to have time for a thorough presentation of his case. Since conscientious objectors made up only a tiny minority of the applicants, and since tribunal members were not likely to have much sympathy for them, it is not surprising that C.O.s often felt slighted. The brevity of the proceedings, the hostile attitude of many tribunals, the ambiguity of the exemption clause, and the assiduousness with which the NCF blanketed the country with tribunal watchers could only spell trouble for tribunals and conscientious objectors alike.

On 8 March 1916 a serving member, Maj. John Newman, asked Herbert Samuel, the home secretary, to "censor in the public press" all reports of tribunal proceedings. Newman

19. Minutes of the Associates' Committee, Croydon Branch of the No-Conscription Fellowship, Edith L. Hayler, secretary, NCF File, SCPC (hereafter cited as Croydon Minutes, with date). Also see *Trib.*, 25 September 1919.

20. NCF circular letters, 6 and 19 February 1916, CAP, and Croydon Minutes, 18 February and 15 May 1916, SCPC.

21. *Military Operations in France and Belgium, 1916* (London, 1932), p. 152.

felt that this censorship was necessary "in view of the exhibition of lack of manhood and cowardice displayed before local tribunals by young men seeking to escape from military service on conscientious grounds." Ironically, on the same day that Samuel dismissed Newman's petition,[22] the NCF published the first of 182 numbers of its four-page weekly tabloid, *The Tribunal*,[23] which became the spearhead of the fellowship's attacks on the tribunals. In the first few weeks of the paper's existence, tribunal watchers provided it with "carefully vouched for details" on dozens of alleged irregular or illegal actions taken by tribunals and hundreds of inane or indiscreet remarks made by individual members. Those not printed in *The Tribunal* were passed on to allied journals like *The Friend* or the *Labour Leader,* or to general-circulation newspapers seeking a sensational story or a bit of comic relief. Tribunal proceedings were reported with a blend of outraged indignation, wounded sensitivity, biting sarcasm, and outright hilarity. A few examples will suffice to give the general tone.[24]

In his instructions to the tribunals, Walter Long had emphasized that members should not allow differences in conviction to bias their judgment of an applicant.[25] Perhaps this sort of objectivity was too much to ask in the superheated atmosphere of war, but unfortunately a minority of tribunal members apparently felt that their chief duty as far as conscientious objectors were concerned was not to judge them

22. 5 H.C., 79:1517–18, 8 March 1916.

23. *The Tribunal* has been reprinted by Kraus from a complete edition in possession of John G. Slater of the University of Toronto (New York, 1970). There are also incomplete collections in CAP, BRA, and SCPC (microfilm). There is some question about the circulation of *The Tribunal.* John W. Graham, *Conscription and Conscience* (London, 1922), p. 191, claimed a distribution of 100,000, and David Boulton, *Objection Overruled* (London, 1967), p. 273, accepts Graham's estimate. But this is an impossible figure that is no doubt based on William J. Chamberlain's note in *Trib.,* 23 March 1916, that the NCF *wanted* a circulation of 100,000. Peter Brock, *Twentieth-Century Pacifism* (New York, 1970), p. 21, gives 10,000 as peak circulation, which seems reasonable, although circulation was only about 2,000 at the end of the war.

24. See NCF circular letter, 19 February 1916, CAP, and *Trib.,* 8 March–1 June 1916.

25. MH 10/80, R. 36, LGB Circular to Local Registration Authorities, 3 February 1916. Long, after hearing strong criticisms of the tribunals' conduct, repeated this point in R. 70, LGB Circular, 23 March 1916.

but to insult them. A member of the Oldbury tribunal told one objector that "there are two things you possess, cowardice and insolence"; another applicant heard from Councillor Hopwood of the Shaw tribunal that he was exploiting God to save his skin and therefore was not only a coward and a cad but "a shivering mass of unwholesome fat." In other cases, unwholesome fat was no barrier to exemption: The Todmorden tribunal granted absolute exemption to a barman named Pharoh on account of "abnormal corpulency" (he weighed 23 stone—322 pounds), with one member remarking on the pity that the applicant could not have fallen on some Germans.[26]

Not unnaturally, tribunals in rural districts had a tender spot for riders after the hounds. The generosity of the Carmarthen tribunal in exempting the whip of the local foxhounds so that he could complete the hunting season was exceeded only by the decision of the Market Bosworth tribunal to exempt the entire membership of the Atherstone Hunt on the grounds that fox hunting encouraged horse breeding. While membership in a hunting club might impress some tribunals, membership in the NCF was generally regarded with suspicion or with downright distaste. When an applicant told the West Glamorgan appeal tribunal that he belonged to the NCF, Alderman Davies replied: "Then you belong to one of the most pernicious bodies in the country. Its members are going all over the place distilling poison, and are greater enemies to Britain than the Germans."[27]

Protests against the illegal or insulting conduct of tribunals, while they momentarily seized headlines, were not the most significant aspect of the NCF's campaign against the tribunals. Even more important were denunciations of the decisions arrived at by the tribunals. Actually, at first glance these decisions might seem quite generous: local tribunals gave some form of exemption to over 80 percent of the applicants for conscientious objection who appeared be-

26. See *Trib.*, 8 and 15 March and 6 April 1916, and *The People*, 19 March 1916. Also see Stanley B. James, *The Men Who Dared* (London, [1917]), pp. 14–15.

27. *Trib.*, 6 April 1916. Also see *Trib.*, 15 March and 20 April 1916; *Daily News and Leader*, 15 March 1916; and Philip Snowden, *Autobiography*, 2 vols. (London, 1934), 1:408.

fore them.[28] The question, however, was not simply one of exemption but of which kind of exemption. The NCF had advised its members to apply only for absolute exemption, but a large majority of tribunals either ignored the possibility of absolute exemption or claimed that they had no right to grant it.[29] The confusion that surrounded the question of absolute exemption is an excellent illustration of the ambiguous guidelines under which the tribunals were forced to work.

In the first Military Service Act, the subsection describing exemptions read:

> Any certificate of exemption may be absolute, conditional or temporary as the authority by whom it was granted think best suited to the case, and *also* in the case of an application on conscientious grounds,may take the form of an exemption from combatant service only, or may be conditional on the applicant being engaged in some work which in the opinion of the tribunal dealing with the case is of national importance.[30]

This subsection was variously interpreted as meaning that any applicant for exemption, including a conscientious objector, could receive absolute exemption; or, while applicants who were not conscientious objectors could receive absolute exemption, C.O.s could only receive exemption if they accepted alternative service or were engaged in work of national importance. *2/05/1*

Cabinet officers evidently started with the assumption that absolute exemption could be granted to any applicant for exemption, including conscientious objectors. Lord Lansdowne, speaking in the House of Lords, emphatically stated that tribunals were empowered to grant absolute exemption to "the out-and-out conscientious objector."[31] One week later, Long, in issuing instructions to local tribunals, stated: "There may be exceptional cases in which genuine convictions and the circumstances of the man are

28. Figures cited by Rae, *Conscience and Politics,* pp. 131–32.

29. NCF circular letter, 31 January 1916, CAP; *Manchester Guardian,* 16 February 1916; and *Trib.,* 23 March 1916.

30. Military Service Act (No. 2) 1916, 2(3). For the discussion of the ambiguity of the conscience clause, see Rae, *Conscience and Politics,* pp. 47–51.

31. 5 H.L., 20:976, 1068, and 1075, 26 January 1916.

such that neither exemption from combatant service nor a conditional exemption will adequately meet the case. Absolute exemption can be granted in these cases, if the Tribunal are fully satisfied of the facts."[32]

At intervals thereafter, especially in response to parliamentary criticism, Long sent further instructions reminding tribunals that total exemption was indeed possible. But another nagging question then arose: What, in fact, was total exemption? The NCF and its supporters in Parliament supposed that absolute exemption meant unconditional release from all military or civilian service under the Military Service Act. But on 6 April 1916, ten days after he had assured appeal-tribunal chairmen that C.O.s could receive absolute exemption, Long stated in Commons: "Then there is the case of the man who is exempted from all service—what is called 'total exemption.' *That is only possible if a man is engaged in work of national importance*" [emphasis added].[33]

Within two weeks, the King's Bench division of the High Court of Justice decided that even Long's narrowing interpretation went beyond the meaning of the law. In the case of *Rex* v. *Central Tribunal* ex parte *Parton,* the high court, in a two-to-one decision, ruled that, under the Military Service Act as written, a tribunal could only grant a conscientious objector exemption from combatant duty. Since the high court's decision effectively changed the obvious intent of the law, the second Military Service Act, which passed in late May and introduced universal conscription, stated explicitly:

> the power to grant special certificates of exemption in the case of an application on conscientious grounds under subsection (3) of section two of the principal Act is additional to and not in derogation of the general power conferred by that Act to grant an absolute, conditional, or temporary certificate in such cases.[34]

32. R. 36, LGB to Local Registration Authorities, 3 February 1916. Also see NCF circular letter, 6 February 1916, CAP.

33. 5 H.C., 81:1460, 6 April 1916. Compare with Long's statement in R. 70, LGB Circular, 23 March 1916, and R. 76, Notes on Conference of Appeal Tribunal Chairmen, 27 March 1916.

34. Military Service Act, 1916 (Session 2), 4(3). For an analysis of the *Parton* decision, see Hawtin, *Military Conscription,* 1:49. Also see ibid., 1:75, 79, and *Trib.,* 1 June 1916.

In practice this clarification meant little or nothing. In early June Long sent out another circular to the tribunals noting that the granting of exemption without any conditions whatsoever would be very exceptional. Also included in this bulletin were a series of questions drawn up by the central tribunal to guide local and appeal tribunals in questioning conscientious objectors.[35] Thereafter, in periodic "Notes on Cases" and other published directives, the central tribunal consistently identified the "extreme objector" as one who had

> proved a genuine settled conscientious objection not only to the actual taking of life but to everything which is assigned directly to assist in the prosecution of the war. Such cases where established, entitled the appellant, in the opinion of the Central Tribunal, to exemption from all forms of military service upon conditions of performing work of national importance.[36]

The apparent sense of this directive was to eliminate absolute exemption despite the specific declarations of the amending act of 25 May 1916.[37]

Two other points of considerable moment to conscientious objectors were also made by the central tribunal in its instructions to the lower tribunals. The first denied the possibility of a political objection such as that held by a socialist who opposed the present war but would fight to create or to

35. R. 84, LGB Circular, 1 June 1916. There is a copy of a central-tribunal questionnaire in BRA; a somewhat different version was printed by Rae, *Conscience and Politics*, pp. 252–53.

36. Quoted by Hawtin, *Military Conscription*, 2:179–80, who also provides (pp. 154–80) an excellent guide to significant cases reviewed by and decided on by the central tribunal.

37. Willis H. Hall, *Quaker International Work in Europe since 1914* (Savoy, 1938), p. 55n, quotes Quakers Hubert W. Peet and John P. Fletcher as believing that only a dozen conscientious objectors received and retained absolute exemption. The official figure given by Lord Peel, 5 H.L., 34:162, 3 April 1919, was over 600. In March 1916 *The Tribunal* listed over sixty cases of men who had received absolute exemption, but undoubtedly many of these exemptions were altered as in the cases of Fletcher (*Trib.*, 20 April 1916) and Barry Brown (*Trib.*, 24 January 1918). Rae, *Conscience and Politics*, p. 130, states that "no more than 350 absolute exemptions were granted and allowed to remain in force."

defend a worker's republic. As the months passed and the basis of the NCF began to shift from passivism to militancy, this decision became increasingly important to the fellowship.[38] Second, the central tribunal decreed that the age of a man claiming conscientious objection should be carefully considered with a view toward ascertaining "whether his objection is so deliberate and settled as to entitle him to exemption." In a strongly worded protest addressed to Long, the Joint Advisory Council of anticonscription groups (JAC) condemned this judgment. Would, the JAC asked, a man who had been forced into the service at eighteen because he was not considered to have a "deliberate and settled" conviction be allowed to claim release from the army at twenty-one if he still held his original convictions?[39] Needless to say, the question was never answered.

On 20 March 1916 the *Morning Post* fearfully pronounced that the NCF had succeeded in "breaking down the machinery of the act." Such hysterical nonsense might unintentionally boost the fellowship's morale, but it was never close to being true. Still, the negative publicity about the tribunals that the NCF had helped to propagate did create a national furor far out of proportion to the numbers of men—though perhaps not to the importance of the principles—involved.

Tribunals and Their Critics

The grosser errors, abuses, and indiscretions committed by the tribunals seem to have been isolated cases, but their widespread exposure made them seem well-nigh universal. In Parliament, questions were continuously raised about the misconduct of one tribunal or another, and Philip Snowden, amply supplied with evidence by the NCF's political committee and private correspondence, offered a detailed indictment of tribunal activities in two substantial speeches.[40] On

38. See Hawtin, *Military Conscription*, 2:179–80, and Rae, *Conscience and Politics*, pp. 116–17.

39. The JAC letter was reprinted in *Trib.*, 14 September 1916; Hawtin, *Military Conscription*, 2:180, quotes the central tribunal.

40. 5 H.C., 81:261–78, 22 March 1916, and 1443–52, 6 April 1916. These speeches were later reprinted as a pamphlet *British Prussianism* (London, 1916).

24 March the Liberal *Daily Chronicle* spoke of the "very grave scandal" Snowden had exposed. The *Chronicle* asked if serious statesmen, upon reviewing the actions of local tribunals, would "be disposed to devolve further decisions of national consequence upon them."

Professional legal journals also took a dim view of the tribunals' proceedings. *The Solicitor's Journal and Weekly Report* warned its readers that the tribunals' attempts to browbeat applicants were a reversion to the style of the seventeenth century. Conscientious objection, said the article, was "neither in fact nor under the statute dependent on religious belief. . . . It is the duty of the tribunals to administer the act impartially, remembering that the exemption clauses have been introduced for the express purpose of preventing the claims of the army from being carried too far." In June 1916 the Hardwicke Society for members of the legal profession passed a resolution stating that "the administration of the law with regard to Conscientious Objectors has resulted in grave abuse and injustice."[41] Beatrice Webb characteristically called the conduct of the tribunals "a scandalous example of lay prejudice—another proof that if you have a law, you must have a lawyer to administer it."[42]

The clergy of the nation, and especially of the Church of England, were widely praised (or condemned) for their nearly unanimous support of the war, but several prominent church leaders expressed grave misgivings about the way in which the tribunals were being conducted. The bishops of Oxford (Charles Gore) and Lincoln (Edward Lee Hicks) both wrote letters to *The Times* asking that conscientious objectors be accorded the protection allowed them by law and the respect due them as human beings.[43] After the appearance of Bishop Gore's letter, Lord Courtney advised Allen to contact Gore through Maude Royden to request that the bishop and about a dozen other prominent clergymen compose another letter on behalf of conscientious objectors. Apparently Allen did, for on 30 March just such a letter ap-

41. Quoted in *Trib.*, 30 March and 15 June 1916.
42. Beatrice Webb, *Diaries, 1912–1924,* ed. Margaret I. Cole (London, 1952), pp. 55–56 (9 March 1916).
43. See *The Times,* 14 March 1916, for Bishop Gore's letter and 4 April 1916 for that of Bishop Hicks.

peared in the *Daily News, Daily Chronicle,* and *Manchester Guardian* signed by the bishop of Oxford and a number of distinguished Free Church ministers as well as by William Temple, who was honorary chaplain to the king and later became the archbishop of Canterbury.[44]

Righteous indignation also burst forth from literary circles. Though he supported the war, George Bernard Shaw could not restrain himself from attacking the "pompous insolence" and "honest barbarism" of the tribunals. He felt that a very sensible conscience clause had been allowed to produce idiotic results and wondered if the government felt satisfied that the Germans were somehow reeling under the shock of the tribunals' persecution of their fellow Englishmen.[45] In an article in the *Sunday Chronicle,* G. K. Chesterton condemned what he called the "daily tomfoolery of the tribunals and the conscientious objectors." Chesterton asserted the impossibility of bringing "two total strangers into one room, where the first is to describe his immortal soul and the other to judge his immortal soul." Such a practice amounted to moral anarchy and from it, he warned, "there will grow . . . something that always and everywhere rises out of anarchy; and that is tyranny."[46]

Thus, the tribunals are historical losers. Characterized as prejudiced, ignorant, insensitive, and unjust—their standing is poor even when compared to that of generals who could not win battles, politicians who failed in their jobs, and conscientious objectors who refused to come to the aid of their stricken country. But whatever the sins of these "novel bodies,"[47] they were not solitary. In many cases, they were committed with the aid and connivance of the very conscientious objectors whom they were allegedly persecuting. Some NCF supporters, for example, took fierce pains to note how the tender consciences of Oxford undergraduates were left

44. "Summary of Conversation Between C. A. (Allen) and Lord and Lady Courtney," undated, CEMP (microfilm). The clergymen's letter was reprinted in *Trib.,* 6 April 1916.

45. From *The Nation,* 27 May 1916, reprinted in George Bernard Shaw's *What I Really Wrote about the War* (London, 1931), pp. 223–24.

46. G. K. Chesterton, "Nonsense, Conscience and the Law," *Sunday Chronicle,* 16 April 1916.

47. *Manchester Guardian,* 8 January 1916.

to the mercies of crass High Street merchants.[48] What these critics seemed to be saying was that, while no one can correctly judge another man's conscience, the consciences of intelligent and sensitive Oxford men were inherently inaccessible to stodgy tradesmen. But could a panel of distinguished dons have any more success deciding the exact state of a man's conscience? And again, would the reverse hold true for less refined men in the mining areas of South Wales? Should every tribunal—even though it supposedly could in no way discover the wellspring of a man's belief— have been geared to the moral and intellectual level of its principal applicants? Many people in the NCF wanted it both ways. They were unwilling to accept any tribunal's right to judge the genuineness of their own feelings, but at the same time they were prepared to ridicule every judgment made by those whom they considered their intellectual or moral inferiors. It was not a happy contest. But it scarcely could have been otherwise when each side operated under a separate, incompatible set of rules.

48. Graham, *Conscription and Conscience,* p. 70. Also see *Trib.,* 24 August 1916.

6

Resistance and Retribution

Repeal the Act!

> FELLOW CITIZENS,
>
> Conscription is now law in this country of free traditions. Our hard-won liberties have been violated. Conscription means the desecration of principles that we have long held dear; it involves the subordination of civil liberties to military dictation; it imperils the freedom of individual conscience and establishes in our midst that militarism which menaces all social progress and divides the peoples of all nations.
>
> We re-affirm our determined resistance to all that is established by the Act....
>
> *Repeal the Act. That is your only safeguard.*[1]

Over the signatures of its national committee, the No-Conscription Fellowship thus announced its intention to resist the operation of Britain's first conscription law and to work for its removal from British life. In formulating a plan against the act, NCF leaders founded their hopes on two fundamental considerations. First, by advertising the fellowship as a defender of Britain's great libertarian tradition and by concentrating on the incompetence of civilian tribunals and the brutality of military officials who were administering the Military Service Act, they hoped to initiate a broad-based revival of the latent spirit of liberalism. Second, they believed that inadequate administration of the act and the opposition such administration would engender, especially among laboring classes, might convince powerful and influential people that the practical difficulties generated by compulsion were actually injuring or inhibiting the war effort.

By any criteria, the NCF was playing a long shot. Un-

---

1. Quoted from an NCF pamphlet, *Repeal the Act* (London, [1916]).

doubtedly, the once-bright flame of nineteenth-century liberalism still flickered in a few dark and quiet places. But it manifested itself only in the occasional speech of a die-hard radical M.P. or in a leading article in the *Manchester Guardian* or *The Nation,* neither of which had much influence on public policy in wartime. Many Englishmen might agree with the London journalist who observed that conscription seemed "a slap in the face to the old British principle of every individual's right to think—and act—for himself,"[2] but they were not likely to transform such vague uneasiness into opposition to the government or to the war. On the other hand, there did seem to be some substance in an appeal to workers. In both the cabinet and the press, there were rumblings of fear about the trade unions' negative attitude toward compulsion. Even the *Daily Express* gave voice to its misgivings about the "grave industrial unrest" that full-scale conscription seemed to portend.[3]

Since the final decision on conscription would be made by Parliament, the NCF employed a considerable part of its resources in attempts to convince that body that conscription could not effectively be extended and indeed should be repealed. NCF members and branches were urged to send letters, petitions, and deputations to their local M.P.s,[4] but really important work at the parliamentary level was done by an elite political committee of associate members. Created and guided by Catherine E. Marshall, this associates' committee included James S. Middleton, H. N. Brailsford, and Bertrand Russell. Middleton, longtime assistant secretary (1903–1935) and later general secretary to the Labour party, provided valuable political assistance, while Brailsford had widespread contacts in the radical press and literary circles. Russell was most important of all.

Because he was beyond military age,[5] Russell could probably have sat out World War I writing philosophy, lecturing

2. Michael MacDonagh, *In London during the Great War* (London, 1935), p. 288. Also see Stephen McKenna, *While I Remember* (New York, 1922), pp. 185–86.

3. *Daily Express,* 29 April and 4 May 1916.

4. NCF circular letters, 31 January and 19 February 1916, CAP.

5. Russell did become eligible for conscription under the Military Service (No. 2) Act (1918), which raised the upper age limit from forty-one to fifty-one years.

at Cambridge, and seeking solace in the warm, brilliant company of the Morrells' Garsington Manor where pacifists could vent their rage against the folly of suffering humanity in a quiet harbor sheltered from the storms of public abuse.[6] From the beginning, however, Russell threw himself into the antiwar movement because, as he has said, "it was my business to protest.... My whole nature was involved."[7] A founding member of the Union of Democratic Control (UDC), Russell organized a Cambridge branch of that organization and worked long and hard to advance its aims.[8] By mid-1915, however, he was finding the UDC "too mild and troubled with irrelevancies," and he told Ottoline Morrell that he would "make friends with the No-Conscription people." The friendship took some time to mature, but by March 1916 Russell was being "bombarded" with letters from Marshall pleading with him to give all possible time to the NCF. Eventually, her entreaties proved so determined, persuasive, or both that Russell succumbed. By April he was, according to Marshall, "working day and night" for the political committee and telling Ottoline: "I can't describe to you how happy I am having these men to work with and for—it is real happiness all day long—I feel they can't be defeated, whatever may be done to them."[9]

6. For comment on the atmosphere at Garsington, see Mary Agnes Hamilton, *Remembering My Good Friends* (London, 1944), p. 7. Keith Robbins, *The Abolition of War: The "Peace Movement" in Britain, 1914–1919* (Cardiff, 1976), p. 88, notes: "In the fastidiousness of his pacifism, Russell typified the superior refinement of that Cambridge–Bloomsbury circle to which he belonged." Russell, says Robbins, differed from others of this group only in the fact that "he possessed both vestigial backbone and a modicum of physical health." This is an extremely curious interpretation of Russell's part in the antiwar movement and one that is overwhelmingly contradicted by evidence available from a wide variety of sources.

7. Bertrand Russell, *The Autobiography of Bertrand Russell*, 3 vols. (London, 1967–1969), 2:18.

8. Russell, *Autobiography*, 2:17–19, and Marvin Swartz, *The Union of Democratic Control in British Politics during the First World War* (Oxford, 1971), pp. 30–31. Jo Vellacott feels that Russell's work with the UDC "is not done justice by any published work on the organization"; see Jo Vellacott Newberry, "Russell and the Pacifists in World War I," in *Russell in Review*, ed. J. E. Thomas and Kenneth Blackwell (Toronto, 1976), p. 40. This excellent article is based on Vellacott Newberry's doctoral thesis, "Bertrand Russell and the Pacifists in the First World War" (McMaster University, 1975).

9. Russell to Ottoline Morrell, 11 June 1915, quoted in Russell, *Autobiography*, 2:52–53; Russell to Ottoline Morrell, undated [29? March] 1916,

Russell's association with the NCF unquestionably cost him a good deal more than he had bargained for, but no member contributed more the indomitable spirit and indeed the very survival of the organization.

During a period of intense activity from mid-March through May 1916, the NCF's political committee embarked on a simple but extremely ambitious program: to apply political pressure against conscription at every level of national life by every available means. Brailsford, for example, took responsibility for drafting a series of petitions to the king, the prime minister, and cabinet members. These petitions were sent to local members of Parliament for presentation to the official concerned. At the same time, a "national" petition was distributed among prominent people who might be sympathetic to the NCF's cause.[10] A number of journalists were enlisted in the campaign to protest against conscription and to publicize the ill-treatment of conscientious objectors. One of these, Henry Nevinson—at Brailsford's request—actually wrote a pamphlet for the NCF and attempted to get Thomas Hardy, John Galsworthy, and John Masefield to sign a memorial on behalf of C.O.s. Galsworthy, at least, supported efforts to aid imprisoned objectors.[11] At the same time, Russell was attempting to line up important people willing to write letters to the national press in support of the C.O.s' cause. In conjunction with the National Council against Conscription (later the National Council for Civil Liberties), the political committee planned possible legal action to forestall the imposition of conscription in any form on those declared to be genuine conscientious objectors.[12]

All this involved considerable effort, but the committee's most important work was at Westminster where Marshall

cited by Vellacott Newberry, "Russell and the Pacifists in World War I," p. 45; Marshall to Gilbert Cannan, 20 April 1916, CEMP (microfilm); and Russell to Ottoline Morrell, 10 April 1916, quoted by Ronald W. Clark, *The Life of Bertrand Russell* (New York, 1976), p. 277.

10. Minutes of NCF Political Committee, 17 and 27 March 1916, CEMP (microfilm).

11. Marshall to Nevinson, 20 April 1916, BRA. For Galsworthy and the C.O.s, see H. V. Marrot, *Life and Letters of John Galsworthy* (New York, 1936), p. 755.

12. Minutes of Political Committee, 17 and 27 March 1916, CEMP (microfilm).

took responsibility not only for organizing deputations to cabinet ministers and friendly M.P.s but also for providing the small group of anticonscriptionists in Parliament with a continuous stream of questions calculated to place the operation of conscription in the worst possible light. The movement's parliamentary spokesmen included Quakers like T. E. Harvey and Arnold Rowntree, a score or so of radical Liberals, and an occasional Labour representative such as Ramsay MacDonald, J. R. Clynes, or W. C. Anderson. But the NCF's real voice in Parliament was Philip Snowden whose pugnacious, vituperative attacks on compulsion and on the officials who administered it filled many a column of *Hansard* with strong words and many a prowar member with rage. Despite the fact that the political committee had decided that it would be wise to limit oral questions on conscientious objectors to the most urgent and important cases, the affairs of various C.O.s engaged an amazing amount of parliamentary time. In fact, at one point, H. J. Tennant, parliamentary undersecretary for war, complained that the volume of questions involving conscientious objectors was so "enormous" that he had been "kept at the War Office the whole morning trying to get answers . . . and . . . was not able to get through by a quarter to three." Gen. Wyndham Childs believed that most of the five thousand C.O.s dealt with by his office would not have been there at all but "for the encouragement they received from Members of Parliament."[13]

The NCF political committee ultimately failed in its objective—to induce Parliament to repeal conscription or at least to prevent its extension—but its lobbying activities were successful in getting the conscientious objectors' point of view across to those who counted in the political realm. The fact that the establishment was not convinced is perhaps not so important as the fact that the NCF's persistence and the necessities of the political system forced them to listen rather more often than they liked.

While the political committee sought to influence opinion at the top, the national committee was organizing local branches throughout the country for "a persistent repeal

13. Minutes of Political Committee, 4 April 1916, CEMP (microfilm); 5 H.C., 82:649, 10 May 1916; and Sir Wyndham Childs, *Episodes and Reflections* (London, 1930), p. 154.

campaign."[14] NCF publications constantly stressed the importance of members' meeting together to discuss their stand and its implications. Ad hoc bodies like the "Greater Manchester Consultative Committee" were formed to give advice and comfort to confused or uncertain objectors. Each night during the crisis period in the spring of 1916, dozens of young men visited this group seeking guidance or just a friendly, sympathetic face. The Croydon branch provided the same service with Edward Grubb acting as father-confessor to the men in that area. Marshall recalled with considerable pride that during these hectic days the NCF had "saved from lifelong remorse many a weaker brother whose loyalty to his conscience was in danger because of the overwhelming odds arrayed against it; it has brought strength and comfort to many a humble soul who thought himself alone in following a light which his companions seemed not to see."[15]

Of course, to achieve its aims the NCF had to do more than ensure that its own members maintained their convictions. Those convictions had to be propagated so widely and so well that the nation would finally acquiesce in them, or would at least concede that such beliefs should not be violated by actions of the state. To this end, the NCF published a series of leaflets, pamphlets, and tracts designed to inform the public of the true nature and purpose of the fellowship's stand. Often these pamphlets took pains to emphasize that the conscientious objector's refusal to participate in the war did not arise from a lack of courage or even of patriotism but rather reflected a belief that war was intrinsically evil and therefore always disastrous to the best interests of the nation and its people.[16]

> We Conscientious Objectors are not out to save our own souls and consciences any more than our own skins; we are out to save the world from war. Conscience is not simply a private scruple which can be satisfied by withdrawal from the evil

14. NCF circular letter, 19 February 1916, CAP.

15. *Manchester Guardian*, 18 February 1916; Croydon Minutes, 18 February 1916, SCPC; and *Trib.*, 15 June 1916.

16. *Compulsory Military Service and Alternative Service and the Conscientious Objector*, NCF pamphlet (London, [1916]), pp. 1–2, and W. E. Wilson, "The Conscientious Objector and Non-Combatant Duty," CAP.

thing. It is a positive and compelling conviction which drives us to active work for the cause we have at heart. We are out for Peace; not the mere declaration of Peace Terms, nor the signing of Peace Treaties, but the creation of that state of mind and spirit which will make it increasingly difficult for nations to go to war.[17]

To some young pacifists, such high-flown ideals could make the NCF "the religious revival for which the churches were looking."[18] Indeed, there was a small positive response to the fellowship's "national appeal" to churches to help those suffering for conscience' sake, especially from the Free Church groups. But the more normal reaction to conscientious objectors, even among clergymen, can be found in the words of a prominent Anglican vicar who noted in *The Times* that "no honest citizen can tolerate these neurotic curiosities. We have no use for them."[19]

The objectors and their friends stressed the role of the popular press in creating such attitudes,[20] but press influence was not decisive. The truth is that, while the NCF was able to enlist prominent radical–liberal support on particular issues and even to force government officials to be aware of its views, pacifist arguments were, by and large, lost on the British public. Even without the sensationalism of the *Daily Mail* or the demagoguery of Bottomley's *John Bull,* hostility to conscientious objectors was part and parcel of the belligerent, semihysterical mood of the civilian populace.[21] One

17. *No-Conscription Fellowship: A Summary of Its Activities* (London, n.d.), p. 3, and "Suggested Circular to Members on Peace Propaganda," undated (probably May–June 1916), mimeographed sheet, BRA.

18. From a speech by John P. Fletcher to the Yorkshire Conference of Young Friends, quoted in *The Friend* 56 (19 May 1916):367.

19. A. W. Gough, vicar of Brompton, *The Times*, 8 April 1916. For Reverend Gough, see *Who Was Who, 1929–1940* (London, 1941), pp. 535–36.

20. For example, see *Trib.*, 4 January 1917; Stanley B. James, *The Men Who Dared* (London, [1917]), p. 20; and Miles Malleson, *The Out-and-Outer,* NCF pamphlet (London, [1916]), p. 11.

21. On the generally hostile public response to pacifists and conscientious objectors, see Thomas C. Kennedy, "Public Opinion and the Conscientious Objector, 1915–1919," *Journal of British Studies* 12 (May 1973):105–19. For a different view, see Vellacott Newberry, "Bertrand Russell and the Pacifists in the First World War," pp. 238–47 passim. She feels that opposition to the war and support for the peace movement, especially among the working class, were much more widespread than is generally believed and that this opposition grew in intensity as the war dragged on. While it is true that NCF and other pacifist propaganda did have a delayed

need not be a C.O. to be a victim of it. When a London
journalist reported that war resisters were being "hunted
and stoned in the country's interest by the common people,"
he may have been referring to the case of George Ernest
Singer. According to an account in *The Times,* Singer was
"mistaken for a German spy and . . . followed through the
streets by a mob of women, who struck him with sticks and
pokers, as they did a number of local residents who tried to
protect him." The unfortunate Singer was later released by a
magistrate who observed that he had had a "miraculous escape."[22]

Rather than being victims of mistaken identity, conscientious objectors deliberately set themselves off from common
opinion. Indeed, there was often a strangely detached and
ethereal quality about much of what C.O.s said and wrote.
As one reporter noted, they seemed unaware that their
country was in mortal danger. Another observed that "such
self-centered and opinionated beings . . . have, however sincere, something repellant and almost inhuman about
them."[23] The NCF seemed to be perched atop some distant
Olympus airily watching the struggles of a desperate and
embattled army and offering critical comments on the wisdom of its deportment. Most Englishmen wanted everyone
on the battlefield below, making the same sacrifices and
sharing the same risks.

Walter Allen, in his marvelous novel-chronicle of a
twentieth-century workingman, *All in a Lifetime,* lets his
hero describe the reasons why "the ordinary sensual man"
could not accept the C.O.'s position:

> I . . . resigned from the I.L.P. when it took the pacifist
> line. . . . I decided that I would rather be wrong with the mass
> of my fellow countrymen than right if to be right separated me
> from them. . . . I profoundly distrusted the rightness that iso-
> lated one from one's fellows. . . . I could not set myself apart
> for a theory.[24]

impact on public opinion in the 1920s and 1930s, during the Great War
hostility toward war resisters seems to me to have been fairly consistent.

22. MacDonagh, *London during the Great War,* p. 100, and *The Times,* 10
February 1916.

23. *Weekly Dispatch,* 9 April 1916, and MacDonagh, *London during the
Great War,* p. 100.

24. Walter Allen, *All in a Lifetime* (London, 1959), pp. 168–69.

The *Daily Sketch* (16 March 1916) caught the same mood in an attack on the NCF: "Theories be damned. Britain is at war. Either we have utterly to crush the oppressor or be enslaved." The gulf between the C.O.s' sensibilities and public attitudes deeply troubled some thoughtful objectors. After the war, Clifford Allen recalled how "a certain spiritual pride" stealthfully made its way into the NCF—"a certain arrogance that stiffened opposition to us and engendered really bitter hatred." "We seemed," he continued, "to wrap ourselves in coil after coil of finely spun logic, to raise our pedestal upon a mountain of phrases and formulas and to be unresponsive to the altered mood of those whose opinions we sought to change."[25]

Conscientious objectors hiding in their "funk holes" were detestable, but when large numbers of them emerged into the light to exercise their rights as citizens of a country they would not defend, they became intolerable. One illustration of this attitude was the press and public response to the NCF's second national convention. Despite the obvious and growing hostility toward conscientious objectors, the NCF's leaders felt that from a tactical and psychological viewpoint the time was ripe for a great national demonstration of the war-resistance movement's unity and strength. The call went out for all NCF branches to select delegates for a national emergency convention to be held in London on 8–9 April 1916.[26]

Some of the leading patriotic journals gave the impending conclave of "pasty faces" and "conchies" considerable play in hopes that NCF delegates would receive a "proper" reception from the outraged citizenry.[27] On 7 April, in keeping with its self-appointed role as provacateur of patriotic fury, the *Daily Express* warned its readers of a "secret meeting of peace cranks" to be held the next day at Devonshire House, the Friends' London headquarters. Because of his concern about the effect of such articles,[28] Allen wrote to the London

25. *Trib.*, 20 November 1916, and Allen ms., chap. 1, pp. 9, 12, CAP.
26. *Trib.*, 15 March 1916, and NCF circular letter, 23 March 1916, CAP.
27. For example, see *Daily Sketch*, 24 March 1916; *Evening Standard*, 23 March 1916; *Western Daily Mercury*, 29 March 1916; and *Leicester Daily Post*, 30 March 1916.
28. See C. P. Trevelyan to Simon (private), 26 November 1915, HO 45/10742/263275/110 in which Trevelyan accuses the *Express* of inciting

commissioner of police informing him of the NCF's strictly private meeting and warning of an organized attempt to halt the proceedings. He noted that the fellowship would have stewards inside the hall and that all delegates and members would be admitted by ticket only at a small side entrance. Nevertheless, he felt compelled to caution the authorities about the possibility of a disturbance.[29]

Police officials responded by setting up a line of officers at the front entrance of Devonshire House facing, as expected, a large and unruly crowd. In the meantime, fifteen hundred NCF delegates—described by the *Daily Mail* as "mild-faced creatures mostly thinnish and large-eyed, with rankish un-trimmed hair ... and ... thin apostolic beards"—slipped into the hall through the side gate. One journalist who dis-covered this passage described it as being "guarded in a way that suggested a secret society with a dark and dreadful con-spiracy to hide."[30]

By all accounts, the convention was an orderly, carefully orchestrated affair. The fellowship's national leaders suc-cessfully balanced emotional appeals and tactical considera-tions to produce the desired effect. In later days, when the NCF was weakened by government pressure and divided by internal strife, many C.O.s would look back to "Devonshire, 1916" as their movement's most glorious manifestation. Allen who later called the convention "a memorable scene in the history of the struggle for freedom in this country," set the tone for the meeting with his firm, quiet style. From her seat in the visitors' gallery, Beatrice Webb saw Allen as "a monument of Christian patience and lucid speech—his spiritual countenance, fine gentle voice and quiet manner serving him well as the President of a gathering of would-be martyrs for the sacred cause of peace."[31]

---

violence against the Union of Democratic Control. Also see *The Attack upon Freedom of Speech*, UDC leaflet 21B (London, [1916]), and Swartz, *Union of Democratic Control*, pp. 110–11.

29. Allen to Commissioner of Police, 6 April 1916, CAP.

30. *Daily Mail*, 10 April 1916. Compare with Beatrice Webb, *Diaries, 1912–1924*, ed. Margaret I. Cole (London, 1952), p. 59 (8 April 1916); *Evening News*, 8 April 1916; and *Reynolds' Weekly Newspaper*, 9 April 1916.

31. B. Webb, *Diaries*, p. 58 (8 April 1916), and Allen ms., chap. 2, pp. 29–31. Also see "Minutes of the National Convention of the No-Conscription Fellowship," 8 April 1916 (transcript from the shorthand notes of Theodore W. Hay), p. 2, CAP.

The morning session began by considering questions and resolutions proposed by various branches as well as by the national committee. These proposals pertained to the fellowship's position on such matters as noncombatant or civilian alternative service, the conduct of tribunals, the campaign to repeal the act, peace propaganda, and agitation for imprisoned C.O.s.[32] In general, debate supported the national committee's view that NCF members should appear before the tribunals but should refuse to accept any judgment except absolute exemption. This debate set the stage for Allen's earnest if overlong speech to the afternoon session. After reviewing the history of the fellowship and reaffirming its determination never to compromise in opposing conscription and militarism, Allen presented a resolution that pledged that all present would bear witness to their convictions regardless of the suffering that might be involved. It passed unanimously, though Mrs. Webb noted that some of the young men present seemed positively dazed by the sacrifices expected of them.[33]

As Allen was concluding his address, the hostile crowd outside the hall raised such a din that he could scarcely be heard. When he sat down, Grubb rose to suggest that the assembly remove one source of provocation of those outside by refraining from further applause and cheering. Thus, when Snowden rose to speak, the audience stood and silently acclaimed him in great swishing whispers of handkerchiefs and papers. The commotion outside had been caused by three sailors and a civilian (reputed to be Mr. Glover of the Anti-German League) who clambered over a locked gate and penetrated the citadel of antimilitarism. The popular press pictured the incident as a pitched battle between sailors and NCF stewards, with bags of flour flying hither and yon and various combatants being laid low. Vigorously denying any violent activity, the official NCF account stated that the invaders were peacefully persuaded to leave after handshaking all around.[34] Sydney R. Turner, who was a

32. See "Agenda for Emergency National Convention," NCF, 8 April 1916, BRA.
33. B. Webb, *Diaries*, p. 58 (8 April 1916), and "Minutes, NCF Convention," pp. 2–15, CAP.
34. For varying accounts of these incidents, see "Minutes, NCF Convention," p. 25, CAP; *Labour Leader*, 13 April 1916; *Evening Standard*, 8 April

steward at the convention, recounts that they left quietly after he had explained the C.O.s' position to them.[35]

After the expulsion of the attackers, the convention resumed audible displays of approval that were amply given to the remaining speakers, including the venerable Free Church leader Dr. John Clifford and Labour pacifist George Lansbury. The exhortations of the speakers, the hostile demonstrations outside the hall, and the incursion by the sailors all helped to create an atmosphere of urgency and unanimity in which the national committee's final proposal for total, no-compromise opposition to conscription received nearly unanimous support. Henceforth, the NCF would recognize the legitimacy of only one classification—*absolute exemption* from any national service except antiwar activity. In other words, the fellowship's convention announced its determination to defy the Military Service Acts and, if possible, to render them inoperative.[36] As Webb noted at the time, such a stand implied not just the

> right to refuse military service, but the inauguration, first in England and then in the world, of a strike against war.... They wanted to smash militarism; they intended, in fact, to use the conscience clause to nullify the Conscription Act... even if all the conscientious objectors, on religious grounds, should be relieved from service.... These men are not so much conscientious objectors as a militant minority of elects, intent on thwarting the will of the majority of ordinary citizens in a national policy.[37]

Obviously, Mrs. Webb did not approve, and just as obviously many rank-and-file C.O.s did not fully appreciate what they had let themselves in for. NCF leaders always referred with pride to the convention's "almost unanimous" resolution, but the apparent resolve of April 1916 faded rapidly—

1916; *Pall Mall Gazette,* 8 April 1916; *Sunday Pictorial,* 9 April 1916; and A. Fenner Brockway, *Inside the Left* (London, 1942), p. 70.

35. Sydney R. Turner, "For Faith and Freedom," handwritten ms., p. 4, SCPC. Turner (1882–?), a designer and rank-and-file member of the NCF, deposited his papers and memorabilia in the Swarthmore College Peace Collection. Also see Brockway, *Inside the Left,* pp. 69–70.

36. "Minutes, NCF Convention," 8 April 1916, pp. 25–31, 38–40, CAP; Allen ms., chap. 2, p. 31, CAP; and *Labour Leader,* 13 April 1916.

37. B. Webb, *Diaries,* pp. 59–60 (8 April 1916).

for a majority, at least—when they realized that the government was actually going to punish them. John Rae blames NCF leaders for "encouraging men to exaggerate the extent of their objection," thus causing unnecessary problems for the government and disrupting attempts to provide suitable alternative service.[38] There is some truth in these accusations, but it would seem to be more to the point to criticize the fellowship for clinging to the concept of the sanctity of human life instead of following C. H. Norman's counsel and openly declaring itself what it truly was: a stop-the-war organization.[39] On the other hand, although such a declaration might have improved the fellowship's consistency, it certainly would not have enhanced its strength or unity. So long as it kept the sanctity of human life as its foundation stone, the NCF could continue to offer a refuge to all conscientious objectors and though ultimately most C.O.s did not share their leaders' absolutist principles, they did not abandon the NCF nor, to the fellowship's credit, were they abandoned by it.

Having resolved to resist every form of conscription and to accept no compromise on alternative service, the NCF took great pains to ensure that the government understood its position. No doubt most cabinet ministers had more pressing matters to consider, but shortly after the convention adjourned, Lloyd George's private secretary was arranging a secret luncheon meeting at Walton Heath between the minister of munitions and NCF leaders, including Allen, Russell, and Marshall.[40] This odd little conclave produced no significant result, though it may reveal something about the nature of British government at the time, or more correctly, about the character of Lloyd George: outside of the

---

38. John Rae, *Conscience and Politics: The British Government and the Conscientious Objector to Military Service, 1916–1919* (London, 1970), p. 93.

39. See extracts from letter of C. H. Norman to A. F. Brockway, [October 1916], FSC Files, FHL.

40. F. L. Stevenson to Catherine Marshall, 10 April 1916, CEMP (microfilm). Also see Russell to Ottoline Morrell, Tuesday [25 April 1916], in Russell, *Autobiography*, 2:62. It has generally been assumed that this meeting took place on 11 April (for example, see Robbins, *Abolition of War*, p. 82), but Jo Vellacott Newberry has made an excellent case for its having occurred two weeks later on 25 April; see Vellacott Newberry, "Bertrand Russell and the Pacifists in the First World War," chap. 6.

landholding aristocracy, Lloyd George had no ideological enemies, only an ever-changing array of tactical opponents.

A week after the convention, the NCF national committee addressed a long letter to the prime minister informing him of their decision on alternative service, asking him to suspend tribunal hearings until an impartial inquiry could be made into their conduct, and warning him of the fellowship's plan "for an insistent agitation on behalf of prisoners, who by their suffering are proving the genuineness of their convictions." In addition, the NCF, in association with the Friends Service Committee (FSC), organized a deputation to convey the decisions of the convention—particularly as regards alternative service—to the House of Commons.[41]

Given the NCF's size and financial circumstances, its campaign of resistance was remarkably successful in publicizing the conscientious objectors' point of view. But at the very moment when the NCF was undertaking its most significant political and propaganda efforts to effect repeal of the Military Service Acts, the call for general compulsion was being transformed into an unceasing roar.

Conscription Now!

During the early months of 1916 military leaders and their political allies were becoming increasingly disaffected by Asquith's refusal to adopt full-scale conscription and by Bonar Law's reluctance to force the prime minister's hand. Asquith seemed impervious to anyone's demands, but a strengthened right-wing faction of Unionist M.P.s, rallying around Sir Edward Carson as leader of the so-called Unionist war committee, was pressing Bonar Law extremely hard as were Lord Milner and his supporters in the House of Lords.[42] Law resisted this pressure because he felt that the dissidents in his party were attempting to maneuver the gov-

41. NCF national committee to Asquith, 15 April 1916, CAP; FSC, Minutes of meeting, 6 April 1916, FSC Files, FHL; and "Notes on Deputation," undated, CEMP (microfilm).
42. For example, see Sir Edward Carson to Bonar Law, 3 April 1916, Bonar Law Papers, 53/1/1, House of Lords Record Office, London; Law to Carson, 4 April 1916, Bonar Law Papers, 53/6/70; and Curzon to Milner, 31 March 1916, Milner Papers, 136, Bodleian Library, Oxford.

ernment into a position where it would have to either accept conscription "all-round" or be removed from office. The Conservative leader claimed to be a supporter of compulsion but not at the price of turning out the coalition government and of forcing a bitterly divisive general election at a crucial point in the war. As he told that most political of generals, Sir Henry Wilson, "the best chance of winning the war is by a Government such as the present [one]."[43]

But while Bonar Law might have successfully stood up to an insurrection in his own party, he lacked the authority to withstand an allied force of Unionist dissenters and Lloyd George. The minister of munitions was a pivotal figure, not because of his strength in the Liberal party but because of the widespread belief that the government could not survive his resignation. At this juncture, he was being assiduously wooed by the so-called Monday night cabal of the Carson–Milner faction.[44] Leopold Amery was especially active in the attempts to convince Lloyd George that it was imperative for him to put aside party labels and to join with those prepared to take any step necessary to win the war: "It really is now or never—you may possibly leave later, but not as a leader."[45]

On 11 April Gen. William Robertson, chief of the Imperial General Staff, presented the cabinet with a memorandum stating that he and the Army Council believed that only full-scale conscription could produce sufficient manpower. Even this "stiff and unyielding" military opinion was not decisive. A report to the cabinet on the "recruiting problem," prepared by a committee that included Tories Austen Chamberlain and Lord Lansdowne in addition to Asquith and Reginald McKenna still insisted that the increased yield of manpower from general conscription would be too small to offset its possible economic and social repercussions. The

43. Law to J. L. Croal, 1 April 1916, Bonar Law Papers, 53/6/69, and Law to Henry Wilson, 31 March 1916, Bonar Law Papers, 53/6/68.

44. For differing versions of the conscription crisis of April 1916, see Alfred Gollin, *Proconsul in Politics: A Study of Lord Milner in Opposition and in Power* (New York, 1964), pp. 332–43; Peter Fraser, "The Impact of the War of 1914–1918 on the British Political System," in *War and Society*, ed. M. R. D. Foot (New York, 1973), pp. 128–30; and Robert J. Scally, *The Origins of the Lloyd George Coalition* (Princeton, 1975), pp. 280–98 passim.

45. Amery to Lloyd George, 6, 13, 14, 16, and 20 April 1916, Lloyd George Papers, D/16/2/3, 5, 7, and 8, House of Lords Record Office, London.

full cabinet rejected this report and demanded a reexamination of the question, but obviously some other means had to be found for ending the impasse.[46]

Within a week, amid growing clamor from the Northcliffe press for men of "courage and character" to put an end to the fetid Asquithian system, events came to a head. On 17 April Lloyd George threatened to resign and to take Kitchener, Robertson, the entire Army Council, and most of the Unionist ministers with him if strong compulsory measures were not implemented.[47] This threat was made more palpable by a letter from Bonar Law to Asquith in which the Conservative leader, still expressing his earnest desire to preserve the coalition, warned that there was "hardly a single Unionist member who does not believe that the needs of the war demand general compulsion." In these circumstances, Bonar Law said, he could now support nothing less.[48]

Asquith's hand was being forced, but even though he was now prepared to give ground on conscription, he could not devise a formula that would satisfy both factions in the cabinet. For two days running—18 and 19 April—the prime minister was forced to admit in Parliament that the cabinet was seriously divided on the question of compulsory service; rumors persisted that he was about to resign. Finally, on 20 April official communiqués announced that cabinet proposals on conscription would be presented to an unprecedented secret session of the House of Commons.[49]

The scheme submitted to Parliament on 25 April was a

46. See CAB 37/145/28, 35–36, and Christopher Addison, *Politics from Within, 1911–1918*, 2 vols. (London, 1924), 1:249.

47. *Lloyd George: A Diary by Frances Stevenson*, ed. A. J. P. Taylor (New York, 1971), pp. 105–6. Also see *The Times*, 14 April 1916. Lloyd George told friends that if he resigned, conscription would serve as the immediate cause but that the overriding issue was the way the war was being run; see Lord Riddell, *War Diary, 1914–1918* (London, 1933), pp. 170–71.

48. Law to Asquith (draft copy), 17 April 1916, Bonar Law Papers, 53/6/73. Also see Riddell, *War Diary*, p. 176.

49. 5 H.C., 81:2241, 2351, 18 and 19 April 1916. The official justification for this extraordinary procedure was to protect the secrecy of Army Council figures on available manpower, but in fact Asquith did not want to risk an open test of strength on the conscription question. In his memoirs John Clynes says that Labour members advised the secret session because of the danger of industrial unrest; J. R. Clynes, *Memoir, 1869–1924*, 2 vols. (London, 1937), 1:199–200.

complicated arrangement that in large part incorporated a plan originally proposed to the cabinet by Lloyd George and subsequently agreed to by Labour ministers. General compulsion was to be adopted in principle, but its implementation would be withheld as long as recruiting figures satisfied army leaders. Asquith added his own unfortunate idea for an immediate call-up of eighteen-year-olds and time-expired veterans.[50] To make matters worse, as this hybrid was being introduced to the House, reports arrived of the Easter Rising in Dublin. Not surprisingly, the measure was greeted with such an outburst of hostility and derision that Asquith had to undergo the humiliation of announcing that the government no longer felt justified in proceeding with it.[51] On the next day the prime minister told the cabinet that the government had "no alternative but to proceed at once with legislation for general compulsion." The cabinet assented unanimously, though there were ominous rumblings about "serious labour trouble" from Arthur Henderson and Walter Runciman. Lloyd George rightly dismissed these fears as exaggerated. The die was cast, and on 2 May 1916 Asquith himself announced the government's intention of introducing a full measure of conscription.[52]

Once the government had committed itself to universal conscription, its passage was a foregone conclusion. The NCF, however, kept up a brave front. A letter from the political committee to local branches urged all members to redouble their efforts to defeat conscription, noting that "nothing is impossible with the NCF."[53] At the national level, activities were considerably more pragmatic. Immediately after the prime minister's announcement, for instance, Marshall organized a deputation of prominent people—most of

50. See Stevenson, *Lloyd George Diary*, pp. 106–7, and Addison, *Politics from Within*, 1:250–52. Also see Peter Fraser, *Lord Esher* (London, 1973), pp. 318–20.

51. 5 H.C., 81:2525–75, 27 April 1916.

52. Cabinet Papers, 1915–1916, 29 April 1916, Asquith Papers (159), Bodleian Library, Oxford, and 5 H.C., 81:2511–16, 2 May 1916. Ireland was not included in the bill ostensibly because it had not been included in the Derby canvass.

53. NCF Honorary Secretary of Political Committee (C. Marshall) to Divisional and Branch Secretaries, 6 May 1916, BRA. Also see NCF Hon. Sec. of Pol. Comm. to Divisional and Branch Secretaries, 23 May 1916, BRA.

whom, like the bishop of Oxford and Clifford, were not officially connected with the fellowship—to press for improved methods of dealing with conscientious objectors. This deputation especially stressed the need to revise tribunal procedures, to limit noncombatant service to those who announced themselves willing to accept it, and to remove all genuine conscientious objectors from the jurisdiction of military law. Although the immediate response to these proposals was not encouraging, the Joint Advisory Council (JAC) and the National Council against Conscription (NCAC) kept up the pressure by suggesting a series of eight amendments to the new bill. These amendments—to be presented by friendly M.P.s—would, if adopted, have effectively eliminated conscientious objectors from the operation of the new act.[54] Some of these proposed amendments, including one that called for the transfer of C.O.s to civil jurisdiction, were debated, though eventually rejected, by the House of Commons. One of them, concerned with clarifying the tribunals' power to grant absolute exemption to conscientious objectors, was, as noted earlier, actually incorporated into the new act.[55]

Although the activities of the political committee and the JAC, plus the stalwart support of some two score anticonscriptionist M.P.s, had made it possible for the conscientious objectors' position to be fully vented in parliamentary debate, the opponents of the second Military Service Act never posed a threat to the measure, which became law on 25 May 1916. Longtime advocates of conscription proclaimed that it had come eighteen months too late and would have been enacted earlier by any decent government, but those with more astute political vision saw that Asquith was probably the only man who could have brought in conscription without causing serious dislocation or industrial unrest.[56] Asquith managed to remain prime minister

54. See "Record of Deputation of 11 May 1916," CEMP (microfilm); "Proposed Improvements in the Method of Dealing with Conscientious Objectors," undated, BRA; and "Amendments to the New Military Service Bill," undated, BRA.

55. See Chap. 5. For presentation of these amendments by T. E. Harvey, see 5 H.C., 82:1182–1230 passim, 15 May 1916.

56. Compare derogatory remarks of *The Times*, 29 April 1916, and L. S. Amery, *My Political Life*, vol. 2, *War and Peace, 1914–1929* (London, 1953),

for another eight months, but as Stephen McKenna has noted, from the day when conscription became law without revolution, "he was no longer indispensable." After watching the prime minister's presentation of the new measure to an "astonishingly cold" Commons, Maurice Hankey, secretary to the Committee of Imperial Defense, noted that "the people who wanted compulsory service did not want Asquith and those who wanted Asquith did not want compulsory service."[57]

The NCF greeted the imposition of universal compulsory service with the same indefatigable spirit (some would say animal stubbornness) that it had demonstrated in every previous crisis. Less than a week after the act became law, the national committee announced:

> We are more strongly of opinion than ever that our Fellowship . . . must not acquiesce in any of these schemes which will assist in establishing Conscription. . . . Everything depends upon uncompromising opposition to each new attempt to rivet [militarism] . . . on our country . . . there is really no method of remedying the present evils so long as Conscription remains law. Freedom of conscience, justice, and liberty cannot exist simultaneously with militarism.[58]

Conscience, Justice, Liberty, and Law

In the "Nightmare" sequence of his autobiographical novel *Kangaroo,* D. H. Lawrence calls the period from 1916 to 1919 the "awful years" when "a wave of criminal lust rose and possessed England . . . a reign of terror, under a set of indecent bullies."[59] During this period, Lawrence was threatened with conscription, humiliated by two army medical examinations, hounded by police and patriotic neighbors, and finally forced to move from a beloved cot-

---

p. 73, with David Lloyd George, *War Memoirs,* 6 vols. (London, 1933), 2:710–11; Stevenson, *Lloyd George Diary,* pp. 106–7; and Bonar Law's acknowledgment in 5 H.C., 92:1392, 4 April 1917.

57. Lord Hankey, *The Supreme Command, 1914–1918,* 2 vols. (London, 1961), 2:476, and McKenna, *While I Remember,* p. 191. Also see Addison, *Politics from Within,* 1:252–53.

58. NCF circular letter, 30 May 1916, CAP.

59. D. H. Lawrence, *Kangaroo* (London, 1935), pp. 238–40.

tage on the Cornwall coast.[60] In retrospect, Lawrence's brooding resentment over the treatment he received seems rather precious and petty, especially when contrasted with the sacrifices of ordinary soldiers and even those of most conscientious objectors. Lawrence does, however, provide a clue to public attitudes that became increasingly harsh and bellicose as the war dragged on.

The campaign for the repeal of the Military Service Act had succeeded in making the position of conscientious objectors widely known, but it had not made that position any more popular. On the contrary, a growing parliamentary distaste for questions and speeches by advocates of the C.O.s' cause[61] reflected the general public's attitude toward "conchies," especially after the Irish uprising and the military disasters in the spring of 1916. Such hostility presented a grave challenge to the NCF, not only because of its demoralizing effect on conscientious objectors but also because it sanctioned and even encouraged governmental actions that would have been unacceptable in ordinary times.

By the spring of 1916 there was an increasing clamor for the outright suppression of the NCF as an "essentially and inevitably treasonable" organization.[62] The sensationalist *Daily Express* implied that the NCF was financed with German money.[63] An outraged *Evening Standard* demanded that "these hordes of cowards organized by the No-Conscription Fellowship be severely dealt with," while a Glasgow journal suggested that all C.O.s be interned until victory had been won and then deported, "their cowardice with them." Apparently, the *Sunday Herald* sought a more definitive solution. In principle, it noted, conscientious objectors were "not worth the powder and shot," but in view of the extreme circumstances "perhaps a few rounds might be spared."[64]

---

60. Ibid., pp. 238–65. For another account of these incidents, see Richard Aldington, *Portrait of a Genius, But...* (London, 1950), pp. 184–203.

61. For example, see Sir Arthur Markham's attack on Philip Snowden, 5 H.C., 82:2179, 15 May 1916.

62. *The Globe*, 30 March 1916,

63. *Daily Express*, 10 April 1916.

64. *Evening Standard*, 23 March 1916; *Glasgow Herald*, 10 April 1916; and *Sunday Herald*, 9 April 1916.

Against the background of the popular press's deep antagonism toward C.O.s, the Home Office was compiling a sizable collection of complaints against the NCF. On several occasions, members of Parliament had called the government's attention to some NCF activity or publication and had demanded to know why this obviously subversive organization was still being tolerated by the authorities.[65] Home Secretary Herbert Samuel generally answered such inquiries by pointing out—as he did in a private letter to Herbert Nield, an M.P. who was chairman of the Middlesex appeal tribunal—that he could proceed against groups such as the NCF only when they openly advocated disobedience to the provisions of the Military Service Act or to some other law.[66]

To many ardent supporters of the war, such a pronouncement seemed nitpicking legalism. With the *Daily Express* (10 April 1916), they felt that people who made statements like those ascribed to members of the NCF "must be either crazy or the agents of the enemy." The fact that the fellowship was permitted to indulge in unsolicited propagandizing with apparent immunity infuriated some patriotic citizens, who proceeded to vent their rage on the government. A former inspector of the metropolitan police reported from Letchworth that NCF pamphlets, such as one entitled *Shall Britons Be Conscripts,* had resulted locally in "a crop of 32 'Conscientious Objectors.'"[67] Another indignant citizen reported that a scurrilous leaflet headed *Repeal the Act* was "placed in our letter boxes at night by women. Can nothing be done to stop this? I have *all* my five sons in the army / all volunteers / hence my anxiety."[68]

As public pressure mounted and concern increased about the possible effect of NCF propaganda on recruiting and on

65. For example, Major Newman's questions, 5 H.C., 81:2100, 2230-31, 17 and 18 April 1916; Ronald McNeill's, 5 H.C., 82:629, 10 May 1916; and statement by Joynson-Hicks, 5 H.C., 82:1161-62, 15 May 1916. Also see HO 45/10801/307402/30 and HO 45/10742/263275/168.

66. See HO 45/10801/307402/50. Also see Samuel's statements on this subject in Parliament, 5 H.C., 81:45, 21 March 1916, and 5 H.C., 82:12, 2996, 3 May and 1 June 1916.

67. H. Rivers Wilson to Lord Robert Cecil, 15 May 1916, HO 45/10801/307402/56.

68. R. H. Hurley to Home Secretary, undated, HO 45/10801/307402/39.

working-class morale, local officials began to crack down on the fellowship's proselytizing activities. During March a member of the NCF's Oxford branch was sentenced to two months (later reduced to fourteen days) for distributing *Shall Britons Be Conscripts*. At Cefn (Merthyr Tdyfil), two men were fined fifty pounds apiece for passing out anticonscription literature.[69] Since these cases were heard by local magistrates and since there was no uniform prosecution for distributing any particular material, the NCF protested such incidents as examples of local officials' overstepping their authority to suppress free speech. The central government, however, not only supported the decisions of local authorities but also, by its own subsequent actions, revealed that in its view the fellowship had overstepped the acceptable bounds of dissent in wartime.

In mid-May 1916 the entire national committee of the NCF—with the curious exception of Allen (Norman was already in custody)—was summoned under the Defense of the Realm Act (DORA) to appear at the London Mansion House for publishing the leaflet *Repeal the Act* that, according to the subpoena, contained material prejudicial to the recruitment and discipline of His Majesty's forces. When the fellowship objected that the home secretary himself had given assurances that repeal agitation was legal, Sir Edward Troup, permanent undersecretary in the Home Office, noted that one sentence in the proscribed leaflet—"We re-affirm our determined resistance to all that is established in the Act"—was clearly an attempt to induce others to disobey the Military Service Act and was therefore intolerable.[70] On 17 May eight members of the national committee were convicted and fined one hundred pounds apiece. The fines of the Reverend Leyton Richards and Grubb were paid by the fellowship, but Fenner Brockway, Will Chamberlain, Walter H. Ayles, Barry Brown, and John P. Fletcher chose to serve two-month sentences instead. After the rejection of their appeal (with Lord Derby and General Childs appearing as

69. For these incidents, see HO 45/10801/307402/53; *Trib.*, 23 March 1916; and 5 H.C., 82:685–86, 2982–83, 3007–8, 10 May and 1 June 1916.

70. Minute by Troup, HO 45/10801/307402/60, and Samuel's statement, 5 H.C., 82:2999, 1 June 1916. Also see "Hostile Leaflet: Circular No. 2," HO 45/10801/307402/53; *Trib.*, 18 May 1916; and Brockway, *Inside the Left*, pp. 72–73.

NCF leaders during the "Repeal the Act" trial. *From left to right:* Walter H. Ayles, John P. Fletcher, William J. Chamberlain, Barry Brown, Clifford Allen, and A. Fenner Brockway. (Courtesy Friends House Library)

witnesses for the prosecution), the convicted men surrendered to the authorities on 17 July.[71]

The proceedings against the NCF's national leadership pointed up the government's readiness—partly in response to public and parliamentary pressure—to use the provisions of DORA to limit or even to eliminate organized agitation against conscription and war. One of the most prominent examples of the state's growing impatience with dissenters was the case of Bertrand Russell. By the spring of 1916 Russell was deeply involved in the work of the NCF. Among the numerous tasks he had performed for the political committee and head office was the drafting of a leaflet protesting and arrest and conviction of Ernest F. Everett, a teacher at St. Helens. Attention focused on Everett because the army court-martial that heard his case had given him two years at hard labor, a sentence of unprecedented severity at the time. Russell's leaflet, which he probably dashed off in a

71. Brockway, *Inside the Left*, pp. 72-73, and *Trib.*, 18 May, 8 June, and 20 July 1916. Morgan Jones was also convicted but at the time was already serving four months for refusing military orders; see *Labour Leader*, 6 July 1914.

few minutes, described Everett's treatment at the hands of the tribunals and the army and concluded with the plea that all who loved liberty join in protest against the sort of persecution that Everett was being forced to endure.[72]

When the leaflet, anonymous but issued on the NCF's behalf, came to the Home Office's attention, the home secretary himself noted that it "appears to me to fall within the scope of [DORA] and should be prosecuted."[73] Subsequently, six men were arrested, fined, or imprisoned for distributing the leaflet. Chagrined that other men should be punished for his unsigned work, Russell placed a short letter in *The Times* stating that, if anyone were to be chastised for the material in question, "I am the person primarily responsible."[74] The government quickly took the bait, and on 5 June 1916 Russell was tried before the lord mayor of London for "statements likely to prejudice the recruiting and discipline of His Majesty's Forces." Russell seemed happy to accept the government's challenge and was confident that his case would be of great use to the NCF's cause, even in the unlikely event that he was convicted. As he told Allen: "I think the Everett leaflet makes a very thin case and I feel disposed not to have a barrister."[75] The printed record of Russell's self-conducted defense reveals a sardonically humorous but withal most impressive performance, concluding with a ringing statement in defense of liberty of conscience. The magistrate, however, was not impressed. First, he cut short Russell's address, noting that the defendant was not permitted to make political speeches, then he pronounced Russell guilty and fined him 110 pounds or sixty-one days.[76] Russell, who had earlier told Allen that "prosecutions are helpful to us and would be especially so if

72. The leaflet is reprinted in Russell, *Autobiography*, 2:63–64. There are also original copies in BRA and SCPC. For reports on Everett's case, see *Trib.*, 30 March and 20 April 1916.

73. Minute by Samuel, HO 45/10801/307402/33. Also see HO 45/10801/307402/53.

74. Printed as "Adsum Qui Feci," *The Times*, 17 May 1916. Also see *Trib.*, 11 and 18 May 1918.

75. Russell to Allen, 30 May 1916, BRA. Also see Russell to Allen, n.d. [early June 1916], BRA, and Russell to Ottoline Morrell, [June 1916], in Russell, *Autobiography*, 2:66–67.

76. The proceedings were reprinted by the NCF as *Rex v. Bertrand Russell* (London, 1916). Also see *Labour Leader*, 6 July 1916.

they ended in imprisonment without the option of a fine,"[77] refused to pay. The government, however, would not accommodate him through imprisonment. Instead, his goods at Trinity College were distrained and sold at auction to satisfy the judgment. Russell lost more than his belongings. On 11 July 1916 the Trinity College council voted unanimously to remove him from his lectureship.[78] If the blow did not seem to fall too heavily on Russell then, it certainly reflected badly on the British academic community.

One reason for Russell's seeming lack of concern may have been the fact that at the time he was sacked from Trinity he was preparing to take a visiting lectureship at Harvard University. Three days after Russell's initial conviction, however, the British ambassador to the United States, Sir Cecil Spring-Rice, informed the president of Harvard that Russell would not be permitted to leave Great Britain.[79]

Actually, from the NCF's viewpoint, the entire affair gave some cause for satisfaction. The fellowship had garnered an immense amount of publicity, had helped to embarrass the government, and had gained the nearly full-time services of one of the country's foremost minds. Indeed, shortly after his conviction, the unemployed philosopher set off on a speaking tour in South Wales on the NCF's behalf.[80] Reports concerning the tour's apparent success no doubt convinced the authorities that Russell's movements should be even further restricted. Henceforth, Russell was to be excluded from certain "prohibited areas," including the entire seacoast; presumably, as he noted, "for fear I should signal to German submarines."[81] This final impediment also meant that Rus-

77. Russell to Allen, 18 May 1916, BRA.

78. Russell tells the story briefly in his *Autobiography*, 2:33, and reprints the official letter notifying him of the council's decision as well as other letters concerning the case, 2:68–71. Also see Prof. C. H. Hereford to *The Nation*, 22 July 1916, and *Trib.*, 20 July and 17 August 1916.

79. Spring-Rice to the President of Harvard, 8 June 1916, reprinted in Russell, *Autobiography*, 2:65. Marshall told Russell, 15 June 1916, BRA: "I always grudge our valuable people going to America.... It seems to me they are always getting up steam there and blowing it off without putting it to any very constructive purpose."

80. See Allen to Russell, 27 June 1916, and I. H. Thomas to Russell, 26 June 1916, which includes an itinerary for 30 June through 4 July, BRA. See Clark, *Bertrand Russell*, pp. 294–97, on the importance of this tour to Russell's emotional life and sense of well-being.

81. Russell, *Autobiography*, 2:33. For an example of the complaints about

sell was prevented from delivering some of the lectures on political ideals that he had arranged in several industrial cities under the auspices of the NCF and the National Council on Civil Liberties. The government did relent sufficiently to say that the restriction would be lifted if he promised not to engage in antiwar propaganda, but Russell would make no such accommodation.[82] All the passages were now closed. Russell himself has said that were it not "for these various compliments on the part of the government, I should have thrown up pacifist work, as I had become persuaded that it was entirely futile. Perceiving, however, that the government thought otherwise, I supposed I might be mistaken, and continued."[83] Thus, by keeping Russell solidly in the enemy camp, the authorities made an unwitting though significant contribution to the NCF's survival.

Pressure against the fellowship continued to increase throughout the summer of 1916. On 5 June, the day of Russell's conviction, the NCF head office was raided, and its records confiscated. By mid-July nearly a score of branch officials had been arrested and prosecuted for distributing "objectionable" material. But as Allen stated in response to the raid on the head office: "When millions of our fellow men are enduring hardships for their sense of duty on the battlefield, shall we stand aside from demanding peace because that way lies persecution?"[84]

Russell's activities, see a report to the home secretary from Capt. Lionel Lindsay, chief constable of Glamorganshire, HO 45/10742/263275/219. Vellacott Newberry, "Bertrand Russell and the Pacifists in the First World War," pp. 238ff, emphasizes the surprising lack of organized or substantial opposition to Russell's public speeches.

82. See Russell's holograph note on the incident in BRA and his account of a conversation with General Cockerill at the War Office; Russell, *Autobiography,* 2:72–73. There is also a scrapbook in BRA containing a pamphlet, *Bertrand Russell and the War Office: A Personal Statement,* dated 1 September 1916. The ban on Russell's movement was widely protested in the liberal press—for example, *Daily News,* 2 and 16 September 1916; *Manchester Guardian,* 2 September 1916; and *Westminster Gazette,* 5 September 1916—as well as debated in Parliament, 5 H.C., 86:825–831, 19 October 1916.

83. Russell, *Autobiography,* 2:33.

84. See HO 45/10801/307402/74; NCF circular letter, 5 June 1916, CAP; and Clifford Allen, "The Conscientious Objector's Struggle: A History of the No-Conscription Fellowship," *Labour Leader,* 20 July 1916. Also see *The Times,* 6 June 1916, and *Trib.,* 8 June 1916.

Did NCF leaders really believe that they were being perse-cuted for the profession of pacifist faith or their defense of conscience and liberty? Rae, for one, considers such com-plaints to be "somewhat disingenuous" given the sophisti-cated nature of the fellowship's political activities.[85] Nonetheless, these cries of persecution were sympathetically heard by an influential minority and point up the manifold ways in which the NCF could provoke an already overbur-dened administration. While the NCF complained of perse-cution, the Home Office was subjected to a barrage of in-quiries and protests from local officials who obviously felt that the government was manifestly derelict in its duty of crushing treasonous dissenters![86]

Whichever view of the government's actions was correct—arbitrary persecution or legitimate police power—certain tragic consequences of the confrontation between conscientious objectors and the state were rapidly becoming apparent. In the midst of raids and prosecutions, accusa-tions and counteraccusations, away from center stage, the minor characters of the drama were beginning to play their most demanding roles. In July 1916 the NCF central office received a letter from a conscientious objector in military custody at Kinmel Park who spoke of the pitiful physical and mental condition of a fellow prisoner, Ernest Everett, the same schoolteacher of St. Helens whose alleged ill-treatment an eminent philosopher had exposed.[87] Russell was still at large and, in the government's view, dangerous. But where were the thousands of Ernest Everetts who had been deemed soldiers, and what was to become of them?

85. Rae, *Conscience and Politics*, p. 93. Compare Robbins, *Abolition of War*, pp. 80–81, 90–91. Robbins also seems to imply (p. 135) that the NCF's major aim was neither to protect the liberty of conscientious objectors nor to stop the war but to prevent the government from winning it.

86. For example, see Lindsay's report to the Home Office in HO 45/10743/263275/284.

87. Cited in COIB Report 30 (28 July 1916):118.

7

Defenders of the Majesty of Conscience

Those Who Were Deemed

As amended in May 1916, the second Military Service Act extended liability for military service to all male residents of Great Britain between the ages of eighteen and forty-one. Men who came under the purview of the act were "deemed to have been enlisted into His Majesty's forces and to have forthwith been transferred to the reserve on an appointed date." This provision allowed the government to make use of the existing Territorial and Reserve Forces Act (1907) in order to call men up from the reserves as the need arose.[1] Thus, the act was not a "selective service" or manpower-procurement plan, but a law that automatically "deemed" every unexempted eligible man to be a soldier.

Although the professed purpose of the second Military Service Act was to gain sufficient manpower for the armed forces, its most notable result was to ensure a means of exemption for those who could not previously have been prevented from enlisting. Thus, conscription was as important for those it kept out of uniform as for those it brought in. In effect, instead of easing the army's problem of securing recruits, the act made competition for available manpower even more acute.[2] Seen in this light, the War Office's deter-

---

1. See William Grist Hawtin, *The Law and Practice of Military Conscription under the Military Service Acts,* 2 vols. (London, 1917-1918), 1:18, and Sir Wyndham Childs, *Episodes and Reflections* (London, 1930), p. 148. The Military Service (No. 2) Act (1918) (8 GEO 5, chap. 5, 18 April 1918), raised the age limit to fifty-one with the proviso that it could be advanced to fifty-six. This act also canceled all exemptions except physical disability or conscientious objection and extended conscription to Ireland. An excellent discussion of the act is contained in the NCF pamphlet, *An Explanation of Procedure under the Military Service (No. 2) Act, 1918* (London, 1918).

2. For a discussion of this anomaly, see John Rae, *Conscience and Politics: The British Government and the Conscientious Objector to Military Service, 1916-1919* (London, 1970), pp. 24, 66-67. Also see A. J. P. Taylor, *Politics in*

mination to question all claims of exemption, especially those of conscientious objectors, seems far less truculent.

In February 1916 single men of military age began receiving army form W. 3236, which instructed them to report for service at a specified time and place. If a man failed to comply after receiving two such notices, he was subject to arrest by the police as a wartime deserter. On 6 April 1916 *The Tribunal* began to print an honor roll of NCF members who had been arrested for failure to report for military duty. NCF leaders hoped to confront the military authorities with an overwhelming flood of C.O.s whose resistance would bring the operation of the Military Service Act to a virtual standstill, but civilian and military officials developed a fairly effective procedure for handling recalcitrant conscripts.[3]

Once a C.O. was refused exemption by the tribunals or had rejected the exemption he was offered, his role became essentially passive: unless he chose to actively avoid arrest, he simply went about his business until the police came to get him. For its part, the NCF counseled members not to avoid apprehension. As one letter to the branch offices noted, "one of the things that has most impressed the Authorities and . . . the public with the sincerity and courage of the C.O. has been that members have quietly awaited arrest without making any attempt to avoid the consequences of their opinion."[4] When a man had been seized by the police, he was taken to the local magistrate's court, which determined whether or not he could legally be deemed to have enlisted. If he was declared a soldier, he was generally fined about two pounds as an absentee and was handed over to a military escort that removed him to the camp of his assigned regi-

Wartime and Other Essays (London, 1964), pp. 23–24, and Lord Hankey, *The Supreme Command, 1914–1918*, 2 vols. (London, 1961), 2:477. *The General Annual Reports of the British Army for the Period from 1st October, 1913, to 30 September 1919* (Cmd. 1193), 1921, pp. 9, 60, not only show that more men volunteered for the army before March 1916 (2.6 million) than were conscripted thereafter (2.4 million) but also reveal that during the first year that compulsion was in force twice as many men were exempted (779,936) as were conscripted (371,500).

3. This procedure is described in the War Office publication, *Registration and Recruiting* (August 1916), pp. 13–15. For an excellent description from a conscientious objector's perspective, see Scott Duckers, *Handed Over* (London, [1917]).

4. Instructions from NCF Political Committee on Branch Activities, 29 July 1916, BRA.

ment. Here, the conscientious objector usually began his resistance by performing some gesture of defiance, for instance, refusing to put on a khaki uniform. If the objector could not be convinced to obey military orders, he was charged with willful disobedience of a lawful order and placed in the guardroom to await court-martial.

Because the military authorities handled most conscientious objectors in a similar fashion, the NCF was able to issue a comprehensive book of instructions called *The Court-Martial Friend and Prison Guide*. This manual, purporting to be "a detailed statement of what a Conscientious Objector needs to know from the time of his arrest onwards,"[5] contained everything from a list of the most useful items to carry along when arrested to a detailed explanation of court-martial procedure. A consistent theme in the fellowship's literature was the necessity of keeping the organization informed as to the whereabouts of members in military custody. As one circular letter noted:

> Parents and relatives should persistently demand . . . information regarding men in the hands of the military and, if the information is withheld, should—if possible—call personally at the War Office and insist upon a reply. . . . Many of our members when isolated may hear little or nothing of what is being done. . . . Let them have confidence that the N.C.F. will exert all its energy and influence on their behalf.[6]

Through the *Court-Martial Friend* and other publications, the NCF attempted to ensure that every conscientious objector was fully aware of his rights. At the same time, NCF members were urged to use every opportunity for propagating pacifist ideals. For example, they were warned not to give themselves up to the police voluntarily since a policeman to whom an absentee surrendered could immediately turn him over to the military without the necessity of a civil hearing, thus denying him his day in court as well as the chance to engage in antiwar propaganda.[7]

Other problems that troubled many objectors once they

5. The NCF published at least two editions of the *Court-Martial Friend*. The earliest version is in the NCF File, SCPC; a later edition is included in CAP. The quotation is from the pamphlet's cover.

6. Clifford Allen and Fenner Brockway to NCF members, 19 April 1916, BRA.

7. NCF circular letter, 1 May 1916, CAP, and *Court-Martial Friend*, p. 2.

were in the hands of the army were when to disobey an order and how to disobey without seeming entirely negative and disrespectful. An NCF circular suggested that C.O.s should "decline to sign any document, to accept any army pay, to undergo medical examination, to put on khaki, or to carry out any instruction to drill." Members were admonished to be "firm and dignified" when refusing to obey orders, to "maintain an attitude of courtesy and good feeling, even under provocation," and never to attempt to meet violence with violence. They were further advised to insist that the charge sheet against them include the fact that they refused orders because of an all-inclusive objection to war, not because of any disrespect for the person giving the order.[8]

The NCF was especially careful to provide detailed instructions on the best methods of preparing and presenting court-martial cases. Because army regulations allowed each prisoner to have a court-martial "friend" to aid in his defense, the fellowship was able to provide experienced help to less-articulate objectors. This help was considered especially important since the court-martial provided C.O.s with "a chance . . . to say exactly how they look at war, at militarism, at duty, at ethics, at morality, at Christianity, and so on." The *Court-Martial Friend* warned, however, that, since an overlong statement might irritate the court, members should try to limit their declarations to about 150 words.[9] Unfortunately, few objectors could adequately cover the envisaged ground in so few words; even the most eloquent court-martial statements were long, and, for the nonpacifist, probably irritating.[10] Still, the general feeling among conscientious objectors seems to have been that military courts gave the accused ample opportunity to present his defense. Certainly, they were credited with a higher standard of justice than that available at civilian tribunals.[11]

But despite all the NCF's advice on proper conduct and all

8. *Court-Martial Friend*, p. 3, and NCF circular letter, 1 May 1916, CAP. Also see Edward Williamson Mason, *Made Free in Prison* (London, [1918]), pp. 31–32.

9. *Court-Martial Friend*, pp. 6–8.

10. For examples, see *Trib.*, 23 March 1916.

11. For example, see Stephen Hobhouse, *Autobiography* (Boston, 1952), p. 158, and T. Corder Catchpool, *On Two Fronts* (London, 1918), p. 139.

its assurances that no member would be abandoned, all objectors could not be adequately prepared for the kind of reception they would receive. At the time of the NCF emergency convention, Beatrice Webb had questioned the ability of conscientious objectors "to survive the mingled coaxing and duress that would be attempted . . . to get them into uniform."[12] Her assessment provided a fairly accurate description of how many C.O.s were handled once they were in the army's hands. Most commissioned and noncommissioned officers did not really understand the conscientious objectors' views, but they did understand malingering and some at least were not adverse to a bit of "horseplay" in order to convince a recalcitrant recruit to "come round." Such horseplay might seem innocent enough to an army corporal, but some C.O.s were profoundly shocked at being treated like "the vilest criminal" because of their devotion to an ideal. In a *Tribunal* editorial, Clifford Allen reminded his followers that the best way of dealing with either physical or psychological pressure was by stoically facing up to the consequences of one's beliefs without rancor or despair.[13] Unfortunately, not all NCF members were capable of following the chairman's advice.

A prominent example of one who did not was Eric B. Chappelow, a writer and NCF member who was handed over to the army shortly after the NCF convention. On 14 April a smiling Chappelow—dressed only in army boots and blanket—was featured on the front page of the *Daily Sketch* as "'Percy,' the conscientious objector who refuses to wear khaki." Apparently, Chappelow's smile hid the near panic that he revealed in a letter written the day before to his old teacher C. P. Sanger.

> [They] strapped a blanket round me and strapped my arms to my sides and marched me off . . . to the orderly room. . . . I shall be in solitary confinement for three or four days, and as there is no heat in the cell, I am shivering. Does a military prison consist of solitary confinement? I feel that if I am faced

12. Beatrice Webb, *Diaries, 1912–1924*, ed. Margaret I. Cole (London, 1952), p. 61 (8 April 1916).

13. *Trib.*, 4 May 1916. Also see A. M. Sanders, "My Experiences as a Conscientious Objector and the Life That Led up to Them," unpublished ms., p. 2, CAP.

with two years, or one year, or even six months of that, with never a sight of my friends or a word from them, I shall go mad and never keep my mental balance. I am so highly strung that to be cut off from the world like a felon would kill me. . . . I feel awful. . . . Urge all our friends in Parliament to spare no efforts for us. . . . I don't think I have deserved this awful treatment. . . . Is the Government going to show us any justice? . . . I don't know how I am going to bear it. I feel I shall break down. . . . The awful part is not being able to hear from one's friends. One has to wait months and never see an end to it, and not know how much they are able to do for you, or are actually achieving for you, and in fact being dead to everything. One feels one will never see one's kith and kin again.[14]

Chappelow's letter is both pathetic and revolting: pathetic because of his obvious hysteria and fright; revolting because it exposes a young man so naive or ill-informed about the nature and seriousness of his actions that he appears ready to collapse under the pressure of minor inconvenience. All talk of high ideals and great causes is drowned out by the whining of an apparently innocent boy who feels awful and pleads for aid from influential friends, while men were suffering and dying on the western front.

In a letter to Bertrand Russell, George Bernard Shaw, who had been asked to help Chappelow, bluntly put the case into perspective.

He seems to have just let things slide, like a child unable to conceive that the law had anything to do with him personally. . . . His letter is not that of a man made of martyr-stuff. . . . I do not blame any intelligent man for trying to dodge the atrocious boredom of soldiering . . . but Chappelow seems to have been too helpless to make any attempt to dodge it; he simply stood gaping in the path of the steamroller. I am sorry for him; but I can only advise him to serve.[15]

14. Eric B. Chappelow to C. P. Sanger (copy), 13 April 1916, BRA. There is also a copy of this letter in the Gilbert Murray Papers, 57, Bodleian Library, Oxford.

15. Shaw to Russell, 18 April 1916, reprinted in Bertrand Russell, *The Autobiography of Bertrand Russell*, 3 vols. (London, 1967–1969), 2:62–63. William Butler Yeats had asked Shaw to help Chappelow, and despite his earlier tone Shaw did write a letter to *The Nation*, 27 May 1916, using Chappelow's case as an example of the government's bumbling failures in dealing with C.O.s.

In fairness to most conscientious objectors, Chappelow's reaction to military methods was not typical. The NCF took great pride in the fact that only two of the first one hundred objectors and twenty-two of the first four hundred gave up the struggle and joined the army. (Indeed, Chappelow himself stiffened his resolve sufficiently to accept a six-month sentence with some show of determination.)[16] And though the fellowship—for obvious reasons—made no great protest over Chappelow's case, it did, as with the tribunals, attempt to expose every possible incident of administrative bungling or physical abuse. During the spring of 1916 *The Tribunal* was filled with tales of military malpractice toward C.O.s. Thus, once again, the NCF unquestionably played an important part in creating the myth of what one author has called the army's policy of "deliberate and calculated brutality."[17]

Taming Lions

In his semiofficial history of the British peace movement during the Great War, John Graham said that the over thirty pages of examples he provided of military abuse of C.O.s were "merely typical" of general army practice.[18] Graham's statement is simply not true. Beyond question, some objectors were badly, even grievously, mistreated by military officials, but far from representing typical cases, their experiences seem to have been decidedly untypical. Indeed, the army expended a remarkable amount of time and energy trying to prevent abuses of conscientious objectors. To some extent, these efforts to ensure equitable treatment for C.O.s were a reflection of the personality and attitudes of Brig. Gen. Wyndham Childs, director of personal services. Childs, a "desk soldier" trained in law, had risen rapidly (he was

16. *Trib.*, 4 May 1916, and COIB Report 7 (12 May 1916), BRA. Chappelow eventually took alternative service as a farm laborer and worked at the Morrells' Garsington estate, where he became something of a laughing-stock. See Robert Gathorne-Hardy, *Ottoline at Garsington* (London, 1974), pp. 125–26, 198.

17. David Boulton, *Objection Overruled* (London, 1967), p. 45.

18. John W. Graham, *Conscription and Conscience* (London, 1922), p. 146. Also see Boulton, *Objection Overruled*, pp. 146–64.

thirty-nine in 1916) as a protégé of Lt. Gen. Sir Nevil Macready, his longtime chief who was adjutant general. When it became obvious that the liberal provisions of the Military Service Act would make it necessary for the army to deal with relatively large numbers of conscientious objectors, Macready created a new branch of the Directorate of Personal Services—AG3 (CO)—and gave Childs responsibility for handling such cases.[19]

Accounts by C.O.s and their friends were filled with negative references to Childs's cold, calculating pursuit of conscientious objectors. Graham felt that Childs was "the official in whom the persecution was incarnated"; Allen referred to Childs as an "arch rascal" who troubled him even in his dreams; another sympathizer called Childs "clever, narrow, like an Inquisitor of old . . . determined at all cost to get the better of the C.O.s."[20] But every writer who criticized Childs also had to admit that the general was as relentless in his attempts to prevent illegal abuses as he was in his desire to destroy the C.O. movement.[21]

Although Childs worked hard to secure proper treatment for conscientious objectors, he did not have the slightest sympathy for them, especially if they were "political"—that is, nonreligious—claimants. Like Macready, Childs had attempted and failed to convince his civilian superiors that "politicals" should be subjected to the full rigors of military law. Since the NCF was the foremost advocate and organizer of politically motivated objectors, Childs and Macready shared Lord Kitchener's view that the NCF was "a growing and menacing body" whose members were committed to a subversive and even treasonous plot to undermine military morale and discipline.[22] In fact, at first Childs was resolved not to make "any investigation as to the treatment of mem-

19. Records of AG3 (CO) are deposited in WO 32/2051–55.

20. Graham, *Conscription and Conscience,* p. 64; Clifford Allen's diary (typescript), 6 and 19 February 1918, CAP; and Margaret Hobhouse to Gilbert Murray, 2 July 1917, Murray Papers, 57.

21. See citations noted earlier for Graham and Mrs. Hobhouse. Also see Allen ms., chap. 3, p. 4, CAP. Nearly twenty years after these events, Allen and Childs exchanged polite reminiscences of their wartime relationship; see letters of 2 and 13 April and 14, 16, and 17 September 1935, CAP.

22. Kitchener Papers, 74/WS/72, PRO. Also see Childs, *Episodes and Reflections,* p. 148.

bers of this organization." Eventually, however, Childs found that he could not ignore abuses against NCF members without abandoning his strong belief that all soldiers should be treated in the manner prescribed by military law. Since these men, despite their protestations to the contrary, were deemed to be soldiers, Childs dealt harshly with anyone proven to have inflicted cruel or illegal punishment on them.[23]

Childs was so determined to ensure correct procedures that he actually formed an unofficial liaison with the NCF in order to track down military offenders and to "take immediate action where cases of brutality were brought to my notice and substantiated."[24] Thus, at the same time that Childs was attempting to snuff out the NCF, he and Catherine E. Marshall were developing a remarkable working relationship. Indeed, some members feared that her constant negotiations and exchanges of information with Childs might compromise the pacifist cause.[25]

Withal, their cooperation did produce significant results, not the least of which was ensuring that military horseplay did not become senseless brutality, as apparently happened in the cases of George Beardsworth, George Benson, and Charles Dukes, three conscientious objectors in the Cheshire regiment. First reports of their mistreatment were published by the NCF in late August 1916,[26] and General Childs, acting on information provided by Marshall, immediately began his investigation. By mid-September statutory declarations made by the three men had been largely substantiated, and Childs issued a stern warning to all district commanders, directing them to deal with acts of insubordination

23. Childs to Macready, WO 32/2055/6923; Childs to Lt. Gen., the Rt. Hon. Sir J. G. Maxwell, 17 August 1917, WO 32/2054/1654; and Childs, *Episodes and Reflections*, p. 152.

24. Childs, *Episodes and Reflections*, p. 152.

25. See Chap. 10. Also see Russell's holograph note on a copy of a letter from Catherine E. Marshall, 2 October 1916, BRA: "Pacifists had moments when they were not solemn. Some of them thought Miss Marshall too fond of negotiations with the above-mentioned General [Childs], so, at a time when Clifford Allen was being court-martialled, they made a riddle: Why did Allen court Marshall? Because she wished to be with Child."

26. COIB Report 39 (29 August 1916). For other accounts, see COIB Report 44 (15 September 1916); *Conscientious Objectors Trial by Torture* (Manchester, n.d.); and Richard B. Graham to Gilbert Murray, 19 and 20 September 1916, Murray Papers, 57.

committed by conscientious objectors in accordance with military regulations and not by physical abuse. Officers disregarding the law, he said, were guilty of "grave dereliction of duty" and would be forthwith removed from their commands.[27] There were, of course, other cases of mistreatment and abuse—some of them quite serious[28]—both before and after the issuance of Childs's letter, but when such cases occurred they unquestionably did as much damage to army morale and to public relations as to the C.O.s involved.

Perhaps the most highly publicized and long-remembered incident was the case of thirty-four conscientious objectors who, despite repeated assurances by cabinet officials that no C.O. would be shot for refusal to obey military orders,[29] were taken to France and sentenced to death for willful defiance of authority in the face of the enemy. The ordeal of these men has been told several times and is generally depicted as a military plot to make a swift end to the C.O. movement by illegally invoking the death penalty.[30] A more recent version by John Rae discounts the idea of a military conspiracy and treats the episode as an attempt to frighten would-be conscientious objectors by imposing the death penalty and then commuting it to penal servitude.[31]

On balance, both the evidence and the argument would seem to favor Rae's version. There was, it seems, little possibility that these C.O.s could actually have been spirited away and shot, despite provisions of the Army Act that made such action technically possible. The NCF, FSC, and certain

27. This letter was read in Parliament by Ian Macpherson, undersecretary of state for war; 5 H.C., 96:873, 23 July 1917.

28. One particularly sensational case was that of Pvt. James Brightmore, a C.O. who in June 1917 was confined to a narrow pit by the camp commandant at Cleethorpes. After investigation, the commander, Brig. Gen. G. S. Elliot, was dismissed from his command. See *Manchester Guardian*, 30 June 1917; 5 H.C., 96:873-75, 23 July 1917; and Rae, *Conscience and Politics*, pp. 144-47.

29. For example, see statements of F. E. Smith, 5 H.C., 78:274, 19 January 1916; Lloyd George, 5 H.C., 81:308, 22 March 1916; and Walter Long, 5 H.C., 81:327, 22 March 1916.

30. See Graham, *Conscription and Conscience*, pp. 111-26; Boulton, *Objection Overruled*, pp. 164-76; and "Rebels in Uniform," *The Observer Weekend Review*, 7 August 1966.

31. Rae, *Conscience and Politics*, pp. 151-56.

prominent individuals like Prof. Gilbert Murray were immediately in possession of the facts of the case and collectively raised such a public and private din that army commanders would have had to risk open confrontation with their civilian chiefs in order to carry out a death sentence. Indeed, on 10 May 1916 Asquith himself, at Murray's behest, directed Gen. Sir Douglas Haig, commander in chief of the British Expeditionary Force, not to confirm any death penalty imposed on a conscientious objector.[32] This order, of course, only forbade the execution of the death sentence, not its imposition. In fact, while the NCF was bombarding the press with information about the case and antiwar M.P.s were harassing H. J. Tennant, the undersecretary of war, for details,[33] thirty-four conscientious objectors were sentenced to death in late June at Boulogne. But these sentences were immediately commuted to ten years' penal servitude, and within a short time all the "condemned" men were returned to Britain and placed in the hands of some civilian agency. It is doubtful whether the NCF fully deserved the credit it later took for saving the thirty-four men from execution,[34] but the fellowship certainly did contribute substantially to adverse publicity about the incident that embarrassed both the government and the army.[35]

Another case was that of C. H. Norman. Norman's attitude or perhaps his mere presence apparently so enraged the commandant of Wandsworth Detention Barracks that, within an hour of his arrival at the prison, Norman was placed in a straitjacket and kept there for over twenty hours. During that time, the commandant, Lt. Col. Reginald Brooke, had Norman forcibly fed as a matter of punishment, called him "a swine, a beast, and a coward," and spat at

---

32. See Gilbert Murray to John Graham (copy), 28 December 1920, and David Davies to Gilbert Murray, 22 May [1916], Murray Papers, 57. Also see David Davies to Catherine Marshall (copy), 12 and 17 May 1917, BRA.

33. For NCF efforts on behalf of the men, see NCF Political Committee, "Conscientious Objectors Sent to France, May 7th," FSC Files, FHL, and Hubert W. Peet, "Are C.O.s to Be Shot" (leaflet), BRA.

34. See A. Fenner Brockway, Catherine Marshall, and Edward Grubb to NCF members and friends, 25 September 1916, FSC Files, FHL.

35. For example, see *Manchester Guardian*, 11 and 30 May and 27 June 1916, and *Daily News*, 27 June 1916.

him three times. All this despite Norman's assertion that he had "not uttered a discourteous or uncivil word to any one."[36] When Philip Snowden, using information provided by the NCF, exposed Norman's treatment in the House of Commons, General Macready immediately dismissed Brooke from his command.[37] Brooke's dismissal seems to have brought about a swift improvement in the treatment of the C.O.s who were prisoners at Wandsworth,[38] but it did not deal with the fundamental problem of keeping conscientious objectors in military custody.

As long as objectors were placed in military detention barracks, they would be forced to endure the explicitly military rules and discipline by which such unlovely places were necessarily governed. Because most C.O.s declared their resolve to resist military orders even in prison, they were subjected to ever-increasing allotments of punishment from which there was no apparent escape. In addition, the kinds of punishments meted out to C.O. prisoners, while commonplace in the army, might be absolutely appalling to the objectors themselves and to a public so long sheltered from the realities of military life. General Childs himself warned an official of the Friends Service Committee that the so-called Quaker chaplains who were permitted to visit C.O.s in military custody should acquaint themselves with *The Rules for Military Detention Barracks and Military Prisons* "lest they be misled into believing that the infliction of statutory punishment required by the rule is a species of cruelty designed to break the spirit of conscientious objectors."[39]

Despite such warnings, the NCF widely and indignantly publicized the unpleasant results of this imbroglio as did Snowden and other C.O. sympathizers in the House of Commons. As a result, a considerable volume of criticism was directed at the army. For example, the well-known non-

36. Norman's testimony of 30 June 1916 before a court-martial at Chelsea Barracks is reprinted in *Trib.*, 6 July 1916. Also see Earl Russell's speech condemning Brooke's conduct; 5 H.L., 22:521, 525-27, 4 July 1916.
37. 5 H.C., 82:2279-80, 25 May 1916. Also see Philip Snowden, *Autobiography*, 2 vols. (London, 1934), 1:411-12, and *Labour Leader*, 22 June 1916. Brooke's defense of his conduct was printed in *Daily Mail*, 4 July 1916.
38. See Duckers, *Handed Over*, pp. 128-29.
39. Childs to Mrs. Bigland, 10 June 1916, FSC Files, FHL.

conformist pastor, Frederick B. Meyer, wrote that he would sooner suffer with the persecuted C.O.s, whose convictions he did not share, than be associated with the noncommissioned officers who mistreated them and whose illegal actions and "filthy language" were "a disgrace to the British Army."[40] The *Daily News* felt that the persecution of conscientious objectors had severely damaged the discipline of the military services: "If the interests of discipline are the concern of the Government, they are manifestly best served by getting these men out of the army as speedily as possible." Even *The Times* commented on the army's handling conscientious objectors "in a singularly crude and ineffective fashion, more worthy of school boys than of a great state."[41] Some American newspapers, having scarcely recovered from Britain's injudicious execution of Irish leaders after the Easter Rising, began to print angry stories about its revolting treatment of war resisters. On 18 May 1916 the *New York Evening Post* commented that war fever had reached such a pitch in England that the government was "now moving legally against a state of mind." It compared the persecution of conscientious objectors to that of William Penn and called the NCF "the true exponent of the liberty of conscience of which the British have always been so proud."[42]

Shaw had appeared as a character witness at Norman's court-martial, and his ever-caustic pen hammered away at official stupidity. In a letter to *The Nation*, Shaw castigated the government for passing a conscription law that created a new crime and then "instead of enacting a penalty for its breach, they hand the criminal over to the military so that he may be physically coerced into compliance with the law, an unprecedented proceeding of which a committee of bargees would, I hope, be intellectually ashamed."[43]

For their part, military officials sought some means of relieving the army from the responsibility and opprobrium of having to deal with hundreds of noncooperating military prisoners. On 15 May 1916 Kitchener circulated to the

---

40. Frederick B. Meyer, *The Majesty of Conscience* (London, [1917]), p. 16.

41. *Daily News*, 16 May 1916, and *The Times*, 6 July 1916.

42. Quoted in *Trib.*, 15 June 1916.

43. Reprinted in George Bernard Shaw, *What I Really Wrote about the War* (London, 1931), p. 233.

cabinet a memorandum written by Macready that recommended that the government take C.O.s who were resisting
military orders out of the army and place them in the custody of some civilian agency "under conditions as severe as
those . . . at the front." The NCF had long lobbied for some
arrangement whereby all genuine conscientious objectors
would be removed from the operation of military law, and
indeed, an NCF deputation to the House of Commons had
presented this argument just four days before the circulation of Macready's memorandum.[44] Despite some cabinet
members' reluctance to give any further concessions, the
army's desire to be well rid of its most troublesome recruits
and the government's hope of silencing its critics won the
day. On 22 May Kitchener, in what was to be his final speech
in the House of Lords, announced that henceforth the army
intended to hand court-martialed C.O.s back to the civil authorities for the execution of their sentences.[45] Three days
later Kitchener issued Army Order X: "A soldier, who is
sentenced to imprisonment for an offence against discipline,
which was represented by the soldier at his trial to have been
the result of a conscientious objection to military service, will
be committed to the nearest public civil prison."[46]

Thus the army had apparently rid itself of the more
bothersome conscientious objectors, while the C.O.s themselves were delivered from the rigors of military detention.
One set of problems was solved, but their solution only
paved the way for the creation of a new and more complicated series of difficulties.

The Struggle Goes On

On 4 July 1916 Marshall wrote to Sir John Barlow, an influential older Quaker and supporter of the NCF, complaining about the increased harassment, official and otherwise,
to which she personally and the NCF collectively were being
subjected. Unofficially, her chief tormentors at the time

44. See CAB 37/147/35; "Record of Deputation of 11 May 1916," CEMP
(microfilm); and "Proposed Improvements in the Method of Dealing with
Conscientious Objectors," undated, BRA.
45. 5 H.L., 22:13–14, 22 May 1916.
46. Army Order X (AO 179, 1916).

seem to have been "Mr. Glover of the Anti-German Union . . . [and] his hooligan New Zealanders," while the official side was represented by shadowy agents of Scotland Yard who snooped about probing for information they might better have discovered simply by asking! In any case, Marshall wanted to set the record straight. "It is no secret," she said, "that I am preparing to take over a considerable part of Mr. Clifford Allen's work when he is removed . . . under the Military Service Act or the Defence of the Realm Act."[47]

The state of Marshall's preparedness is well illustrated by a memorandum among her papers outlining the publicity campaign to be undertaken immediately after Allen's arrest.[48] The thoroughness of these plans and the determination reflected in her letter to Barlow are characteristic of Marshall's activities in the NCF. Once she had decided—after long and anguished consideration and despite the criticism of revered former colleagues like Maude Royden[49]—that her work for the NCF must supersede all other causes, Marshall contributed more to the fellowship's success and survival than any other individual. She was truly a human dynamo who threw herself into the work with absolutely reckless abandon. While this devotion may be partly explained by her deep personal feelings for Allen, such concentration was typical for Marshall. Months before she became involved with Allen or the NCF, Marshall's worried father had told her: "If you only had the wisdom to take care of yourself, you would be of far more value to the causes to which you dedicate yourself."[50]

Marshall did not heed her father's advice, but she did provide a tonic for the NCF. From the summer of 1916 until the end of 1917, the fellowship's policies and activities were largely shaped and directed by her hands. Her devotion to this work reflected her conviction that the NCF stood "for something far wider than mere personal refusal to bear arms" and therefore ought to operate on a scale equal to the

47. Catherine E. Marshall to Sir John [Barlow] (copy), 4 July 1916, BRA.
48. Undated memorandum, CEMP (microfilm).
49. See Maude Royden to C. E. Marshall, 10 July 1916, CEMP (microfilm). Also see Marshall to Bertrand Russell, 7 and 15 July 1916, BRA.
50. Mr. Marshall to Catherine Marshall, 11 April 1915, CEMP (microfilm). Also see Chap. 11.

significance of its message. "I think," she told Helena Swanwick of the Women's International League, "that I have been able to help them in some degree to develop and make good the positive and constructive ideals involved in their attitude about war."[51]

During the spring and early summer of 1916, while the bulk of the NCF's leaders of military age were being taken by the authorities, there was deep concern about the fellowship's ability to carry on. But when most of the original national committee was jailed in late July and Allen was arrested in early August, a new committee composed mainly of associate members took up their duties. With Marshall as honorary secretary showing the way, they maintained and even broadened the scope of the fellowship's activities. When Allen "emerged from silence" after his first prison sentence, he wrote that the work of the new committee "eclipses anything we used to take in hand in the good old days." It gave him great comfort, he said, to know that the administration of the NCF was "on a larger and more perfect scale than ever."[52]

One important reason for this seemingly effortless transition was the quality of the men and women who took over the positions of leadership. In addition to Russell who served in a variety of ways before he became acting chairman in 1917,[53] Marshall could call on the services of Dr. Alfred Salter, a socialist physician who had foresaken a promising career in bacteriology to minister to the physical and spiritual needs of the poor in Bermondsey. During his three years of unstinting service to the fellowship, including a term as interim chairman, Salter was a sometimes controversial and always formidable figure of whom an NCF colleague once said: "not a soul could look at his powerful jaw and feel unafraid."[54]

Serving at one time or another as chief administrative as-

51. C. Marshall to H. M. Swanwick, 7 September 1916, CEMP (microfilm).

52. Allen to Catherine Marshall, 28 November 1916, CAP.

53. For a complete discussion of Russell's activities in 1916 and 1917, see J. Vellacott Newberry, "Bertrand Russell and the Pacifists in the First World War" (Ph.D. diss., McMaster University, 1975). Also see Ronald W. Clark, *The Life of Bertrand Russell* (New York, 1976), pp. 273–357 passim.

54. A[ylmer] R[ose] to Allen, 20 January 1918, CAP.

sistant to both Russell and Salter was Ernest E. Hunter, a product of the Bethnal Green slums, who became an important figure in the postwar Independent Labour Party (ILP) and lobby correspondent to the *Daily Herald*. Hunter was a curiosity not only because of his bohemian habits but also because he was literally always a man on the run. Alone among those who guided the NCF after 1916, Hunter was of military age. Though he was sought by the authorities for two years, he continued to coordinate the activities of various NCF departments until he was finally caught two weeks before the war ended. Even then he escaped imprisonment. Mary Agnes Hamilton—under whose bed Hunter sometimes hid NCF documents—remembers him as "short, stout, cheery, rather vulgar, very astute . . . he had the resilience of a rubber ball; was constantly in difficulties but always got out of them." To Hunter, a born conspirator, the rules of the game were less important than the fun he got from playing.[55]

A steadier, if less dramatic, influence during this period was Edward Grubb. Working quietly behind the scenes, Grubb kept the organization solvent through all its adversity. The glamor surrounding men like Allen would occasionally bring in sizable donations, but, for the lifeblood of its material existence, the NCF depended on the contributions of the wealthy Quakers whom Grubb persistently solicited. Doubtless one important reason why benefactors generally maintained their pledges was Grubb's ability to prove that their generosity would bear abundant fruit. In a letter of June 1918 Grubb pointed out that, for an expenditure of about seventy-five pounds per week, the various departments of the NCF were providing manifold services not only for imprisoned C.O.s but for the peace movement in general. He asked friends of the group to look at the record and then to decide if they could in conscience allow the NCF to fail.[56] One way or another, he usually got the money.

55. Mary Agnes Hamilton, *Remembering My Good Friends* (London, 1944), pp. 165–66. Also see Robert E. Dowse, *Left in the Centre: The Independent Labour Party, 1893–1940* (London, 1966), pp. 82, 85n, and *Trib.*, 31 October and 7 November 1918 and 9 January 1920.

56. See Edward Grubb, "War Resistance," in *We Did Not Fight*, ed. Julian Bell (London, 1935), and Grubb to Friends of the NCF (printed letter), June 1918, NCF File, SCPC.

The value of these people's contributions to the NCF be-
comes all the more significant when one realizes that the
administration of local branches, which had always been
somewhat irregular and haphazard, declined markedly in
the spring and summer of 1916. By September Marshall was
complaining that "as a rule only 50 percent of the forms sent
out asking for information are returned." Decent results
could not be expected, she said, until the other 50 percent
began to shoulder some responsibility.[57] The head office
included carefully worded instructions with nearly every
form it dispatched and continued to offer the services of
representatives from headquarters who could give inspiration and instructions to local members, but invariably only a
small percentage of members were really active and helpful.[58]

In order to compensate for the general lack of local initiative, the national committee decided to completely reor-
ganize the central office staff to redistribute the work that
had hitherto fallen almost exclusively on the political committee and to allow the national office to maintain closer
supervision of local activities. The political committee was
replaced by seven new departments, each of which handled
some specific phase of the fellowship's national operations.
Marshall retained control of the record department and its
offshoot, the Conscientious Objectors Information Bureau
(COIB) as well as the visitors (later investigation) department. Her place as chief correspondent with division and
branch officials was filled by J. A. Harrop who headed the
organization and propaganda department. As overseer of
the parliamentary department, Charles G. Ammon, a future
Labour M.P., became the NCF's chief lobbyist at Westminster, while B. J. Boothroyd served as director of the legal
department and as editor of *The Tribunal.* Assisting Boothroyd were two former suffragists, Violet Tillard, head of the
publication or literature department, and Lydia Smith, chief
of the publicity (press) department. Ada Salter, who (with
Tillard) had directed the NCF maintenance program from

57. NCF, Hon. Sec. of Political Comm. to NCF Branch Secs., 29 June
1916, BRA, and NCF, Hon. Sec. Political Comm. to NCF Branch Secs.,
5 September 1916, FSC Correspondence, 1916, FSC Files, FHL.
58. See Aylmer Rose (NCF general secretary) to Branch Secs., 21 July
1916, BRA, and NCF letter on branch activities, 29 July 1916, FSC Files,
FHL. See App. A for a list of branches and secretaries.

the beginning, retained control of that department from a separate office in Lincoln's Inn Fields.[59] Among these multifarious operations, Marshall's work with the record and visitors departments needs to be carefully examined because of its importance to the organization and also because of the controversy that it eventually created.

The record department's major responsibility was the compilation of a complete and accurate report on each C.O.'s progress through the various courts and prisons. Information about imprisoned objectors was largely gathered through a network of "visitors" that had been established soon after the first C.O.s were arrested. According to this arrangement, each army camp, barrack, and military prison (and later civil prison) had an assigned visitor or group of visitors. The job of these volunteers was to advise and cheer C.O.s in places of detention, to make careful records of all men passing to or from these places, and to glean every possible bit of information about the prisoner's welfare, about the conditions of imprisonment, and about possible irregularities committed by the authorities.[60] A special instruction book for visitors, published by the Joint Advisory Council (JAC) of the NCF, FOR, and FSC, noted that "every Conscientious Objector should be in the care of some visitor and that it should be impossible for him to be removed from one place to another without the visitor having early knowledge of it."[61] One of the methods of obtaining this early knowledge was through a series of pickets set up outside Wormwood Scrubs and most other major prisons.[62] The

59. The new organizational scheme is outlined in a letter from Marshall to Branch Secretaries, 21 September 1916; department heads are listed in a directive from J. A. Harrop to Branch Secretaries, 1 November 1916, FSC Files, FHL. The NCF's internal organization is discussed by Graham, *Conscription and Conscience*, pp. 183–87, and by Boulton, *Objection Overruled*, pp. 177–79, but both provide an incomplete and somewhat inaccurate picture.

60. See *NCF Souvenir*, p. 25; *The No-Conscription Fellowship: A Record of Its Activities* (London, [1916]), pp. 5–6; and Croydon Minutes, 15 May 1916, SCPC.

61. "The Visitation of Conscientious Objectors in Detention or Prison," mimeographed booklet, CAP.

62. See *NCF Souvenir*, p. 25, and *Trib.*, 16 August 1917. Also see Hannah M. Clark to Elizabeth Ellis, n.d. [June 1917], FSC Correspondence, 1917, FSC Files, FHL, which notes that "some of them [NCF pickets] are always outside W.[ormwood] Scrubs so I suppose they will be at Wandsworth, too."

idea, then, was that visitors, through observation and investigation, should provide material that would allow the NCF to compile a detailed and accurate record on each conscientious objector in military or civilian custody.[63]

To enhance this operation and to protect NCF records from possible seizure by the authorities, the JAC also created the COIB, nominally a separate office but actually under Marshall's control. The COIB used the information gathered by the NCF to publish a series of "Reports on Conscientious Objectors" that attempted to provide up-to-date statistics on all C.O.s in custody as well as bits of information on individual prisoners.[64]

Of course, the intelligence collected by the NCF could have other uses, which were the cause of a considerable controversy among pacifist allies. By the autumn of 1916 Marshall had thoroughly integrated the work of the record office and the COIB with the operation of the visitors or investigation department. As a result, the collection of records and statistics was being carried on hand in glove with the investigation and exposure of official incompetence and brutality. To Marshall, this seemed a perfectly reasonable combination of activities, just as it seemed right to cooperate with officials like General Childs to prevent illegal acts being perpetrated against conscientious objectors. Others, however, felt that, in her zeal, Marshall was going beyond the bounds that should be maintained by a legitimate peace movement.[65]

In addition to its other projects, the NCF made every attempt to keep up the spirits of imprisoned C.O.s, even to the point of organizing special choirs to sing inspirational songs outside the walls of Wormwood Scrubs and other prisons.[66]

63. Despite myths, mainly perpetuated by pacifist and socialist writers about the accuracy of NCF records (see Graham, *Conscription and Conscience*, pp. 182–87, 204n, and Boulton, *Objection Overruled*, pp. 177–78), later investigation would reveal that the NCF record office either lost track of or was never informed about a considerable percentage of conscientious objectors; see Chap. 10 and Chap. 10, n. 44.

64. See App. B for a summary of COIB Reports on Conscientious Objectors, July 1916–June 1917. So far as I know there is no complete file of these reports though there are incomplete collections in CAP, SCPC, and FSC Files, FHL.

65. See Chap. 10.

66. See Allen's note of thanks to those who sang outside Wormwood Scrubs, Christmas, 1916, *Trib.*, 4 January 1917. Also see *Trib.*, 30 November

Probably the most important morale builder, however, was the NCF maintenance committee's support for the families of C.O. prisoners. Although the army insisted on recognizing conscientious objectors as soldiers, it made no allowance for their families after they were arrested. If dependents became destitute, they had only the poor-law guardians to turn to for relief. Toward the end of 1915 the NCF had created the machinery for instituting maintenance and relief work among dependents of C.O.s, and by February of 1916, a national maintenance subcommittee headed by Tillard and Ada Salter was formed to direct and coordinate the branches' relief work. Branches, however, were slow to establish their own maintenance committees, and at first the aid offered to C.O.s' families was uneven at best.[67]

Despite the efforts of the maintenance subcommittee to improve poor administration and sagging revenues,[68] by midsummer of 1916 the situation for many dependents had become so perilous that some new approach was obviously needed. In this emergency, a group of prominent London socialists and Friends, headed by Ramsay MacDonald, formed a committee that raised sufficient money from C.O. sympathizers to establish a central maintenance fund that could supplement the maintenance work of the NCF and FSC. When it established this fund, the MacDonald committee took pains to note that the purpose of its effort was "not to encourage anyone who would not otherwise object to Military Service, but to prevent the sufferings of the supporters of families being shared by their dependents."[69] In response to this private initiative, the NCF national committee reorganized the fellowship's maintenance machinery by directing local and divisional officers to establish joint mainte-

---

1916 and 17 and 24 May 1917, and *Manchester C.O.'s Journal*, January 1918, p. 3, NCF File, SCPC.

67. See NCF circular letter, 9 December 1925, CAP; *NCF Souvenir*, p. 79; and *NCF Summary*, pp. 13–14. Also see *Trib.*, 8 March 1916, and Croydon Minutes, 11 March 1916, SCPC.

68. For example, V. Tillard to NCF members, 9 June 1916, and Ada Salter, Sec. of Maintenance Sub-Committee, to Maintenance Secretaries, 21 July 1916, BRA.

69. Quoted in *Trib.*, 8 March 1917, and in *NCF Summary*, p. 14. The major source of funds for the Central Fund was probably the Central Financial Committee of the Meeting for Sufferings; see printed notices from Central Financial Committee, Hubert W. Peet Papers, FSC Files, FHL.

nance committees in conjunction with the FSC, ILP, FOR, and other pacifist groups in each divisional and local branch area. They emphasized that the central fund was to be used only when local needs could not be met from local funds and that, in any case, the fund was to be used only for dependents and not for conscientious objectors themselves. As a general rule, the rates paid to dependents of C.O.s were based on those paid to dependents of soldiers on active service.[70] Whether or not (as opponents charged) this maintenance system created any new conscientious objectors, it certainly did provide a modicum of mental peace for those who were resolved not to give in.[71]

Thus, the NCF was generally able to fulfill its oft-repeated promise to never abandon even the least of those who were fighting to uphold the cause. But each person reacts to adversity in his own way, and for all of their ability and dedication, some NCF leaders made the dual error of predicting how all conscientious objectors would respond to their way of pain and then of demanding that this prophecy be fulfilled. This illusion eventually caused the first chink in the moral armor of the British peace movement and presented the NCF with a dangerous internal crisis.

70. See four-page mimeographed report of Maintenance Committee, 14 September 1916, FSC Files, FHL. Also see J. H. Hudson and Ada Salter to Maintenance Committee, 14 September 1916, FSC Files, FHL.

71. See Sanders, "My Experiences," p. 4, CAP. A cabinet memorandum on "Pacifist Propaganda" published in 1917 noted that the NCF was no longer able to provide support for dependents of C.O.s "owing to lack of funds"; CAB 24/4, G 173 (secret).

8

Divided Counsel: Absolutists and Alternativists

The Alternative-Service Question

Army Order X removed the bulk of conscientious objectors from military detention, but the government still had to decide what to do with them. Few officials relished the idea of filling up civil prisons with a special kind of political prisoner, and indeed, Herbert Samuel, the home secretary, had earlier spoken strongly against such a course.

> Is it really contemplated that now, when for the first time you are making military service compulsory in this country, it should be accompanied by the arrest and imprisonment of a certain number of men who unquestionably, by common consent, are men of the highest character, and, in other matters good citizens? I am sure Hon. Members would not wish to ... have this body of men locked up in the gaols of this country![1]

On the other hand, almost no one was willing to accept the idea of simply releasing conscientious objectors from the army, thereby terminating not only their military careers but also any further inconvenience suffered because of the war. Such a procedure would obviously be a clarion call to shirkers more than willing to exchange a brief period of unpleasantness for the horrors of the western front.

The solution adopted by the cabinet, in keeping with General Macready's recommendations of 15 May,[2] was to instruct the central tribunal to review the case of each C.O. in custody and to ascertain whether he was sincere in his views. Those who were adjudged "genuine" by the central tribunal and who indicated their willingness to perform civilian alternative service would be released from custody and permitted to undertake nonmilitary work of national impor-

---

1. 5 H.C., 79:449, 19 January 1916.
2. CAB 37/147/35.

tance. A special committee appointed by the home secretary and chaired by William Brace, Labour M.P. and under-secretary at the Home Office, was to establish the type and conditions of work and to generally supervise the men. Objectors who accepted this Home Office scheme, as it was called, were released from military discipline, though they were transferred to Section W of the army reserve as "soldiers whose service is deemed . . . more valuable to the country in civil than in military employment."[3]

In presenting this proposal to the House of Commons, the prime minister stated that all honest objectors "ought to be and will be able to avail themselves of the exemption provided by Parliament."[4] The scheme was indeed similar to proposals drawn up by the National Council against Conscription (NCAC). But there was one glaring and ominous difference: the NCAC maintained that objectors who could not accept alternative service should not, in any case, be put back under military control.[5] Asquith, however, ended his address by noting that if there were any C.O.s who would use the conscience clauses "as a pretext and a cloak to cover their indifference to the national call and . . . [were] therefore guilty of the double offence of cowardice and hypocrisy, [they] should be treated . . . with the utmost rigour."

This is precisely what Childs and other hard-liners at the War Office had in mind.[6] After the introduction of the Home Office scheme, the decision was made to test the mettle of those who were found insincere by the central tribunal or who refused to cooperate with its proceedings. Henceforth, such "absolutists" would be subject to the imposition of repeated sentences at hard labor for what was literally, though not technically, the same offense.[7]

3. Quoted from Army Order 203/1916. The other original members of the Home Office committee on alternative service were Sir Thomas Elliott, K.C.B., and Sir Matthew Nathan, G.C.M.G.; see 5 H.C., 83:1915, 29 June 1916.

4. 5 H.C., 83:1915, 29 June 1916.

5. "Proposals for Dealing with the Problem of Conscientious Objectors," 31 May 1916, BRA.

6. Childs's "Notes for the Prime Minister on the History of Army Order X," cited by John Rae, *Conscience and Politics: The British Government and the Conscientious Objector to Military Service, 1916-1919* (London, 1970), p. 160.

7. For the announcement and defense of this policy, see Asquith's state-

The announcement of the government's intention to classify conscientious objectors according to their willingness to cooperate with the state's designs caused such a serious rift in the NCF's ranks that many pacifists saw the Home Office scheme as a government plot to divide the antiwar forces. In fact, the difficulties that arose over alternative service were far more a reflection of differences within the pacifist movement than of government chicanery. Considering that the NCF's members had widely divergent reasons for becoming C.O.s, it is not surprising that the fellowship was racked by disagreements about how far to carry its protest. The NCF might criticize the government's inability to define conscientious objection, but the fellowship had little more success in determining the exact principles that guided its dissent or the limits to which they should be taken. Beyond opposition to the war and conscription, any attempt to create dogma was almost certain to alienate some portion of the membership and thus to threaten the organization's unity. Nowhere is this more clear than in the national leadership's efforts to impose a single concept of acceptable service on all NCF members.

The fellowship's opposition to conscription and to the war had evolved from its original declaration of the sanctity of human life to an assertion of opposition to all forms of alternative service.[8] But while the NCF had declared its collective resolve to resist the war absolutely, it also felt constrained to add that individual members should be "left entirely free to follow what course they considered right." In a letter to members issued shortly after the convention of April 1916, the NCF national committee added that no one should "from a mere sense of loyalty to the Fellowship ... decline service he can conscientiously accept." Likewise, Clifford Allen noted that it would be a "grave error" to classify C.O.s "according to whether they are or are not prepared to accept alternative service." One did not serve the principle of freedom of conscience, he said, by

---

ments in 5 H.C., 84:644, 17 July 1916, and 1673-74, 26 July 1916, and Forster's reply to Snowden, 5 H.C., 85:1832-33, 16 August 1916. Also see Allen ms., chap. 3, p. 12, CAP.

8. See Chap. 6.

judging others in the terms of one's own commitment or by expecting a uniform sense of duty from all.[9]

While NCF leaders felt the need to recognize freedom of conscience within the organization, most of them assumed that uncompromising opposition would be the norm for the fellowship. They were no doubt encouraged in this belief by the failure of the Non-Combatant Corps and other early forms of alternative service to attract many NCF members.[10] The Home Office scheme, however, was a horse of a different color. It seemed designed to strike at the heart of the NCF's declared intention to render the machinery of conscription inoperable. Indeed, the new scheme was obviously intended to lubricate that machinery by offering an apparently honorable alternative to military service. Furthermore, the scheme was offered after the government had shown its determination to punish and imprison those who refused to cooperate with the Military Service Act. The alternative to imprisonment at hard labor contained in the Home Office scheme was unquestionably a decisive factor for some conscientious objectors who had been in prison or who were presented with the possibility of being put there.[11]

Faced with these developments, many of the NCF's national leaders felt obliged to make the question of alternative service the basis for the success or failure of the fellowship's resistance. In so doing, they seemed to be demanding from conscientious objectors the sort of conformity that they felt the state had no right to impose. As Allen later said: "Crude ideas grew up as to our being a kind of Church, in which all who took different views from the articles of our established faith were heretics." Such an attitude, he added, resulted in a "stultifying rigidity" that created confusion, consternation, and, eventually, deep-seated bitterness.[12]

Indications of impending difficulties could be seen im-

---

9. *The No-Conscription Fellowship: A Summary of Its Activities* (London, n.d.), p. 7; NCF circular letter, 1 May 1916, CAP; and *Trib.*, 11 and 25 May 1916.

10. See Clifford Allen, "Alternative Service," *Ploughshare* 1 (May 1916): 101–4, and "The Solution," *Trib.*, 22 June 1916. Also see W. E. Wilson, "The Conscientious Objector and Non-Combatant Duty," CAP.

11. See Allen's comments on this; Allen ms., chap. 3, p. 10, CAP.

12. Ibid., chap. 1, pp. 11–12; chap. 2, pp. 31–32; and chap. 4, p. 2.

mediately in the contrasting reactions to the Home Office scheme by various would-be allies in the anticonscription camp. While most parliamentary supporters of the C.O. movement, including Philip Snowden, were inclined to look on the Home Office scheme as "the defeat of both the military machine and the Military Service Act,"[13] the reaction of the Joint Advisory Council (JAC) of war resisters was almost completely negative. In a letter to Asquith, the JAC characterized the scheme as a veiled and cynical continuation of the same persecution that it claimed to be ending.[14] To reemphasize the defiant tone of this letter, Allen wrote in *The Tribunal* that the victory or defeat of militarism in England would depend on those C.O.s who refused to "enter into a bargain with the Military Service Act" by accepting alternative service.[15]

These comments were only the preliminaries. The first indication of a serious split on the alternative-service question occurred in late July when *The Tribunal* published messages from T. E. Harvey, the Quaker M.P., and Gilbert Murray, pleading with conscientious objectors to accept alternative service. The crux of Murray's argument was that the NCF had won its point in making the government revise its methods. Therefore, he felt, they ought not to "behave in a manner which savours less of brotherly love than of insatiable pugnacity." Harvey added that the Home Office scheme was not a subtle plot to divide C.O.s since they were "neither numerous enough nor important enough, in the eyes of statesmen, to be treated by such . . . methods." Smarting, perhaps, from the insinuation that the NCF was not important enough to be the target of government plots, the national committee answered this appeal with a searing editorial in *The Tribunal* that implied that the two distinguished friends of the NCF had been duped. Because alter-

13. Philip Snowden to C. H. Norman, 12 September 1916, FSC Files, FHL.
14. "The Prime Minister and Conscientious Objector," 4 July 1916, CAP; also printed in full *Trib.*, 6 July 1916, and signed by Allen and Brockway for the NCF, Robert O. Mennell and Hubert W. Peet for the FSC, and Henry T. Hodgkin and Richard Roberts for the FOR. Also see the remarks of Joseph King, 5 H.C., 83:1015, 29 June 1916.
15. *Trib.*, 6 July 1916.

native service was not harmless civil work but a compulsory substitute for military service or for prison, its acceptance contradicted the fellowship's fundamental principles.[16]

The *Tribunal* article simply reinforced an "Open Letter to Some Would-Be Friends of the Conscientious Objector" that had already been issued, unsigned, by the NCF central office. This document—which pictured absolutist C.O.s as, among other things, the sole guardians of liberty of conscience and of the ethical principles of the Sermon on the Mount—had about it a distinctly unpleasant aura of self-righteousness. For example:

> We find among too many of our would-be friends a tendency to substitute themselves as the Tribunal in place of those set up by the law. We would respectfully suggest that, in drawing up schemes which they believe capable of meeting the difficulty, they should endeavour to ascertain the views and feelings of . . . the conscientious objectors themselves—the more so as they are often falsely supposed to be speaking for us. . . . No scheme is satisfactory which does not free *all* conscientious objectors from persecution. . . . We appeal to you once more to recognize the value of the ethical conviction which has made the conscientious objectors stand firm, and to restore that liberty of conscience for which, in other days, many of your own ancestors suffered . . . persecution.[17]

Another letter from the political committee instructed all NCF branch secretaries to

> *impress upon friends who go upon deputations not to offer suggestions either of a temporary or final character without the fullest consultation with Branch officials. Proposals for the temporary mitigation of persecution have often added new complexities to the problem resulting only in the delay of a final solution, thus adding to the sum total of suffering.*[18]

16. The remarks by Harvey and Murray and the NCF reply are in *Trib.*, 27 July 1916. Harvey later told Murray that he believed the letter had had "its effects on a good many C.O.s, though not of course the strong Absolutists"; Harvey to Murray, 29 October 1916, Gilbert Murray Papers, 57, Bodleian Library, Oxford.

17. "An Open Letter to Some Would-Be Friends of the Conscientious Objector" (copy), 28 June 1916, BRA.

18. NCF, Hon. Sec. to Political Committee [C. Marshall] to Branch Secs., 10 July 1916, BRA.

At about the same time that the quarrel over alternative service was becoming public, the central tribunal began to interview conscientious objectors at Wormwood Scrubs prison in London. At once it became evident that the tribunal was going to accommodate the War Office—and the Home Office scheme—by accepting the vast majority of C.O.s who appeared before it as genuine.[19] Most of these objectors readily agreed to abide by the conditions (as yet unspecified) laid down by the Home Office's Brace committee in exchange for their release from imprisonment. Clearly, the uncompromising absolutism that the NCF national committee had hoped for was being undermined. No doubt, some C.O.s who agreed to do civilian work under civilian control were so desperate to get out of prison that they put their original convictions aside, but probably the great majority of over four thousand who eventually accepted the Home Office scheme were sincere.[20] Still, from the beginning, all "Home Office men" had to face a double-edged charge of shirking—from their country in the eyes of the public and from their principles in the eyes of their pacifist comrades.[21]

Even the most humane figures among the absolutists were at times moved to rebuke alternativists for their lack of perseverance. T. Corder Catchpool believed that men who chose the Home Office scheme were left with "a haunting sense of having chosen a spiritually 'second best.' . . . I am not sure that Christ's agony in Gethsemane was not essentially a struggle to refuse 'alternative service' to Calvary." Another absolutist tells of the pathos of seeing man after man give up the fight and agree to the scheme. They gave

19. During 1916 the central tribunal approved 89.1 percent of the C.O.s interviewed as genuine. Report of the Central Tribunal, February 1919, p. 24, cited by Rae, *Conscience and Politics,* app. G.

20. Allen ms., chap. 3, p. 13, CAP. In all, 4,522 men were released to work under the Brace committee. Of these, 4,126 were actually engaged in some type of employment under the Home Office scheme; *Statistics of the Military Effort of the British Empire during the Great War, 1914–1920* (London, 1922), p. 673.

21. For example, see John W. Graham, *Conscription and Conscience* (London, 1922), p. 234. Edward Williamson Mason, *Made Free in Prison* (London, [1918]), p. 133, noted that prison officials "scorned" the men who took alternative service.

themselves away, he said, by the look in their eyes—"that was the sign of spiritual defeat, the curse of the furtive eye."[22]

Absolutists were upset because they saw their intractable position as the only practical method of achieving victory. If the government found itself faced with a continuing stream of obstinate conscientious objectors, they reasoned, the sheer weight of numbers might compel it to grant them absolute exemption, or at least, to release them from prison after the completion of their sentences. Such an occurrence would not only free C.O.s for peace work but would also illustrate the state's inability to deal effectively with war resisters. Widespread acceptance of the Home Office scheme reduced the number of imprisoned objectors to more manageable proportions, and some of those remaining in prison felt that they had been sold out. One absolutist told his brother: "I am sorry to say it but our friends are really our enemies . . . if C.O.s had refused the Scheme the Government would have given in weeks ago. They would not have had enough prisons to put us in."[23]

This same tone persisted in a series of articles by Fenner Brockway who had become acting chairman after Allen's arrest in early August 1916. While giving somewhat grudging promises to aid alternativists, Brockway noted that the national committee "wholeheartedly endorsed the Absolutist attitude" and added that the conditions of alternative service "must make acceptance difficult for any self-respecting person who understands them."[24] The struggle reached a crucial stage in late August when C. H. Norman, formerly considered the ultraextremist, wrote to inform the national committee that he had accepted alternative service. He had done so, he said, because he considered the Home Office scheme not as an alternative to military service but as an

22. T. Corder Catchpool, *On Two Fronts* (London, 1918), pp. 154–55, and Mason, *Made Free in Prison*, p. 137. Compare with Mason's own struggle over alternative service; *Made Free in Prison*, pp. 111–13. Also see Allen's comments in *Trib.*, 31 August 1916; Edith J. Wilson, "Alternative Service," *Ploughshare* 1 (August 1916): 203–5; and COIB Report 47 (29 September 1916), p. 176, which commented on the "agony" of the men who had taken the Home Office scheme.

23. Sydney Turner to Guy Turner, undated, Sydney R. Turner Papers, SCPC.

24. *Trib.*, 17 and 31 August 1916.

alternative to prison work and as such a continuation of his punishment. If he had refused the scheme, he should also logically have refused to do prison work.[25] After his release from prison, Norman appeared personally before the NCF national committee to explain his position, but his arguments carried little weight. Indeed, the committee showed its disagreement with—if not scorn for—him by adopting a resolution "reiterating its opposition to Alternative Service to military service." Brockway underlined this attitude by calling the scheme "a form of slavery" that denied "that sense of the worth of human personality which is the foundation of all we are doing."[26] Stung by the intimation that he had compromised his principles, Norman wrote a snarling rejoinder reminding certain members of the national committee that the dilemma over alternative service had arisen from their compromise in deciding to appear before the tribunals. He himself had not been so accommodating and it was gross dishonesty to brand him a backslider.[27] In a personal letter to Brockway, Norman added that the deteriorating effects of prison were in themselves good reason for removing active pacifists from such an environment. There was, he said

> not the least doubt, in my mind, that the effects of prison and detention have been very grave on many... [C.O.s] in an insensibly corrupting and unbalancing way.... The issue must be faced, as to whether the present refusal to face facts is not doing the peace movement the ill-service of shattering the morale of a good many splendid men of character whose sense of idealism has become clouded and embittered by prison and detention.[28]

Norman's fellow alternativists likewise accused the national committee of abandoning them simply because its concept of duty was different than theirs—hardly a convinc-

25. Norman's letter is printed in *Trib.,* 24 August 1916. Although Norman's argument with respect to prison work was practically howled down at the time, apparently Allen later saw considerable logic in it, although he came to a somewhat different conclusion; see Chap. 11.
26. See report on the national committee's resolution and Brockway's article in *Trib.,* 7 September 1916.
27. *Trib.,* 28 September 1916.
28. Extract of letter from C. H. Norman to A. Fenner Brockway, 16 October 1916, FSC Files, FHL.

ing advertisement for liberty of conscience. One group noted that the extension of the fellowship's original principles embodied in the committee's stand had never been considered by the national conventions. Another man wrote that Home Office C.O.s were accepting the reality of the situation without haggling over technicalities. If the Home Office scheme was slavery, he said, was not prison even more so? A former secretary of the London branch expressed the view that many C.O.s had undertaken alternative service because they saw the need of doing useful work for the community: "We felt . . . that the war was a catastrophe in which we were all involved and for which none of us could claim to be entirely free from blame."[29]

For a time, the absolutist–alternativist controversy, with all its attendant bitterness, threatened to undermine the NCF completely. Fortunately for the fellowship, at this critical juncture Marshall and Russell took the lead in counseling moderation and reconciliation. While both of them strongly favored the absolutist position—Russell told Ottoline Morrell he got a sense of failure because so many C.O.s chose alternative service[30]—both also realized that the breach had to be sealed if the fellowship were to survive as an effective organization. They believed that the negative implications of Brockway's articles and the national committee's resolution would not only further divide the NCF but would also allow the government to administer the Home Office scheme free from the fellowship's watchful criticism.

While Allen awaited court-martial at Worley Barracks, Marshall pressed him to make whatever conciliatory gestures he could toward the alternative-service faction. Allen, who had gradually moderated his own hard line against alternative service,[31] was greatly upset by the crisis that he had, in part, helped to create. After he had been convicted

29. Statement by alternative-service men at Keddington, *Trib.*, 7 September 1916; F. E. Edwards to *Trib.*, 19 October 1916; and statement by Maurice Webb, *Trib.*, 4 January 1917. Also see *NCF Souvenir*, p. 69.

30. Russell to O. Morrell, September 1916, reprinted in Bertrand Russell, *The Autobiography of Bertrand Russell*, 3 vols. (London, 1967–1969), 2:74.

31. Compare Allen's *Trib.* article of 6 July 1916 with his "farewell" message of 3 August 1916 and his letter to H. Peet, undated [August 1916], CAP, in which he noted that alternative-service men would need "very sympathetic understanding."

and sent to Wormwood Scrubs, the former chairman slipped a series of concilatory messages out of the prison.

> Let Miss Marshall know that I want National Service men treated with utmost care. . . . Give them more attention than us men who have refused! I want us all to look back upon this time . . . with nothing but joy and gladness. . . . Let us do nothing, inside or outside prison, that may divide us from one another, or that we shall have any reason to look back upon with regret.[32]

Allen's words seemed to have the desired effect. Brockway's articles assumed a gentler tone[33] and the national committee passed a resolution noting that it had "not intended to express or imply censure on those members . . . who do not share the Committee's view regarding the non-acceptance of alternative service or work under the Home Office scheme, recognising that this matter is a question for each member's individual conscience as to what is right for him and best for the community."[34]

Russell contributed a front-page article to *The Tribunal* that reminded conscientious objectors that, ultimately, they stood for something outside of and infinitely greater than the organization they had created: for "the sanctity of human life and the brotherhood of man," for "a change of heart and soul in the world." What men decided, Russell said, mattered far less than the fact that they decided honestly.

> If you disbelieve in alternative service, stand out against it, no matter what the Government may do to you; if you believe in it, take it, no matter what the absolutists may say to you. . . . So long as the spirit of our actions is that for which the Fellowship stands, our loyalty is unimpaired whatever outward form our actions may take. But no outward form will preserve true loyalty if the inward spirit has been lost.[35]

The cumulative effect of these various pleas for unity eventually drove absolutist–alternativist arguments out of

32. Allen's messages were printed in *Trib.*, 21 and 28 September 1916. Also see extract of Allen's message from Wormwood Scrubs, 21 October 1916, FSC Files, FHL, and Allen ms., chap. 3, p. 14, CAP.
33. For example, see Brockway's editorial in *Trib.*, 21 September 1916.
34. Printed in *Trib.*, 5 October 1916. Also see *Trib.*, 28 September 1916.
35. *Trib.*, 12 October 1916.

the pages of *The Tribunal,* so that, if nothing else, they were pushed underground. By mid-November 1916 Brockway could congratulate the membership on the fact that the alternative-service controversy had been resolved (or, more accurately, superseded by other difficulties).[36] This declaration may have been premature, but at least there was little further public debate about whether Home Office men were still entitled to full-fledged membership in the fellowship. Nonetheless, the controversy had burned itself deep into the NCF, and, though the wound was sutured on the outside, it continued to fester within.[37] Many alternativists remained resentful of the superior attitude of the no-compromise faction. Some even renounced their membership in the NCF and joined the Alternative Service Guild, an organization formed by Percy Redfern, the NCF's first national treasurer. Redfern's group caused no large-scale defections from the NCF, but inevitably there was bad blood between the two organizations.[38]

By the autumn of 1916 it had become abundantly clear that the NCF's attempt to maintain a solid front against the Home Office scheme had failed. Henceforth, in order to recover its unity as well as its equilibrium, the fellowship's support of the Home Office men would have to be as vigorous as it was for the absolutists. As the months passed and the full operation of the Home Office scheme unfolded, NCF leaders discovered that this new responsibility was a formidable challenge.

The Home Office Scheme

As originally conceived by the cabinet and envisioned by the Brace committee, the Home Office scheme should have presented few serious problems. Sincere—if wrongheaded—conscientious objectors who had been certified as genuine by the central tribunal would diligently perform civilian

36. *Trib.,* 16 November 1916. See also Chap. 10.
37. See Allen's comments, Allen ms., chap. 3, p. 17, CAP.
38. For the Alternative Service Guild, see P. Redfern to Bertrand Russell, 30 June 1917, and R. W. Crammer to Russell, 15 July 1917, BRA. Also see "Work of National Importance, Memorandum of Low Wages and Bad Conditions," by P. Redfern, Murray Papers, 57.

work of national importance, thankful, no doubt, for having been released from confinement without having to violate their conscientious convictions. In the ideal, it seemed so simple; in practice, it was a wholly different matter.[39]

The difficulties began when the central tribunal chose to adopt a leisurely standard for deciding the genuineness of C.O.s. This procedure satisfied the army, which wanted to deal with as few objectors as possible, but it also meant that the Brace committee would have to deal with men who had no intention of abiding by the agreements they had made. Herbert Samuel added to the committee's difficulties by insisting that the men be assigned to work in large groups under conditions that would convince public opinion that at least some sacrifice was being required of them. "Equality of sacrifice" was part of the cant of Britain at the home front, but here, as in most other instances, it proved to be a troublesome and elusive bogey. When the Brace committee attempted to find suitable employment for the released men, they discovered meager pickings. Almost all private employers refused to have anything to do with C.O.s. Only after much searching did the committee manage to secure positions for some hundreds of men on such projects as quarrying, road building, tree felling, and the maintenance of a gasworks in South Wales. By November 1916 nine Home Office camps had been established and over nine hundred conscientious objectors set to work,[40] but the problems had only begun.

When the Home Office scheme was first proposed, *The Times* (6 July 1916) had insisted that conscientious objectors be assigned to "a form of arduous and unremunerative public service." If it accomplished little else, the scheme did provide over four thousand conscientious objectors with just such labor. The Brace committee did its best under adverse circumstances, but from the viewpoint of the C.O.s, its best was simply not good enough. Not only was the work generally difficult and demeaning, but the circumstances also re-

39. The best description of the political and administrative difficulties involved with the Home Office scheme is Rae, *Conscience and Politics*, pp. 162–90.

40. A description of the kinds of work done at various Home Office camps is given in a "Report on Home Office Centres," NCF Record Department, 16 November 1916, FSC Files, FHL.

Home Office men on a rock-breaking gang. (Courtesy Friends House Library)

quired restrictions on personal liberty that many objectors were unwilling to accept. They came to feel, with some justice, that the Home Office looked on them, not as sincere dissenters for conscience' sake, but as political prisoners released on good behavior and liable to be sent back to prison for the slightest breach of an arbitrary code of conduct.[41] Furthermore, the men were paid only eight pence per day or one-third less than the rate (equal to that of an army private) that Samuel had originally proposed. No extra provisions were made for dependents except that a small grant could be recommended by the poor-law relieving officer. In such cases, the men's wages were reduced to two pence.[42] Taken altogether—the low wages; the difficult, wasteful work; the poor living conditions; and the application of semimilitary discipline—the operation of the Home Office scheme was not calculated to induce enthusiasm even among the most well-intentioned C.O.s.

The Brace committee suffered the consequences—in the form of criticism, disaffection, and obstructionism—for

41. Herbert Samuel's remarks would seem to support this interpretation; see 5 H.C., 88:356–57, 29 November 1916.
42. Ibid.

conditions that were largely beyond its control. At the same time, the committee was attacked from the other side by those who felt that the scheme treated C.O.s too leniently. An example of this attitude was a motion presented to the House of Lords by Lord Latymer objecting to the fact that the government paid the Home Office men's national health insurance.[43] The frustration and harassment to which the committee was subjected led Brace to declare, after one particularly insulting attack on him, that "as chairman of the committee . . . I accepted a responsibility very distasteful to me, and it has been one of the most critical problems which I have ever been called on to face since I entered public life."[44] A few examples of the actual working out of the scheme should suffice to illustrate the authenticity of Brace's complaint.

The first camp for Home Office men was established in August 1916 at the village of Dyce near Aberdeen in northern Scotland. Approximately 250 C.O.s were brought there to quarry, crush, and transport stone for the construction and repair of roads in the area. Trouble began almost immediately. The Brace committee's contract with the local road board stipulated that the conscientious objectors would work ten hours a day. But many of the men had just been released from prison, and most of them had little experience at hard physical labor. Feeling that the men were simply not up to such an assignment, a committee elected to represent the C.O.s' interests negotiated a new agreement that limited work to five hours per day. This unauthorized action not only angered the Brace committee but also failed to satisfy the men, who still felt that the work was useless. Nor were they happy about their accommodations, housed as they were in surplus army tents that were ineffective shelters against the area's damp climate. Then, amid continuing complaints about the generally unhealthy and unnecessarily restrictive conditions, one of the C.O.s working at Dyce died. According to the other men in the camp, the dead man, Walter Roberts, had never received adequate medical atten-

43. 5 H.L., 25:856–60, 19 July 1917. Also see *Trib.*, 26 July 1917.
44. 5 H.C., 93:186, 30 April 1917. Brace was answering an attack by Sir C. Kinlock-Cooke, M.P. for Devonport, 5 H.C., 93:180–85.

tion. They naturally blamed his death on the negligence of camp authorities.[45]

Roberts's death gave the C.O. movement its first authentic martyr; it also provided the NCF with a tool for helping to patch up the differences between the absolutist and alternative-service factions. Brockway eulogized Roberts as a "brave bearer of the banner of Peace" and an inspiration for renewed strength and unity in the struggle against war.[46] At the same time, the fellowship greatly expanded its activities on behalf of the Home Office men. In response to a suggestion from Allen, a special committee was established to keep watch on Home Office camps.[47] Members of the national committee also visited various work centers on fact-finding tours and the COIB issued periodic reports on the men's living and working conditions.[48] Eventually, Marshall took on the added responsibility of conveying all important intelligence to the various camps as well as of being the chief agitator for improvement of conditions there.[49]

Actually, by this time the situation at Dyce had become a national issue. Ramsay MacDonald had already visited the camp and had reported to the House of Commons on the "shocking" conditions he had found there. Other M.P.s, such as C. B. Stanton, were perhaps begging the question when they scornfully compared the "horrible" conditions at Dyce with the horrors of the western front.[50] But such com-

45. See *The Granite Echo: Organ of the Dyce C.O.s* 1 (October 1916): 1-2, NCF File, SCPC, and *Trib.*, 14 September 1916.

46. *Trib.*, 14 September 1916.

47. See NCF, Hon. Sec. of Political Committee to Branches, 5 September 1916; "Notes on Proposed Change of NCF Policy," 9 November 1916; and Allen to Marshall, 28 November 1916, CAP.

48. See Report to the National Committee by W. J. Roberts on South Wales Home Office Camps, BRA; COIB Report 45 (19 September 1916):167-68; 46 (22 September 1916):170; 50 (6 October 1916):181-82; "Report on Home Office Centres," NCF Record Department, 16 November 1916, FSC Files, FHL; and C. Marshall to B. Russell, 1 June 1917, BRA.

49. See Catherine Marshall to Secretaries of Camps and Settlements Established under the Home Office Scheme, 15 November 1916, FSC Files, FHL. The NCF record department evidently did not have an accurate account of all men in Home Office centers since the 926 men employed in mid-November 1916 were "far in excess of the names reported to the Record Department"; NCF Record Department, 16 November 1916, FSC Files, FHL.

50. For the debate, see 5 H.C., 86:802-39 passim, 19 October 1916.

parisons do help to explain why public opinion was scarcely outraged about the death of one conscientious objector or about the poor accommodations in Home Office camps.

In any case, the Dyce camp was closed down, and its inhabitants sent elsewhere.[51] This action did not, however, cause any abatement in complaints about the scheme's operations. By early October, Norman, having helped to escalate the NCF's internal struggle over alternative service, was attempting to lead resistance within the Home Office camps. As chairman of the men's committee at the Risbridge camp, Norman became involved in a series of acrimonious disputes involving the possible military significance of the work being done there and the restrictions being imposed on the men. On 26 October Norman sent a letter to all Home Office men eliciting their opinions on the possibility of a mass repudiation of the scheme.[52] Apparently, Norman received little support for his proposal, but the Brace committee's patience was wearing thin as it faced the dual problem of maintaining control over the men and of providing them with some kind of work. The committee had been most successful at fulfilling these needs at work centers located in the disused prisons at Wakefield and Warwick. As discipline problems increased and work projects failed or closed down, the committee pleaded for use of still another abandoned prison. In February 1917 it received authorization to occupy Dartmoor prison, which, rechristened as Princetown Work Centre, became the largest and most controversial of all the Home Office camps.[53]

The center at Dartmoor was inevitably a breeding ground for trouble. Although the locks were removed from the cell

51. A Report from E. Jope, Hon. Sec. of Dyce Men's Committee, 22 October 1916 (copy), FSC Files, FHL, said, among other things, that the men used money earned from a "Dry Canteen" store to finance "agitation" and that "we never had any idea of obeying [the Camp rules] re. hours at night and week-end leaves and such childish restrictions of liberty."

52. See "Matters of Principle," submitted by C. H. Norman to Brace Committee on 11 September on behalf of C.O.s at Risbridge; Statement of Events at Risbridge House Camp, Kedinton, Haverhill, on 11 and 12 October 1916; and mimeographed letter from C. H. Norman, 26 October 1916, FSC Files, FHL.

53. According to Brace, 5 H.C., 98:1957, 6 November 1917, there were twelve hundred "schemers" at the Princetown center in the autumn of 1917.

doors and the men were allowed to move about freely, the ancient prison's grim aspect and the generally penal character of the work reminded many men of the jails from which they had only recently been released. As one man reported to friends:

> Much of the work done by the C.O.s is similar to that imposed by our penal codes. . . . When "efficiency" is called for on every side we are confronted by the spectacle of men skilled in various trades and professions, called upon to perform work for which they are quite unsuitable, both by training and temperament, and doing such work by antiquated methods, which would be condemned by commercial, agricultural or business experts.[54]

In a letter to the *Manchester Guardian*, Lydia Smith, who had investigated the Princetown center for the NCF, reported that the work performed there, far from being of national importance, was of little use to anyone. Dozens of men were assigned tasks that one horse could have done better in half the time, and every attempt to speed up the work or to improve working conditions was thwarted by government supervisors. Such conditions, she said, were not calculated to help the country but to discourage and exhaust the men. One man told her: "we are merely keeping the place going till the convicts return . . . no one can pretend that it is work of 'national importance.'" The Home Office, she concluded, was manufacturing malcontents out of men who might otherwise be doing meaningful work for the community.[55]

After receiving Smith's report, the NCF national committee adopted a resolution calling for "a vigorous campaign exposing the penal character of the work in Home Office camps, and demanding that the government should provide in its place real work of social utility."[56] The fellowship also sponsored the writing and publication of two pamphlets that argued that, in effect, Home Office men were being treated in essentially the same way as the absolutists remaining in prison. Both groups, as Ernest E. Hunter noted in *The Home*

54. Howard Marten, Secretary of Dartmoor Men's Committee to Friends (copy), 5 May 1917, BRA. Also copy in FSC Correspondence, 1917, FHL.
55. *Trib.*, 17 May 1917. Also see *Trib.*, 28 June 1917.
56. Quoted in *Trib.*, 24 May 1917.

Office Compounds, were being "punished and persecuted," and none of the men were allowed to use their talents in serving the nation. It was the "finality of futility" that in a country making desperate efforts to increase its food supply and to eliminate waste, thousands of men anxious to be of service were left languishing in penal settlements. The nation, he said, was being "deprived of much useful endeavour in order to satisfy the stupid malice of those who wish to make the path of a minority a hard one."[57]

The NCF's attacks on the Home Office scheme had some validity, but the general reaction to Home Office centers throughout the country was not sympathy for the men, but outrage that the government would countenance the establishment of these "C.O.'s Cosy Clubs." A series of clashes among the C.O.s themselves and between off-duty "schemers" and local residents were widely and indignantly reported in the press. The *Daily Mail* was especially fierce in its attacks on the "coddled Conscience men" and "pampered pets" who were being permitted to carry on subversive activities in the Princetown center on Dartmoor.[58] Apparently such attacks had an effect. At a public meeting in Plymouth Guildhall, Alderman J. Y. Woolcombe protested the lenient treatment afforded C.O.s at the Princetown center, noting that nine-tenths of them were "disloyal men [and] anarchists" who professed "a sort of bastard socialism . . . I cannot understand why . . . they are not put up against a wall and shot."[59] While no one took Alderman Woolcombe precisely at his word, some of the "Dartmoor Do-Nothings" at Princetown were assaulted by the outraged citizens of neighboring towns.[60] After these attacks, the Brace committee restricted the Dartmoor C.O.s to the prison grounds. This action partially assuaged public opinion but probably exacerbated the difficulties in controlling noncooperative or openly rebellious men within the center.

57. Ernest E. Hunter, *The Home Office Compounds: A Statement as to How Conscientious Objectors Are Penalized*, NCF pamphlet (London, n.d.), pp. 5–6, 11–12. Also see C. G. Ammon, *Waste of National Resources* (London, [1917]), and *Trib.*, 21 July 1917.

58. See *Daily Mail*, especially 23–30 April 1917.

59. Quoted in *Trib.*, 3 May 1917.

60. See *Trib.*, 26 April 1917, for reports of attacks on C.O.s at Tavistock, Yelverton, and Walkhampton. Also see *Trib.*, 19 April 1917.

Supporters of the NCF sometimes blamed disputes and disorders on police spies and agents provocateurs, but even Marshall admitted to a representative of the War Office that a small minority of Home Office men advocated a policy of "sabotage."[61] Stanley Keeling, a C.O. at Dartmoor, reported to the FSC that some men had refused to abide by any rules since the center opened. "They ate their food, took remuneration, but did nothing to justify it." There was, he added, "a 'rabid' type of socialism stalking about here—not the real socialist of the Barry Brown type—but a more obstructionist and semi-anarchist, who opposes things from within and without! To me, these are the greatest enemies of our movement . . . because they do not care about the standard to be kept up."[62] Keeling singled out Norman as a particularly evil influence. The more moderate men, he noted, were forced to expend "all their time and endeavour . . . to keep sanity and coolness prevailing. Norman's natural food seems to be 'strikes.' I see him as a real danger here." Russell received similar reports from the Wakefield center.[63]

By early March 1917 an accumulation of reports of this kind moved the NCF national committee to issue a policy statement that condemned obstructionism and emphasized that there were only two honorable alternatives open to Home Office men: to fulfill the conditions of their agreement or, if unable to do so in good conscience, to return to prison.[64] Perhaps in response to this message and certainly in keeping with its tone, a general meeting of Dartmoor C.O.s passed a resolution repudiating the charge of slacking and promising "to perform work provided in a reasonable spirit." But the men still objected to the penal character of the work they were doing and demanded "civil work of real importance with full civil rights."[65]

Despite such attempts at regularizing the behavior of

61. Extract from letter of C. Marshall to Major Thornton, 27 April 1917, BRA. For charges that the government planted agents provocateurs, see the statement of Joseph King, M.P., 5 H.C., 91:654, 8 March 1917.

62. Stanley V. Keeling to Dr. [Henrietta] Thomas, [May 1917], FSC Correspondence, 1917, FHL.

63. Ibid., and R. W. Crammer to Russell, 14 October 1917, BRA.

64. Extract from letter of C. Marshall to Major Thornton, 27 April 1917, BRA. Also see Howard G. Marten to Bertrand Russell, 23 May 1917, BRA, and Keith Robbins, *The Abolition of War: The "Peace Movement" in Britain, 1914-1919* (Cardiff, 1976), pp. 124-25.

65. Quoted in *Trib.*, 24 May 1917.

"schemers" and improving conditions in the work centers, the Home Office scheme continued to deteriorate. In July 1917 the Home Office committee on employment of conscientious objectors was reorganized in response to continuing complaints about its lack of control over the men. Brace remained as chairman, but the other two members were replaced by retired majors—one of whom had previously served as a prison warden. These changes in personnel were accompanied by changes in regulations that imposed a near-military standard of discipline.[66]

There were some complaints, especially from organized labor, about the new direction that the scheme seemed to be taking. In October 1917 members of seventy local Labour parties and trades councils endorsed a resolution signed by ten trade-union secretaries, including Herbert Morrison, that condemned "continual attempts to militarize the control" and to impose a system with all the aspects of dreaded industrial conscription.[67] A more widely read and popular view, however, was presented at about the same time by the bishop of Exeter, Lord William Cecil. The bishop was apparently so outraged by what he had seen in a visit to the Princetown center that he felt compelled to write to *The Times,* warning of a vile conspiracy being hatched there. "Sacks of letters," he noted, "come and go, no doubt conveying instructions for those plans of bloodshed which may at some future time bring, according to their view, liberty, and to our view, ruin, to England." The bishop's suggestion for dealing with this state of affairs was to release all genuine religious objectors as "good citizen[s] with fanatic views" and to treat all political objectors "as enemies to our commonwealth" to be shipped, "without money or rations [to] . . . that portion of England which is frequently visited by the enemy aeroplane."[68]

Answering for the NCF, Russell noted that since the bishop's obvious intent was

> to turn men aside from love and to stimulate hate, we cannot deny that he adopted an admirable method towards that end;

66. Parliamentary Papers (House of Commons and Command), 1917. Committee on Employment of Conscientious Objectors: Rules (Cd. 8627).
67. Reprinted in *Trib.,* November 1917. Also see "Summary of News for Prisoners," September–October 1917, FSC Files, FHL.
68. *The Times,* 8 October 1917.

but we would beg him not to be disappointed if, in their first fumbling efforts to adopt that gospel of hate which, as we all know, is the true interpretation of our Lord's teaching, the object of their detestation is not exactly that he indicated. We cannot all become perfect at once, but those who have learnt to hate a bishop may in time acquire the more difficult act of hating a German.[69]

So the debate descended, and with it the men's morale. In November 1917 the Home Office introduced a plan for "exceptional employment" that would allow men who had served satisfactorily for twelve months to be released and to take up outside employment on an individual basis. Men released under this plan were forbidden to engage in any antiwar or anticonscription propaganda, but otherwise they were free from control except for the requirement that their employer send a monthly report to the Home Office committee.[70] While this arrangement worked out fairly well, the twelve-month rule for eligibility was strictly applied, and the release of the most cooperative men from work centers did not satisfy the grievances of many who were left behind. In February 1918, for example, some five to seven hundred men, again led by Norman, staged a work strike at Princetown to protest the death of a C.O., whom, they claimed, had died as a result of gross neglect on the part of the center's physician.[71] The incident ended with the C.O.s back to work, the medical authorities cleared of negligence, and Norman and another man returned to prison. But the adverse publicity arising from these events lingered on.[72] Such publicity, along with military setbacks in the spring of 1918, no doubt contributed to renewed violence directed against C.O.s at the Knutsford and Wakefield work centers in May. Several C.O.s were injured in both places, and the Wakefield operation was shut down as a result of attacks on men there.[73]

69. *Trib.*, 18 October 1917.

70. See 5 H.C., 100:2122, 20 December 1917; *Trib.*, 3 January 1918; *NCF Souvenir*, p. 70; and C. H. Norman, *A Searchlight on the European War* (London, 1924), pp. 99–100.

71. See *Trib.*, 14 and 21 February 1918. Also see 5 H.C., 103:1223–27, 26 February 1918.

72. 5 H.C., 103:1628–31, 28 February 1918, and *Trib.*, 28 February and 21 March 1918.

73. See account by J. F. Wade printed in *Manchester C.O.'s Journal*, 6 July

During the final months of the war, the majority of Home Office men were gradually released for exceptional employment,[74] but the last were not released until April 1919 when the work centers were finally shut down.[75] By most criteria, the Home Office scheme would have to be accounted a dismal failure. Certainly, few of the 4,126 men[76] who worked under the scheme had any endearing memories of it, and Brace must have looked on its demise as the removal of an enormous weight from his back. Taxpayers had contributed around 150,000 pounds to an experiment whose utilitarian results were meager at any cost.[77] The NCF had also paid dearly for its involvement. As Allen later recalled, the internal struggle over alternative service

> led to every kind of spasmodic disorder and sectional movement, which bewildered the Government and the public, and brought the name of the objector into some disrepute. To have done our duty by all sections would have only served to strengthen the position of those who intended to resist to the end. . . . As it was, from the day that liberty of conscience was somewhat overlooked in our midst, there began a gradual disintegration of the movement.[78]

Whatever effect the Home Office men had on the NCF, they were only one of the factions to which the fellowship had to minister. There was, in addition, that small, but even more difficult, body of men whom the journalist Henry Nevinson once described as the "logicians of conscience, the extremists of peace"[79]—the absolutist prisoners.

1918, NCF File, SCPC; *Trib.*, 30 May 1918; and Graham, *Conscription and Conscience*, pp. 233–34. Also copy of letter from C.O.s at Wakefield to Home Secretary, 23 May 1918, concerning the provocations of the *Wakefield Express* in urging citizens to intimidate the men at the Knutsford center, Murray Papers, 57.

74. COIB Report 98 (25 May 1918), p. 273, listed only 183 men on exceptional employment.

75. See *Military Statistics, 1914–1920*, p. 673.

76. Ibid.

77. This estimate is based on the fact that from 16 August 1916 to 31 October 1917 the scheme cost £92,306 11s. 11d.; 5 H.C., 99:560–61. Also see *Trib.*, 13 December 1917.

78. Allen ms., Chap. 2, p. 32, and chap. 8, p. 17, CAP.

79. Henry W. Nevinson, "The Conscientious Objector," *Atlantic Monthly* 118 (November 1916):690.

9

"The True Place for a Just Man"

Under a Government which imprisons anyone unjustly, the true
place for a just man is also in prison.—Henry David Thoreau

Absolutists in Prison

In the autumn of 1916 the NCF moved its central offices
from Salisbury Court in Fleet Street to 5 York Buildings,
Adelphi Terrace. According to Barry Brown, however, the
"spiritual headquarters of the Fellowship" was Wormwood
Scrubs prison where the majority of the absolutists were still
holding out.[1] While some alternative-service men might
have disagreed, it is not surprising, given the circumstances,
that many absolutists thought of themselves as a kind of
moral elite. Certainly, British public opinion, which at first
derided the "out-and-outers" as obstructionist cranks, came
to judge the entire pacifist movement according to the standard set by the absolutists.

The average age of the first one thousand imprisoned
conscientious objectors was twenty-one, and, while the NCF
raised a considerable din about the government's callousness
in dealing with such young and inexperienced men, some
objectors departed for prison like schoolboys beginning a
holiday. Such a mood pervaded William J. Chamberlain's
lighthearted, almost silly account of his prison experience,
which was serialized in *The Tribunal*. Chamberlain's waggish
banter about the "great fun" one could have fooling the
warders or sending secret messages seemed to place the
whole business in the realm of a colossal joke.[2] For more

---

1. *Trib.*, 23 November 1916.
2. Chamberlain's prison memoirs appeared in seven installments between 21 September and 2 November 1916 and were later published as *A
C.O. in Prison* (London, [1916]), a copy of which is in CAP. Also see A.
Fenner Brockway, *Inside the Left* (London, 1942), p. 68; T. Corder Catch-

spiritually minded objectors, prison seemed fraught with possibilities of a great religious adventure, a monastic retreat from the world—"A Home whereby I can meditate upon Him."[3] The realities of continued imprisonment would disabuse most C.O.s of any radiant expectations about a free soul's overcoming its caged environment. The NCF soon ceased to give optimistic appraisals of prison life and began to prepare its members for the sort of treatment they could actually expect.[4]

Most objectors were sentenced to hard labor in what was called the "third division."[5] A term in this division exposed a man to the most stringent conditions an English convict could be forced to endure. For the first twenty-eight days, a prisoner was kept in "separate confinement," working alone in his cell at hard labor (usually sewing mailbags) and seeing no one except warders and perhaps the chaplain. For a fortnight, the prisoner slept on a plank and was fed a meager "A" diet consisting mainly of bread and porridge. After a month's good behavior, he gained the privilege of "associated" but silent labor for part of the day. At this point, the prisoner became eligible for participation in the so-called progressive stage system, whose benefits included the possibility of writing one letter of eight hundred words and receiving one twenty-minute visit on completion of two months' imprisonment. Thereafter, the interval between letters and visits was gradually reduced to one month. In addition, a prisoner could earn "remission marks" that might cancel up to one-sixth of his sentence. The progressive stages and remission marks were, of course, contingent on the prisoner's good behavior.[6]

---

pool, *On Two Fronts* (London, 1918), pp. 111–13; and Stanley B. James, *The Men Who Dared* (London, [1917]), pp. 69–70.

3. See Catchpool, *On Two Fronts*, pp. 112–13, and letter from "G," 24 November 1916, printed in COIB Report 58 (1 December 1916), p. 211, NCF File, SCPC.

4. For example, see *Trib.*, 5 October 1916.

5. The three divisions in English prisons were a reflection of the class system. Conditions were progressively better in the second division, while in the first they could be almost luxurious. There were sporadic but unavailing attempts to get C.O.s placed in the second division; for example, see Allen to J. A. Whitehouse, M.P., 1 June 1916, BRA.

6. For discussions of conditions in the third division, see *The Court-*

In his seven-by-twelve-foot cell, the prisoner was allowed a few eating utensils; a Bible and some other religious books; four small, unframed photographs; and a slate and chalk, but no regular writing materials. Next to the silence rule (prisoners were not permitted to speak except when addressed by prison officials), inability to record and preserve thoughts and ideas was probably the greatest hardship for C.O.s.[7] In addition, conscientious objectors gained little from the progressive stages since at first they were generally given repeated short sentences of three to four months. Thus, they only had time to reach the first few stages before they were released, resentenced, and forced to begin the rigorous purgation all over again.

Another constant source of worry among C.O. prisoners was the physical deterioration that was a nearly inevitable consequence of prison life. A bland, barely adequate diet; lack of exercise (forty-five minutes per day); and damp, ill-heated, ill-ventilated cells greatly increased the incidence of real or imagined ailments among the men. Prison medical officers were supposed to make weekly visits to each prisoner and to give regular reports on the condition of every man being treated,[8] but this procedure was not carefully adhered to. Because of the war, doctors were in short supply, and those who were available generally had little sympathy for conscientious objectors. C.O.s probably fared no worse than other prisoners, although some men were apparently allowed to develop serious illnesses before treatment was begun.

Taken altogether, the singular lack of beauty, of generosity, and, most of all, of normal verbal communication was far more degrading and debilitating than most C.O.s had imag-

---

Martial Friend and Prison Guide, NCF pamphlet (London, [1918]), pp. 10-12; a mimeographed "Memorandum on Conscientious Objectors in Prison," CAP; and Stephen Hobhouse, *An English Prison from Within* (London, [1919]), p. 15.

7. See Hubert W. Peet, "112 Days' Hard Labour," published as a supplement to *The Ploughshare* (April 1917), pp. 6-11; Hobhouse, *An English Prison,* p. 19; and Chamberlain, *A C.O. in Prison,* pp. 24-25. It should also be noted that these conditions apply only to English prisons. Scottish penal institutions were more harsh; see *Trib.,* 13 December 1917, and "Memorandum on C.O.s in Prison," CAP.

8. *Court-Martial Friend,* p. 14.

ined. The craving for color to disperse the sameness; for a bit of kindness, taken or given, to soften the remorseless, calculated inhumanity; and for companionship to relieve oneself of the perpetual company of one's own morbid thoughts could have severe effects on the mental balance of even the most stable C.O. Indeed, at one time or another, most absolutists found their prison experience almost beyond the limit of their endurance.

A prominent example of how prison life could destroy the health and try the faith of the most resolute C.O. is the case of Clifford Allen. Allen managed to remain out of jail for a considerable time by using every debating trick and legal maneuver he could devise. But finally on 11 August 1916, after his last appeal had been disposed of,[9] he was taken into custody and began a sixteen-month period of imprisonment that very nearly killed him.

Before Allen was sentenced, Edward Grubb, the NCF's elderly treasurer, wrote to say that he felt "like having a good cry" when he considered the possibility of Allen's frail body being subjected to the rigors of imprisonment.[10] On the other hand, the chairman's presence gave a considerable boost to the morale of those men already behind bars. Years later, one former C.O. told Lord Allen how he felt when he saw penciled on the wall of the lavatory the news that the chairman had been brought to Wormwood Scrubs. "Can you understand the thrill that passed through us all and how we then trod the exercise ring with a lighter step?" Outside, Allen had been the prophet and inspiration for a movement that was slowly taking on almost religious overtones; within prison walls he became, as Jennie Lee later recalled, "the very embodiment of . . . martyrdom. . . . I should not have been surprised if he had suddenly sprouted wings and a halo."[11] Allen seems to have had a similar effect on his jailers. Soldiers guarding Allen while he was in military custody gave up their pillows to make a mattress for his plank bed.

9. A typescript of Allen's hearing at the Lavender Hill police court on 31 July 1916 where he received a ten-day reprieve can be found in CAP. Also see *Trib.*, 10 August 1916, and Arthur Marwick, *Clifford Allen: The Open Conspirator* (Edinburgh, 1964), p. 33.

10. Grubb to Allen, 14 June 1916, CAP. Also see *Trib.*, 22 June 1916.

11. Charles Tritton to Lord Allen, 13 January 1938, CAP, and Jennie Lee, *Tomorrow Is a New Day* (London, 1948), p. 50.

The chaplain of Winchester prison, where Allen spent his third and most difficult sentence, wrote to an NCF official: "For Mr. Clifford Allen I have the very greatest sympathy and respect. I consider him a very lovable character and a powerful influence for good, . . . [however] mistaken in his present attitudes; he is a very dear fellow." Apparently, Allen's influence also brought about considerable relaxation in the strict administration of Winchester prison hospital when he was a patient there.[12]

However much Allen reminded so many diverse people of a saint, no ministering angel came, as had come to Paul and Silas, to spirit him away to freedom. After completing his first sentence of 112 days, Allen was twice returned to the hands of the army and sentenced. In December 1916 he received a second 112 days' sentence, and the following May he was given the maximum term of two years' hard labor. These repeated imprisonments did not weaken his faith in the C.O. movement nor his will to resist,[13] but they did remove, absolutely and for all time, any delusions he may have had about the purifying effects of imprisonment. Two months after his arrest, Allen wrote from Wormwood Scrubs:

> This experience has been a greater strain than even I thought. Solitude is a terrible thing when it is enforced. It is torture to receive thoughts and ideas you cannot commit to paper, then to forget them and start chasing them, to know they were yours but have flitted. I have been the victim of sleeplessness and changing moods. . . . I have yearned for things I never had time for when free—like music; it has been tragic to be idle when plans of action crowded upon my mind.[14]

In a letter to Catherine E. Marshall, written in the middle of his second prison term, Allen noted his concern about references to the joys of prison life in the letters that the NCF received from imprisoned objectors. He feared that these messages gave those on the outside an overly sanguine pic-

12. Allen ms., chap. 3, p. 9, CAP; Chaplain H. I. St. J. Thrupp to [G. Rinder?] of Visitation Committee, n.d., FSC Files, Correspondence of Visitation of Prisoners Committee, JAC, FHL; and typewritten statement by John Mitchell, a C.O. in the same ward with Allen at Winchester prison hospital, CAP.

13. See Allen's defense before his third court-martial, reprinted as *Why I Still Resist*, NCF pamphlet (London, [1917]).

14. Typed extract from letter of 21 October 1916, FSC Files, FHL.

ture and did not prepare prospective prisoners for the "very harassing" life that would soon be thrust upon them. He admitted that the introspection induced by isolation could bring "moments of spiritual exultation that neither hills, nor sea, nor sky, nor music, nor great gatherings of men have ever given me, when in some way or another the more conscious I am of the curbing of my freedom . . . the more content I seem to become."[15] Yet Allen believed that such feelings of peace and joy were dangerous, unhealthy sentiments that would slowly incline a man toward inertness and thereby destroy the possibility of his making any positive contribution toward ending the war. For this reason, he looked on times of "intense mental and spiritual torture," and even of physical pain, almost as a salvation, not because he retained any belief in the redeeming qualities of suffering, but because such periods helped him to remember why he was in prison and how far the movement was from gaining ultimate success.

"There were," he said, "moments of unutterable loneliness and anguish when I seem unmindful of the very purpose that has brought me here." A prisoner could never expect to hear a polite or compassionate word; his only companions were his own incessant, unrelenting thoughts.

> You cannot stop thinking for an instant. And if you seem to, it is only to listen intently to the beating of your heart drumming in your ears. You cannot escape thinking about the most trivial matters of routine. I think of the very knots in the boards every time I scrub them, until I could scratch them out of the floor to rid myself of their arrogant insistence upon themselves.[16]

Like Allen, all absolutists were faced with the possibility of months and even years of solitude, enforced silence, and creeping physical and mental degeneration. And like him, most were ultimately driven to rebel, either overtly or covertly, against those prison regulations that preyed most heavily on them. Of all the calculated discomforts of prison life, none so thoroughly dispirited the average inmate as the silence rule. Created in some blinding flash of Victorian righteousness, enforced silence was supposed to produce a rehabilitating effect by compeling the prisoner to turn his

15. Allen to Marshall, 24 March 1917, CAP.
16. Ibid.

thoughts toward the heinousness of his offense against society. In fact, the primary result was that it drove prisoners to extravagant lengths to defeat the system. Most conscientious objectors quickly fell into the habit of exchanging furtive confidences at every opportunity. For some, beating the warders at their own game became a kind of indoor sport. Fenner Brockway, while admitting that habitual deception was dangerous, encouraged NCF members to make use of every possible means of communication.

To supplement the limited opportunities for verbal expression, Brockway also organized a campaign for smuggling pencils into prison so that written messages could be passed. Before going into prison, many NCF members received from their local branches a packet containing a supply of pencil leads and a corn plaster. The plaster, which could survive the hot bath given every incoming prisoner, was attached to the arch of the foot with the leads beneath it. Thousands of leads were gotten into prison in this fashion before the authorities detected the ruse toward the end of the war.[17] There were also other methods. A. M. Sanders brought a pencil into Maidstone prison hidden "under my top lip and moustache," and Chamberlain concealed one in his hair.[18]

Unimportant as they may seem, these writing materials were significant morale builders because they gave enterprising C.O.s the wherewithal to launch a series of fugitive prison newspapers. Brockway began a twice-weekly journal called the *Walton Leader* that ran to forty issues handprinted on toilet-paper pages. After four months, he was detected and sentenced to six days' bread and water for "production of a prison newspaper." The *Leader*, which survived this setback and eventually had over one hundred editions, was only one of over a half-dozen prison journals produced by conscientious objectors.[19]

Despite the distracting and morale-building qualities of

17. A. Fenner Brockway, *Prisons as Crime Factories* (London, 1919), p. 8, and *Inside the Left*, pp. 92–96, 96n.

18. A. M. Sanders, "My Experiences as a C.O. and the Life That Led up to Them," unpublished ms., p. 10, CAP, and William J. Chamberlain, *Fighting for Peace* (London, [1928]), p. 96.

19. Brockway, *Inside the Left*, pp. 98–101, and *The C.O. Clink Chronicle* (London, n.d.), pp. 1–2.

such things as prison newspapers, the cumulative effects of prison life bore down heavily on C.O.s behind bars. Hubert W. Peet, for example, believed that prison was even worse than the army: army regulations allowed for much that was inherently human, but the "civil penal code is . . . calculated, scientific, soulless cruelty—Prussian in the true meaning of the term."[20]

Cat and Mouse

For the last two years of the war, only the steadfast dedication of a hard core of women and older men kept the NCF alive. During this time, the fellowship's unfree hard core—the absolutists—had none of their comrades' opportunities for adventure or exhilaration in carrying on the struggle against the government, the military, and the police. For them, prison life continued at the same remorseless pace, broken only by intervals during which absolutists who had served out their sentences were released. In practice, as soon as he had passed through the prison gates, the "released" absolutist was taken in tow by an army escort and delivered back to his assigned regiment. If a man retained his conscientious convictions, he would naturally again refuse to follow military orders. Such men would be placed in custody, court-martialed, and sentenced to begin the same grim process all over again.

Although there was no limit to the number of times a soldier might be court-martialed, Section 68(2) of the Army Act did state that no offender on conscientious grounds could be subject to imprisonment for more than two consecutive years. The army contravened this proviso through the simple legal fiction of allowing a released prisoner one day's "liberty" in camp, thus breaking the continuity of his confinement.[21] Therefore, a man might, with an occasional day of "freedom," be condemned to remain in prison for an interminable period. The result was that, while two years

20. Peet, "112 Days' Hard Labour," p. 12.
21. *The Court-Martial Friend*, p. 16, and *Scraps of Paper*, NCF pamphlet (London, n.d.), p. 6. See, for example, the case of Allen by Marwick, *Clifford Allen*, p. 38, and Martin Gilbert, ed., *Plough My Own Furrow* (London, 1965), pp. 73–74.

was the maximum allowable punishment at hard labor, some absolutists actually served more than three years under this regimen.

These circumstances caused a growing number of protests from C.O. sympathizers and liberal-minded people who supported the war but deplored what seemed an unconscionable persecution of a tiny minority. Blame for the way in which conscientious objectors were treated fell especially on the person and eventually the administration of David Lloyd George, who by the summer of 1916 had become the personification of evil for the British peace movement.[22] To some extent Lloyd George brought these attacks on himself, especially because of one widely publicized statement about the treatment of absolutists: "With that kind of man I personally have absolutely no sympathy whatsoever.... For my part, I will take no step that will make it easy for a man to get out of his national obligations ... [and] I shall only consider the best means of making the path of that class a very hard one."[23] This statement, as A. J. P. Taylor has said, "drove the first nail in the coffin of Lloyd George's Radical reputation."[24]

Yet for all of this, Lloyd George was to some extent unjustly accused. He may not have overburdened himself in considering the question, but as John Rae has noted, it was under his administration that the sustained effort to gain relief for the absolutists bore at least some fruit.[25]

From the summer of 1916 the NCF's campaign on behalf of the absolutists had received help from a number of predictable sources—Free Church leaders like the Reverend Frederick B. Meyer;[26] prominent liberals like Gilbert Murray, Lord Courtney, and H. A. L. Fisher;[27] and even indi-

22. For example, see A. Fenner Brockway, "Sentence of Death," *Trib.*, 24 August 1916.

23. 5 H.C., 84:1758-59, 26 July 1916.

24. A. J. P. Taylor, *English History, 1914-1945* (Oxford, 1965), pp. 54-55, and *Politics in Wartime and Other Essays* (London, 1964), p. 41.

25. John Rae, *Conscience and Politics: The British Government and the Conscientious Objector to Military Service, 1916-1919* (London, 1970), p. 206.

26. See Frederick B. Meyer's pamphlet, *The Majesty of Conscience* (London, [1917]).

27. A memorial to Asquith, 4 October 1916, was signed by all the above and others; FSC Files, FHL, and *Trib.*, 12 October 1916. Also see G. Lowes

vidualistic conservatives like Lord Parmoor and Lord Hugh Cecil.[28] Bertrand Russell believed that the government's "demented" treatment of absolutists constantly increased the number of C.O. sympathizers; "each stage in the persecution [he said] had lasted just long enough to win the reluctant respect from the public for its victims." By the spring of 1917 Russell reported that "signs are not wanting that the public conscience is beginning to be seriously troubled by the dreary repetition of court-martials and imprisonments."[29] Until the fellowship acquired the support of an unexpected ally, however, the question of relief for absolutists was not raised in the highest circles of government.

In April 1917 Stephen Hobhouse, Quaker absolutist and scion of a prominent family, was court-martialed and sentenced to a second prison term.[30] At about the same time his mother, Margaret Hobhouse, wife of the Right Honorable Henry Hobhouse and elder sister of Beatrice Webb, entered the lists on behalf of her son and his fellow absolutists. Mrs. Hobhouse did not share her son's pacifist convictions— indeed, she was a Conservative who strongly supported the war—but she was as persistent in her attempts to gain release for the absolutists as she was in her advocacy of the national cause. In a handwritten note found among his wartime papers, Russell provides some insight into the tenacity of her character: "Her son persuaded her that Christianity and war are incompatible, so she gave up Christianity."[31]

Sometime in late April 1917 Margaret Hobhouse approached Lord Milner, who had stood as proxy godfather at Stephen's baptism, and asked him to intercede. Milner obviously put his private secretary, Major Thornton, to work on the case, for on 2 May 1917 Marshall wrote to Thornton of

---

Dickinson to G. Murray, 31 August 1916, Gilbert Murray Papers, 57, Bodleian Library, Oxford.

28. See Lord Hugh Cecil to C. Marshall, 2 June 1916, BRA. Also see 5 H.L., 25:324–30, 24 May 1917, for Lord Parmoor's speech on behalf of absolutists.

29. *Trib.*, 17 August 1916 and 17 May 1917.

30. *Trib.*, 2 and 9 April 1917.

31. BRA. The story of Margaret Hobhouse's efforts on behalf of the absolutists is ably told by Rae, *Conscience and Politics*, pp. 207–25. My account, following Rae's, is largely devoted to Mrs. Hobhouse's campaign as it involved or affected the NCF.

her willingness to give information that might be helpful to the cabinet's reconsideration of the C.O. problem. She added that she would appreciate "an opportunity of seeing Lord Milner personally before the government was committed to any fresh scheme, so as to give him, at first hand, some of my personal knowledge of the types of men concerned."[32] On this occasion, Milner voiced his misgivings about the treatment of obviously genuine C.O.s to the war cabinet (there was also a debate in the House of Lords) but relief for the absolutists was strongly opposed by General Childs, and Milner's thrust was turned aside.[33]

Temporarily thwarted at the cabinet level, "that pernicious woman Margaret Hobhouse," as Childs called her,[34] launched the second maneuver in her campaign—an assault on public opinion. In early June, after she had made a contribution to the NCF, Mrs. Hobhouse outlined her plans to Russell. Decrying the long-suffering passivism of the Quakers, she emphasized the need to expose "the injustice of continuing punishment and the barbarity of the punishment. Englishmen are tender-hearted and cannot bear cruelty... one would advise the... authorities that it is a dangerous policy to play at injustice, even with rebels, and that which Russia will not tolerate, England will in the end repudiate."[35] In reply, Russell cautioned Mrs. Hobhouse not to expect too much from an investigation then being conducted by Philip Kerr at the behest of the prime minister. Russell saw Kerr's inquiry as a diversionary tactic stressing prison reform when the only policy that would satisfy the vast majority of absolutists was "unconditional release."[36]

As it turned out, Russell was correct about Kerr's report. It came into General Childs's possession before reaching the cabinet, and through his influence its final effect was to induce the War Office to discontinue the practice of commut-

32. Marshall to Major Thornton (copy), 2 May 1917, BRA.

33. See Milner's memorandum to the war cabinet, CAB 24/12/677 and 5 H.L., 25:324-40, 24 May 1917. The question was discussed in the war cabinet on 22 May; see CAB 23/4/257(3).

34. Childs to Wigram, 11 October 1917, Royal Archives, GV 5910/5, cited by Rae, *Conscience and Politics*, p. 225.

35. M. Hobhouse to Russell, 4 June 1917, BRA. Also see Catherine Marshall to M. Hobhouse, 1 June 1917, CEMP (microfilm).

36. Russell to M. Hobhouse, 6 June 1917, BRA.

ing heavy court-martial sentences to 112 days, thus reducing the number of second and third sentences for C.O.s. This action, of course, neither reduced the total number of imprisoned C.O.s nor mitigated their punishments.[37]

Undeterred, Mrs. Hobhouse turned to the mass of "tender-hearted" Englishmen by publishing a sensational tract on the plight of the absolutists called *I Appeal unto Caesar*. The book's cover page identified the author as Mrs. Henry Hobhouse, but some fascinating detective work by Jo Vellacott makes it clear that the book was largely written by Russell.[38] In any case, this little volume, which had an introduction by Murray; supporting declarations by Lords Parmoor, Selborne, Henry Bentinck, and Hugh Cecil; and a favorable endorsement from *The Times*, sold eighteen thousand copies in four months. One of these was given to the king by Lord Milner.[39]

The launching of *I Appeal unto Caesar* was accompanied by a series of carefully solicited protests from prominent people. On 12 June, for example, George Bernard Shaw's letter to the *Manchester Guardian* asked if the public was aware that death was the only escape from the repeated sentences of hard labor given to C.O.s. Shaw felt that the government's aim was to continue sentencing and confining men like Allen and Hobhouse until they died of "exhaustion, starvation and close confinement. . . . Anyhow, here are two gentlemen in a fair way to be killed because the public has no knowledge and the authorities no sense. If we wish to kill them, cannot we shoot them out of hand and have done with it, Dublin fashion?"[40]

37. See WO 32/2051/3307 and "Summary of News for Prisoners," September–October 1917, FSC Files, FHL. Also see Forster's announcement of the new policy; 5 H.C., 95:358–59, 27 June 1917, and *Trib.*, 5 July 1917.

38. Jo Vellacott Newberry, "Russell as Ghost Writer, a New Discovery," *Russell* 15 (Autumn 1974):19–23.

39. See Gilbert Murray to M. Hobhouse, 21 and 25 June 1917, Murray Papers, 57; *The Times*, 8 September 1917; W. David Willis, *Stephen Hobhouse: A Twentieth-Century Quaker Saint* (London, 1972), p. 43; and Rae, *Conscience and Politics*, p. 215.

40. Shaw was referring to the execution of fifteen Irishmen for their part in the Easter rebellion of April 1916. Also see Arthur S. Peake, *Prisoners of Hope: The Problem of the Conscientious Objector* (London, 1918), pp. 80–88.

A meeting in early August at which Lord Derby and General Childs, as spokesmen for the War Office, discussed the absolutist problem with Asquith and McKenna, representing independent M.P.s, had more political significance. Asquith stated his belief that the government could and should devise some administrative means for obtaining the release of obviously sincere C.O. prisoners.[41] Before any action was taken on Asquith's proposal, Milner circulated a second memorandum in the war cabinet on the "quite indefensible" manner in which some absolutists were being treated. Culminating this flurry of activity was a note from Derby urging "that some decision should be arrived at with regard to the future treatment of conscientious objectors, either by maintaining the *status quo,* or else by some form of legislation which would give effect to Mr. Asquith's views."[42]

At this point, leaders of the NCF felt that both the public and private campaigns on behalf of the absolutists were going "extraordinarily well." In her news summary for prisoners in military custody, Marshall noted that the C.O.s' stand was "making steady headway in impressing itself on public opinion. All kinds of new people are interesting themselves in the question and realising . . . that a C.O. is not a man who is merely desirous of saving his own skin." She added that, while some people outside the C.O. movement were trying to get first-division treatment for absolutists, even government officials now admitted that this would not meet the case of the real C.O. On the other hand, she said, the "chief opponent of the proposal made in May" was apparently softening his attitude toward the administrative release of all genuine conscientious objectors.[43]

41. CAB 24/23/1799.
42. For Milner's memo, see CAB 24/24/1833; for Derby's, CAB 24/27/2167.
43. "Summary of News for Prisoners," September–October 1917, FSC Files, FHL. The "chief opponent" of whom Marshall spoke would seem to have been Derby or Childs, probably the former since Rae insists that Childs never relinquished his view that the release of absolutists would spell disaster for the army; *Conscience and Politics,* pp. 123, 213–14. Also see Russell to R. W. Crammer, 3 September 1917, and to C. H. Norman, 17 September 1917, BRA. Crammer wrote to Russell asking about the validity of "all kinds of stories . . . to the effect that Mrs. Hobhouse has twice interviewed the King and that the only obstacle to the release of the absolutists is Lord Derby's opposition"; 14 October 1917, BRA.

Public opinion also seemed to be softening. Certainly *The Times*, which had previously taken a hard line on C.O.s, had come round a long way, as a lead article of 25 October illustrated.

When a man has deliberately refused to avail himself of two alternative ways of escape from prison labour; when he has more than once, of his own deliberate choice, gone back to gaol; when he shows himself resolute to go back again and again rather than submit to that military service against which he asserts that his conscience raises for him an insuperable barrier—when he thus proves repeatedly his readiness to suffer for what he proclaims to be his beliefs, is it either justifiable or politic to go on with the punishment?

Russell greeted *The Times* as "Saul among the Prophets" and joyously reflected on the fact that even the Northcliffe press now admitted that the persecution of minorities was not the most efficient way to conduct a war.[44] When *The Times*'s declaration was followed by memorials from a group of prominent Anglican churchmen and from the Howard Association asking for the release of genuine C.O.s, J. A. Hobson wrote to *The Tribunal* expressing his satisfaction that

—Their understanding
Begins to swell; the approaching tide
Will shortly fill the reasonable shores
That now lie foul and muddy.[45]

Certainly, as Russell noted, Mrs. Hobhouse's intervention had been decisive in focusing public attention on the plight of the absolutists. Eventually, in addition to securing Milner's support, she was able to enlist the services of Jan Smuts and, amazingly, of Lord Curzon.[46] But Margaret

44. *Trib.*, 1 November 1917. Rae, *Conscience and Politics*, pp. 219-20, believes that the article was placed in *The Times* by Milner in cooperation with its editor Geoffrey Dawson while Lord Northcliffe was in the United States.

45. See *Daily News*, 29 October 1917, for a letter from fourteen Anglican leaders and *Trib.*, 8 November 1917, for a reprint of a memorial on C.O. prisoners from the Howard Association. Hobson's lines are from *The Tempest*.

46. *Trib.*, 15 November 1917, and Smuts to M. Hobhouse, 3 July 1917, in *Selections from the Smuts Papers*, ed. W. K. Hancock and Jean Van Der Poel, 4 vols. (Cambridge, 1966), 3:535. Also see Rae, *Conscience and Politics*, pp. 220-25.

Hobhouse could not accomplish miracles. The final result of all her exertions and those of her "lobby" was a compromise treaty, not complete victory. Under strong prodding from Milner and Curzon, the War Office agreed to a major concession with regard to the absolutists: any C.O. prisoner acknowledged by a prison doctor to be medically unfit would be released and transferred to the army reserve. This policy was announced in the House of Lords by Curzon on 4 December.[47] Four days later Stephen Hobhouse was released from Exeter prison. He had been preceded into the free world by Allen, who was in such a precarious state of health that he was simply transferred from Winchester prison hospital to a nursing home. Allen and Hobhouse were among the first of over three hundred medically unfit men released during the next eighteen months.[48] Allen, however, believed that the government was merely attempting to relieve itself of responsibility for a group of half-dead C.O.s by resurrecting the old "Cat and Mouse" (Prisoners Temporarily Discharged for Ill-Health) Act of 1913. As he told Russell shortly after his release: "You are not right in saying in this [week's] *Tribunal* that Hobhouse and I are both released under the New Army Reserve scheme. He is, I am a 'mouse.' "[49]

Another concession announced by Curzon gave conscientious objectors a second opportunity to establish their right to absolute exemption. On 2 January 1918 the local government board sent out a circular to all tribunals noting that the Army Council had been informed that there were men serving in the army who would have been given absolute exemption if their tribunals had been aware of their power to grant such exemption. If such cases existed in the records of any tribunal, the local government board wished to be so informed.[50] The NCF hoped that this circular would "reopen a large number of cases," but it was unrealistic to sup-

47. 5 H.L., 27:56, 4 December 1917. Also see 5 H.L., 26:1011, 14 November 1917.

48. *Trib.*, 6 and 13 December 1917, and Stephen Hobhouse, *Autobiography* (Boston, 1952), p. 171. *Trib.*, 8 January 1920, lists 333 released under this scheme, and *NCF Souvenir*, p. 37, says 334. The government never published a figure.

49. Allen to Russell, 17 December 1917, BRA.

50. R. 168, LGB circular, 2 January 1918.

Clifford Allen just after his release from prison in 1918. (Courtesy Allen Papers, University of South Carolina)

pose that tribunals at any level would readily admit their past errors. Indeed, both the local government board and the Scottish office reported that they had discovered no case of a man denied absolute exemption through a tribunal's ignorance of its power to grant such exemption.[51]

The government's response seemed generous to the influential people involved in the Hobhouse case, but the uneven application of the release policy and the failure to admit possible errors in withholding absolute exemption raise serious questions about the policy's apparent magnanimity. First, while it is obvious that the government reacted positively to the complaints of prominent people and of organs of opinion, it is questionable whether, in the light of hostile public feelings toward C.O.s, it was willing to respond to the suffering of unknown men without influence. Many absolutists, apparently as ill or even more ill than Hobhouse, remained in prison until after the war had ended.[52] But most damning of all is the excellent case Rae has made for the view that the War Office's agreement to release some medically unfit C.O.s was directly connected with the government's acceptance of an amendment to the Representation of the People Act (1918) that disqualified conscientious objectors from voting in local or parliamentary elections for five years. Such a proposal had long been advocated by Tory back-benchers and by the popular press, but the government had resisted the idea until the debate over the fate of the absolutists.[53]

In any case, the situation of the majority of absolutists, who had been proclaimed "fit" and were thus still in prison, changed very little. The last concession allowed by the government was that absolutists who had served twelve months' imprisonment would receive certain privileges under the so-called Churchill Rule (Prison Rule 243A), which had orig-

51. Catherine Marshall, NCF Acting Hon. Sec., to Friends, 10 January 1918, FSC Correspondence, 1917, FHL, and "Forty-seventh Annual Report of the LGB, 1917–1918," (Cd. 9157), pt. 4, p. 51.
52. See speech by Joseph King accusing the government of favoritism in the Hobhouse case; 5 H.C., 103:1597, 28 February 1918. Also see *Trib.*, 27 December 1917 and 3, 17, and 31 January 1918.
53. See Rae, *Conscience and Politics*, pp. 222–26, and 5 H.C., 99:1135–52, 20 November 1917.

inally been devised for imprisoned suffragettes. Probably the most important concession allowed C.O.s two exercise periods a day during which they were permitted to talk. In addition, a man could have his own books ("except those bearing on current events"), could write and receive a letter once a fortnight, and could have one visit a month in a private room, if one were available.[54]

While these policies were certainly an improvement, their value was limited by the manner in which they were carried out. The fortnightly letter, for instance, could only be half as long as the former monthly one, and the monthly visit was at first limited to fifteen minutes instead of the half-hour previously allowed. Also there was no improvement in the C.O.s' diet, and they were still denied any kind of writing materials. Russell attacked the "farcial inadequacy" of the new privileges that, in his opinion, were given not to do justice to conscientious objectors but to quiet government critics. He repeated the NCF's long-standing demand for absolute exemption and called on all friends of the fellowship to continue their protests with unstinting vigor.[55]

At Maidstone prison, seven C.O.s, including Sanders, refused to recognize any amelioration of conditions because they, like Russell, were convinced that the so-called privileges were merely a subterfuge.[56] Others accepted the concessions for the sake of their mental balance but noted that in effect the improvements were a tacit admission by the government that C.O.s had been unjustly imprisoned. The NCF national committee took the position that, for health's sake, the concessions should not be refused unless they involved a compromise of principle. In its public pronouncements on the subject, however, the NCF maintained that the concessions were a pittance that merely added insult to injury. What the fellowship's leaders most feared was that the commitment of those who had previously signed resolutions

54. See 5 H.L., 26:1011, 14 November 1917, and 5 H.L., 27:54–56, 4 December 1917.
55. "The Government's 'Concessions,'" *Trib.*, 13 December 1917. Also see Marshall's long letter in *Trib.*, 3 January 1918, criticizing the concessions as "a sham," and Allen ms., chap. 3, p. 21, CAP.
56. Sanders, "My Experiences," p. 13, CAP.

of protest would weaken under the new conditions. The NCF begged them not to be "tempted to think that 'persecution with kid gloves' ceases to be persecution."[57]

One of those who did not relent in her struggle on behalf of the absolutists was Margaret Hobhouse. Members of the cabinet who had assisted her in obtaining her son's release thereafter seemed to lose interest in the problem,[58] but no one could accuse her of flagging in her efforts. A year after Stephen had been set free, she wrote to Murray: "One feels so horribly helpless to do anything for these most unfortunate men, and they remain a kind of deadweight on my conscience since I was able to get my own son out a year ago."[59] When Margaret Hobhouse died in 1921, all the absolutists had long since been released, but in the interval some of them decided that becoming sick unto death was not the most efficacious way to be restored to freedom. Their eventual revolt forms a last chapter in the dreary tale of the absolutist objectors to the First World War.[60]

57. *Trib.*, 14 and 28 February 1918.
58. Rae, *Conscience and Politics*, p. 227.
59. M. Hobhouse to G. Murray, 14 January 1919, Murray Papers, 57. Also see Mrs. Hobhouse to Murray, 30 January and 8 February 1918, Murray Papers, 57.
60. See Chap. 12.

10

Trouble among the Peacemakers: The NCF and the FSC

Diverging Roads to Peace

One of *Punch*'s wartime cartoons depicts two men fighting in the street, causing a spectator to remark: "They ought to be at the Front. That's the sort they want there." To which another replies: "They won't go, sir. They're Conscientious Objectors."[1] In thus announcing his disdain for "conchies" and other peace cranks, "Mr. Punch" had accidentally stumbled on a grim reality for British pacifists—because of personal and ideological difficulties, opponents of the Great War spent considerable time squabbling among themselves.

From the summer of 1915 until mid-1916 the No-Conscription Fellowship (NCF) and Friends Service Committee (FSC) worked closely and harmoniously in common cause. Communications between the two organizations reveal a genuine amiability and sense of camaraderie. In his report to the London Yearly Meeting of May 1916, FSC chairman Robert O. Mennell expressed "a sense of debtedness to Clifford Allen . . . and to his Committee of the No-Conscription Fellowship for their inspiring leadership and their devoted work. The Cause of Peace had . . . no braver or truer advocates. . . . It had been a great privilege to stand with them and to catch something of the infection of their immense energy."[2] Such sincerely given praise further strengthened the relationship between the two organizations and helped the NCF to obtain substantial contributions from wealthy Quakers for its expanding anticonscription activities.[3]

---

1. *Punch*, 2 February 1916, p. 81.
2. "R. O. Mennell's Observations in Introducing FSC Report to Yearly Meeting, May 1916," R. O. Mennell Papers, FSC Files, FHL.
3. For example, see Hubert Peet to R. O. Mennell, 28 March 1916, and R. O. Mennell to Sir James Reckitt, 29 March 1916, Hubert W. Peet Papers, FSC Files, FHL.

This early solidarity, blooming under the pressure of public hostility and government harassment, made the two organizations seem more alike than they were. From its inception, the FSC, unlike the NCF, was united by the fundamental religious commitment of its members and the long-standing pacifist tradition of their society. The FSC had only twenty original members and, though it later expanded to include women as well as men, it remained very small. On the other hand, the NCF had not only to fashion principles that a large and diverse membership might adhere to but even had to create the sense of fellowship that would make that adherence possible. Thus, NCF policies could never be fixed and constant. They had to evolve gradually in response to changing circumstances and intermittent crises. Although it was not apparent in the early months of the struggle against the war, the controversies that damaged the British peace movement had their roots in these essential differences.

During the latter months of 1916, while the dispute over alternative service still raged within the fellowship,[4] the seeds of an even more damaging quarrel between the NCF and its Quaker ally were being planted. Since the imprisonment of the first conscientious objectors, Catherine E. Marshall and her associates' political committee had set out to detect and expose any ill-treatment of C.O.s by the authorities. When military personnel were disciplined for brutality or for other illegal actions as a result of NCF publicity, the patriotic press depicted these incidents as examples of "conchies" squealing to obtain special treatment.[5]

In fact, some of the absolutists involved resented attempts by the NCF, or anybody else, to obtain their release or to mitigate their punishment as long as the war continued. As one of them said in a rather brutal letter to his mother: "I wish no sort of preference or privilege. . . . I am not trying to 'get out' of anything, and . . . rather than make any compromise I shall repudiate the efforts of those nearest and dearest to me." Another supporter of the NCF, the feminist leader Maude Royden, told Marshall that she felt

4. See Chap. 8.
5. See, for example, *Daily Express*, 10 April 1916; *Evening Standard*, 23 March 1916; and *Daily Sketch*, 14 April 1916.

horribly uneasy about your whole method of campaign. It seems to me . . . just like the old militant [suffragette] plan of creating impossible situations and forcing persecutions, and then making a fearful uproar about it. And this plan, in our case, has the enormous disadvantage of being compared with the sacrifices made by the soldiers. . . . I do most deeply disagree with the line that the NCF has taken. It seems to me that if anything *can* destroy the effect of persecution and suffering of the C.O.s, it is advertising and demonstrating about it. After all, the army, as a whole, doesn't demonstrate and the contrast is too glaring.[6]

Though Marshall always emphasized that NCF protests about the mistreatment of conscientious objectors as well as its negotiations with government officials were undertaken solely to protect C.O.s from illegal brutality, the FSC, like Royden, was highly sensitive to criticism about special considerations being shown to imprisoned war resisters. In their view, once British militarism had succeeded in establishing its ultimate weapon of conscription, there were only three effective means of continuing war resistance: refusing to acquiesce in any activity that might advance the war effort, engaging in ceaseless antiwar propaganda to persuade the public of the necessity for peace, and, finally, suffering in prison as silent but willing witnesses to the destructive immorality of war. Only such an uncompromising approach could, they believed, preserve a "true" pacifist movement.

By the summer of 1916 the FSC, which had earlier contributed funds to support Marshall's work,[7] was becoming fearful that the public might conclude, however inaccurately, that conscientious objectors, including Friends, cared more about their personal convenience than about witnessing their pacifist faith. Furthermore, the FSC had been informed by a Quaker M.P. that the War Office was making "a strenuous effort to discriminate between 'political agitators' and real C.O.s."[8] Always chary of "being identified . . . with

6. Scott Duckers to his mother, quoted in Miles Malleson, *The Out-and-Outer* (London, [1916]), p. 9, and A. M[aude] R[oyden] to C. Marshall, 24 April 1916, BRA.

7. Notes on Committee Meeting, 4 May 1916, and Summary of FSC Meeting, 8 June 1916, FSC *Minutes* 1 (June 1915–July 1916): 73, 78, 86, and Mennell to Marshall, 9 May 1916, Mennell Papers.

8. The M.P. was T. E. Harvey. See Edith Ellis to R. O. Mennell, 18 June

any political agitation,"[9] FSC leaders believed that Marshall's activities were providing the War Office with a prime example of "political" pacifism and thus with an opportunity for differentiating between "true" (religious) pacifists and mere political objectors. They did not believe that the pacifist movement should attempt to obtain exemptions for C.O.s, to secure their release from custody, or to prosecute their tormentors. Instead, they felt that the movement's sole effort should be aimed at trying to stop the war. For these reasons, they wanted Marshall's activities to be severely restricted, and, for a time, they got their way.

Led by Barry Brown and John P. Fletcher, the Quaker faction convinced the NCF national committee that Marshall's department should limit itself to the collection and dissemination of unadorned facts about the treatment of war resisters. This limitation meant, of course, that Marshall should suspend negotiations aimed at improving conditions for C.O.s, and so forth. To help salve any wounds inflicted by the virtual suspension of Marshall's political work, the FSC announced its determination "to help the NCF in any manner possible." It immediately put this promise into effect by releasing its secretary, Hubert W. Peet, with pay, to help Marshall to organize and operate an expanded but nonpolitical press department that would simply report the "pilgrim's progress" of each arrested conscientious objector.[10]

Marshall was deeply chagrined that "the minority," as she called them, should dismiss the bulk of her labor as useless to the real cause of peace. As she told Bertrand Russell at the time, she was willing to turn over her political and parliamentary tasks to the Quakers. But, while they wanted to formulate policy, they did not, it seemed, want to take charge of the work that needed to be done. "I think," she continued, "Mr. Barratt Brown ought to throw up everything else and be prepared to do this [work]. . . . I was dismayed at the irresponsibility of forcing on a Committee a policy which its executive members believed to be unwork-

---

1916, Mennell Papers. Also see memorandum on "Conscientious Objectors," 1 June 1916, Kitchener Papers, WO 30/57/74, WS/73, PRO.

9. Mennell to Marshall, 24 February 1916, Mennell Papers.

10. Notes on Meeting of Service Committee, 6 July 1916, FSC *Minutes,* 1 : 100, FHL.

able and being content to leave it there instead of themselves shouldering executive responsibility."[11]

The tone of Marshall's letter would seem to indicate that at least some members of the NCF national committee questioned the wisdom of the FSC's view. But if so, this doubt was not reflected in the fellowship's public pronouncements. Two articles by NCF chairman Clifford Allen, for example, emphasized that it would be "almost indecent" to use the group's time and talents chiefly to advertise "the trifling sufferings" of C.O.s; the NCF's dedication to peace was more important. With the fellowship's internal structure firmly established and provisions made for the dependents of its persecuted members, the chairman believed that the time was ripe for members to reassert their positive sense of citizenship by redoubling their efforts to obtain peace.[12]

In its last meeting before the majority of its members were imprisoned for their "Repeal the Act" conviction, the national committee issued "An Urgent Call to Members." This message began by noting that more than a few of the sixteen hundred NCF members in custody had written to say, "do not think of me. Think of the millions suffering by the war." With this in mind, the national committee felt that "the time has come to throw the full weight of the NCF into active, organized participation in the Peace movement." The letter went on to recommend that each NCF branch appoint a propaganda secretary and establish contact with all other organizations working for peace. "Now and henceforth," the message concluded, "our lives must be devoted to an impassioned service for Peace."[13]

All that had transpired would seem to indicate that the FSC's view had been officially adopted as NCF policy, but in fact the Quaker faction's triumph was less than complete. While the NCF national committee accepted the primacy of the peace campaign, they would not accept its singularity. Because of the diversity of opinion within the fellowship and its constant assertion of the necessity for liberty of con-

11. Marshall to Russell, 12 July 1916, BRA. Also see Marshall to Russell, 7 July [1916], BRA.

12. *Trib.*, 13 and 20 July 1916, and Clifford Allen, "The Conscientious Objector's Struggle: A History of the No-Conscription Fellowship," *Labour Leader*, 20 July 1916.

13. *Trib.*, 20 July 1916. Also see NCF national committee, "Suggested circular to members on Peace Propaganda," undated, BRA.

science, a majority of the committee also voted for a separate resolution that acknowledged the fellowship's continued responsibility to support all conscientious objectors in their attempts to secure "those forms of exemption they can conscientiously accept."[14] As soon as this reservation was announced, Fletcher resigned from the NCF national committee because he was convinced that the only legitimate activity of any pacifist organization was "to awaken the sleeping soul and conscience of the nation." If superficial attempts to ease the burdens of persecuted C.O.s also eased the public conscience, then, in Fletcher's view, these attempts were actually harmful to real pacifism.[15]

The national committee accepted Fletcher's resignation with regret but set out to prove that the NCF could effectively work for peace as well as for the well-being of individual conscientious objectors. A national peace-campaign department was established to coordinate propaganda activities within the NCF and to establish liaisons with other pacifist groups. Instructions and suggestions poured out of the central office, reminding branches that

> none of our other work on behalf of prisoners will be worth-while unless we also make a sustained effort to stimulate the desire for Peace. . . . It is in the service of Peace that our members have faced what they have faced, and there is not a man in prison cell or guard-room who is not far more concerned about securing the realization of his principles than the release of himself.[16]

In the weeks that followed *The Tribunal* featured editorials and articles emphasizing that the fellowship's real work was stamping out the "slavery of militarism."[17]

14. *Trib.*, 20 July and 3 August 1916. Also see A. Fenner Brockway, "The Policy of the NCF," *Trib.*, 16 November 1916.

15. *Trib.*, 3 August 1916. Also see "The NCF," *Ploughshare* 1 (November 1916): 323, and Hubert W. Peet, "Alternative and 'National' Service," *Ploughshare* 2 (June 1917): 142–43.

16. NCF, *Branch Activities* (Instructions to Branches from Political Committee), 20 July 1916, and NCF national committee to members, 4 September 1916, FSC Files, FHL. Also see *Trib.*, 20 July 1916, and *The No-Conscription Fellowship: A Record of Its Activities* (London, 1916), p. 8.

17. For example, "The National Religion," *Trib.*, 26 October 1916. Also see A. Fenner Brockway, "The Principles of the NCF," *Trib.*, 19 October 1916, and other Brockway articles, *Trib.*, 5 October and 23 November 1916.

But despite a continuous barrage of exhortations, cajolery, and even harassment from national headquarters, the peace campaign created little enthusiasm. In early September a letter from the political committee noted that local branches were lagging badly on the peace campaign. Few of them had taken even "the most urgent preliminary step" of convening a joint conference of peace organizations in their areas. Three months later J. A. Harrop, secretary of the organization department, scolded branch secretaries because only two branches had reported on their local peace-campaign activities.[18]

Reasons for the dismal failure of the much-vaunted peace campaign are not difficult to discern. As more and more members of the fellowship were dragged off to prison to undergo a cruelly demoralizing demonstration of state power, the thoughts of the majority increasingly concentrated not on how their suffering might help end the war but on the possibility of their obtaining relief or, if possible, release from their ordeal. These men, many of whom were newly drawn to pacifism, saw the NCF as their one link with the free world, their best hope for succor. Therefore, they and their relatives and friends on the outside wanted the fellowship to pursue a vigorous policy of agitation on behalf of the prisoners. Those charged with directing NCF policy felt constrained to respond to the desires of the members. By the late summer of 1916 Marshall had fully resumed the political work that had momentarily slackened under pressure from the FSC.[19] As a result, the FSC again protested that in permitting such activity the NCF was abandoning "the witness for Peace which . . . [it] had come into existence to bear" and was becoming merely a "society for prevention of cruelty to C.O.s."[20] FSC representatives on the NCF na-

---

18. Hon. Sec. of Political Committee to Branch Secretaries, 5 September 1916, and J. A. Harrop to Branch Secretaries, 6 December 1916, FSC Files, FHL. Also see Harrop to Branch Secretaries, 1 November 1916, FSC Files, FHL.

19. By late. September 1916 the peace-campaign department had become the organization and propaganda department. See Marshall to NCF Branch Secretaries, 21 September 1916, FSC Files, FHL.

20. FSC Records, "Notes of Committee Meeting," 2 November 1916, 2: 16; R. O. Mennell to Daisy Harland, 25 October 1916; and Peet to Mennell, 1 November 1916, Mennell Papers.

tional committee wanted some clarification. Was the fellowship going to lead the peace movement or degenerate into a prisoners' aid society?

The Pacifists' Dilemma

The FSC's protests came at a time when many NCF leaders were already gravely concerned about losing touch with the fellowship's rank and file. The Quakers and their allies on the national committee had advocated the rejection of the Home Office scheme and the primacy of the peace campaign, but these directives obviously did not reflect the views of most NCF members. Indeed, the strongest remaining link between national headquarters and local branches seemed to be the work being done on behalf of the conscientious objectors in custody—just the sort of activity the FSC faction was questioning. There was, then, a growing feeling that Quaker influence had caused the NCF to adopt policies that endangered the future of the organization. Clearly, some means had to be found to restore confidence in the fellowship's leaders and to establish priorities in keeping with the views of the majority. But how was this to be done without an open confrontation that would further weaken the peace movement?

One way of resolving this dilemma might be to hold another national convention, but, since so many NCF members were already in custody, such an event might not be well attended and, given the public mood, might even be dangerous. In these circumstances, NCF leaders decided that the best hope for reviving a spirit of unity in the fellowship was to hold a series of divisional conventions in various parts of the country. These conventions were asked to consider several vital questions that troubled the organization and to select a new national committee that would better represent local opinion. This new committee was to include one individual elected from each of the nine NCF regional divisions, in addition to six "national" members elected at large. During this time, a referendum was also held to test the opinions of the entire membership on the fellowship's future direction.[21]

21. NCF national committee to Divisional and Branch Secretaries, 4 Oc-

In the end, these activities proved to be of little help in shaping NCF policy. The results of both the conventions and the national referendum were so indecisive or incomplete that the retiring national committee decided to let the newly elected committee "lay down the policy to be pursued in the future." Nothing was effectively resolved, and the controversy over priorities was left smoldering.[22] In early December 1916, for example, when FSC chairman Mennell stated that "the aim of the FSC has been to create a real and strengthening sense of fellowship *among those who, by their uncompromising fidelity, in action as well as in word, are bearing witness to the Truth* [my italics]," his remarks did not appear calculated to strike a balance between opposing views.[23] Indeed, Mennell's remarks ran counter to a gradual but perceptible shift within the NCF's leadership back to the view that no conscientious objector, whether he was in prison or in a Home Office camp, could be ignored and that, in fact, efforts to secure his release or to mitigate his punishment were an integral part of the fellowship's protest against militarism and the war.

Allen, writing from a military guardroom after the sobering experience of a prison term, openly attacked the idea of making the NCF an extension of the Society of Friends. To abandon any group of conscientious objectors to their fate, he said, was the surest way to destroy the unity of the organization. It was foolish to imagine that all C.O.s had an equal ability to withstand the rigors of imprisonment. Once the men in prison realized that they were on their own, the weaker ones would take alternative service, the stronger ones would become demoralized, the NCF would begin to break apart, and there would still be no real hope of bringing peace.[24]

Allen felt that the NCF had an important contribution to make to peace propaganda; it consisted, he said, of its members "being" C.O.s. Their suffering was a practical demonstration of pacifist ideals, and the NCF was fulfilling a special need by bringing that demonstration to the public's atten-

---

tober 1916; NCF circular letter, 10 October 1916, FSC Files, FHL; and *Trib.*, 26 October 1916.

22. *Trib.*, 16 November 1916.

23. Robert O. Mennell, FSC Report, 1 December 1916, Mennell Papers.

24. Allen to Catherine Marshall, 23 November 1916, CAP.

tion. Just before he began serving his second sentence, Allen noted in *The Tribunal* that the government "will not dread the No-Conscription Fellowship . . . if we are merely carrying on peace propaganda." The government's weak spot was not in waging the war but in mistreating conscientious objectors. Some members, Allen concluded, seemed to have the idea that the NCF's success should be measured by the number of men who were jailed. His idea of resistance, however, was not to "take the consequences" but to destroy conscription, and its destruction was scarcely aided by passive acquiescence in its evil results.[25] Allen felt so strongly about this matter that he advised Marshall to return to her work in the women's movement if the Quaker faction gained the upper hand.[26]

When the newly elected NCF national committee, headed by Russell as acting chairman,[27] took office in 1917, its FSC members apparently believed that the time had come for a definitive resolution of the question of priorities. At the first meeting of the new committee, Brown moved "that the Fellowship make a practice of giving full publicity . . . to the witness of its members, but make no efforts, direct or indirect, to alleviate their conditions or obtain for them exemptions of any kind, devoting its energies solely to arousing the public conscience on war and conscription."[28] The resolution's defeat by eight votes to three was probably a fairly accurate reflection of NCF opinion in general. Certainly, the vote expressed Russell's conviction that no work should take priority over "a vigorous agitation" on behalf of the absolutists who still languished in prison. Russell felt that this effort was especially important because the public had been led to believe that the Home Office scheme had all but solved the C.O. problem.[29]

25. Ibid.; *Trib.,* 14 December 1916; and Allen ms., chap. 3a, p. 29, CAP.

26. "Notes on Proposed Change in NCF Policy," 9 November 1916; Allen to Marshall, 28 November 1916; and Allen's notes on Barry Brown's suggestions on policy, CAP.

27. Most of the members of the sitting committee were substitutes elected to represent members who had been imprisoned. Lists of the newly elected national committee members and their substitutes are given in *Trib.,* 18 January 1917.

28. Reprinted in *Trib.,* 21 June 1917.

29. *Trib.,* 1 February 1917. Also see *Trib.,* 1 March 1917, in which Russell discussed a special propaganda committee that was to work on behalf of imprisoned objectors.

The defeat of Brown's resolution did not silence the FSC Quakers' attacks on what they considered to be a serious distortion of the NCF's original principles. Why, asked one letter to *The Tribunal,* should absolutists be singled out as objects of pity when conditions for men at the front were far more pitiable and morally abhorrent? Absolutists, said the writer, should be envied rather than pitied for they were sustained by a "spiritual strength which keeps them free and happy, even in gaol, and makes persecution ridiculous." Several prisoners, including Walter H. Ayles and Stephen Hobhouse, wrote to ask that members not waste time and energy on attempting to help them—"think not of us, but work for peace."[30]

In defending the national committee's policy, Russell pointed out that, while the liberation of all soldiers was the ultimate goal and could only be reached by working for peace, some of the most sincere and articulate antiwar people were still in prison. Demanding their exemption or release to work for peace was not acquiescing in the war any more than signing a petition for the commutation of a public hanging was acquiescing in capital punishment. Even apart from the damage done to the men themselves and to the peace movement through their loss, Russell noted, members should also remember the damage to the community whose conscience had to be awakened if the "sad cruelties" of persecution were to be stopped.[31]

Russell received considerable support. Fenner Brockway wrote from military detention to say that, while most C.O.s were more concerned with peace than with being set free, there were, nevertheless, few men in prison who would not prefer to be free. The physical and mental strain of prison life was reason enough to aid objectors. Brockway also repeated Allen's earlier warning that the isolation of prison could lead to a sense of fanciful contentment that was very close to spiritual death. Another correspondent noted that it was fine for Ayles, Hobhouse, and company to say, "Do not agitate for me!" But it was presumptuous of them to say, "Do not agitate for anybody!" Being an absolutist was difficult enough, he said, without the added burden of knowing that

---

30. See letters of S. V. Bracher and Walter Ayles, 15 March 1917, and A. B. Brown and S. Hobhouse, 22 March 1917, *Trib.*
31. "The Evils of Persecution," *Trib.,* 29 March 1917.

you were left entirely on your own.[32] Russell also received a personal letter from the wife of an absolutist thanking him for his attempts to expose the "evils of persecution" whose terrible effects she could see working on her husband. "I am glad," she concluded, "that the NCF has your restrained and healthy mind to guide it through the present troubled times."[33]

Although the policy of mixing peace propaganda with open support for every variety of war resister had apparently won the day within the NCF, the FSC Quakers refused to accept it. By remaining steadfast in the view that pacifists should take no official action on behalf of imprisoned C.O.s, the FSC not only disrupted relations with the NCF but troubled its own house as well. While most imprisoned Quakers were ready to repudiate any attempts to alleviate their situation,[34] not all Friends in or out of prison supported this view. One who did not was Edward Grubb who from the first had warned against Friends' attempting to prescribe a standard for all war resisters.[35] Grubb felt that the FSC's position partially repudiated the Society of Friends' traditional defense of liberty of conscience. In March 1917, when Grubb received a letter from a young Quaker prisoner decrying the FSC's refusal to help absolutists, he decided to use the occasion to press for a modification of FSC policy. Grubb gave the letter to the FSC secretary, Edith Ellis, adding his own strong endorsement of its contents.[36] Thus challenged by co-religionists, the FSC agreed to reconsider its stand, but the ensuing discussion concluded with a resolution declaring that it was "not the function of any pacifist body to agitate for the release of conscientious objectors till the public de-

32. Brockway and "Regular Reader" to *Trib.*, 29 March 1917. For other letters supporting Russell and the national committee, see *Trib.*, 29 March, 5 April, and 7 June 1917.

33. "Wife of a C.O." to Russell, 4 April 1917, BRA.

34. See, for example, H. Peet to E. Ellis, 28 February 1917, Edith Ellis Papers, FSC Files, FHL. Also see Russell Frayling to E. Ellis, 27 February 1917, Ellis Papers, and E. Ellis to E. Grubb, 21 March 1917, FSC General Correspondence, 1916–1917, FHL.

35. See Edward Grubb, "Suffering for Conscience Sake," *The Friend* 56 (28 April 1916): 284–85.

36. Wilfred Hinde to Grubb (copy), 11 March 1917, FSC *Minutes*, 2: 44, FHL, and Grubb to E. Ellis, 14, 17, and 22 March 1917, FSC General Correspondence, 1916–1917, FHL.

sires it."[37] This decision did not, however, end the controversy within the society. Indeed, Friends who opposed the FSC position could and did point to the historical precedent of a similar debate in 1675. At that time, a Quaker conference on persecution had advised Friends "to take such courses for relief and ease to the oppressed as may not be prejudicial to Truth's testimony."[38] In this instance, the FSC (and the influential Meeting for Sufferings, which supported the FSC's policy) apparently interpreted "Truth's testimony" as the silent acceptance of continued imprisonment until the war could be ended or until public opinion spontaneously demanded the release of C.O. prisoners.[39]

At first, the FSC's hard-line position had little effect on the NCF's day-to-day activities. The fellowship continued to spend the bulk of its time, energy, and money on exposing conditions in prisons and Home Office camps and on attempting to alleviate them or to secure the release of those who were being victimized. However, soon after the FSC had reasserted its adherence to the no-protest principle, Brown, the most prominent Quaker representative on the NCF national committee, resigned his office. Brown said that he felt compelled to step down because the fellowship's policy was "quite opposed to my conscience and my judgment," moving, as he believed, "from step to step along . . . a downward path."[40] Allen, then in military custody, was disappointed by Brown's action and correctly predicted that it would widen the fissure between the two organizations. Nevertheless, he believed that the NCF had to maintain its

37. Notes on FSC meeting, 29 March 1917, FSC *Minutes*, 2: 48, FHL.

38. Quoted in William Charles Braithwaite, *The Second Period of Quakerism* (London, 1919), pp. 283–84. For examples of protests, see James Crawshaw to E. Ellis, 6 June 1917, FSC General Correspondence, 1917, FHL. I must express my thanks to Edward Milligan, librarian to Friends House, for making me aware of this precedent.

39. See notes of FSC meetings, 3 May and 6 September 1917, FSC *Minutes*, 2: 50, 76, FHL, and *Proceedings of the Meeting for Sufferings, Summary, 1917–18* (London, 1921), p. 45. The Meeting for Sufferings was established in 1675 "to have the oversight of all cases of suffering, whether by persecution or misfortune"; from Margaret E. Hirst, *The Quakers in Peace and War* (London, 1923), p. 64n.

40. Brown to Allen and Brown to Marshall, 23 May 1917, CEMP (microfilm). Also see Brown's letter of resignation, dated 2 June 1917, in *Trib.*, 21 June 1917.

stand for the sake of its imprisoned members and because of its distinctive duty "to stress . . . the struggle for liberty and therefore first and foremost for liberty of conscience."[41]

Brown had taken pains to stress that his resignation was a personal decision and was not intended to influence other members of the Society of Friends. Soon, however, other FSC Quakers began reappraising their relationship to the fellowship. Although FSC officials acknowledged that "the Government would be delighted if Friends withdrew their support from the NCF," apparently this was exactly what a number of them were considering.[42] The major question at issue once again concerned Marshall's activities.

For some time, the FSC and individual Friends had been providing support for the COIB, a sort of central repository for all information on C.O.s. Supposedly, the COIB was an independent organization but, in fact, it was simply a partially disguised version of the NCF record office and was still operated by NCF personnel. Early in 1917 a report from Marshall on the functions of the COIB made many in the FSC suspect that she was mixing the COIB's business and its funds with her continuing political work for the fellowship.[43] In other words, Marshall was using funds earmarked for information gathering and record keeping for projects that the FSC had specifically disavowed. Particularly upsetting was Marshall's liaison with the director of personal services at the War Office, General Childs, for the purpose of protecting C.O.s from illegal treatment by army personnel. Furthermore, they felt that Marshall's concentration on negotiating with officials and on aiding prisoners had contributed to a serious breakdown in the record-keeping system.[44]

41. Allen to Marshall, 17 June 1917, BRA.

42. E. Ellis to Brown, 31 May and 4 June 1917, and E. Ellis to Harrison Barrow, 31 May 1917, FSC General Correspondence, 1917, FHL.

43. Marshall's report was submitted to and accepted by the Joint Advisory Council on 23 February 1917. A separate copy was sent to the FSC on 1 March 1917; the controversy began when its executive committee refused to endorse the report. See Marshall to Dr. [Henrietta] Thomas, 1 March 1917, and handwritten notes on "Conscientious Objectors Information Bureau and the Visitation and Information Department," FSC Files, FHL.

44. One FSC member (probably Brown) wrote that the "official unofficial touch with the Government . . . and the NCF . . . has now become practically the same as the touch between Government Departments." See

Under pressure from the FSC, the NCF national committee was, according to Brown, "quite severe" with Marshall
and "arranged to stiffen up relations" with the War Office.[45]
FSC leaders were, however, still concerned that their money
might be tainted by being used in projects that they could
not in conscience approve. Therefore, during the latter
months of 1917, with most of their national officers in
prison and government harassment of the peace movement
intensifying, the NCF and the FSC were engaged in an
exhaustive round of meetings, investigations, and reports to
decide how the keeping of records could conform to the
ideological requirements of both groups.[46]

While this tedious process was being carried on, donations
to the NCF by FSC members and other Friends, which had
formerly been very generous, were drying up. In early June
NCF treasurer Grubb wrote to Ellis who, with her sister
Marian, had been a major contributor to the NCF, appealing
for a renewal of her support. In reply, Ellis stressed the
differences between the FSC and the NCF that needed to be
resolved before she could make a further pledge.

> We are all united in believing that militarism is wrong and
> conscription is the evil which you and we are unitedly attack-
> ing. Most of the leaders of the NCF believe that . . . [by] accept-
> ing Absolute Exemption only they are helping best in this ob-
> ject. Many of the members have accepted Conditional Exemp-
> tion feeling it right for them to undertake it and others have
> felt the same with regard to the H.O. Scheme. None of us want
> these men to go against what they feel they ought to accept. We
> however feel that an organisation founded to protest against
> conscription weakens its own position and also that protest, if
> it . . . takes on the position of intermediary between the men
> who have accepted these schemes and the Government when
> they prove to be unsatisfactory. . . . Till there is a change of

memorandum on "Matters upon which the line to be taken needs to be
more clearly defined," n.d., FSC Correspondence, 1917, and "Report of
Charles L. Leese on file of absolutists in NCF Record Office," 2 May 1917,
FSC Correspondence, 1917, FHL. Also see *Trib.*, 21 June 1917.

45. Brown to E. Ellis, 17 and 21 June 1917, FSC Correspondence, 1917,
FHL, and Notes on FSC meeting, 8 June 1917, FSC *Minutes*, 2: 57, FHL.

46. There is an immense body of material relating to problems of control
over the COIB in the FSC *Minutes*, Correspondence, and Files in FHL. For
one NCF official's view of the dispute, see E. Grubb to Bertrand Russell, 17
September 1917, BRA.

heart in the Nation regarding the bigger matter of War, we feel there is real danger of our object being obscured by action such as the NCF has thought it right to take. Believing this very strongly we cannot unite with you in some things which may seem to you unimportant details but to us they are included as part of the witness against war.[47]

In his response, Grubb admitted that some of the methods adopted by the NCF "may have been of doubtful wisdom," but he emphasized that the fellowship's financial situation was "getting serious" and that it was most difficult for him to plan ahead

when our good friends help us with lavish generosity one year and find the next year that their available supplies are otherwise engaged. . . . If you and your sister are out of sympathy with our policy so much that you do not feel it would be right to continue the support you so kindly gave us, perhaps you would let me know soon, as I must keep things going if I anyhow can.[48]

But the Ellis sisters would not be pressed,[49] and this was evidently where the matter stood until the NCF agreed to place the COIB under the actual control of the Joint Advisory Council to ensure that none of the information collected there would be used in a manner odious to the FSC.[50]

The NCF managed to find alternative means of support for carrying on its own work in its own way, but the difficulties with the FSC took their toll in time, temperament, and spirit. In September 1917 Marshall broke down completely under the strain of overwork and growing criticism.[51] Russell, who already felt temperamentally unsuited for the administrative burdens he had to bear as acting NCF chairman, was dispirited, confused, and not a little angered by the FSC's attitude. "I wish," he wrote to Ellis,

47. Grubb to Ellis, 5 June 1917, and Ellis to Grubb, 18 June 1917, FSC Correspondence, 1917, FHL.

48. Grubb to Ellis, 20 and 21 June 1917, FSC Correspondence, 1917, FHL.

49. Ellis to Grubb, 28 June 1917, FSC Correspondence, 1917, FHL.

50. The final settlement of the records question was outlined in a "Further Report to the J.A.C. by the Commission Appointed to Investigate the Work of Records," 5 September 1917, FSC Files, FHL, but it was not fully implemented until October or November 1917.

51. See Chap. 11.

I could make you feel the problem in the way I do. I think it
very likely the FSC attitude is right in dealing with Friends, but
I am sure it is not right for our membership.... To my mind, a
duty of human kindness is involved and it is essential to remember that many of our people have come with difficulty to
pacifism, through the insights of their best moments; many of
them really need friendly support, or else they would feel de-
serted. I feel we are in some way developing the cruelty of
fanaticism, which is the very spirit that supports the war.

Ellis seemed puzzled by Russell's letter, referring him to
Brown's recent assertion that the FSC had always retained
"the human touch."[52]

For all the obvious sincerity of these FSC Friends, one
cannot help concluding that, on this question, they suffered
from a fatal blind spot. Did they ever really understand the
extent of the diversity within the NCF or appreciate the vital
fact that, for the fellowship, support in time of need must
always supersede unity of belief? Probably they did not. Certainly, many of them saw every NCF policy with which they
disagreed as the abandonment of some fundamental principle of *the* pacifist faith. Allen's postwar reflections on this are
most telling.

[The Quakers] had been to a very large extent responsible for
the gradual break up of the NCF. First, they had not recog-
nised the fundamental difference in the structure and function of the Friends' Service Committee and the NCF, the
former being an ad hoc Committee with practically no democratic membership, the latter being a semi-political organisation with a constitution and branches and membership controlling the National Committee. Secondly, the FSC only included
people of one denomination, while we represented every
shade of opinion under the sun.... Our business was more
definitely to engage in a fight with Conscription than theirs,
which was more in the nature of a testimony to certain accepted and traditional opinions about war. Barry had once said
that we were a kind of Church; I believe I had been foolish
enough to say the same. But we were not, and by trying to
resemble one we had become as fanatical and harsh and for-
mulaesque as the worst of the Calvinists, and had repelled the
community as much as they had. It had been argued that we
must accept casualties in our membership, but that we must

52. Russell to Ellis, 11 September 1917, and Ellis to Russell, 22 September 1917, FSC Files, FHL.

disregard this, making sure above all things that we did not desert our principles in the minutist respect. (God knows how many principles our different groups held.) They had argued that by preserving liberty of conscience amongst ourselves and seeking the kind of conditions desired by our different groups under the different government schemes, we should not effectively fight Conscription. As a matter of fact by allowing our membership to fall aside in all directions and shift for themselves, we had thoroughly muddled public opinion, which had tended to watch the scattered groups we had left behind far more than the advance of the so-called main army, and we had left these scattered groups to be exploited by the sundry irresponsible leaders who had cropped up. Consequently, we had repelled the public, who believed us impossible harsh fanatics, we had not appreciably influenced the Conscription situation, and we had let down many of our own people, who were capable of much finer performances.[53]

During the last months of 1917 differences between the NCF and the FSC were patched up sufficiently to allow them to work together on schemes to provide care, maintenance, and rehabilitation for C.O. prisoners released from confinement as well as to establish a conscientious objectors' employment agency.[54] The relative harmony of these efforts may have been partly due to the influence of Dr. Alfred Salter, a convert to the Society of Friends, who became acting chairman of the NCF after Russell's resignation.

Still, none of the outstanding differences between the pacifist allies were effectively resolved. The FSC remained opposed to agitation on behalf of C.O. prisoners, and in December 1917, after the Meeting for Sufferings had again refused to sanction intervention on behalf of absolutists, the FSC issued a statement explaining its position in considerable detail.[55] This document failed to convince all pacifists or

53. Typed extract from Allen's diary, 1 February 1919, CAP. Also printed in Gilbert, ed., *Plough My Own Furrow*, pp. 128–29. Keith Robbins, *The Abolition of War: The "Peace Movement" in Britain, 1914–1919* (Cardiff, 1976), p. 166, takes issue with Allen's statement, noting, incorrectly, that tension between "religious" and "secular" objectors did not arise until 1918.

54. FSC *Minutes* and Files, 1918–1919, FHL, contain voluminous material on these projects. Also see *Trib.*, 10 and 24 October 1918, 23 January and 24 April 1919, 1 and 15 May 1919, and Chap. 12.

55. The letter was signed by Edith Ellis and Robert Davis and was reprinted in *The Friend*, 2 November 1917, pp. 838–39, and *Trib.*, 27 De-

even all Friends that the FSC was following the correct course. Within a few weeks J. E. Hodgkin, a former member of the FSC, wrote to express his grievous disappointment that, because of FSC influence, the Society of Friends as a body was doing little to help C.O. prisoners. As a result of Hodgkin's letter, the FSC tortuously reconsidered the question but again refused to alter its position.[56] The NCF national committee responded to this by reassuring an increasingly aggravated and restless group of C.O. prisoners that the fellowship would maintain "its un-remitting agitation for absolute exemption and unconditional release of all C.O.s in prison and Home Office Camps."[57] And it continued to do so until the war ended.

In retrospect, it is not surprising that pacifist groups of such diverse origins should experience difficulties maintaining a unified front, but to the outsider—even over a half-century later—quarrels among pacifists often seem to involve the narrowest sort of hairsplitting by people who were already too precious and self-righteous for their own good.[58] Such internecine conflicts clearly weakened an already tiny minority and, more significantly, pointed up the impossibility of a unified peace movement's surviving the war.

---

cember 1917. Also see J. P. Fletcher to Thompson Elliott (copy), 16 August 1917, FSC Correspondence, 1917, FHL. It is interesting and somewhat ironic to note that when Brown himself was finally imprisoned as a C.O. an appeal was made to the War Office on his behalf—though probably not with his agreement—by Sir Oliver Lodge, principal of Birmingham University; see Rae, *Conscience and Politics,* pp. 227, 227n.

56. FSC meetings of 28 February and 1 March 1918, FSC *Minutes,* 3: 3, FHL. For the continuing debate on the Quaker position within the NCF, see *Trib.,* 17 January, 14 and 28 February, and 21 March 1918.

57. Resolution of the NCF national committee, printed in *Trib.,* 18 April 1918.

58. For example, see Robbins, *Abolition of War,* pp. 90–92, 121–25, 217.

11

The War of Attrition

"A Cancer at the Heart"

Late in 1916 Catherine E. Marshall, who had traveled to the military camp at Newhaven to be with Clifford Allen while he awaited his second court-martial, wrote a long letter to Bertrand Russell. In it she told him, among other things, that he would "have to be interim chairman" since Barry Brown had refused the job and no other acceptable candidate was available.[1] Even though Russell had already been fined, dismissed from his job, and prohibited from traveling in certain areas—and despite the fact that he had expressed misgivings about the usefulness of his efforts[2]—he dutifully accepted this new responsibility.

Russell's decision to become chairman might be explained by his feeling that the NCF was the only sufficient outlet for his obsession with stopping the war or simply by the fact that as an unemployed academician he had nothing better to do. Probably what influenced him most, however, was the combination of genuine admiration and paternal devotion that Russell felt for the young people who belonged to the fellowship.[3] Though that initial enthusiasm unquestionably waned amid the troubles and controversies of the latter half of 1916, Russell must have been buoyed up by the expressions of respect and admiration showered on him by NCF leaders. In his last message before entering Wormwood Scrubs, Allen told Russell: "I want you to know how grateful I am to you for the strength you and your ideas have given me." A year later Fenner Brockway was equally appreciative. "All of us," he said, "feel tremendously indebted to you—not only for your NCF work, but for all that you have given up for your pacifist principles." Emrys

1. Marshall to Russell, 3 December 1916, BRA.
2. Bertrand Russell, *The Autobiography of Bertrand Russell*, 3 vols. (London, 1967–1969), 2:33, 74.
3. See Chap. 6.

Hughes, son-in-law of Keir Hardie, a future Labour M.P. and an NCF leader in South Wales, wrote from prison thanking Russell "for helping us to understand the first principles of . . . the pacifist ideal . . . those of us in prison will go on much more confident knowing that the work outside is in the hands of people who can be relied upon so well."[4]

All these men were absolutists. Russell also maintained close contact with men in Home Office camps during the time when many suspected that the NCF might abandon them. In May 1917 Russell visited the Home Office center at Princetown and throughout his tenure as chairman he provided a steady stream of advice and sympathy to Home Office men.[5] Russell's willingness to act as arbiter of the NCF's internal disputes[6] and to communicate with members at every level concerning any sort of difficulty gave a considerable boost to the fellowship's always precarious morale.[7] But if his leadership was a great boon to the NCF, it was also, by his own testimony, one of the most difficult and disagreeable episodes in his life.

Of all those with whom Russell associated in the NCF, none worked with him more closely, admired him more deeply, or clashed with him more frequently than Marshall. Their relationship is fascinating and rather bizarre. From the beginning she seemed determined to retain her independence of spirit and action and not to be overawed by Russell's reputation or by his powers of persuasion. As she told him in the summer of 1916:

> I would do a great deal to try to deserve "admiration and affection" from you, but your plea that I should act as *you*

4. Allen to Russell, 25 August 1916; Brockway to Russell, 7 September 1917; and Hughes to Russell, 4 March 1917, BRA.

5. See especially Russell's correspondence with Howard Marten at Dartmoor (Princetown) and R. W. Crammer at Wakefield, BRA.

6. Keith Robbins, *The Abolition of War: The "Peace Movement" in Britain, 1914-1919* (Cardiff, 1976), p. 90, implies that Russell was of little help in solving problems within the NCF; Russell obviously did not resolve all difficulties, but he was in fact a great steadying force.

7. The BRA contains a great volume of correspondence that Russell carried on with a wide variety of NCF members. He was also much in demand as a speaker; see, for example, Dorothy Gittins (Leicester branch) to Russell, 11 January 1917, and Emily Cox (Northwest Divisional Council) to Russell, 19 May 1917, BRA.

think I ought to act in order not to disappoint you is unworthy of you. O Mephy. You know you would not respect me if I allowed myself to be guided by it. . . . It w[oul]d be contrary to your whole philosophy. No, I must take my chance of losing what I greatly value, though I don't deserve it. But please, Mephy, try not to be disappointed in anything more than my judgement if I make what you think a wrong decision. It won't be for lack of caring.[8]

But despite this declaration of independence, Marshall came to depend on Russell far more than she had intended. In the autumn of 1916, after Allen, with whom she had fallen in love, had been imprisoned and while the debate over alternative service was raging, the strain of constant worry and an enormous self-imposed work load began to tell on her. Apparently overwhelmed by a fit of depression, she dispatched a distress signal to Russell.

S.O.S.

I am drowning in a sea of loneliness—parched in a barren desert—imprisoned between walls I can't see over. I don't know what is the matter, but I want some help very badly . . . [to] get over this fit of unfruitfulness . . . I don't often feel helpless like this—and shouldn't now if C. A. were here, or if I were not so tired.[9]

As luck would have it, Russell was on his way to see her on another matter before he received the letter, and he must have provided some immediate commiseration. On the next day she sent along a cheery note of thanks: "I am tickled," she said, "at the idea of your writing out notes with sub-headings, for a talk with me, just as I do for an interview with General Child [sic] or Lloyd George."[10]

Later, after he assumed the acting chairmanship of the NCF, Russell worked with Marshall nearly every day in the fellowship's central office where Russell assumed what was, for him, the distasteful and fatiguing job of managing affairs. Unfortunately, the more closely he and Marshall worked together, the less compatible they proved to be. A sensitive, highly strung woman, Marshall was, by the spring

8. Marshall to Russell, 7 July 1916, BRA. "Mephy" stood for Mephistopheles, Russell's nickname on the NCF national committee.
9. Marshall to Russell, 1 October 1916, BRA.
10. Marshall to Russell, 2 October 1916, BRA.

of 1917, well into a second year of working too hard on too many projects. In addition to carrying on a continuing series of negotiations with the War Office and with politicians concerning specific cases and general policy, she also directed the COIB and the record office, wrote for *The Tribunal,* and helped with head-office administration. She bore these burdens under steadily increasing internal pressure and criticism.[11] Russell supported her endeavors but, nervous and anxious in his unfamiliar work, he found it increasingly difficult to accept her methods.

When he had to deal with Marshall on a day-to-day basis, Russell found her not simply assertive but positively overwhelming. As Jo Vellacott has noted in her excellent analysis of their relationship,[12] Marshall personally imposed a regimen on Russell—to the point of posting a daily list of his assigned tasks—the like of which he had probably never endured before or after. If Russell failed to complete his work to her satisfaction, Marshall apparently subjected him—just as she did other office staff—to a withering barrage of criticism. On Good Friday, 1917, Russell told Ottoline Morrell that C. E. M. was being "very difficult—bullying everyone, dilatory, untruthful, hating to part with power."[13] Shortly thereafter, following what must have been a particularly caustic reproach, Marshall wrote to beg Russell's forgiveness for her petulance. "I do love and admire you so much, and owe you so much—I can't bear to find myself constantly being horrid and cantankerous with you, or associating you with feelings of exhaustion or irritation on my side. We must not let circumstances and over-work drive us into getting on each other's nerves."[14]

For Russell, however, their difficulties had gone far beyond merely getting on each other's nerves. Marshall's attacks had become a near-obsession with him, robbing him of

11. See Chap. 10.
12. Jo Vellacott Newberry, "Russell and the Pacifists in World War I," in *Russell in Review,* ed. J. E. Thomas and Kenneth Blackwell (Toronto, 1976), p. 48. Also see her doctoral thesis, "Bertrand Russell and the Pacifists in the First World War" (McMaster University, 1975). Vellacott Newberry is presently writing a biography of Catherine E. Marshall.
13. Russell to O. Morrell, Good Friday, 1917, quoted by Ronald W. Clark, *The Life of Bertrand Russell* (New York, 1976), p. 330.
14. Marshall to "Mephy," 1 May 1917, BRA.

sleep and driving him to the edge of despair. By the time he received her letter of 1 May he had evidently decided that his mental health absolutely required some resolution of their differences. Russell's answer, composed on 3 May, vividly expressed his preoccupation with the office situation. He began by admitting shortcomings in his work, adding that he disliked it "so much that I should be overjoyed if I could have a painful and dangerous illness from now until the end of the war." On the other hand, said Russell, Marshall was not equally aware of her deficiencies and if someone did not inform her of their effects, the entire head-office staff might be driven to resign. "After you have been criticizing," he noted, "I have to go round consoling and persuading people that they are not so incompetent that they ought to retire." She treated them this way, he felt, "because instinctively you regard us as subject to your authority. The feeling of authority is one that a pacifist should root out from his instincts." Furthermore, her methods of handling the work simply added to the difficulty: "You have an immense amount of system which you never adhere to; and let all routine matters drift, because there is always a crisis." Russell concluded by admitting that he would have no initiative until the war was over,

> partly due to fatigue, partly to the fact that my instinct is oppressed by the sense of public hostility, partly by dread of your onslaughts, which I find absolutely paralysing. . . . I had hoped to save you from a breakdown by taking over your work but that proved impossible, so I have no longer the same motives for attempting to do things that are unnatural for me.[15]

Russell's criticisms of Marshall were no doubt mainly justified. But in her overwrought condition such an attack, especially from a man she admired so much, might literally have destroyed her. Russell realized her vulnerability, and after venting his spleen, he put the letter aside to be read by posterity instead of by his momentary tormentor. This incident is perhaps a small one but the letter is important because it not only reveals something of Russell's state of mind during the war but also illustrates his deep-seated sense of responsibility and humanity. Marshall troubled days and

15. Russell to Marshall, 3 May 1917 (not sent), BRA.

nights that, for Russell, were already afflicted by frustration and futility over the war, but, much to his credit, he did not lessen his burden by adding to hers.

Russell's decision not to confront Marshall directly may have been noble, but it did not solve the difficulties between them. Thus, in mid-May, during a time of momentary calm when Marshall had gone down to the army camp where Allen was awaiting his third court-martial, Russell drafted a letter of resignation to the NCF national committee. Nowhere in this four-page document did he even hint at his troubles with Marshall, though he did cite his deficiency "in administrative and executive matters" as the first of four reasons why he had for some time "felt uncomfortable about my position as Acting Chairman of the NCF." His other reasons were essentially political and ideological, but taken together they led him to the conclusion that he was "not the right person to be Acting Chairman."[16]

It is doubtful whether the NCF national committee ever saw this letter; certainly, they never acted on it. Russell may have been brought up short by the impending resignation of Brown,[17] but the decisive factor was probably a letter he received from Allen exhorting him

> to give a great deal of yourself to the Fellowship. To know you are doing this will make me so much more confident that it is doing things of value and that our efforts in prison are being pressed home. I plead with you to make Catherine Marshall successful by bearing with the things that anger you. I am so sure she can do for the movement what very few others can.[18]

Russell would have found it difficult to reject Allen's plea, but what probably clinched his decision was a note from Marshall that indicated that she had decided to return to her family home in Dernwater for a rest cure, promising to reappear in August "frightfully vigourous . . . and able to do your work as well as my own."[19]

---

16. Russell to the Members of the National Committee, 18 May 1917 (original handwritten draft and typed copy), BRA.
17. See Chap. 10.
18. Allen to Russell, 31 May 1917, BRA. Russell later told Ottoline Morrell that he remained NCF chairman chiefly for Allen's sake; 18 December 1917, cited by Clark, *Bertrand Russell,* p. 330.
19. Marshall to Russell, 1 June 1917, BRA. Jo Vellacott Newberry has

So Russell stayed on. Still, the temporary end to one personal and organizational crisis simply opened the way for another, and very soon he became embroiled in a political qua literary incident that nearly became a national scandal before its quiet, rather pathetic conclusion.

Dulce et Decorum Est

> And am I not myself a conscientious objector with a very seared conscience.... —Wilfred Owen[20]

In mid-June 1917—while labor and socialist elements were making their first rumblings about the establishment of soldiers' and workers' councils in the wake of the March Revolution in Russia[21]—Russell was approached by 2d Lt. Siegfried Sassoon whose recently published volume of war poems, *The Old Huntsman,* was already a sensation. Sent to Russell by the Morrells, Sassoon informed him that after spending two years in the trenches and having been decorated for conspicuous gallantry, he was convinced that he must make some public protest against the relentless slaughter that was being uselessly prolonged.[22] After questioning the young poet closely about his motives and convictions, Russell advised him to write a short personal statement outlining his reasons for opposing the continuation of the war. He promised to have this statement printed and widely publicized by the NCF and other pacifist organizations but warned Sassoon that the price of any meaningful propaganda would be court-martial and imprisonment. A soldier behind bars for refusing to acquiesce in further killing, Rus-

---

suggested that by late 1917 Russell was again so desperate to have Marshall out of the office that he encouraged her in a plan to have herself arrested and jailed as a means of obtaining a rest cure; fortunately the scheme died aborning. Evidence for such a plan is located in Russell's correspondence with Helena W. Swanwick of the Women's International League, BRA. See Vellacott Newberry, "Russell and the Pacifists in World War I," p. 50.

20. Quoted in Harold Owen and John Bell, eds., *Wilfred Owen: Collected Letters* (London, 1967), p. 461.

21. See the discussion later in this chapter.

22. What follows is largely based on accounts given by Sassoon in *Siegfried's Journey, 1916–1920* (New York, 1946), pp. 73–85, and in *Memoirs of an Infantry Officer* (New York, 1920), pp. 263–322, and by Robert Graves, *Good-bye to All That,* 2d rev. ed. (Garden City, N.Y., 1957), pp. 256–64.

sell believed, might play a useful part in the struggle against the war. Sassoon understood all this and remained undeterred.

After considerable soul-searching and repeated failure, Sassoon managed to draft a brief declaration that began

> I am making this statement as an act of wilful defiance of military authority, because I believe that the war is being deliberately prolonged by those who have the power to end it.

And ended:

> On behalf of those who are suffering now I make this protest against the deception which is being practised on them; also I believe that I may help to destroy the callous complacence with which the majority of those at home regard the continuance of agonies which they do not share and which they have not sufficient imagination to realise.[23]

Russell took the statement and Sassoon to H. B. Lees-Smith, an antiwar Liberal M.P., who promised to raise a question about the statement in the House of Commons; it was also printed and circulated by Francis Meynell at the Pelican Press.[24] Having completed the preliminary spadework, Sassoon dispatched the protest to his superior and awaited the inevitable showdown.

Up to this point everything about the tight little pacifist conspiracy seemed to be falling into place. Then the crusty machinery of the English class system began ponderously clanking into operation, and the old-boy network of schoolmates, family friends, and compassionate spectators launched a counterconspiracy to deny Sassoon his painful day in court. Things began to go awry when the major temporarily in command of Sassoon's unit—"a man of great delicacy of feeling" as Sassoon later said—refused to place him under arrest and instead sent him to a hotel in Liverpool to await further instructions. While Sassoon spent three days in Liverpool contemplating his fate—and throwing his

23. Complete statement in Graves, *Good-bye to All That,* p. 260, and 5 H.C., 96:1797-98, 30 July 1917. The BRA contains a draft copy of Sassoon's statement with Russell's suggested revisions as well as Russell's most favorable personal assessment of Sassoon in a letter to Helena Swanwick, 20 July 1917.

24. See Russell to O. Morrell, 7 July 1917, cited by Clark, *Bertrand Russell,* p. 328.

224 / The Hound of Conscience

Military Cross into the sea—his friend and fellow poet Robert Graves was pulling strings with friends at the War Office who made arrangements to convene a special medical board to hear the case.[25] Graves felt that it would be relatively simple to convince this board that a man with Sassoon's distinguished record could only have acted as he did because of a complete mental collapse.

Having thus made all the necessary arrangements to save Sassoon from himself, Graves raced to Liverpool where he attempted to persuade his friend that the protest declaration was being squelched and that he owed it to himself and to the men with whom he had served to appear before the medical board. Sassoon gave in.

With Graves as chief witness, the medical board voted to send the would-be mutineer to a convalescent home for shell-shocked officers near Edinburgh. So the case closed with Sassoon—still troubled in heart and mind over a war that he could not stop by killing or by refusing to kill—in "Dottyville," as he called it, and the government saved all but a few uneasy moments when Lees-Smith belatedly read Sassoon's statement in the House of Commons and it was finally printed in some national newspapers.[26] Some good did emerge for English literature, since one of Sassoon's fellow patients in the hospital was Wilfred Owen, whom Sassoon encouraged to begin seriously writing war poetry.[27]

The villain of the piece, at least so far as Graves was concerned, was Russell. Graves felt that Russell had taken unfair advantage of Sassoon while he was depressed and confused.

> Sassoon has been forced to accept a medical board and is being sent to a place in the country as suffering from nerves . . . as anybody can easily see. . . . His opinions are still unchanged, but there is nothing further for you to do (with him for your cause)—I blame you most strongly for your indiscretion in having allowed him to do what he had done, knowing in what state of health he was. . . . Now you can leave things alone until

25. Sassoon, *Memoirs of an Infantry Officer*, p. 308, and Graves, *Good-bye to All That*, p. 262.

26. Graves, *Good-bye to All That*, p. 264; 5 H.C., 96:1797–99, 1804–6, 30 July 1917; and *The Times*, 31 July 1917. *Trib.* did not mention the case until 16 August 1917.

27. Sassoon, *Siegfried's Journey*, pp. 86–108 passim.

he's well enough again to think calmly about the War & how to end it.[28]

Russell did not mention the incident in his *Autobiography*, but, given his own melancholy state, such a letter from a young man who in other circumstances might easily have been one of his undergraduate students must have inflicted some pain. Sassoon had, of course, come to Russell who took the time to ascertain that he was, as Graves also knew, both sane and serious in his intentions. In any case, Russell apparently did not become involved in such a situation again, although other NCF leaders detected and attempted to take advantage of an increased sympathy and respect for the C.O.s' stand among fighting men. In November 1917, for instance, William J. Chamberlain, in an "open letter" to Lloyd George, warned the prime minister that if he really wanted to know how soldiers felt about the war, he should tour the army camps disguised as a conscientious objector. Certainly, verbally and sometimes even by leaflet, the seeds of pacifism were being sown in guardrooms and detention barracks all over England, but they seem to have fallen chiefly on barren ground.[29] Occasionally a soldier like Lt. Max Plowman[30] would defy military authority and change sides, as it were. But most such men were probably as uncomfortable among C.O.s as Sassoon had been because, as he later said, any man who had seen the worst of the war "was everlastingly differentiated from everyone except his fellow soldiers." Certainly there were few soldiers who did not hate the war, but many no doubt agreed with Graves that the pacifists were as big a humbug as the politicians. Their loyalty to their comrades or to the men they led demanded

28. Graves to Russell, 19 July 1917, BRA; also see *Good-bye to All That*, p. 261.

29. Chamberlain's letter was printed in *Trib.*, 15 November 1917. Also see Stephen Hobhouse, *Autobiography* (Boston, 1952), p. 157, and Vellacott Newberry, "Russell and the Pacifists in World War I," p. 46, who cites the case of Joseph Dalby, a C.O. who spent his time between court-martials passing out pacifist propaganda to members of the Non-Combatant Corps.

30. On Plowman, see *Trib.*, 11 April and 2 May 1918, and Dorothy L. Plowman, ed., *Bridge to the Future* (London, 1944). For other cases of officers who became conscientious objectors, see *Trib.*, 23 May and 3 October 1918.

that they continue to acquiesce in the insanity of slaughter until somehow it ended or ended them.[31] This attitude speaks volumes about the mood of Britain in the years between the wars.

As for Russell, however badly the Sassoon affair turned out, at least he retained the saving grace of humor. In the late summer of 1917, when a member of the York branch of the NCF sent a letter complaining in particularly outraged terms about poor service in the head office, Russell replied, "in consequence of certain complaints, chiefly from Yorkshire, a . . . reorganisation of the office with a view to a greater efficiency is being considered, but—as in Russia— even the most beneficient revolution does not produce an immediate increase of fighting efficiency."[32]

The Russian Revolution had a greater effect on the NCF than increasing efficiency at the head office. It created a new spirit as well as a new controversy, and, as Peter Brock has said, it "brought to the fore the question whether continued alliance was possible between those who actively supported violent revolution and those who believed in nonviolent means, even if they might . . . share the same enthusiasm for the ultimate goal of a classless society."[33]

Conscience and the Call of Revolution

When word of the Russian Revolution began to filter into England in March 1917, many conscientious objectors in and out of prison saw the cataclysm as a sign of their own approaching deliverance. In a letter to Russell, Marshall described the effect of the good news on her and on the prisoners she was visiting.

> Wasn't yesterday wonderful. I felt simply intoxicated with a sense of freedom and joy and *frustration*—the frustration of all the heroism and sacrifice and suffering that has been preparing for this miracle in Russia—the joy it was to tell the pris-

31. Sassoon, *Memoirs of an Infantry Officer*, p. 280, and Graves, *Good-bye to All That*, pp. 262, 275-76.

32. Herbert P. Bell to Russell, 5 September 1917, and Russell to Bell, 6 September 1917, BRA.

33. Peter Brock, *Twentieth-Century Pacifism* (New York, 1970), p. 35.

oners about it. The warden let me talk without interruption &
I told them . . . *everything* & saw *them* go back to their cells
radiant and with renewed *vitality*.

Prisoners indeed rejoiced! Brockway, for one, had a vision
of prison doors being flung open "by comrade workers and
soldiers."[34]

Writing in *The Tribunal*, Russell, with transparent optimism, reflected on the possible effects of these momentous
events for all "lovers of freedom."

> It is not our cause in isolation that will triumph, but the univer-
> sal cause of Liberty, Equality and Fraternity. The British na-
> tion is growing weary of its self-imposed servitude. Our an-
> cient liberties can be recovered to-morrow if the people have
> the courage to demand them. When the new spirit begins to
> stir among those who have hitherto submitted to tyranny with
> scarcely a murmur, we must be ready to help in every battle for
> freedom. . . . The world is moving, and there is hope at last of a
> real peace by a fraternal conciliation of the awakening
> peoples.[35]

On behalf of the NCF and all C.O. prisoners, Russell dispatched a fraternal message:

> To our comrades in Free Russia, we send cordial congratula-
> tions, as lovers of freedom who honour the heroism of the long
> struggle, and feel the world a happier place for your final
> victory. As believers in the brotherhood of all men, we are
> filled with the fervent hope that recent events in Russia will
> lead to a peace founded on good-will and fraternity between
> all nations now at war.[36]

For the moment, then, exhilaration and euphoria seemed
to be the general reactions. But for a supposedly pacifist
organization like the NCF, the Russian Revolution raised
some serious questions that would inevitably have to be

34. Marshall to Russell, undated [March 1917], BRA, and A. Fenner
Brockway, *Inside the Left* (London, 1942), p. 97. An excellent account of the
NCF reaction to the first Russian Revolution is Vellacott Newberry's "Ber-
trand Russell and the Pacifists in the First World War," chap. 10 passim.
Also see her article on "Anti-War Suffragists," *History* 62(October
1977):423.

35. "The New Hope," *Trib.*, 5 April 1917. Also see *Trib.*, 22 March 1917.

36. The message was sent on 6 April and printed in *Trib.*, 3 May 1917.

faced. The leaders of the revolution had issued a charter of freedom that promised what many in the fellowship considered their own fundamental goal—complete liberty of conscience. To obtain that end the Russians had used violence and they were evidently willing to continue using it (they had not even withdrawn from the war!). What *was* the essential condition—freedom or peace? What was the object lesson of the revolution? Was it indeed true, as one young Russian wrote to his C.O. brother in England, that the "moral of the Revolution is what a wonderful thing force is when it is on the right side, the side of the people"? Certainly, it did seem strange as this same brother told Marshall "that in a country to which my parents went to escape religious persecution, I should be awaiting further punishment for refusing to do what to me is wrong."[37] The NCF itself had consistently held that British liberty had been mercilessly suppressed by the forces of rampant militarism. Now when revolution was in the air, what was to be done about it?

Russell felt that the Russian Revolution presented a moment in history that had to be grasped by those who truly desired human freedom and social progress. This attitude was an important consideration in his abortive decision to resign as acting chairman of the NCF since, as he said, the fellowship was "not a suitable body for action in general politics." There were, he believed, "thousands [who] desire an end to the present war for every one who accepts the extreme pacifist position." Russell himself had never accepted that position and indeed had publicly stated in his lectures on "Social Reconstruction" that the use of armed force might become necessary in the struggle to overthrow an oppressive or militarist government.[38] Previously, this had been a "merely academic reservation, without relevance to the actual situation," but events in Russia had made it "a

37. Letter from "Elsa" printed in *Trib.*, 19 April 1917, and S. Weinstein to Marshall (copy), 2 April 1917, BRA.
38. Russell to Members of the National Committee, 18 May 1917, BRA. In November 1916 the Tottenham branch of the NCF withdrew their nomination of Russell as NCF vice-chairman because members had noted Russell's condoning of armed force in one of his lectures on "Social Reconstruction" and they felt that this view contradicted the fellowship's basic principle of the sacredness of human life; see E. J. Ford, secretary of Tottenham Branch, to Russell, 5 November 1916, BRA.

pressing practical consideration." Furthermore, those events had led him to the conclusion that progressive forces were compelled to help infuse British society with the sort of political and industrial spirit that the Russian Revolution had engendered, even at the risk of violence.[39] Russell persisted in this view, even while he continued to serve as NCF chairman.

Others in the fellowship also recognized the significance of the revolutionary spirit. While he did not disavow the principle of the sacredness of human life, Allen did feel that the upheaval in Russia was a harbinger of worldwide revolution. He felt that if imprisoned C.O.s continued to supinely accept whatever punishments the government chose to inflict on them, they would be scorned by the more militant sections of labor and would be cut off from the growing spirit of revolution. Therefore, he concluded: "Just because it is so important that we should use our influence to restrain violence in the new revolutionary movement, it is vital we should keep alive the revolutionary spirit in our own movement." Patience and long-suffering, he said, would gain no more for the C.O.s' cause than "the Quakerism of centuries" and would cause objectors to fall into "the trap of passivism" that he apparently believed had already ensnared too many Friends.[40]

The imprisonment of conscientious objectors, he said, had ceased to be a test of sincerity and had become a means for ensuring the continuation of compulsory service; the army was using the persecution of C.O.s to frighten ordinary conscripts into submission. Men were being court-martialed two, three, and four times in order to completely crush the spirit of resistance. By acquiescing in this system, Allen concluded, the NCF was actually aiding the administration of conscription and was dampening the fires of resistance at a time when they should be blazing out of control.[41]

Because the situation had changed so drastically, Allen perceived the necessity for some dramatic gesture that

39. Russell to Members of the National Committee, 18 May 1917, BRA.
40. Allen's "Notes on Prison Policy," with comments by Chamberlain and Brockway, CAP, and Allen ms., chap. 3a, pp. 19-20, 23, CAP.
41. Allen's letter from Maidstone Prison (copy), 21 April 1917, CAP. Also see Allen ms., chap. 3, pp. 17, 30, and chap. 3a, pp. 18-22, CAP.

would change the pitch of the nonviolent revolutionaries. He predicted that when the war ended and hordes of disillusioned soldiers returned, "Revolution of some kind must come and then the Supreme need will be to give spiritual expression to gigantic material forces. This can only be done if those who have seen the visions are . . . the keenest of all men and women when . . . action is called for."[42]

Allen set forth what he had in mind in a long letter to Russell. He proposed that the NCF national committee sponsor and organize a C.O. prisoners' work strike. This step should be undertaken, he said, because absolutists were becoming increasingly aware that their prison labor freed non-C.O. prisoners to do war work; in essence, the men who had not accepted the Home Office scheme were doing as much to assist the prosecution of the war as those who had.[43] A work strike would be a dramatic means of fixing national attention on the fact that there were over a thousand C.O.s undergoing an indefinite series of imprisonments. The idea of this demonstration would not be to improve the lot of the absolutists—indeed, the result would be the exact opposite—but to advance the NCF's revolutionary leadership and to prevent the government from reaching an easy solution to the conscription problem.[44]

The chairman's proposal was certainly dramatic, but it also flew in the face of all previous NCF pronouncements on prison conduct. From the beginning it had been assumed that a C.O. should obey prison rules as part of his punishment, and during the previous autumn a poll of branch opinion indicated that most members felt that prison work should be accepted. Allen himself had earlier declared that he could see no reason to decline prison work as long as it was part of the regular routine and had not been devised especially for conscientious objectors. There had been minor work strikes early in 1917, but these were based on specific issues and ended when the issues in question were resolved.[45] What Allen proposed not only was a new departure

42. Letter from Maidstone Prison, 21 April 1917, CAP, and Allen to Marshall, 17 June 1917, BRA.
43. This was, of course, the argument advanced by C. H. Norman when he accepted the Home Office scheme. See Chap. 8.
44. Allen to Russell (and national committee), 17 May 1917, CAP.
45. Hon. Sec. of Political Committee to Branches, 5 September 1916,

but also could lay the fellowship open to charges of conspiracy.

The NCF national committee's immediate reaction was distinctly negative. Brown, even though he was about to resign from the national committee, wrote to "implore" Allen "not to think of attempting theatricals ... [that] would *just spoil an increasingly effective witness.*" Charles G. Ammon, NCF parliamentary secretary, thought the idea "ill-advised and impossible to turn to good account." Even Marshall thought it "essentially and profoundly wrong ... contrary to the basis of the NCF, and to a real sense of Human brotherhood." Shortly after receiving Allen's letter, the committee passed a resolution opposing any organized work strike, though promising to "support those who adopt the practice as a matter of conscience."[46]

This rejection of Allen's new strategy placed him in an awkward position, for while he wished to maintain the unity of the fellowship, he also felt that his policy was absolutely necessary to carry forward its revolutionary aims. He could see no wrong in attempting, by nonviolent means, to compel a state to cease doing "an unjust thing for an unjust purpose." The informed and committed minority, he said, had a duty to force the government to discontinue its unjust actions, even if the general public, through ignorance, misunderstood their intentions. Allen was convinced that he had a moral obligation to end the stalemate in the struggle between the government and conscientious objectors. Therefore, he resolved to carry out his policy even if it meant acting alone and against the wishes of the entire national committee.[47]

On 31 May 1917 Allen forced the issue with a long, rambling "open letter" to Lloyd George explaining the reasons why he would refuse to do prison work during the two-year sentence that had just been imposed on him. His chief motivation, Allen said, was to reassert the gathering spirit of

---

FSC Files, FHL; Agenda of NCF National Convention, 29–30 November 1919, p. 9, CAP; and *Trib.*, 28 September 1916, 8 February, and 22 March 1917.

46. Brown to Allen, 23 May 1917, and Ammon to Marshall, n.d. [May–June 1917], CEMP (microfilm); Marshall to Edith Ellis, 30 April 1917, FSC Correspondence, 1917, FHL; and *Trib.*, 14 June 1917.

47. Allen ms., chap. 3a, pp. 23–25, CAP.

revolution that the government was attempting to smother by imposing a permanent system of conscription.[48] This document, whose discursive, convoluted, and repetitive style no doubt reflected the effects of Allen's imprisonment, contains some valuable insights into the workings of the minority mind. Even so sober a thinker as Allen somehow imagined that the prime minister and his cabinet invested anticonscriptionist–antiwar activities with the same importance as members of the NCF did. The continued imprisonment of conscientious objectors was, for Allen, proof of the state's "secret determination" to maintain conscription whatever the cost. The notion that the war cabinet's center of attention should be exactly the same as that of the No-Conscription Fellowship was, of course, preposterous. The fact that Allen assumed that it was helps to explain not only the single-mindedness of many C.O.s, but also their inability to appreciate the government's honest, albeit muddling, attempts to solve the problem.

In any case, Allen's letter to the prime minister brought him into conflict with the vast majority of NCF leaders who were not in custody. Russell reported that the fellowship's special propaganda committee considered the letter "a very poor document." Russell had defended Allen but was overcome "by an unholy alliance between Salter and the extremists. . . . [Salter's] view is that the letter should not be published at all in 'The Tribunal.' He is doubtful whether we should even mention Allen's decision, and holds that if we do mention it, we should strongly repudiate it. In all these views he has much support."[49]

When the "open letter" was finally published, Allen took pains to explain both in the text of his message and in a special boldface notice, that his action was strictly personal. The national committee, however, apparently felt compelled to include a rebuttal. In the same issue in which Allen's letter appeared, Dr. Salter published a rejoinder that rather unkindly began by comparing Allen's proposal with Jesus's second temptation in the wilderness. Salter went on to urge members to use "methods of all-persuasive reasonableness" in dealing with the government rather than coercion or vio-

48. "Open Letter to Lloyd George" (copy), 31 May 1917, CAP. Also reprinted in *Trib.*, 14 June 1917.
49. Russell to Marshall (copy), 6 June 1917, BRA.

lence, which had been "thoroughly discredited" when attempted by suffragettes before the war. He also emphasized that prison work was practically the only means by which absolutists could maintain their physical health and mental balance, adding that nearly every C.O. who had hitherto attempted a work strike had become insane.[50]

Allen was deeply hurt by what he considered a personal attack. Why, he asked bitterly, did Salter condemn a general work strike when that had never been publicly advocated? Salter's questioning not only of Allen's policy but of his motives was even more galling. This, Allen said, was the unkindest cut, especially from a Christian like Salter who should have known that

> there comes to most individuals sometime or other a demand from "conscience" that they sho[uld] not merely abstain from evil but actively engage in doing right. The position and temper of the different sections of the F.[ellowship] being now what it is [*sic*], I should have failed the movement & been false to myself if I had acted otherwise. All the way through this struggle our most delicate problem has been to combine vigour and constructive effort with an unmistakable willingness to endure to the end & an honest recognition of the power of sweet reasonableness. Unless we wisely & fearlessly combine these, we may prove the worth of the C.O. & achieve little else.[51]

As so many times before, the disagreement on policy at the top reverberated throughout the organization. Advocates on both sides of the issue argued their respective cases with considerable vehemence. One of the strongest retorts to Salter's letter and to the national committee's stand was issued on behalf of the Kennington branch by its honorary secretary Nellie Best, a former suffragette. Best concluded a stinging attack on Dr. Salter's biblical interpretation, medical statistics, and antifeminism by noting that it was the business of C.O.s "to follow God and their own intelligence . . . not Dr. Salter," as it was "the business of the National Committee to give sympathy to strikers and non-strikers."[52]

Writing from prison, Chamberlain cautioned NCF com-

---

50. *Trib.*, 14 June 1917.
51. Allen to Marshall, 15 June 1917, BRA. Also see Allen to Marshall, 22 June 1917, and Allen's "Notes on Prison Policy," CAP.
52. *Trib.*, 5 July 1917. Also see *Trib.*, 26 July and 20 September 1917.

rades against becoming embroiled in another dispute like the one over alternative service. He added, in support of the national committee, that the NCF oath bound its members to accept any penalties that resulted from their stand.[53] Brockway agreed with Allen's view that resistance was an essential next step, but he wanted to wait until the precise "psychological movement" when revolutionary feeling had developed sufficiently for an organized work strike to have national impact, especially on the labor movement. Brockway's position was partially predicated on his belief that at least 75 percent of his fellow absolutists would join such a strike.[54] Some of the men in the Home Office work centers, in reaction to the Russian Revolution, claimed that they were ready to repudiate the scheme and to join Allen in his mission. As one of them said: "Clifford Allen is right . . . we must decline to work in prison, and to acquiesce in prison discipline. The atmosphere is demoralising and the only way to better the conditions of prisoners generally is—to refuse to do anything that will *keep such slavery in vogue.*"[55] Despite such exhortations there was little practical support for Allen, who felt that C.O.s failed to back him up because they refused to "allow themselves to face new developments."[56]

Allen, however, was still determined to carry through with his demonstration. As he told Russell: "Try and make something for public propaganda out of my mission. I must do it even if I fail."[57] Thus, when he was returned to Winchester prison on 1 June, he commenced a work strike. The authorities retaliated by placing him in solitary confinement with little exercise and three days of every four on bread and water. Almost at once he began to suffer from severe headaches. By mid-June the prison doctor informed him that he had tuberculosis of the spine that was being greatly aggravated by his meager diet and by hours of sitting on a

53. *Trib.,* 19 July 1917. Also see Chamberlain's comments in the "Notes on Prison Policy," CAP. Chamberlain's letter was answered by Marshall who defended Allen's motivation and sincerity; *Trib.,* 2 August 1917.
54. "Notes on Prison Policy," CAP.
55. Selwyn Hayes to H. Thomas, 16 June 1917, FSC Correspondence, 1917, FHL. Also see note from Ernest C. Everett, 24 June 1917, FSC Correspondence, 1917, FHL.
56. Allen ms., chap. 1, p. 10, CAP.
57. Allen to Russell, 31 May 1917, BRA.

prison stool with no back. If Allen continued his resistance, the doctor warned, he faced almost certain death. But Allen refused to give in and indeed seemed to be mainly interested in how his situation could best be used to aid NCF propaganda. As he told Marshall: "I suggest the best way to rouse opinion re the Absolutists (out of my case) is to wait until I have had about 30 to 40 days . . . [with] no exercise and punishment cell and 60 or 90 days solitary confinement, etc. Then all this following upon the Doctor's original fear of serious consequences might provide material for 'Scandal propaganda' . . . on the Absolutists' persecution."[58] But a prison inspector scotched Allen's plans by ordering him into the prison hospital where he remained virtually incommunicado for five months.[59]

In all that was chiefly important to him, Allen's work-strike policy must be accounted a failure. It did cause a number of questions to be raised in the House of Commons that eventually helped to secure his release from confinement,[60] but the larger issues were not broached. No revolutionary manifestations rose from his actions. Few fellow absolutists joined him, and the leaders of the NCF remained firmly opposed to his stand. Indeed, in November 1917 the national committee issued a resolution reiterating its opinion that "under present conditions resistance to prison regulations . . . is not likely to secure release, and is undesirable from the point of view of policy."[61]

What then was a desirable policy? While the national committee was rejecting Allen's plan for taking advantage of the revolutionary spirit abroad in the land, the committee was seeking to mobilize that same spirit on behalf of peace by incorporating the fellowship into the larger labor and socialist movement that rose in the wake of the first Russian Revolution.

As noted earlier, the NCF had been instrumental in

58. Allen to Marshall, July 1917, quoted in Martin Gilbert, ed., *Plough My Own Furrow* (London, 1965), p. 86; Allen to Marshall, 22 June 1917, and Allen to Will Chamberlain, 4 August 1917, CAP.

59. *Trib.*, 12 July 1917, and Allen to Will Chamberlain, 4 August 1917, CAP.

60. 5 H.C., 95:1272, 5 July 1917; 5 H.C., 95:1647-52, 6 July 1917; and 5 H.C., 96:1227, 25 July 1917. Also see Chap. 9.

61. *Trib.*, 22 November 1917.

spreading propaganda that pictured the March Revolution as the opening round in a series of upheavals that would ultimately end the war and would sweep away European militarism. When various working-class, radical, and progressive sympathizers organized a national conference at Leeds on 3 June 1917 in support—and hopefully imitation—of the Russian example, the NCF was well represented. Russell received an enormously enthusiastic reception from the assembled delegates who good-naturedly forced him to speak from the platform rather than from the floor.[62] It seemed a great moment, representing, as Ramsay MacDonald predicted, the first step in the restoration of labor's lost initiative. Now, he said, the "Russian Revolution has given you the chance.... Let us lay down our terms, make our own proclamations, establish our own diplomacy."[63] In response to MacDonald's challenge, the delegates passed four resolutions. The first three congratulated the Russian revolutionaries, demanded that British foreign policy be in harmony with that of the new Russia, and called for a revival of British civil liberties in accordance "with the democracy of Russia." The last resolution, moved by W. C. Anderson of the ILP, proposed the establishment of councils of workers' and soldiers' delegates on the Soviet model "in every town, urban, and rural district" to carry out the policies of the conference.[64]

The "spirit of Leeds" certainly moved among the NCF leaders who attended the conference. It was infectious and it was indeed revolutionary. But in the view of one anonymous writer in *The Tribunal*, the coming revolution would not mean "bloodshed and hatred and bitterness" but rather "a permanent and democratic peace," established and main-

---

62. The best source on the Leeds conference is a pamphlet, *What Happened at Leeds,* published by the Council of Workers' and Soldiers' Delegates (London, 1917), but it is most difficult to find. The BRA, for example, only has a xerox copy. Also see the account of Lady Constance Malleson, who attended the conference with Russell and her husband, in *After Ten Years* (London, 1931), pp. 113–14. Both of these sources are quoted and discussed in John G. Slater, "What Happened at Leeds?," *Russell: The Journal of the Bertrand Russell Archives* 4(Winter 1971–1972):9–10, which has been superseded by Stephen White, "Soviets in Britain: The Leeds Convention of 1917," *International Review of Social History* 19/2 (1974):167–93.

63. Quoted in David Marquand, *Ramsay MacDonald* (London, 1977), p. 209. Also see *Trib.,* 7 June 1917.

64. See Slater, "What Happened at Leeds?," p. 9, and *Trib.,* 7 June 1917.

tained by methods of peace.[65] Russell was also moved to rhapsody by the splendor of the moment. In his chairman's editorial immediately after the Leeds conference, Russell told the membership:

> The control of events is rapidly passing out of the hands of the militarists of all countries. . . . A new spirit is abroad. All who were at the Leeds Conference must have realised that British tyranny will soon go the way of the tyranny of the Tsar. When the day of freedom dawns, we shall want the comradeship and help of those who have borne the long weariness and enforced inaction of prison. For the sake of the nation . . . it is imperative that the Absolutists should be liberated. The time has come when this can be achieved in spite of all the Lord Derbys and Lloyd Georges in the world.[66]

In a letter informing NCF branches that they would soon be asked to elect delegates to the divisional conferences of the workers' and soldiers' councils, Russell was a good deal more circumspect than he had been in the immediate afterglow of Leeds. The chief thrust of his presentation was to warn NCF members that they should be prepared to take a realistic view of the possible actions of the workers' and soldiers' councils and should not expect them to be so exclusively devoted to pacifist principles as the fellowship was.

> The new movement will be at least as much concerned with economic reconstruction as it will be with the question of peace. But probably a large majority of members of the NCF would agree that a great change in our economic system is implied in the principles which underlie our basis. We should therefore be not going seriously outside our province by joining in the advocacy of some changes, though as pacifists we should wish to do all in our power to secure that the changes should occur without the use of force and not in the spirit of violence or hate. The new movement will aim, as the Russian Government does, at bringing the war to an end by a general peace, but it will not be an out and out pacifist movement, and *if it were it is not likely it would succeed in securing peace.* We cannot therefore demand the whole of our basis shall be embodied in its programme, but we may . . . very reasonably demand that its programme shall include such items as the abolition of conscription.[67]

65. *Trib.*, 7 June 1917.
66. "Lord Derby and Leeds," *Trib.*, 7 June 1917.
67. Russell to branch secretaries (draft), n.d. [June–July 1917], BRA.

At its 13 July meeting the NCF national committee recommended that the fellowship branches send delegates to the district conferences organized by the National Workers' and Soldiers' Council. On the next day a joint conference of the NCF, FOR, and FSC broached the subject and though the two religious-pacifist bodies declined to make any official commitment to the workers'-and-soldiers'-council movement, two leaders of the FSC and one from the FOR did contribute to a special *Tribunal* supplement consisting of four essays on the theme of peaceful revolution.[68] Brown's effort was characteristic in emphasizing that pacifists, by maintaining their principles, could "achieve a revolution by the irresistible method of non-resistance." Russell struck a similar chord:

> It is through the new revolutionary spirit that peace is being brought nearer; and as peace comes nearer, it grows more important for those who hate violence to realise what is implied by their principles in the way of economic reconstruction. . . . The unjust privileges of the rich are supported by the force of the police and the criminal law; without force they would melt away. . . . To secure their abolition force is not necessary, any more than it is to dethrone the militarists. All that is necessary is that men should refuse to use force for the carrying out of unjust laws.[69]

Letters from the NCF head office to the branches outlined the procedures and schedules for the district conferences that were to establish workers' and soldiers' councils in every town and to make straight the path of nonviolent revolution.[70] But it was not to be. There was neither revolution nor an end to violence. Indeed, in his *Autobiography* Russell recalls how drunken soldiers and other patriots stormed the Brotherhood Church in Southgate Road where a group had gathered to select delegates to the workers' and soldiers' council.[71] The first hurrah of revolution proved to be the

---

68. *Trib.*, 19 July 1917, with four-page supplement. Contributors to the supplement were Russell, Barry Brown, Edith Ellis, and Henry T. Hodgkin. Also see Edith Ellis to Henry Hodgkin, n.d. [July 1917], FSC Correspondence, 1917, FHL, and Agenda for Joint Conference of Conscientious Objector Bodies, 14 July 1917, FSC *Minutes*, 2:69, FHL.

69. *Trib.*, 19 July 1917.

70. J. A. Harrop, NCF Organizing Secretary, to Branch secretaries, 17 July 1917, BRA.

71. Russell, *Autobiography*, 2:31–32.

last as well. Few local councils were given birth and none grew to maturity. For one brief shining moment it all seemed so simple and so clear, but as the pure revolutionary vision faded into the reality of violence, terror, and civil strife in Bolshevik Russia, the No-Conscription Fellowship was plagued by recurring debates about whether the socially responsible pacifist could support violence if his goal was socially necessary change.[72] It was an old, hard, and relentless question, and in the end it harried the fellowship into its grave.

72. See Chap. 13.

12

A Struggle on Two Fronts: The NCF in and out of Prison

DORA and the NCF

The *Manchester Guardian* once commented that the government, if it wished, could use its broad umbrella of powers under the Defense of the Realm Acts to prosecute the management of every "intelligent" newspaper in Great Britain—and, it might be supposed, unintelligent ones as well.[1] DORA (as the accumulated acts were affectionately called) was another "first" for the Great War—the first comprehensive attempt in a modern democracy to tip the legal balance against long-standing traditions of free speech and a free press in favor of the now-ubiquitous "national security." However valuable and necessary these acts were to Britain's war effort, there is no question that hydralike DORA sprouted two new heads with every real or imagined threat to the well-being of the empire. The No-Conscription Fellowship was considered to be among those threats and at least part of DORA's growth and development was in response to groups like the NCF.

The fellowship had, of course, long been the target for a considerable range of police and internal-security operations. Its head office had been periodically raided and searched as were the homes of some 150 branch officials.[2] In addition to the prosecution of Bertrand Russell and most of

1. 9 November 1916. The government did, in fact, suspend the operation of some "unintelligent" papers—the right-wing *Globe* for predicting that Kitchener planned to step down as secretary of state for war and the left-wing journals *Forward* and *Vanguard* for publishing embarrassing, though largely accurate, reports of Lloyd George's debacle when he met with striking Clyde workers on Christmas Day, 1915. See Chris Wrigley, *David Lloyd George and the British Labour Movement: Peace and War* (Hassocks, 1976), pp. 154–56.
2. See *The No-Conscription Fellowship: A Summary of Its Activities* (London, n.d.), p. 12, and Chap. 6.

the fellowship's national committee, many less-famous members and associates were arrested, fined, or imprisoned for publishing or distributing antiwar materials. These sporadic reprisals seemed to have had little effect on the fellowship's propaganda activities. Allen once commented, "if the Government is going to sweep down on every effort—however constitutional—to stir public opinion in favour of peace . . . , it is merely encouraging responsible persons to take risks."[3]

Some government officials, however, believed that even DORA was an inadequate instrument for dealing with the NCF. General Childs, for instance, felt that the fellowship could be properly broken only if its leaders were dealt with under the provisions of the Incitement to Mutiny Act.[4] One member of the war cabinet who was deeply concerned about pacifist activities was Sir Edward Carson (who was himself something of an expert at subversion). On 3 October 1917 Carson introduced a memorandum to his colleagues linking pacifist propaganda with labor troubles and asking that the cabinet inquire into the possibility that German money was being used to support agitation by pacifist groups such as the NCF, UDC, and ILP.[5] One week later G. H. Roberts, the minister of labor, reported to the cabinet that evidence amassed by his department indicated that Carson's fears were unwarranted. Groups like the UDC and NCF, he said, "command the support of very wealthy Quaker families" whose contributions enabled them to carry on their activities.[6]

Unappeased by Roberts's appraisal, the war cabinet directed the Home Office to undertake an "investigation of all pacifist propaganda and . . . submit a full report to the War Cabinet."[7] Sir George Cave, the home secretary, assigned this task to Basil Thomson, assistant commissioner of met-

3. *Trib.*, 1 June 1916.
4. Sir Wyndham Childs, *Episodes and Reflections* (London, 1930), p. 149.
5. See "Memorandum on Pacifist Propaganda by Sir Edward Carson," 3 October 1917, CAB 24/4/157. Attitudes and activities arising out of Carson's memo are fully described by Marvin Swartz, *The Union of Democratic Control in British Politics during the First World War* (Oxford, 1971), pp. 180–92.
6. Memorandum by Roberts, 10 October 1917, CAB 24/28/2274.
7. CAB 23/4/253 (1).

ropolitan police and head of the criminal-investigation division of Scotland Yard. Thomson's reports on the NCF, based, it would seem, on a curious admixture of confiscated material and personal prejudice, described the membership as incorporating "a number of long-haired men of the type of Wycliffe Preachers ... , many genuine conscientious objectors," and a large group of professional dissidents who sometimes exhibited a "strong revolutionary spirit." Despite such manifestations of socially disruptive behavior, Thomson concluded that there was no evidence of enemy financial support and that the NCF was "conducted in an unbusinesslike way by cranks." Indeed, Thomson was so unimpressed by the fellowship that he ranked it only fourth in order of importance among pacifist and revolutionary groups, trailing after the UDC, the ILP, and the Socialist party.[8]

Despite such findings, Cave still wanted some more effective means of stifling pacifist literature. He therefore recommended to the war cabinet a new regulation under DORA requiring that all literature "relating to the present War or the conclusion of peace ... bear the names and addresses of the author or printer, and ... be submitted to the Press Bureau for approval." This requirement "would not be an interference with freedom of opinion and speech," Cave reasoned, because such materials were not expressions of opinion "but propaganda intended to influence others."[9] The home secretary's request was quickly approved as Regulation 27(c) under the Defense of the Realm Act.

Liberal opinion was outraged by the grave implications of this action. The *Manchester Guardian* thundered against those "among our governors who think that every time they trample upon a British liberty they are defeating the enemy."[10] Organizations like the NCF and the FSC saw the new regulation as a threat to the essential purpose of their existence—akin to having a rope looped around their necks with the government able to tighten the noose at will.

8. See "Pacifist Propaganda," 13 November 1917, app., CAB 24/4/173, and B. Thomson, "Pacifism," 13 December 1917, CAB 24/55/2980. Also see HO 45/10801/307402/78, which notes a police raid on NCF headquarters on 14 November 1917.

9. See "Pacifist Propaganda," Cave's note, 13 November 1917, CAB 24/4/173, and 5 H.C., 99:557, 15 November 1917.

10. *Manchester Guardian*, 16 November 1917.

For its part the FSC resolved to defy Regulation 27(c) and publicly demonstrated its intentions by printing and distributing, without reference to the Press Bureau, nearly seventy-five thousand copies of a pamphlet called "A Challenge to Militarism." The government accepted the challenge by prosecuting three FSC officials—Edith Ellis, Harrison Barrow, and Arthur Watts—for violating the new regulation. All three were convicted and, after appeal, sentenced to fines and imprisonment.[11] Thus the state established its right to control or to suppress antiwar propaganda, and having moved successfully against religious pacifists, the Home Office could feel confident in acting against political pacifists as well.

The NCF made no direct challenge to government censorship, though it continued to publish highly provocative attacks on the Lloyd George ministry. Russell's weekly editorials in *The Tribunal* were particularly pungent as, for instance, his mocking satire on a mythical peace treaty between British and German imperialists. The chief tenets of this imaginary pact were to be the "division of spoil and combination against the forces of progress everywhere." The British imperialists, Russell noted, were somewhat worried about labor trouble, but they consoled themselves with the hope that they soon would have "an American garrison in the country ready to shoot down strikers."[12]

Such outbursts were perhaps a reflection of Russell's determination to make the most of his remaining tenure as a full-time pacifist agitator. He had already decided to give up not only the NCF chairmanship but most of his other work as well and to return to the more congenial tasks of writing and lecturing on philosophy.[13] In January 1918 Russell joyfully turned over the acting chairmanship to Dr. Alfred Salter and his journalistic duties on *The Tribunal* to Lydia Smith who with Joan Beauchamp had become coeditor.

---

11. Barrow and Watts received six-month sentences and Edith Ellis, refusing to pay a hundred-pound fine and fifty guineas in costs, served out a three-month sentence. For a detailed account, see the FSC pamphlet *The Story of an Uncensored Leaflet* (London, [1918]). Also see FSC *Minutes*, Meetings of 4 April and 22 May 1918, 3:4, 8, FHL, and *Trib.*, 18 April, 2 and 30 May, and 11 and 18 July 1918.

12. "Imperialist Anxieties," *Trib.*, 30 August 1917.

13. Russell to Gilbert Murray, 15 February 1918, and to Lord Russell, 27 May 1918, BRA.

As a favor to them, and a parting shot at the powers that be, Russell wrote editorial articles in the first two *Tribunal* issues of 1918. The first of these on "The German Peace Offer" harkened back to his diatribe of the previous August and warned trade unionists of plans the Allied governments might be hatching to keep them under control: "The American Garrison which will... be occupying England and France, whether or not they will prove efficient against the Germans, will no doubt be capable of intimidating strikers, an occupation to which the American Army is accustomed when at home."[14] With this final blast, Russell prepared to take his leave. In early February Allen, now released from prison, expressed his fear that Russell might become completely immersed in academic life: This "would be a disaster for the breezy young people like me; we are so dependent upon you for compelling us to think carefully and act honestly and fearlessly."[15]

Russell's own mood at this time seemed lighthearted and effusive as he wrote to Allen of his delight with the success of the Bolsheviks and his feeling that the world grew "more full of hope every day." But as a kind of postscript to this same buoyant letter, he warned Allen:

> The police are on the track of *The Tribunal.* Two detectives visited me yesterday when I was in my bath and asked if I had written an article (about a month ago) called "The German Offer" [*sic*], and in particular a certain sentence about the Americans being useful for intimidating strikers. So I said I had. They then asked me if I edited *The Tribunal;* so I said I didn't. I thought they would ask me who did but they didn't; they went away, after saying it was about *The Tribunal* they were inquiring.[16]

Russell was mistaken. The government was not really after *The Tribunal*—at least not yet—they were after *him.* Within a week of the first police inquiries, he and Beauchamp were on trial before a Bow Street magistrate on the respective charges of writing and publishing material concerning the use of American troops as strikebreakers

14. "The German Peace Offer," *Trib.,* 3 January 1918.
15. Allen to Russell, 6 February 1918, BRA.
16. Russell to Allen, 2 February 1918, BRA.

that, according to the prosecutor, could have a "diabolical effect" on the morale of the Allied armies. Despite the fact that he introduced a U.S. Senate report that confirmed the use of troops against strikers, Russell was convicted and sentenced to six months in the second division without option of fine. Beauchamp was fined sixty pounds and costs. In pronouncing sentence the presiding magistrate noted that "Mr. Russell seems to have lost all sense of decency and fairness, and has gone out of his way to insult by a deliberate and designed sneer the army of a great nation which is closely allied to us. . . . The offense is a very despicable one."[17]

For the next three months Russell miserably awaited the hearing of his appeal. Full of bitterness because the government had prosecuted him just after he had let it be known through his brother Frank that he was withdrawing from pacifist activities, Russell was also assailed by doubts about his ability to endure a prison sentence without books or companionship.[18] Even the well-intentioned efforts of young compatriots in the NCF oppressed him. When, for example, the exuberant, if sometimes boorish, Ernest E. Hunter informed Russell of plans for a banquet honoring him, Russell told Allen that having Hunter in the chair would be "*quite* intolerable . . . and will make me suffer to a degree I can't contemplate calmly; he threatens—e.g., to recite an ode of his own composition."[19]

Allen agreed to chair the proposed banquet, though he had also probably contributed to Russell's despondency by outlining a strategy according to which Russell would personally defend himself at his appeal (which would, of course,

17. Quoted by Alan Wood, *Bertrand Russell: The Passionate Sceptic* (London, 1957), p. 112, but also see Clark, *Bertrand Russell,* p. 339, who notes that the magistrate Sir John Dickinson expressed regret at having to carry out an unpleasant duty. For accounts of the proceedings, see *Trib.,* 14 February 1917, and Bertrand Russell, *The Autobiography of Bertrand Russell,* 3 vols. (London, 1967–1969), 2:1. Also see Clifford Allen's diary, 11 February 1918, typescript copy, CAP.

18. Russell to Gilbert Murray, 15 February 1918, BRA. Reprinted in Russell, *Autobiography,* 2:81–82, and also see p. 33.

19. Russell to Allen, 9 March 1918, BRA. Also see Hunter to Russell, 12 February 1918, BRA. Jo Vellacott Newberry, "Russell and the Pacifists in World War I," in *Russell in Review,* ed. J. E. Thomas and Kenneth Blackwell (Toronto, 1976), p. 33, quotes a limerick that may have been Hunter's poem for Russell.

fail) and then go on to prison with "a great fight and a great case for propaganda left behind."[20] Marshall added a cheery note in a similar vein: "I can't help hoping that you *will* go to prison for a time (though not a long time), because I feel sure you will be so glad afterwards to have been, and think it might well be of value internationally."[21]

What Allen, Marshall, and others did not seem to comprehend was that Russell did not want to go to prison at all. Propaganda and international implications aside, he simply had no desire to be a martyr. There was indeed almost a touch of panic in Russell's letter to Gilbert Murray, telling how six months in the second division had turned E. D. Morel's hair snow white.[22] Russell had no qualms about assisting friends who were attempting to influence the government to drop the case[23] or, failing that, to at least get his sentence altered to the first division. Murray seems to have been the key figure in persuading Arthur Balfour to intervene and to have Russell, whose appeal was dismissed on 1 May, placed in the first division.[24] There he was allowed his own clothes, furniture, and all the books and writing materials he wanted. Thus, none of Russell's worse fears were realized and though his stay in prison had certain unpleasant aspects, on the whole it passed "very fruitfully," given over almost completely to reading and writing.[25]

Russell's exit from the NCF was accompanied by a chorus

20. Allen to Russell, 11 February and 11 March 1918, BRA. Also see Allen to Russell, 10 April 1918, BRA.

21. Marshall to Russell, 30 April 1918, BRA; also see Marshall to Russell, 23 March 1918.

22. Russell to Murray, 27 March 1918, BRA. Also in Russell, *Autobiography*, 2:82. Swartz, *Union of Democratic Control*, p. 179n, says that "the story that Morel's hair turned white because of his prison experience may be discounted."

23. A letter protesting Russell's sentence, signed by Arthur Henderson, J. H. Thomas, the Webbs, and George Bernard Shaw, among others, was addressed to the prime minister and home secretary; copy in the NCF File, SCPC. Also see *Trib.*, 16 May 1918.

24. Bertrand Russell to Lord Russell, 6 May 1918 (copy), CAP, and Russell, *Autobiography*, 2:34. Joan Beauchamp's appeal was also dismissed, and when she refused to pay her fine, she was sentenced to one month in the first division.

25. Russell, *Autobiography*, pp. 34–37, in which he prints extracts from some of his prison letters. There are copies of his letters to Lord Russell and Gladys Rinder in BRA and CAP.

of letters praising his services and sacrifices for the fellowship. One of Allen's expresses the general tone.

> One of the moments I look forward to most is . . . when the
> men in prison are free and we can unite in telling you what we
> feel about the things you've done and the way in which you've
> done them. . . . If ever I contribute anything of value to the
> world, it will be in great measure due to the fact that you were
> willing to help me understand my own mind without patronizing with yours.[26]

When Russell emerged from prison in September, the belligerent nations were staggering toward their last decisive battles, and the NCF was still locked in its final struggle with the wartime government.

Once the authorities had temporarily disposed of the NCF's leading agitator, they began to move decisively against the fellowship's chief vehicle for agitation, *The Tribunal*. The NCF newspaper had been subject to a considerable campaign of harassment since its inception, and from July 1916 it had been banned from overseas shipment on the grounds that it was being used for enemy propaganda. The question of suppressing the paper completely arose from time to time, but government officials had restrained themselves until shortly after Russell's conviction in February 1918.[27] On 14 February *The Tribunal* featured an article, "The Moral Aspects of Conscription," that was concerned with the opening of official brothels for the use of British soldiers in France. Although signed by Beauchamp, the article consisted largely of reprints from other sources including an editorial in *The Times* and the speeches of two bishops in the House of Lords. The fatal indiscretion, it seems, was the inclusion of a rhetorical question: "Have not the British Military Authorities always encouraged vice?"[28] The Home Office decided that the NCF had finally gone too far. On the next day police officers raided the NCF's head office, removed all copies of *The Tribunal*'s current issues, and seized

26. Allen to Russell, 11 March and 10 April 1918, BRA. Also see Edward Grubb to Russell, 12 February 1918, and Violet Tillard to Russell, 30 April [1918], BRA.

27. See *Trib.*, 20 and 27 July 1916; HO 45/10742/263275/178; and HO 45/10786/297549/51a.

28. *Trib.*, 14 February 1918.

the names and addresses of subscribers and distributors of the paper. Simultaneously, they descended on the London offices of the National Labour Press and began dismantling the equipment on which *The Tribunal* was printed. Officers went to great lengths to find and destroy every possible copy of the paper—in one case waiting for the mail to arrive at a subscriber's house so that even his single copy could be eliminated.[29]

Rather than being dismayed by this setback, Smith and Beauchamp, the paper's editors, seemed to revel in it. They quickly obtained the services of an independent printer, S. H. Street, and *The Tribunal* turned up one week later still snorting defiance in an editorial that stated that the paper had been singled out for retribution solely because it advocated peace and freedom of conscience.[30]

After *The Tribunal* twice printed full-page ads (on 7 March and 11 April) calling on citizens to "throw off the bondage of conscription" and to "stop the war," the authorities struck again. As recounted by Street, the police entered his printing shop at 3:00 P.M. on 22 April and, after ascertaining that he had in fact printed *The Tribunal* of 11 April, proceeded to render his equipment inoperable, breaking up what they could not easily take apart. Street estimated his loss at five hundred pounds. At the same time detectives were also ransacking the NCF head office, and one of them told Smith: "We have done for you this time."[31]

Three days later a one-page leaflet appeared with the saucy headline: "Here We Are Again." *The Tribunal* had returned on schedule still proclaiming its defiance of DORA and the government.

> The press in this country is no longer free, it is . . . the servile tool of those who would fasten militarism upon us. But . . . we are not daunted. We shall go on with the message we believe it is our duty to deliver. We are trying to show the world— Scotland Yard included—the vision of that new way of life in

29. *Trib.*, 21 February 1918. Also see Snowden's question concerning the raid; 5 H.C., 103:472–74, 18 February 1918.

30. *Trib.*, 21 February 1918.

31. Statement by S. Howells Street, *Trib.*, 25 April 1918. Also see *Manchester Guardian*, 10 June 1918.

which the methods of violence have no part. We have no fear of the ultimate results of the conflict between the spirit of violence and the ideal for which we stand.[32]

The paper survived because the NCF had stayed one step ahead of the authorities. After the enforced shutdown of the National Labour Press in February, Smith had been commissioned by the NCF national committee to buy a small hand-press, type, and a stock of paper. This equipment, hidden in the home of a sympathetic printer, was brought into action when Street's press was dismantled. For almost a year this clandestine press, manned by a volunteer printer and compositor, produced the weekly edition. Since Scotland Yard was constantly on the lookout for the secret press, these men were obliged to be extremely careful in their operations. On at least one occasion the press had to be moved when neighbors began to comment about odd noises.[33]

Through the use of various ruses and improvisations, *The Tribunal* escaped detection until the police ceased to look for it.[34] The government nonetheless kept unrelenting pressure on the NCF. The fellowship's acting honorary secretary Violet Tillard was charged, under Regulation 53 of DORA, with refusing to divulge the name and address of the printer of the March 1918 edition of a monthly *NCF News Sheet* that was circulated to district and branch officials. She insisted that the *News Sheet* was a private document and therefore not subject to the regulation in question. The magistrate disagreed and after an unsuccessful appeal and her refusal to pay a fine, Tillard was sentenced to sixty-one days in Holloway prison where she immediately refused to obey prison rules.[35] *The Tribunal* remarked that the Tillard case was the first instance of a prosecution under DORA to force

32. *Trib.*, 25 April 1918.
33. *NCF Souvenir*, p. 85; A. Fenner Brockway, *Inside the Left* (London, 1942), pp. 70–71; and Lydia S. Smith and Joan Beauchamp, "Ave atqua Vale," *Trib.*, 10 April 1919.
34. See John W. Graham, *Conscription and Conscience* (London, 1922), pp. 201–3, and David Boulton, *Objection Overruled* (London, 1967), pp. 271–72, for descriptions of some of these incidents.
35. For reports on the case, see *Trib.*, 8 May, 25 July, and 15 August 1918; V. Tillard to Bertrand Russell, 30 April [1918], BRA; *NCF Souvenir*, p. 83; and *NCF News Sheet*, March 1918, NCF File, SCPC.

someone to give private information that could in no way affect the defense of the realm: "If the safety of the British Empire is indeed dependent upon members of the NCF not knowing what their fellow members are doing, ruin must surely be near at hand."[36]

The final episode in the saga of the NCF's struggle to maintain a public forum for its views involved a long and futile effort by the government to discover the printers of *The Tribunal*. In August Beauchamp was again summoned to appear at Bow Street Police Court to answer charges that she was responsible for printing the 4–25 July issues of *The Tribunal*. The basis for the summons was a hitherto uninvoked law—the Newspapers, Printers and Reading Rooms Repeal Act (1869)—that provided that every newspaper give "the name and place of abode of the printer." From the time that the NCF's secret press had begun printing *The Tribunal*, the paper had listed the following publishing information: "Printed by J. Beauchamp . . . and published at 5, York Buildings Adelphi, W.C." The state's case was predicated on the assertion that this information was false and it presented as evidence the fact that Beauchamp could not be the printer since she was constantly under close surveillance by police officials.[37]

When a dour Beauchamp appeared in court, she asserted that, though she did not operate the machinery, she was in fact the printer and publisher of the paper in question. She added that "in view of the destructive propensities of this freedom-loving Government, I think it advisable not to say where that press is located." The presiding magistrate, however, refused to recognize Beauchamp as the printer and ruled that because of her deliberate attempt to suppress the name of the real printer, she should be fined two hundred pounds and twenty-five guineas costs. However, on an appeal to Quarter Sessions, Beauchamp's attorney pointed out that the act in question provided penalties only for "the publisher . . . of each copy of the publication printed by him." Since the court had upheld the view that Beauchamp was not the printer of *The Tribunal*, it was therefore impossible to inflict any penalty on her. The judge agreed and upheld the appeal—a signal victory for the NCF.[38]

Determined to have some satisfaction, the government appealed the case and it hung on in the courts for another year. Finally, in January 1920, Beauchamp was convicted, not on the original charge, but for contempt of court because she refused to tell the judge the name of the actual printer. In the end she served only eight days of a twenty-one-day sentence and no doubt took pleasure in the knowledge that her personal struggle with DORA and the Home Office had helped *The Tribunal* to survive long enough to report the outcome of her case in its final edition.[39]

Revolt on the Inside

Even after the widely publicized concessions of December 1917, certain individuals, newspapers, and organizations kept up their protests against the continued imprisonment of absolutists. Edward Lee Hicks, the bishop of Lincoln, for example, railed against the "cruelty and absurdity of the . . . treatment of conscientious objectors." George Bernard Shaw told readers of the *Manchester Guardian* that "nothing but sheer inertia and incompetence . . . [prevents] us from applying to conscientious objectors the same protection from excessive rigor enjoyed by burglars, incendiaries, homicides, child torturers and utter unmentionables."[40]

When the seventeenth annual Labour party conference met at Nottingham in late January 1918, it unanimously adopted a resolution calling for the immediate release of all C.O.s, and in April the ILP annual conference followed suit.[41] On 21 March the *Manchester Guardian* remarked that

---

38. *Trib.*, 29 August and 17 October 1918. Also see "Rough Account of the Trial of Miss Joan Beauchamp at Bow St. on Aug. 22nd," by J. A. Nielcolfe (?), FSC Files, FHL.

39. *Trib.*, 8 January 1920. Also see Brockway, *Inside the Left*, p. 71.

40. Edward Hicks to Lord Parmoor, 27 February 1918, Gilbert Murray Papers, 57, Bodleian Library, Oxford, and G. B. Shaw to *Manchester Guardian*, 15 March 1918.

41. Report of the Annual Conference of the Labour Party, 1918 (London, 1918), p. 136; *Trib.*, 31 January 1918; and Report of the Annual Conference of the ILP, 1918 (London, 1918), p. 72.

"the law of the land" ought to replace "a senseless persecution of which the better part of public opinion is becoming steadily more ashamed." Taking all such protestations together, *The Tribunal* could insist in April that "indignation at the treatment of conscientious objectors has been steadily growing."[42] But this supposedly growing indignation was no doubt largely swept away by the frightening success of the German spring offensives. Indeed, *John Bull* may have more accurately caught the national mood when on 4 May 1918 it printed a cartoon showing a smug C.O. sitting in an easy chair warming his feet by the fire. The caption read: "This little pig stayed at home."

Whatever the public attitude, the absolutists were tending to feel increasingly isolated or even abandoned. Their restlessness engendered a growing spirit of resistance not simply to war service but to the prison system that was gradually beating them down. Some decided to rebel to make that system inoperative; others, seeing the prison system as the ultimate expression of capitalist coercion, wished to smash it completely. Many a nonresisting socialist or civil-disobedience libertarian was transformed into an outraged militant by his prison experiences.[43] Gradually, this spirit of resistance and rebellion began to have considerable influence on the future direction and policy of the No-Conscription Fellowship.

One of those who belatedly felt the need to resist was Fenner Brockway. The example of the March and November revolutions in Russia and the cruel realities of prison life had brought the founder of the NCF a long way from the attitude he expressed when first entering prison in October 1916: "When the prison gates close upon us, we must accept confinement as 'forty days in the wilderness,' a period of quiet meditation and spiritual strengthening in preparation for the days of service that lie ahead."[44] Several factors influenced Brockway's decision to revolt, but probably the most important was the creeping suspicion that the routine of imprisonment was slowly crushing his mental

42. *Trib.,* 11 April 1918.
43. For example, see C. H. Norman, *A Searchlight on the European War* (London, 1924), pp. 97–98, and *Manchester C.O.'s Journal,* 6 July 1918, p. 3, SCPC.
44. *Trib.,* 26 October 1916. Also see Brockway, *Inside the Left,* pp. 91–92.

awareness and spiritual strength. Prison routine so influenced his mentality that he unwillingly began to fear the consequences of breaking prison rules. The threat of a few days of bread and water kept him awake at night, though he had no reasoned fear of a punishment diet. For Brockway the breaking point came when a warder shouted at him to keep silent. "Was I," he asked himself, "so spiritless that I would allow anyone to forbid me the elementary right of human speech?" His answer was a resounding *no,* and having made his peace with himself, he proceeded to make war on the prison system.[45]

On 12 May 1918 Brockway wrote to his wife that he had now accepted Allen's views and that his pacifism was "no longer passive!" Henceforth, he said, he and the six men who had decided to join him would be "mentally and spiritually free" regardless of what punishments the government inflicted on them.[46] The next day Brockway informed the home secretary of his intention to break all prison rules that he considered to be "inhuman and immoral," especially the silence rule. The warden of Walton prison, where Brockway was confined, warned him and his companions that they could be charged with mutiny and punished by flogging, but they were not deterred. When the mutineers began to talk openly, they were rounded up and put into an isolated area of the prison, but they continued to talk. Indeed, their example spread even to non-C.O. prisoners.[47]

The result of Brockway's rebellion was an almost complete disruption of prison routine. All C.O.s at Walton were confined to one hall, and for ten days they ran this hall according to their own rules. Brockway recalled it as "a gay and exciting time" when self-expression came alive again, but the victory was short-lived. The uprising was successfully isolated and the ringleaders removed to other prisons. Brockway blamed himself for not having the foresight to spread the word of the revolt. A general and simultaneous resis-

45. Brockway, *Inside the Left,* pp. 103–8.
46. Extract of a letter from Brockway to his wife, 12 May 1918, CAP.
47. Brockway to Sir George Cave, 13 May 1918 (copy), CAP. Also see *Trib.,* 23 May 1918, and Brockway, *Inside the Left,* p. 108. When it printed Brockway's letter, *The Tribunal* urged relatives of men in Walton prison to write to the warden if they did not hear from the prisoners.

tance among the absolutists would, he believed, have brought significant concessions from the prison authorities. Brockway himself continued to resist prison rules until he was finally released in 1919.[48]

Although the example of Walton prison was not widely followed, there was a marked increase in isolated individual incidents. By mid-1918 the idea of a work strike, which had seemed so radical and unpacifist the year before, was considered too mild a form of resistance by some prisoners. Many of these adopted the old suffragette practice of hunger strikes in order to become so weak that the authorities would release them. A few C.O.s had refused to eat almost from the time they reached prison, but most of those who went on hunger strikes only took up the tactic during the bitter, frustrating days of 1918. Of course, this policy was never endorsed by the NCF leaders. Even those, like Allen and Brockway, who had previously ignored the advice of the national committee drew the line at hunger striking. As Brockway said: "We were not justified in forcing our liberation by threatening to take our own lives."[49]

Nonetheless, the government was faced with an increasing number of C.O. hunger strikers and struck back at them as it had at the feminists—by forcible feeding. The most astounding example of the use of this extremely unpleasant process on a C.O.—and perhaps the most amazing in any instance—was the case of a Manchester objector named Emmanuel Ribeiro. From 24 January 1917 until late June of 1918 Ribeiro underwent almost daily forced feeding. The case was repeatedly brought up in Parliament, but the authorities insisted that Ribeiro's health was good and they refused to release him until he was too weak to stand.[50] In commenting on this case the *Manchester Guardian* noted that

the whole process is stupid, useless, wasteful and disgusting. If anything more need be said it may perhaps not be irrelevant to remind the Government that by this sort of senseless persecu-

48. Brockway, *Inside the Left*, pp. 108–15. Also see *Trib.*, 8 and 22 August 1918.

49. Brockway, *Inside the Left*, pp. 111–12, and *NCF Souvenir*, pp. 66–67. Also see Allen to Russell (national committee), 17 May 1917, CAP, and *Trib.*, 27 March 1919.

50. For example, 5 H.C., 103:715, 20 February 1918. Also see *Trib.*, 4 October 1917 and 20 June 1918, and *Manchester C.O.'s Journal*, 21 February 1918, SCPC.

tion they are doing more perhaps than in any other way to ruin
their credit with great numbers of thinking men and [to] shake
their confidence in the justice of a cause for the support of
which such measures are deemed . . . necessary.[51]

There were numerous other cases of forcible feeding and at
least one instance of a C.O. who died after undergoing the
process. But after the middle of 1918 the government generally handled hunger strikers by discharging them under
the "Cat and Mouse" act. By March 1919, 115 C.O.s had
been released for hunger striking and 103 of them were still
at liberty.[52]

Although the hunger strike was the most extreme form of
prison resistance, the number of C.O.s who undertook such
a course was not large enough to cause the government
more than occasional minor embarrassment. During the last
months of the war, after the military situation in Europe had
quite obviously turned in the Allies' favor, and amid growing
difficulty with absolutists, the government decided on one
final effort to mollify both public protests and restive C.O.
prisoners. Home Office officials had somehow gained the
impression that the amelioration of prison conditions for
absolutists would bring about a cessation of the problems
that increasingly plagued prison authorities. Early in September absolutists who had served the equivalent of two
years' hard labor were assembled at Wakefield prison. Lately
abandoned as a Home Office scheme work center,
Wakefield was in the process of being transformed into a
kind of modified internment camp. Why the authorities
supposed that such a policy would solve their difficulties is
something of a mystery. Certainly no official of the NCF had
ever supported internment.[53] While still a prisoner, Allen

51. *Manchester Guardian,* 18 February 1918. Also see *Trib.,* 21 February
1918.
52. W. E. Burns died in Hull prison after being forcibly fed; see *Manchester Guardian,* 22 March 1918, and *Trib.,* 27 February, 4 and 18 April, and 30
May 1918.
53. John Rae, *Conscience and Politics: The British Government and the Conscientious Objector to Military Service, 1916–1919* (London, 1970), p. 228, n. 3,
suggests that Lord Parmoor may have influenced Home Office policy. If
anyone consulted Marshall, with whom both the Home Office and the War
Office had ready communication, she must certainly have deprecated the
idea just as she did in a letter to Dr. Alfred Salter, 21 May 1917, CEMP
(microfilm). Also see Lilla Brockway to Marshall, 27 May 1917, CEMP
(microfilm).

had specifically condemned such an idea, and as late as 1 July 1918 the national committee had announced its opposition "to any efforts being made in the direction of substituting internment for imprisonment of C.O.s."[54] Nevertheless, the Home Office pressed on.

Men arriving at Wakefield were told that they were to receive better food, a shorter work day, and free access to the buildings from 5:30 to 9:30 P.M. In addition, they would be provided with pocket money and would be allowed to open a canteen where they could buy tobacco, candy, writing materials, and so on.[55] For men who had spent two years in silent, narrow prison cells on a disgusting diet and without the most basic amenities, Wakefield must have seemed like a paradise. But this initial reaction quickly wore off and difficulties began to arise. The men were doubtlessly aware of a message from the NCF national committee, issued in mid-July, warning absolutists of a new attempt to split their ranks by an offer of special privileges: "We are of the opinion that acceptance of any such scheme by absolutists would not be in conformity with the attitude you have hitherto taken up, and we would urge you to persist in your refusal to barter your principles for any release based upon terms and conditions."[56]

By 12 September over a hundred men had been brought to Wakefield, but because the warden had not yet received his instructions from the Home Office, they had no idea what promises the government wanted from them in exchange for their improved situation. Pending the disclosure of such terms, the men held a general meeting at which they elected an advisory council headed by Walter H. Ayles. The council then began to organize work parties that were to maintain the operation of the jail on a strictly voluntary

54. See Allen's statement on internment, n.d., BRA, and NCF national committee on "The Suggested Internment of C.O.s," 1 July 1918, Murray Papers, 57. Also see Alfred Salter to Edith Ellis, 6 December 1916, in which Salter told of his interview with "a shocking old pagan" of an archbishop who had proposed internment, FSC Correspondence, 1917, FHL; and Emrys Hughes to Russell, 15 January 1918, BRA.

55. For details, see *Trib.*, 12 September 1918, and *NCF Souvenir*, p. 67.

56. Printed in *Trib.*, 18 July 1918. For the NCF's official reaction to the Wakefield scheme, see Dr. Salter's press release of September 1918, CAP, and *Trib.*, 26 September 1918.

basis, but it warned the men not to undertake any industrial or other type of prison work.[57]

Finally on 15 September instructions from the Home Office arrived and were communicated to the men in a mass meeting. The conditions laid down were essentially like those of the Home Office scheme except that the Wakefield C.O.s did not have to sign any promises and could not leave the premises.[58] In another general meeting on 17 September the men decided by a vote of 102–1 to reject the government's plan. They also drew up a manifesto outlining their reasons for refusing to do collectively what they had already refused to do individually. The affair ended in confusion and disorder when a Home Office inspector arrived with instructions to enforce the regulations. Those men who still refused to cooperate—112 out of 125—were put into locked cells in one wing of the prison and gradually returned to regular civil prisons.[59]

Thus once again the government was thwarted in its attempt to deal with the absolutists. The executive committees of both the NCF and the FSC sent laudatory "victory" messages to the Wakefield absolutists praising their "clear-sighted faithfulness and unflinching courage."[60] On the other hand, the actions of the conscientious objectors at Wakefield had again mystified and irritated the public and at least temporarily relieved pressure for further measures on the absolutists' behalf. In addition, all absolutists who had been at Wakefield were "redirected" to the first stage of hard labor, with the loss of remission marks and all privileges. The final irony of the Wakefield fiasco was that even those few men who had agreed to abide by the prescribed conditions were returned to regular prisons by mid-October.[61]

57. See undated copy of handwritten memorandum from Wakefield prisoners' committee (Wakefield Memo), BRA. Also see *Manchester Guardian*, 17 September 1918, and *Trib.*, 26 September 1918.

58. See *Trib.*, 26 September 1918, for a list of the conditions. Also see Wakefield Memo, BRA.

59. The Wakefield Manifesto was printed in *Trib.*, 26 September 1918; there is a copy of it in CAP. Also see *Trib.*, 2 October 1918; *NCF Souvenir*, p. 67; and *Manchester Guardian*, 27 September 1918.

60. *Trib.*, 26 September and 31 October 1918, and FSC *Minutes*, 3 October 1918, 3:14, FHL.

61. *Trib.*, 10 and 17 October 1918. For Allen's observations on the

Six weeks after the failure of the Wakefield experiment, the armistice was signed. There was no peace, however, for imprisoned conscientious objectors. Many had doubtless expected to be released once the war ended, but when it became obvious that the government had no intention of loosening its grip, some absolutists—approximately 130 of the 1,100 who remained in custody—staged a full-scale rebellion.[62]

All-out resistance occurred at several prisons including Maidstone, Newcastle, and Winchester, but the center of the prisoners' insurrection was Wandsworth prison. Beginning with a work strike, the men at Wandsworth slowly escalated their resistance and with each step demanded concessions in exchange for their promises to desist. On Christmas Eve and Christmas Day, 1918, the C.O.s organized concerts that the warders were evidently powerless to stop. One of the programs for these concerts has been preserved in the Swarthmore College Peace Collection. Written on toilet paper, the program lists thirty-eight separate performances and exhorts prisoners to "join in choruses" and to obey the directions of the chairman. Significantly, the program began with the "International" and ended with "The Red Flag." Sydney R. Turner, one of the participants, described the event.

> The glass of the spy holes to all the cells in the wing were smashed. The chairman called on the prisoner either to sing, recite or speak as he had promised, this was done by standing close to the hole. The applause was given by banging the cell doors with either stools or bedboards.
>
> Many friends took part in this unique performance which was very good considering the very difficult conditions under which it was held.[63]

The Wandsworth C.O.s proved to their own satisfaction and to the horror of the government that English prisons were simply not sufficiently staffed to deal with a large-scale,

---

Wakefield scheme, see Allen ms., chap. 3, p. 22, CAP. Also see Elizabeth Fox-Howard, *After Two Years—The Absolutists at Wakefield* (London, n.d.).

62. Allen ms., chap. 3, p. 23, CAP, and Graham, *Conscription and Conscience,* p. 291. On 6 February 1919 the FSC declared that it "could not in any way encourage or help" an organized strike against prison discipline; see FSC *Minutes,* 6 February 1919, 3:20, FHL; also see 6 March 1919, 3:21.

63. Note in Sydney R. Turner Papers, SCPC. The chairman was Victor Beacham. Also see *Trib.,* 27 February 1919, 6 and 20 March 1919.

well-organized uprising. In response to the chronic trouble at Wandsworth, the Home Office appointed a new warden to the prison, with orders to institute a get-tough policy. The new warden, Major Blake,[64] was evidently even more severe than the authorities had intended and, as a result of his handling of the situation, a parliamentary investigation was held. In his report Albion Richardson exonerated Blake,[65] but the result was dubbed "the Wandsworth Whitewash" by *The Tribunal,* and the *Manchester Guardian* called it "about as humiliating a document as ever a Government has had to spend public money in printing . . . it reduces to greater absurdity than any of its predecessors the handling of the rebels against military service."[66]

There was another sordid footnote to the events at Wandsworth. After hearing the chief warder derisively say that conscientious objectors not on strike were enjoying privileges won by those who had resisted, one of the prisoners who had refused to join the strike unleashed his frustration by smashing his cell windows and furniture and declaring himself on a personal work and hunger strike. Apparently because he was acting on his own, this man was treated with considerable brutality and forced to remain almost twenty-four hours in a straitjacket without even the opportunity to relieve himself.[67] His case was an object lesson in the efficacy of communal rather than individual resistance.

The punishment meted out to rebellious prisoners at Wandsworth did not deter other conscientious objectors from continuing the struggle. One of the NCF's early leaders, James H. Hudson, imprisoned at Manchester, wrote a memorandum that urged a general strike of all C.O. prisoners on May Day, 1919. He felt that the members of the NCF must do this to illustrate to the labor movement that the fellowship would never acquiesce in tyranny.[68] Hudson's old comrade Allen was in full agreement with this view.

---

64. Turner calls Blake "a bad lot" who later stood in the dock at Old Bailey; Sydney R. Turner to author, June 1967.
65. Wandsworth Prison (Allegations against Acting Governor), (1919 Cmd. 131), 27, 831.
66. *Trib.,* 15 May 1919, and *Manchester Guardian,* 8 May 1919.
67. This prisoner's statement was printed in *Trib.,* 23 January 1919.
68. Cited by Graham, *Conscription and Conscience,* p. 292. Also see letter from Richard Pennifold in *Trib.,* 13 March 1919.

I am convinced . . . that if you wish to make a real impression upon the future of conscription, every effort must be made to break through the net of the conscription system so that you create a precedent, not only . . . that militarism cannot *break* men, but even more that conscription cannot *hold* a man who is determined. The measure of our success in this case is the measure of our freedom from conscription.[69]

The NCF was, however, still not able to break through the finely woven net of conscription. While it continued its efforts to secure the release of the absolutists, it was hounded by the nagging questions of its past achievements, present worth, and future possibilities.

What contribution had the imprisoned absolutists made to the No-Conscription Fellowship and to the British war-resistance movement? It must be admitted that, in their prison cells, the absolutists did little to strengthen the NCF. Indeed, control of the organization had been taken completely out of their hands, and when they were finally released, their altered moods would significantly contribute to the demise of the fellowship.[70] Furthermore, the absolutists had not achieved the NCF's original goal of breaking down the machinery of the Military Service Acts by inundating the nation's prisons with thousands of unyielding idealists. They were, to be sure, a fly in the ointment, but, however irritated, the state managed to cope.

In evaluating the role of the absolutists and in contrasting them with the peace-by-negotiations wing of the antiwar movement, one scholar recently noted that "the course they followed . . . led them from the main theatre of political struggle to the by-path of moralistic martyrdom."[71] This unhappy conclusion is not entirely accurate. For while it is

69. Allen ms., chap. 4a, pp. 11–12, CAP.
70. See Chap. 13.
71. Howard Weinroth, "Peace by Negotiation and the British Anti-War Movement, 1914–1918," *Canadian Journal of History* 10(December 1975): 374. Some absolutists were martyrs in the literal sense. The government listed only nine C.O.s who died in prisons or Home Office camps; see 5 H.L., 34:161, 3 April 1919. But the NCF claimed that ten men died in custody and that the deaths of more than sixty others could partly be traced to the consequences of their imprisonment. In addition, thirty-one C.O.s became temporarily or permanently insane, and an undisclosed number committed suicide; see *NCF Souvenir*, p. 5.

essentially correct that the absolutists' resistance led to martyrdom rather than to any lasting effect on government policy or on the conduct of the war, it is also true that the extremist faction of the NCF provided the British peace movement with its most lionized and most influential heroes during the interwar period. Whether absolutists were thought of as miserable shirkers or as honest nuisances during the war years, by the 1930s an increasingly large number of people saw these extreme war resisters as possessed of a vision that more Britons and peoples elsewhere would have done well to adopt. During the so-called appeasement era, the delayed effect of NCF's resistance and propaganda caused at least a considerable minority to see the absolutists in the same light as these "prisoners for conscience" had seen themselves during the war. In other words, the silent sufferers for peace were eventually heard and though their message may have been inappropriate for the time when it was received, it was certainly not without effect.

13

Why Have We Fought?

Victory!—Or Defeat?

During the last year of the war the No-Conscription Fellowship, despite maintaining the services of a dedicated band of workers, was, both physically and psychologically, a badly depleted organization. As month followed dreary month and all hopes for peace were continually frustrated, the mood in the NCF became increasingly harsh and bitter. Bertrand Russell had long since warned members against allowing their mental attitudes toward the government to become like those that most Englishmen had toward the Germans, but growing disaffection seemed inevitable. Late in 1917, for example, Catherine E. Marshall felt obliged to rebuke the anonymous author of an hysterically antipatriotic article in *The Tribunal* for his "monstrously unjust assumption that pacifists are the only people who realize and suffer from the horror and tragedy of war."[1]

Even in the highest circles of the fellowship, morale was being lowered not only because of diminished chances for peace (in light of the failure of the Stockholm conference, the blunting of the pope's peace initiative, and the American entrance into the war) but also because of continued squabbling within the organization. Although differences with the FSC were temporarily resolved (or at least left dormant), new problems arose over the administration of the central office. In early September Bryce Leicester, a veteran worker in the London office, issued a memorandum on "Work in Headquarters" that took nearly everyone from Marshall to Edward Grubb to task for their alleged shortcomings. Grubb responded with an earnest defense of his work, but Marshall did not even reply to the charges

1. "Resistance and Service," *Trib.*, 3 May 1917; the unsigned article entitled "Pro Patria" appeared on 27 September 1917, and Marshall's reply was in the issue of 8 November 1917.

against her.[2] Russell was again caught in the middle and, no doubt, suffered in the knowledge that his own incapacity for administrative work had contributed to the strain.

In December 1917 an attempt was made to rally the fellowship's scattered and dissident forces and to regain some of the fire and camaraderie of earlier days by issuing a "Second Manifesto" that exhorted members to continue work for peace and brotherhood "in a spirit of true loyalty to our country and to humanity as a whole."[3] But all this seemed a bit pale, especially when compared to the Bolshevik revolution, then in its inspiring infancy.

Even the crisis brought on by the passage in April 1918 of a new conscription act failed to revive the fellowship. The Military Service (No. 2) Act of 1918[4] raised the age limit of those liable for conscription to fifty-one and also extended compulsory military service to Ireland. Theoretically, the act should have opened up a vast new field of endeavor for the NCF, but in the end nothing of particular significance transpired. Simultaneous divisional conferences were called throughout the country to protest the new measure, and *The Tribunal* boasted that these meetings "did much to bring back the enthusiasm of earlier days," but this alleged enthusiasm bore little fruit. Older men did not rush to fill the antiwar ranks[5] and the anticonscription movement in Ireland was, from its inception, controlled by militant Republicans rather than by nonviolent pacifists.[6]

---

2. Grubb to Russell, 17 September 1917, and C. Marshall to Russell and Ernest E. Hunter, 17 September [1917], BRA.

3. *Trib.*, 6 December 1917.

4. 8 GEO 5, chap. 5, 18 April 1918. See *Trib.*, 2 May 1918, and *Annual Register*, 1918, pt. 1, pp. 71–75, for detailed explanations of the act.

5. *Trib.*, 9 May 1918. On 26 August 1918 Edith Ellis of the FSC told Evangeline Barratt: "I am sorry to say that so far very few of the older men are taking up the Absolutist position. . . . the Tribunals are treating them much more leniently than the younger men . . . and quite a number have got absolute exemption"; FSC Files, FHL.

6. The conscription question as it relates to Ireland is a fascinating topic unfortunately beyond the scope of this study. The NCF had few members and little influence in Ireland although there were some interesting contacts between NCF and Irish prisoners; see A. Fenner Brockway, *Inside the Left* (London, 1942), p. 76. For a good general discussion of the Irish anticonscription movement, see George Dangerfield, *The Damnable Question* (Boston, 1976), pp. 251–84 passim. Also see *Trib.*, 23 May and 18 July 1918.

Still, the new acting chairman of the NCF, Dr. Salter, was not easily deterred. In a front-page article in *The Tribunal* he called on older men to join him in resisting the new act, not by invoking the conscience clause as younger comrades had done but by standing up "courageously, unflinchingly and unitedly in the name of simple Human Right, against the tyranny and devilry which are threatening to engulf the whole of Western Humanity in one common desolation and ruin."[7] Salter's sermon may have cheered some NCF members, but people such as Russell, Allen, and Marshall raged at its blustering irrelevancy.[8] Equally useless in their view was an NCF manifesto condemning the new act. This document, which stressed the Inner Light and other religious manifestations of pacifism, ranged rather far from the socialist and libertarian views held by most NCF members.[9]

Whatever doubts these former leaders had about the efficacy of Dr. Salter's pacifist fundamentalism, the direction of the NCF was effectively out of their hands. Besides, there were other matters of more immediate concern. Russell, of course, was faced with imprisonment, and Allen, narrowly rescued from death's door by his premature release from prison, was threatened by permanent disability. Marshall, who had never fully recovered from her breakdown of September 1917, was probably as badly off as Allen was. Certainly, he thought so. She had raced to his side as soon as he was released from prison, but within a month Allen was telling Russell of his concern for her health: "I am having a terrible tussle with her. She is nearer Conscientious Objection Mania than anyone I've yet met and *must* be prevented from coming down to the next national committee meeting."[10]

7. *Trib.*, 18 April 1918.
8. See Marshall to Russell, 30 April 1918, and Russell to Allen, n.d. [late April 1918], BRA. Russell said of Salter: "I should entertain him with examples of unsuccessful martyrdoms. What caused Xianity [Christianity] to grow was episcopal organisation and promiscuous charity on a large scale. Every persecution carried a great set-back. You should read Chap. XV of Gibbon. No one who has not done so is competent to take an intelligent part in the Labour movement."
9. Published in *Trib.*, 6 June 1918. There is also a copy in FSC Files, FHL. Also see FSC *Minutes*, 2 May 1918, 3:6, FHL. The FSC decided against signing the manifesto, although they entirely agreed with its contents.
10. Allen to Russell, 2 January 1918, BRA.

One manifestation of Marshall's "mania" was the obsessive fear that Allen was being turned against her by the Ellises, a Quaker family who in January had taken him into their home on the Yorkshire coast. As she told Russell: "I am very unhappy about C. A. . . . Miss Ellis . . . is definitely trying to sow misunderstanding and mistrust between us. This would not matter in the least if we were together—she would be powerless to do anything of the kind. But as it is . . . she has a certain amount of power to make mischief." All this put her into another mood of black despair. "Everything," she said, "seems dead or futile or not worthwhile."[11]

Marshall's frame of mind doubtless improved at the end of February when Allen left Yorkshire to join her and her parents in Keswick. But he was in fact a very sick man, deeply troubled in mind and body, subject to fits of sleeplessness, and oppressed by "disconsolate memories."[12] The diary Allen kept and the letters he wrote during this time when he was trying to sort out and to justify his wartime experiences reveal a doleful, unsettled mood. Certainly he had moved a long way from the view that violence was innately evil and that nothing was more sacred than human life. Russell's influence is clearly visible in Allen's increasing stress on libertarian rather than strictly pacifist principles. A newly revived interest in guild socialism also reflected his growing distrust of the power of the state, even the socialist state, over the individual. On 29 January he wrote:

> I want my country to be great amongst the nations of the world—great by virtue of its loyalty to freedom and tolerance; still the world home for men and women exiled because they insist on thinking or speaking as they believed right. . . . And just because I love and respect the spirit of my country, I hate to see her persecuting free opinion.[13]

Three months later he added:

> For me the struggle for liberty for the individual in the state played a more important part . . . than an objection to war and . . . this led me to decide my action not so much by drawing lines between different kinds of war work as by considering

11. Marshall to Russell, 23 January 1918, BRA. Also see Marshall to Russell, 3 February 1918, BRA.
12. From incomplete typescript of Allen's diary (3 March 1918), CAP.
13. Allen's diary, 29 January 1918, quoted in Martin Gilbert, ed., *Plough My Own Furrow* (London, 1965), p. 105.

whether we ought as good citizens to admit the wrongful interference of the state with individual freedom and choice.[14]

And in a letter to Russell he said:

> Of course I hate all the rubbish a good many of our own
> people talk about the resistance of a handful of young pacifists
> being the way to prevent war. . . . I am sick to death with the
> endless discussion about drawing lines between different kinds
> of national service and keep a very open mind upon so-called
> bargains of that kind, but that's because my resistance is far less
> directed against the war than it is to preserving liberty.[15]

During these last sad months of the war, Allen stayed
chiefly with Marshall's family, venturing out with her in August for a three-week holiday in Scotland. Soon after returning he discovered that he had contracted tuberculosis of the
right lung and would be a partial invalid for the rest of his
life.[16] Then the war ended.

Allen's reaction to the news of the armistice gave profound expression to the loneliness and disillusionment of a
conscientious objector with lingering doubts about the significance of what he had done during the war years. "I have
never longed so intensely as then to be one with the rest of
the nation and to share its rejoicings and its reasons for
rejoicing. . . . I too was glad that the war was likely to be over,
but I had no share in the achievement over which everyone
was exulting."[17] Thus, the coming of peace was a kind of
psychological defeat not only for Allen but for the NCF—a
realization that victory had eluded them even as their fond-
est hope was fulfilled.

But the NCF had never won great victories. Its chief merit
had always been the ability to organize itself to deal with a
number of ever-changing specific problems, and some of
this strength carried over into the postwar period.

The first problem that faced the NCF after the war was
the parliamentary election of 1918 in which Lloyd George,
nationally celebrated as "the man who won the war," asked
the voters to extend the mandate of his coalition govern-

14. Allen's diary, 2 May 1918, quoted in ibid., p. 113.
15. Allen to Russell, 27 June 1918, BRA.
16. See Arthur Marwick, *Clifford Allen: The Open Conspirator* (Edinburgh,
1964), pp. 49, 51.
17. Allen ms., chap. 4, pp. 4–5, CAP.

ment. Since the prime minister had become the bête noire of all pacifists, there was grave anxiety that the postwar government would be dominated by men determined to fasten permanent conscription onto the British nation.[18] In attempting to meet this new challenge, the NCF had a special disadvantage. According to Section 9(2) of the Representation of the People Act (1918), any person who was exempted from the army as a conscientious objector or who, as a member of the forces, refused to obey orders because of conscientious objection to military service was to be disqualified from voting in local or parliamentary elections for five years after the end of the war.[19] The fellowship faced a further liability in that its extreme antiwar stance had alienated it from every political party except the numerically insignificant ILP. *The Tribunal* therefore called on its readers to support first of all those M.P.s who had voted against the various Military Service Acts. Where these men were not standing (almost everywhere), members were urged to help Labour candidates since Labour's election manifesto included the release of all conscientious objectors and the abolition of conscription.[20] While the NCF's support of anticonscription candidates obviously had little effect on the Lloyd George coalition's sweeping victory,[21] in a sense the fellowship did accomplish one of its principal aims. Whether because of the pacifist campaign or because of some more general outcry, conscription did become an election issue, and ultimately Lloyd George disavowed any intention of permanently maintaining compulsory military service.[22]

18. See *Trib.*, 24 October and 14 November 1918.

19. Since the war did not officially end until August 1921, the clause was in effect until August 1926. In practice, the disqualification of C.O.s seemed to have been ineffective; see John Rae, *Conscience and Politics: The British Government and the Conscientious Objector to Military Service, 1916-1919* (London, 1970), pp. 234–35.

20. *Trib.*, 14 November–12 December 1918.

21. Eighteen conscientious objectors, including Salter and James Maxton, contested seats, but only Neil Maclean, who stood for the Govan District in Glasgow, was successful. See *Trib.*, 16 January and 13 February 1919. Ramsay MacDonald told Russell that the "coming of victory has put us in the wrong from a platform point of view"; Russell to Allen, 14 October 1918, BRA.

22. See statement giving Lloyd George's position in *Trib.*, 19 December 1918.

After the election the NCF gave much of its attention to a campaign for securing the release of the men who remained in prisons and Home Office work centers. The "hard-faced men" of the new Parliament were not likely to be moved to compassion by the fellowship's pleas for clemency. Indeed, through the early months of 1919 the government maintained the position that conscientious objectors would be held to their military obligation so long as that obligation was incumbent on other members of the forces.[23] The cabinet feared that the release of C.O.s would increase the bitterness among men still detained in military service and would give C.O.s preference in obtaining employment.[24]

The NCF responded by establishing a new department, directed by Gladys Rinder and supported by a "Set Them Free" campaign fund, to coordinate propaganda and agitation for the release of prisoners. Rinder was able to organize a memorial, signed by 162 prominent people and presented to Lloyd George by the Reverend E. W. Barnes, master of the Temple; Gilbert Murray; John Buchan; and Lord Parmoor, that decried the continued imprisonment of C.O.s and asked for their immediate release.[25] The prime minister also received a petition from eighty members of Parliament urging him to set the tone for the rebuilding of British society by releasing all conscientious objectors. Another petition containing 130,000 signatures gathered by *The Herald* was personally handed to the home secretary by *Herald* editor, George Lansbury.[26]

The liberal press was also outraged by what it considered a

23. See statement by Sir George Cave, 5 H.C., 110:1592, 31 October 1918.

24. On demobilization, see Stephen R. Graubard, "Military Demobilization in Great Britain following the First World War," *Journal of Modern History* 19 (December 1947):297–311, and Martin Gilbert, *Winston S. Churchill*, vol. 4, *1916–1922: The Stricken World* (Boston, 1975), pp. 181–96.

25. Reprinted the *Trib.*, 9 January 1919. There is a copy in the Lloyd George Papers, F/95/1/1, House of Lords Record Office, London. Those signing included Hilaire Belloc, Arnold Bennett, G. K. Chesterton, John Galsworthy, George Bernard Shaw, C. P. Scott, J. M. Keynes, R. H. Tawney, H. G. Wells, Lord Crewe, Lord Morley, and seventeen bishops. Also see FSC *Minutes*, 6 March, 3 April, and 5 June 1919, 3:21–22, 26, FHL.

26. See *Trib.*, 28 November and 5 December 1918 and 13 March 1919. Also see *The Herald*, 8 March 1919, and FSC *Minutes*, 5 December 1918 and 2 January 1919, 3:19–29, FHL.

crass attempt to pander to the mob. *The Nation* noted that the release of conscientious objectors was becoming "a first class political question" that would finally force the cabinet to take some belated action.[27] Nor were conservatives entirely silent. Lord Hugh Cecil was particularly prominent in efforts to obtain the release of C.O.s, just as he had been in denouncing their disfranchisement through the Representation of the People Act. With nearly two thousand conscientious objectors still in prison or in Home Office centers, Cecil wrote a stinging letter to *The Times* castigating the government for "extreme wickedness" in allowing the "prejudices and complaints" of ignorant people to be put before simple justice. A few days later Cecil and six other M.P.s organized a bipartisan group to pressure the cabinet on the C.O. question. These seven men organized a meeting on 25 March at which about fifty M.P.s adopted a resolution calling for an end to the imprisonment of conscientious objectors. To underscore this resolution Cecil and a select committee of those attending the meeting sent a letter to Lloyd George warning him that the inevitable turning of public opinion would make the continued punishment of conscientious objectors "as impolitic as . . . it has always been wrong."[28]

A few days after this parliamentary protest, Secretary of State for War Winston Churchill announced that demobilization had progressed sufficiently to allow the gradual release of conscientious objectors.[29] Even five months after the war's end, however, the cabinet would not release C.O.s en masse. On 8 April the first absolutists were set free, but only those who had served two years' imprisonment were allowed to go. Others were to be released on completion of their current sentences or after two statutory years (twenty months), whichever came first. Those remaining in prison were usually young boys or older men who had been called up late in the war. Indeed, if the original scheme had not

27. Quoted by *Trib.*, 3 April 1919. Also see *Trib.*, 6 February and 13 March 1919.
28. *The Times*, 10 March 1919, and *Trib.*, 20 March–10 April 1919 passim. Also see *Daily News*, 7 March 1919.
29. Churchill had previously advocated the release of C.O. prisoners but was rebuffed by his cabinet colleagues; see CAB 24/75/6873, CAB 23/9/537(5), and CAB 23/9/545(1). The decision to release conscientious objectors was made on 3 April 1919; see CAB 23/10/553(1).

been modified, some C.O.s would have had to remain in prison until February 1920.

After an initial rush, the process of release slowed down to a snail's pace. By mid-May over three hundred C.O.s remained in prison, and other objectors were still being court-martialed.[30] Finally on 30 July 1919 Churchill announced that all conscientious objectors had been released. Thus ended the first stage of the NCF's battle against conscription.[31]

Actually, the freeing of the absolutists left one group of conscientious objectors still in the hands of the military. Many of the men in the Non-Combatant Corps were kept in France until late 1919 or early 1920. When the pay of the army of occupation was raised, the NCC men received none of the extra benefits. As General Childs pointed out at the time, it was a mean and petty way to treat men who had exercised a legal right specifically provided for them by the government.[32]

Many of the men who finally emerged from prison in 1918 and 1919 were not in a physical or psychological condition to cope with the outside world. Most, even those healthy enough to work, were without immediate prospects of employment. Pacifist leaders had not been unmindful of this situation. As early as March 1917 Marshall had suggested to the Joint Advisory Council (JAC) that it should prepare a file of men who might need employment after the war as well as a list of firms who would be willing to hire them. In February 1918, at the instigation of the FSC, the JAC met at Devonshire House to discuss, among other things, plans for providing convalescence, training, and employment for released C.O.s.[33] In June the Fellowship of Reconciliation

30. *Trib.*, 1 May 1919. One C.O. was court-martialed for desertion as late as 11 September 1919; see *Trib.*, 25 September 1919.

31. 5 H.C., 118:2001-2, 30 July 1919, and *Trib.*, 7 August 1919. All C.O.s remaining in Home Office centers were unconditionally released in April 1919; see *Trib.*, 24 April 1919.

32. Sir Wyndham Childs, *Episodes and Reflections* (London, 1930), p. 154. Also see Rae, *Conscience and Politics*, p. 194, and *Trib.*, 3 April, 5 June, 21 August, 4 September, and 20 October 1919.

33. FSC *Minutes* and Files, 1917–1919, contain voluminous material on these projects; see especially FSC to J. A. Harrop [of NCF], 17 March 1917, FSC General Correspondence, 1916–1917; FSC, Minutes of meeting (Manchester), 7–8 January 1918; and Notice of Joint Conference of NCF, FOR, and FSC held at Devonshire House, 8–9 February [1918], FSC *Minutes*, 3:1,

began to take steps to set up an employment bureau for men needing immediate employment.[34] This Conscientious Objectors Employment Agency (COEA) was not firmly established until the autumn of 1918 when the FSC took chief responsibility for finding work for those who had lost their positions because of conscientious convictions. Offices were set up in London and Manchester, and by late January 1919 the COEA had obtained employment for 155 men or about one-third of those who applied. In addition to its employment work, the FSC also provided vocational and educational training for released men.[35]

Eventually, these cooperating agencies were able to establish a fairly regular routine in caring for released conscientious objectors. Upon his release, each prisoner was handed a letter informing him of the help available and directing him to an address in the vicinity of the prison where he could receive immediate aid. Friends of the movement were asked to contribute money (it was estimated that four thousand pounds would be required), clothing, and, if possible, housing for recuperating objectors.[36]

The housing situation was most acute but was considerably relieved by Dr. Salter's farsightedness. Late in 1917 Dr. Salter began soliciting funds for the purchase of a twenty-acre country estate, Fairby Grange, at Harley, Kent. The estate was to be used initially as a convalescent home for C.O.s released on medical grounds and would eventually be developed as a holiday camp where youth and families from the London slums could enjoy healthy outdoor living without being subjected to the nascent militarism of groups like the Boy Scouts.[37] The manor house at Fairby Grange could

FHL. Also see *Trib.*, 10 and 24 October 1918 and 23 January, 24 April, and 1 May 1919.

34. *NCF Souvenir*, pp. 78–80, and FSC *Minutes*, 6 June and 3 July 1918, 3:10–11, FHL. Also see *Trib.*, 30 January and 1 May 1919.

35. FSC *Minutes*, 30 October and 18 November 1918 and 2 January 1919, 3:14, 19, 24, FHL. Also see *NCF Souvenir*, pp. 80–81, and *Trib.*, 17 October 1918 and 30 January 1919.

36. *Trib.*, 9 May 1918 and 23 January and 1 May 1919, and Joint Advisory Council, "Provision for Convalescent C.O.s," 9 January 1919, Gilbert Murray Papers, 57, Bodleian Library, Oxford.

37. For a full description of Fairby Grange and its operation, see two letters from Alfred Salter to Friends and Subscribers, undated [early 1918] and October 1918, FSC Files, FHL. Also see A. Fenner Brockway, *Bermondsey Story* (London, 1949), pp. 69–70.

accommodate about thirty men, in addition to a C.O. staff that provided them with special care and medical treatment. It was even possible to set up open-air facilities for tuberculosis patients, and Dr. Salter personally supervised the treatment and diet of the men.[38]

When the large-scale release of C.O. prisoners began in April, a joint board for assistance of conscientious objectors and their dependents was established to coordinate relief services, with Dr. Salter as chairman, Grubb and Ramsay MacDonald as treasurers, and Ernest E. Hunter as secretary. The joint board made an immediate appeal for £10,000 and this goal was nearly achieved. From 1 June 1919 to 30 April 1920 the board received £9,775 in contributions and spent £7,185 in direct relief. During this time it provided holidays for almost 150 men, paid weekly maintenance grants to 200 unemployed ex-prisoners, and helped C.O.s to pay debts that had accumulated while they were in prison. After April 1920 the joint board continued its operations from the NCF's old headquarters at 5 York Buildings and until the end of 1920 distributed another £2,000 in aiding 100 "incapacitated or victimized" objectors.[39]

The Future of the No-Conscription Fellowship—The Last Phase

Even while the NCF was engrossed in its efforts on behalf of imprisoned or newly released C.O.s, some members detected the growth of new and formidable challenges from the military establishment. They believed that within the coalition government certain elements led by Churchill—the newly emerging archvillain of the pacifist left—were attempting to establish conscription as a permanent fixture in British life. *The Tribunal* (8 May 1919) called Churchill "a man who will stick at nought to strengthen the hold which militarism has gained upon this country during the last four

38. Report of COIB, 21 August 1918, p. 2, CAP; *NCF Souvenir*, p. 81; *Trib.*, 24 October 1918 and 1 May 1919; and Brockway, *Bermondsey Story*, pp. 69–70.

39. NCF Trustees: Annual Report—January to December 1920, NCF File, SCPC; *NCF Souvenir*, p. 81; and *Trib.*, 24 April, 14 May, and 12 June 1919.

years." In the eyes of anticonscriptionists, this assertion was well warranted by events.

Despite Lloyd George's campaign promises, the king's speech opening the new parliamentary session carried the implication that continued conscription would be necessary "to reap the full fruits of victory and to safeguard the peace of the world."[40] A week later Churchill, speaking at the Mansion House, stressed the necessity of prolonging conscription in order to ensure that Germany could not undertake a war of revenge.[41] The fears and suspicions of anticonscriptionists were confirmed on 6 March 1919 when Frederick Guest, chief coalition Liberal whip and Churchill's cousin, presented to the Commons a stopgap conscription measure embodied in the Naval, Military and Air Force Service Bill. Defenders of the bill emphasized that it was absolutely necessary to keep some semblance of a military establishment until the peace was signed and that, in any case, its provisions would expire on 30 April 1920. Both Labour and the "Wee-Free" Liberals opposed the bill, but it passed easily and received royal assent on 16 April.[42]

In the eyes of the NCF, Churchill had thus been provided with the means to carry out his nefarious scheme to crush the forces of progress wherever they arose—in Russia, in Ireland, or along the Clyde. Added to this danger C.O.s saw another, more insidious threat. NCF propaganda had long warned of the militarists' attempts to rivet their ideas on the country by leading astray the younger generation. After the war *The Tribunal* constantly warned of conscriptionist efforts to impose some type of compulsory military training on the British school system. The possibilities ranged from a compulsory cadet corps to another attempt to link the Boy Scouts with the War Office.[43] In *The Tribunal*, Hunter warned

---

40. 5 H.C., 112:48, 11 February 1919. For articles on the dangers of continued conscription, see *Trib.*, 12 December 1918 and 4 January and 6 February 1919.

41. *The Times*, 20 February 1919. For Churchill's plans for maintaining an army of considerable size, see Gilbert, *Churchill*, 4:184–93.

42. See 5 H.C., 113:687–787, 6 March 1919, for the debate. Also see *Annual Register*, 1919, pt. 1, pp. 30–31.

43. See *Trib.*, 12 December 1918 and 6 February 1919; H. P. Adams, *Pacifism as a Practical Policy*, NCF pamphlet (London, n.d.), pp. 4, 7; and a circular letter of 6 December 1917 signed by Bertrand Russell, Edward Grubb, and Harry Snell warning of "immoral coercion" being exerted on

that "the militarists are at work preparing once again to lead the next generation into the slaughterhouse. Ours is the task of frustrating their devilish designs and showing the people that better way which substitutes cooperation for competition in the councils of nations."[44]

In the light of these postwar developments, some members of the NCF felt that the future of their fellowship was every bit as important as its past. They saw the organization as a leader in defending against further assaults on the liberties of the people and in rebuilding a more humane, equitable, and durable social order.[45] On the other hand, many members believed that the NCF had run its course and should disband after discharging its duties toward its members who had suffered in upholding pacifist principles. This faction felt that conscientious objectors could more effectively fight militarism and aid society by returning to the various organizations from whence they had come. Conferences on the future of the movement had been held intermittently from January 1918,[46] but no coherent plans had emerged. During the early months of peace, opposing views were presented at great length in the columns of *The Tribunal*. Taken together, they form a fairly accurate mosaic of the diverse elements that had shaped the NCF throughout its history and that finally made its survival impossible.

Those who saw an important future for the NCF formed at least a sizable minority of the fellowship, but when it came to describing the precise role the postwar organization should play, they dissolved into a dozen squabbling factions. Some members of the national committee like Brockway, Salter, and William J. Chamberlain at first believed that the NCF should combine the best of socialism with the best of Christian pacifism and become in Brockway's words: "a great missionary body inside the Socialist and Christian movement." By linking antimilitarism with international

youth to join the "Cadet Corps" and other military-training groups, BRA. Also see *Trib.*, 31 January and 18 July 1918, 24 January and 27 February 1919.

44. "The Next War," *Trib.*, 17 July 1919. Also see Hunter's editorial on "The Fallacy of Military Training," *Trib.*, 26 June 1919.

45. See statements by Morgan Jones and Frank Lloyd, *Trib.*, 2 January 1919. Also see *Manchester C.O.'s Journal*, November 1918, SCPC.

46. See FSC *Minutes*, 7 and 8 January 1918, 3:1, FHL, and Ernest E. Hunter to E. Ellis, 26 February 1918, Edith Ellis Papers, FSC Files, FHL.

brotherhood, the fellowship could be the rallying point for a worldwide organization of war resisters. At one time or another, supporters for this utopian view ranged from Quakers like Hubert W. Peet to freethinkers like Hunter.[47] But what of those who had emerged from prison talking about the "dictatorship of the armed proletariat"? Did they, with Stephen Hobhouse, still believe in "the sacredness of human life . . . and . . . the power of passive resistance?" C. H. Norman, for one, wanted an international organization, but one willing to employ the "Activism of the general strike" as the proper method of resisting war. Never again should it succumb to the futility of merely passively resisting militarism since "the Passivism of the NCF weakened [its] influence . . . among the masses."[48]

Noting the wide divergence in views about the future of the fellowship, Chamberlain presented a novel suggestion. Since the position of the absolute pacifists and that of the militant anticapitalists were clearly incompatible, he felt that it would be "quite correct" to divide the fellowship into antimilitarist and militant-anticapitalist sections. Chamberlain added his personal view that he would prefer one thousand members who were against armed force to ten thousand who were merely opposed to the militarism of capitalism.[49] Still other members believed that the NCF's dilemma might be solved if the central organization were dissolved, leaving the branches to carry on the fight against militarism as each thought best. Finally, there were men like Hunter who seemed to believe that the NCF should be preserved regardless of which specific ideas it espoused. Hunter felt that the only basis for membership in the organization should be opposition to conscription, regardless of the basis of that opposition.[50]

47. See articles by W. J. Chamberlain, "On Christianity and War," *Trib.*, 5 September 1918, and A. Fenner Brockway, "What of the Future?," *Trib.*, 24 April 1919. Also see articles by Hubert W. Peet and Ernest E. Hunter, *Trib.*, 29 May and 19 June 1919.

48. "The Future of the NCF," *Trib.*, 8 May 1919. For Hobhouse's view, see *Trib.*, 2 January 1919; for Philip Snowden's, see *Trib.*, 4 September 1919.

49. "What is Anti-Militarism?," *Trib.*, 22 May 1919. Chamberlain did in fact carry through with this suggestion in 1921 when he helped to found the No More War Movement.

50. The suggestion that the NCF be resolved into independent local branches was made by Robert O. Mennell of the FSC, *Trib.*, 22 May 1919,

Amid this plethora of proposals and counterproposals over the future of the NCF, there were some who were prepared to say that the fellowship had no future at all. One of these was Aylmer Rose who had been the first organizing secretary of the NCF. Rose believed that the chief function of the fellowship had been to oppose conscription and that any secondary functions could be better carried on by other bodies more qualified for such work. He personally would be unwilling to associate with the "revolutionary pseudo-C.O. who wants Russian Revolutions." In a perceptive passage, Rose summed up the argument for those who believed the NCF had outlived its usefulness.

> The contracting of our thoughts into a single channel . . . has tended to produce in us defects and injuries more serious even than loss of health or energy or memory. To be narrow, sectarian, bitter, bigoted, short-sighted or out of touch with broader interests of humanity, are the gravest deficiencies which can be imputed to internationalists, reconcilers and peacemakers. It is precisely because these are the faults into which . . . we are . . . liable to fall . . . that I should be glad to see our concentration in a single organisation broken up.[51]

Rose's view received considerable support from those who agreed that it served no useful purpose to sentimentally cling to what was in essence "an emergency corps in search of an emergency."[52] But a far more useful demonstration of Rose's arguments for disbanding were the controversies raging through the fellowship even as he wrote. The most prominent example of high-level feuding was an exchange between perpetual malcontent Norman and Grubb. In the course of an article reviewing "the series of errors that has . . . represented the policy of the NCF since 1916," Norman chose the Society of Friends as the special target for his dissatisfaction. He noted that the NCF had depended on subsidies from Quakers

> with the inevitable result that an anti-militarist organisation, founded on pacifist principles, became transformed into a

---

and by an anonymous correspondent, *Trib.*, 8 May 1919. Also see Hunter's article, "An Appeal for Unity," *Trib.*, 20 February 1919.

51. *Trib.*, 8 May 1919. Also see Rose to Allen, 23 February 1919, CAP.

52. Frank Milland, "The NCF and Its Future," *Trib.*, 19 June 1919. Also see *Trib.*, 10 July and 4 September 1919.

non-resistance organisation inspired by passivism and submissiveness. . . . In the past those who have paid the piper have called the tune, with the consequence that the song of the organisation has been keyed rather lower than the spirit of the members in the early days justified. If we are to go on, that must not be permitted to recur.

Grubb's reply was almost vehement. Since becoming treasurer in July 1915, he said, he could recall no time when a subscriber not in the membership had attempted to influence or to control NCF policy. Grubb also denied that the NCF had ever become passive rather than activist for fear of losing wealthy subscribers.[53]

While this confrontation was unfortunate from a personal view, it did serve to illustrate the gulf that divided various sections of the NCF. Another illuminating example also involved Rose who, because of his outspoken opinions, was rapidly becoming persona non grata to some leftist members. In July 1919 Rose wrote an article outlining his reasons for being an anti-Bolshevik. The following week he was hotly attacked by readers who felt that his opinions were worthless because he was "an *intellectual* university man" and therefore too far removed from the class struggle.[54]

After observing and sometimes partaking in several months of fierce contention, the national committee decided to call a convention in London for the purpose of deciding the future of the NCF.[55] To frame recommendations for convention delegates, conference of representatives from all past national committees would be held. This preconvention meeting took place at Jordans, a Quaker estate near Beaconsfield, late in July. In reading his report on the condition of the fellowship to its assembled leaders, Hunter merely recounted what most of them already knew: the NCF was perilously close to collapse. Memberships were falling off, branches were closing, and *The Tribunal*'s circulation was declining rapidly. Past and present dissensions, lack of

---

53. See Norman's attack in *Trib.*, 8 May 1919, and Grubb's rejoinder on 15 May. Grubb may have been technically correct in his assertion of independence, but his own correspondence with Edith Ellis in 1917 (see Chap. 10) would seem to indicate some attempt by wealthy contributors to restrict NCF activities.

54. See Aylmer Rose, "Why I Am an Anti-Bolshevik," *Trib.*, 17 July 1919, and Ernest Cant's letter attacking Rose, *Trib.*, 24 July 1919.

55. *Trib.*, 29 May 1919.

communication between younger and older members, and the widespread feeling that the NCF had outlasted the crisis for which it was created—all convinced a majority of those at Jordans that there was "no future for the fellowship along present lines." As Fenner Brockway noted, members had "been brought together from different points of view and it is according to these points of view that we regard the future."[56] Not surprisingly, the two most obvious points of view were roughly parallel to those that had motivated and divided the FSC and the NCF during the war: one wishing to emphasize "the pacifist doctrine of life" as a means of abolishing war, and the other desiring a more diverse and active policy to ensure the establishment of social justice as well as world peace.[57]

Mindful of what had transpired at Jordans, the national committee met on 2 August, fixed the dates for the convention at 29-30 November, and drafted its recommendations to the delegates. In essence, the committee recommended that the NCF be dissolved and that it be replaced by three committees: one "to initiate a new organization to associate all those who will resist conscription"; a second to create a new group that would form the British section of an international pacifist organization; and finally a third committee to deal with any attempts to introduce military training into the educational system. As was his wont, Norman dissented and later noted that the national committee's action seemed to "risk the destruction of the little permanent value the movement has had."[58]

In summarizing the majority view for *The Tribunal*, Allen noted that the chief objective of former C.O.s should not be to save the NCF but to further disseminate the ideals and principles on which that ad hoc body had been founded. Events during the war years, he continued, had made the

56. *Trib.*, 7 August 1919, which included a listing of those attending the Jordans meeting. Also see Allen ms., chap. 3a, pp. 25-27, CAP.

57. See Clifford Allen, "The Future of the NCF," *Trib.*, 14 August 1919, and Edward Grubb, "The 'Political' Conscientious Objector," *Trib.*, 21 August 1919. Also see FSC *Minutes*, 3 September 1919, 3:31, FHL.

58. See "Minutes of the National Committee of the NCF," 2 August 1919, CAP; NCF leaflet on the national committee's recommendations, CAP; and *Trib.*, 2 October 1919 and 20 January 1920. For other dissent against the committee's proposals, see *Trib.*, 30 October 1919.

fellowship an even more divergent body than it had been in the beginning. Some members were even willing to risk bloodshed to ensure the destruction of the capitalist system. Clearly, these men could not feel at home with those who believed that even strikes were an improper method of compelling a man to do something before he believed in it.[59] Because of this type of intellectual dispersion, Allen concluded, the NCF should be willing "to declare its triumph and hand on the wider work to others."[60]

The national committee made careful plans to ensure that the coming convention would not be merely a large-scale reiteration of the controversies that troubled the NCF. Considerable space in *The Tribunal* was devoted to articles exhorting the membership "to make the Convention . . . a great Festival of Fellowship."[61] Allen noted that the convention had two major objectives: to provide a reunion for all resisters and to enable those present to rededicate themselves to the service of their fellow men from whom they had been isolated for so long: "I think we have often intensified that isolation by our intolerance and by a certain spiritual pride which almost always develops in those who are persecuted. Only life service can establish our resistance as an act of citizenship and fulfill the hopes which were renewed in our prison cells."[62] Finally, groundwork for the final meeting was laid in a series of divisional conferences that were to thrash out questions to be considered at the convention. In spite of some disaffection, these meetings apparently all agreed to recommend acceptance of the national committee's views.[63]

The size of the delegation that met at Devonshire House on 29 November reflected the diminished circumstances of

59. Allen's point here referred especially to Dr. Salter; see Allen ms., chap. 3a, pp. 25–27, CAP.
60. *Trib.*, 14 August 1919. Also see Dr. Salter's article in *Trib.*, 13 November 1919.
61. A. Fenner Brockway, "The Convention," *Trib.*, 28 August 1919. Also see *Trib.*, 24 July and 4 September 1919.
62. Allen, "The Future of the NCF."
63. *Trib.*, 11 September 1919, and *NCF Souvenir*, p. 86. Also see *Trib.*, 30 October 1919, for complaints about the high-handed manner in which the national committee's recommendations were forced through at the London divisional conference.

the fellowship. There were about four hundred delegates, each representing at most ten branch members,[64] a depressingly small figure compared to the ten thousand represented at the convention of April 1916.

Allen opened the convention with a ringing address in which he traced the history of the movement, admitted its shortcomings, praised its successes, and urged the members to redouble their efforts on behalf of peace and social justice. He concluded by proposing a resolution that read in part:

> We acclaim the new hope of human liberty now challenging ancient tyrannies in industry, within the State and between the nations, and dedicate the liberty we have regained, to such service as shall contribute to the building of a world rooted in freedom and enriched by labour that is shared by all.
>
> It is in this spirit that we go forth to meet new tasks, confident that through its long and bitter suffering mankind must yet come into the way of love.[65]

There followed a great number of speeches—some critical, most laudatory—but the most significant developments occurred on the second day when the national committee's recommendations were debated. The first serious challenge to the committee's view was a resolution from the Glasgow branch that the proposed international pacifist union should "work for the overthrow of the capitalist system." Brockway opposed the resolution because, he said, the NCF should not attempt to establish a rival Socialist International, and it was easily defeated. Another critical vote was on an amendment moved by the Dundee branch, which advocated the continuance of the fellowship as "a united anti-militarist organisation." Norman, perhaps opting for leadership among the rebels, spoke in favor of this resolution, but the final count, taken after lengthy debate, was 244–171 against the Dundee proposal. The NCF had, in effect, voted itself out of existence.[66]

64. NCF Souvenir, p. 87, and John W. Graham, Conscription and Conscience (London, 1922), p. 331, both state that there were 400 delegates. The agenda for the convention, however, lists only 333 delegates as of 18 November 1919; see "Agenda for NCF National Convention, 29–30 November 1919," pp. 26–30, CAP. Also see Trib., 25 September 1919.
65. Trib., 8 January 1920.
66. See Trib., 8 January 1920, p. 6, for a summary of the debate.

Thus, the convention accepted the national committee's recommendations *in toto* and at the close of the meeting all that remained of the organization were three watchdog committees—an anticonscription committee, a pacifist's union committee, and a committee to oppose military training in schools. There was also a board of trustees that consisted of members of the last national committee. At the end of 1920 these trustees issued a report that gave a full account of the activities and the fate of the committees.[67]

The anticonscription committee decided in March 1920 that the danger of conscription was so slight that, for the time being at least, no further anticonscription society was needed. In August, however, it reacted to the government's anti-Russian policy by forming a resist-the-war committee. This group registered forty-eight hundred citizens who pledged not to partake—directly or indirectly—in any government action directed against the Soviet Union. The resist-the-war group felt that it could take at least partial credit for the failure of Churchill's anti-Bolshevik crusade.[68]

The committee to consider the formation of an international pacifist union met a few times and finally dissolved after passing a resolution recommending that NCF members interested in peace attach themselves to one of the existing pacifist societies. The committee to resist military education was called on three occasions but could never raise a quorum. After 1920 all that was left of the No-Conscription Fellowship was a commission for social reunion that arranged periodic reunions for ex–conscientious objectors.[69] The hound of conscience had found rest at last.

67. "NCF Trustee's Report, 1920," NCF File, SCPC. The names of the various committee members are listed by Graham, *Conscription and Conscience*, p. 340.
68. "NCF Trustee's Report, 1920," SCPC, and *NCF Souvenir*, p. 51.
69. "NCF Trustee's Report, 1920," SCPC.

14

The NCF in Modern British History

Epilogue

The release of conscientious objectors and the dissolution of the No-Conscription Fellowship did not conclude the story of those who resisted the Great War. For one thing, recriminations lingered. All ex-conscientious objectors, aside from those in the Non-Combatant Corps, were disfranchised for five years after the end of the war (officially from 1921 to 1926), though in practice this restriction seems to have been difficult to enforce effectively.[1] More meaningful for a small number was the fact that conscientious objectors who had been civil servants were temporarily barred from reappointment; absolutists were permanently excluded. This particular development prompted an outraged *Westminster Gazette* to note that "if Civil Servants are to be victimised for their moral convictions, men holding political opinions of any sort which are obnoxious to the Government of the day will be in danger of dismissal."[2] In 1922 a parliamentary committee was selected to investigate the question of prejudicial treatment of ex-C.O.s in the civil service; the recommendations of this select committee not only confirmed discriminatory practices but commended them. Conscientious objectors, said the committee, should not be promoted over the heads of army veterans, and any reduction in staff should be "made first at the expense of. . . Conscientious Objectors." Finally, any C.O. applying for a position in the civil service was to be preemptorily rejected.[3] This policy remained in force until 1929 when,

1. See John Rae, *Conscience and Politics: The British Government and the Conscientious Objector to Military Service, 1916-1919* (London, 1970), pp. 234-35.
2. Quoted by *Trib.*, 14 August 1919.
3. *Report from the Select Committee on the Civil Service (Employment of Conscientious Objectors)*, in Parliamentary Papers, April 1922 (69) and (69 Ind.), 4, 967.

under the second Labour government, the restrictions on promotion and employment were eased.[4] But for some absolutists discrimination did not end even then. In January 1932 Clifford Allen—lately become Lord Allen of Hurtwood—received a pathetic letter from Thomas Drayton, secretary of the Dismissed Men's Association of ex-Civil Service C.O.s, asking his aid in securing their reinstatement. There is no evidence in Allen's papers that he was able to help.[5] Thus, a few conscientious objectors continued to suffer economic deprivation for their opposition to the war, but, of course, economic deprivation was not an uncommon occurrence in the interwar period: many veterans of the Great War left the ranks of honorable service only to fill the ranks of the permanently unemployed.

In assessing the two wartime governments' performances with regard to conscientious objectors, it must be said that official resentment and public hostility adversely affected the treatment of war resisters. Furthermore, the inability of some prominent Liberal politicians to resist the pressure of popular distaste for C.O.s was at least a symptom of the decline of traditional liberal ideals and, with them, of the old Liberal party. It was not a happy moment in British history when some hundreds of men were severely punished for following their conscientious convictions. Neither was it a matter of pride that in punishing the most steadfast of these men, there was no alternative to a prison system whose silent inhumanity was scarcely dreamt of in proper society.

On the other hand, if there were shortcomings and failures in the treatment of conscientious objectors, one should not forget that incidents of gross brutality and culpable neglect were the exceptions and, more significantly, that Great Britain pioneered the concept of legal conscientious objection to military service. In 1940 as in 1916 legal recourse for conscientious objectors existed only in Britain and in the British Empire. During the two world wars of the twentieth century, only Great Britain and the United States recognized the legal possibility of conscientious objection. In America, however, conscientious objection was restricted to the reli-

4. Treasury Circular E 1206/4, "Civil Service and the Conscientious Objector," 10 September 1929.
5. Thomas Drayton to Clifford Allen, 6 January 1932, and Allen to Drayton, 13 January 1932, CAP.

gious realm and could not, as in Britain, be based solely on moral or ethical considerations.

Furthermore, the much improved administrative machinery for the treatment of British conscientious objectors during World War II indicated that public officials were sensitive to past deficiencies. There were over three times as many C.O.s in the Second World War as in the first, but the 60,000 in 1940 made far less impact than the 16,500 in 1916. The absence of an organization similar to the NCF that could unify anticonscription activities and propaganda may in part account for this situation, but in some measure it was due to the tolerance with which objectors were treated by the public and to the sensible administration of the law by the authorities. Changes in recruiting procedures and the establishment of separate semiprofessional tribunals to deal with C.O.s made the government's task simpler and allowed the individual objector's conscience to be more readily satisfied. There were cases of obvious injustice and brutal treatment, but these were rare.[6]

It has been noted that the NCF won no great victories in its struggle against conscription and militarism, but in this instance one might feel justified in modifying that conclusion. Because of its refusal to acquiesce in what it considered inadequate provisions for conscientious objectors, the NCF helped to make a significant contribution to the development of Anglo-American civil-rights law. Eventually, public officials became convinced of the necessity for treating pacifists in a special way, not only to enhance the war effort and to reduce their own burdens but also—and this was a considerable "also"—to preserve in British society the libertarian ideal of freedom of conscience. During the Second World War the government tacitly admitted that the "extremists" of the NCF had been correct in their insistence that forcing citizens to partake in war involved a different and higher order of things than forcing them to pay taxes or to buy licenses for their dogs. To be sure, it is an unusual, and

6. The best and most detailed account of the treatment of conscientious objectors in the Second World War is the later chapters of J. M. Rae, "The Development of Official Treatment of Conscientious Objectors to Military Service, 1916-1945" (Ph.D. diss., University of London, 1965). Also see Peter Brock, *Twentieth-Century Pacifism* (New York, 1970), pp. 154-71.

perhaps even illogical, legal code that demands recognition of "the majesty of conscience" and "the sanctity of human life" in the midst of a vicious, murderous war. But one can legitimately doubt that many Britons are embarrassed by such eccentricity.

Perhaps the best summary of the moderation and good sense of this policy during World War II was provided by Winston Churchill, whom C.O.s had considered their implacable enemy in 1919. When a question arose about the possibility of unjust treatment of some conscientious objectors, the prime minister noted: "Anything in the nature of persecution, victimisation, or man-hunting is odious to the British people."[7] And so it proved to be.

The NCF and Liberty

The No-Conscription Fellowship was one of a kind. There had never been an organization like it prior to 1914, and although conscription and world war were repeated within twenty years of its demise, no pacifist body in the Second World War came close to emulating the passionate, unyielding opposition of the NCF, let alone its accomplishments in political organization and propaganda. But to say that the fellowship was unique is not necessarily to say that it was significant. The importance of the NCF must be measured by other criteria, the most obvious of which is its ability to accomplish the goals it set for itself.

One particularly stirring piece of rhetoric that issued forth from the NCF headquarters at the height of its struggle against conscription and militarism emphasized that conscientious objectors were "not out to save . . . our own skins, we are out to save the world from war."[8] That objective proved to be beyond the capacity of a few thousand dedicated pacifists. In point of fact, the struggles and sufferings of conscientious objectors and other war resisters played no discernible part in bringing the war to an end. And the final military victory denied them even the vicarious joy that other stay-at-homes derived from their roles, however

7. 5 H.C., 370:284, 20 March 1941.
8. *Trib.*, 20 July 1916.

minor, in helping to win the war. In his *Autobiography* Bertrand Russell has summarized his own bitter sense of disillusion: "When the war was over, I saw that all I had done had been totally useless except to myself. I had not saved a single life or shortened the war by a minute. I had not succeeded in doing anything to diminish the bitterness which caused the Treaty of Versailles."[9]

No doubt this sense of futility was what motivated many of those who argued for the NCF's preservation in 1919. They must have felt that there was surely something more to be achieved or at least to be learned. After being insulted, hounded, hated, humiliated, and imprisoned for perservering in principles that they believed would have saved millions of lives, war resisters grasped for some permanent consequence or at least some soothing balm. But unless objectors had gained spiritual strength from their ordeal—as did perhaps the hundreds of C.O.s who were newly drawn to the Society of Friends[10]—there seemed to be little solace beyond the personal satisfaction of having refused to surrender. The continued search for enduring results may have inspired those ex-conscientious objectors who founded the NCF's direct descendant, the No More War Movement (NMWM). Formed in February 1921 as, in the words of its first chairman, "the spear-head of the *real* Peace movement in this country," the British NMWM associated itself with the War Resisters International and demonstrated its purity of principle by requiring a pledge of absolute pacifism.[11] Of course, it remained small in numbers and in influence, the merest shadow of the NCF in its great days.

Indeed, one might venture to devise a rule of thumb for peace groups during the twenties: the more explicit their pacifist doctrines, the smaller their membership. The only organization with impressive membership figures was the League of Nations Union (LNU). Because it played down

9. Bertrand Russell, *The Autobiography of Bertrand Russell*, 3 vols. (London, 1967-1969), 2:40.

10. See FSC *Minutes*, meetings of 5 December 1918 and 1 January 1920, 3:18, FHL.

11. William J. Chamberlain, *Fighting for Peace* (London, [1928]), pp. 118-29, and Brock, *Twentieth-Century Pacifism*, p. 109. Founders of the NMWM included Chamberlain, Fenner Brockway, Walter H. Ayles, and Wilfred Wellock, all former members of the NCF.

differences and emphasized sources of unity for its potential members, the LNU could make a home for absolute pacifists, liberal internationalists, doctrinaire socialists, and conservative supporters of collective defense, all of whom were supposedly working for the same ends. But while the total number of people affiliated with it seemed immense, the LNU, as events of the thirties tragically revealed, was singularly lacking in the capacity for effective united action.[12]

During the thirties the somewhat delayed reaction to the horrors of the Great War (partly inspired, perhaps, by fears of another) seemed to offer a promise of meaningful popular support for pacifist ideals, but the ultimate disintegration of the movement should have surprised no one. The scenario had been played out in the wartime quarrels within the NCF and between the fellowship and the Friends Service Committee. These disputes were not the cause of pacifist failures in the interwar years, but they were a somber portent of the persistent factionalism that undermined the peace movement.[13]

Still, if the No-Conscription Fellowship had been unsuccessful in either accomplishing its more grandiose wartime aims or in sustaining the intensity of its wartime resistance, both its aims and its resistance had some effect. For just as the internationalist ideas of the Union of Democratic Control influenced interwar foreign policy,[14] so the trials and sufferings of conscientious objectors helped to inspire a widespread revulsion against the monstrous evil that war

12. See Donald Birn, "A Peace Movement Divided: Pacifism and Internationalism in Inter-war Britain," *Peace and Change* 1 (Spring 1973):20-24. By 1933 the LNU claimed 1,000,000 members but, as Birn notes, that figure resulted from "a rather dubious form of double bookkeeping." The actual number of paid subscribers at the time was 388,255; ibid., p. 23. Birn's full-length study of the LNU is eagerly awaited.

13. On this theme, see Louis Bisceglia, "Norman Angell and the Pacifist Muddle," *Bulletin of the Institute of Historical Research* 45(1970):105-21, and Brock, *Twentieth-Century Pacifism*, pp. 126-30.

14. See Henry R. Winkler, "The Emergence of a Labour Foreign Policy in Great Britain, 1918-1929," *Journal of Modern History* 23 (September 1956):247-58; A. J. P. Taylor, *The Troublemakers: Dissent over Foreign Policy, 1792-1939* (Bloomington, Ind., 1958), pp. 156-200 passim; and Marvin Swartz, *The Union of Democratic Control in British Politics during the First World War* (Oxford, 1971), pp. 217-22.

288 / The Hound of Conscience

had inflicted on Britain and the world. In 1931 when George Bernard Shaw said "as far as the question was one solely of courage, the Conchy was the hero of the war," a growing number of his countrymen agreed.[15] Conscientious objection, far from being a bar to political success, was a stepping-stone to Parliament for at least a dozen former members of the NCF, among them some of the most admired and respected figures of the British political left.[16] Eventually, three of the four men who had served as chairmen of the fellowship became peers of the realm: Russell, as heir to his brother in 1931; Allen as a "National Labour" supporter of MacDonald in 1932; and Brockway, after a distinguished career in Commons, as a life peer in 1964. Ironically, however, just as the pacifist ideals of the NCF seemed to be gaining influence with public opinion, these former absolutists were discovering that the pacifist philosophy they had adhered to during the Great War was an inadequate response to the circumstances of the 1930s.

Allen abandoned absolute pacifism because of his support for a strong League of Nations and the realization that the league would need armed might to enforce its sanctions against aggressor states. When the league collapsed, Allen became one of Britain's leading amateur appeasers. Indeed, his final illness came on as a result of a private mission to convince Czech leaders of the necessity for international arbitration of the Sudeten question.[17]

Throughout most of the interwar years, Russell main-

15. George Bernard Shaw, *What I Really Wrote about the War* (London, 1931), pp. 214–15. For development of this theme, see Joyce Avrech Berkman, "Pacifism in England, 1914–1939" (Ph.D. diss., Yale University, 1967), pp. 49ff.

16. Former NCF members in Parliament included Morgan Jones (1921), Charles G. Ammon (1922), Alfred Salter (1922), C. H. Wilson (1922), Walter H. Ayles (1923), James H. Hudson (1923), A. Fenner Brockway (1929), Wilfred Wellock (1929), Arthur Creech-Jones (1935), Emrys Hughes (1946), and George Benson (1929). Other M.P.s who had been C.O.s were Herbert Morrison, F. W. Pethick-Lawrence, and Sidney Silverman.

17. For a good summary of Allen's views on interwar foreign policy, see his pamphlet *Peace in Our Time* (London, 1936). Lord Allen's attempts at personal diplomacy are discussed in Thomas C. Kennedy, "'Peace in Our Time': The Private Diplomacy of Lord Allen of Hurtwood, 1933–38," in *Doves and Diplomats*, ed. Soloman Wank (Westport, Conn., 1978), pp. 217–39.

tained the position he had held during the war, which he reiterated in *Which Way to Peace?* (1932), namely, that a true international government could legitimately use force to ensure peace; for all national armies, he still advised conscientious objection. In 1936 Russell joined the Peace Pledge Union and ostensibly became an absolute pacifist,[18] but with the coming of "Hitler's War" Russell abandoned pacifism altogether because he believed that a world controlled by Nazis would be even worse than a world in the throes of war.[19]

Brockway remained close to the heart of the peace movement for a long time. In 1921 he helped to organize the NMWM and later served as its chairman and as chairman of its parent organization, War Resisters International. During the late 1930s, however, Brockway gradually realized that he could not reconcile pacifism with his support of Republican Spain nor with the awful fact that fascism would never succumb to nonresistance. Hence, he forsook a principle to which he had passionately devoted most of his adult life and supported the Second World War as a necessary evil.[20] Indeed, with the notable exception of Alfred Salter, every major leader of the NCF during the Great War, including Catherine E. Marshall, accepted the necessity of using every means possible to defeat Nazi Germany.

Viewed from the perspective of 1940, then, survivors of the No-Conscription Fellowship could not claim to have fulfilled the primary objectives that they had pursued from 1914 to 1918. For just as all the sacrifices, all the earnest propaganda, and all the witness for peace through suffering had not availed to end or even to shorten the first war, so the spread of pacifist ideals during the interwar period had not created sufficient strength or resolve to prevent the second. Thus in 1940 the NCF veteran—by now, like most of his

18. Keith Robbins, *The Abolition of War: The "Peace Movement" in Britain, 1914–1919* (Cardiff, 1976), p. 212, citing Ponsonby ms., Russell to Ponsonby, 31 October 1936. Russell makes no mention of this incident in his *Autobiography*.

19. Russell, *Autobiography*, 2:191–92.

20. See A. Fenner Brockway, *Inside the Left* (London, 1942), pp. 130ff, and *Outside the Right* (London, 1963), pp. 17–18. Also see his statement in the foreword written for Denis Hayes, *Challenge of Conscription* (London, 1949), p. viii.

former leaders, probably a reluctant supporter of the war—might legitimately look back at the old struggle and ask despondently: "What real good came of it?"

In retrospect, what did come of it all was perhaps less meaningful than members of the NCF had hoped in 1916 but also probably more important than most imagined it to be twenty-five years later. Founded by and largely consisting of socialists who were dedicated to the international solidarity of the working classes and to the triumph of collectivist principles, the fellowship, unconsciously and almost by default, became Britain's most prominent defender of the liberal principle of freedom of conscience. And, in the final analysis, the success as well as the significance of the NCF lies in its contribution to the struggle for the preservation of human liberty.

The difficulties encountered by the NCF in attempting to articulate a universally applicable statement of principles, the internal disputes over policy, the hairsplitting over the rightness or purity of pacifist beliefs all pointed the way toward the ineffectiveness of the much larger but even less-cohesive interwar peace movement. Indeed, the inability of the peace movement to adopt some agreed-upon set of standards has recently been cited to illustrate the fact that during World War I "pacifists did not really know what peace was" and were therefore foolish ever to have tried to live by principles they could not define, let alone agree on. "Brave but rather silly" seems to be the verdict.[21] Such a view is singularly inadequate. Even before the end of the First World War, the NCF's most perceptive and realistic thinkers had come to appreciate that what they were truly struggling to obtain was not the establishment of a regime of international peace or the dictatorship of the unarmed proletariat. They fought instead for the preservation of the quintessential liberal ideal that all human beings have the right and the duty to decide their own actions in keeping with the dictates of their own consciences.

Russell has said that he resisted the war because his "whole nature was involved." Unquestionably, in 1914 pacifism was part of his nature, induced by the irrationality and brutality of war and most of all by his "unbearable pity for the suffer-

---

21. Robbins, *Abolition of War*, p. 122 and passim.

ing of mankind."[22] Socialism was also a part of his nature, impelled by his distaste and disdain for the injustice and inhumanity of a mature capitalist system. But the most important part of Russell's resistance was his passionate devotion to the dignity and worth of the individual human personality. Elie Halévy was surely correct when he said in 1935 "that if in fifty or a hundred years someone writes a history of modern English thought, he will class Bertrand Russell among the individualists and libertarians, not among the socialists." Russell himself told Constance Malleson in 1916: "I don't like the spirit of socialism—I think freedom is the basis of everything."[23]

Though he had a deeper ideological attachment to socialism, Allen followed his friend and mentor in concluding that "the struggle for personal liberty and thus for general liberty" was the most important aspect of the NCF's stand. The preservation of freedom of conscience would, he felt, ultimately be of "immense value" to all of society.[24] Allen's realization that the No-Conscription Fellowship had accomplished more in fighting for liberty of conscience than against conscription and militarism is certainly apparent in the preface he wrote for John W. Graham's *Conscription and Conscience*. When, in this essay, Allen summarized the attitude of the modern state toward the individual—"Make him work, make him kill, make him die, but don't make him important."—it was not only the capitalist state of which he spoke. (He had seen Lenin's Soviet state in 1920.)[25] Allen's hope was, therefore, that the No-Conscription Fellowship would be remembered and respected not because of its valiant failure to end militarism and to bring about the triumph of socialism, but because the fellowship sought to make each

22. Russell, *Autobiography*, 2:18, 1:13.

23. Elie Halévy, *The Era of Tyrannies*, trans. R. K. Webb (New York, 1965), p. 201, and Russell to Constance Malleson, 29 September 1916, in Russell, *Autobiography*, 2:74–75.

24. Allen's diary, 31 March 1918, incomplete typescript in CAP and quoted by Martin Gilbert, ed., *Plough My Own Furrow* (London, 1965), p. 111. Also see ibid., p. 95, where Russell comments on Allen's belief "that it is only through liberty that human beings can develop."

25. For Allen's trip to Russia, see Arthur Marwick, *Clifford Allen: The Open Conspirator* (Edinburgh, 1964), pp. 46–65. The quotation is from Allen's introduction to John W. Graham, *Conscription and Conscience* (London, 1922), p. 20, which strongly emphasized guild-socialist ideas.

person and the dictates of each conscience more important and more free.

What of the rank-and-file conscientious objectors who were caught up in the drama of the NCF? Were all of them also staunch defenders of liberty? Not all of them, certainly. Some fought always for a workers' state; some always in the name of God; and some undoubtedly were afraid or insincere or just did not want to be bothered. Still, most of them suffered enough to refute accusations of hypocrisy or sloth. Indeed, one cannot help admiring their steadfastness and their devotion to principle, especially if they were absolutists. But there is often a disquieting impression that Promethean courage and animal stubbornness are so closely entwined as to make it nearly impossible to decide which was most influential. Allen, whose body was permanently and perhaps unnecessarily ravaged by imprisonment, confessed in later days that the NCF's campaign "was carried on by the resisters far too often in a spirit of half-arrogant pride, not far removed from the militarism they sought to overthrow."[26]

Frequently, members of the fellowship, while demanding that the state recognize conscience as a two-way street, refused to admit the possibility of honesty in those who did not agree with them. This sort of intolerance was indignantly revealed by one clergyman who wrote to protest *The Tribunal*'s apparent attempt (following Shaw) to classify men of the cloth as neither pharisaical "disciples of Mars" (supporters of the war) or true Christians (opposed to it). "Why and how," asked the Reverend J. A. Douglas in ironic outrage, "can you bespatter me with persecution and abuse because I . . . act according to my conscience?"[27] The answer, of course, was that conscientious objectors, like ministers of every gospel, felt that they had a mission to save society and an ideal that could provide salvation. They were the few gathered in an upper chamber on whom the fiery tongues had descended, but when they went out to teach the redeeming word, they were greeted with scorn, hatred, and persecution. That made it difficult even for the truest believers. For them the No-Conscription Fellowship performed the great human service of letting some few despised and

26. Graham, *Conscription and Conscience*, p. 23.
27. *Trib.*, 17 and 31 August 1916.

troublesome people know that they were not entirely alone. Had the NCF never existed, there would, no doubt, have been fewer conscientious objectors, but one may legitimately wonder if there would not also have been fewer clear consciences.

Liberty of conscience is a great reward, but it was not the only one for the ordinary folk who followed the NCF's banner. From among them there emerged at least one characteristic feeling—they looked on their connection with the fellowship as the great adventure and the supreme achievement of their lives. The No-Conscription Fellowship linked them to a movement that, for all its shortcomings, rose above the mundane concerns of conventional lives and conformist thinking. It gave them some assurance that in their resistance to the awesome power of patriotic militarism, they had been more intelligent, more civilized, and more humane than generals, leaders, and kings. The Welsh schoolteacher, Emrys Hughes, writing from his prison cell, spoke for each of them:

> When I think of my life before I was arrested, of trying to fit into the environment of one of those soul-killing schools in the Rhondda Valley, of disheartening little encounters with the headmasters of the old regime and all the dismal shabbiness of life in a South Wales village, I feel a thrill to think of how we have challenged it all, refused to fight for the foul old ideas and tried to show the way to a better world.[28]

28. Emrys Hughes to Russell, 4 March 1917, BRA.

Appendix A

Divisional (7) and Branch (150) Secretaries of the NCF, 1917*

Division 1	For Divisional Secretary, see Glasgow
Barrhead	E. Ross Griffiths, Springhall View, Barrhead
Blantyre	Geo. Russell, 20 Clark St., Blantyre
Cowdenbeath	Tom Muir, 3 Roseberry Terrace, Perth Rd., C'Beath
Darnel	Wm. Dears, Wilson Place, Newmilns
Douglas Water	J. C. Welsh, 2 Carmichael St., Douglas Water
Dunfernline	J. MacInnie, 131 Chalmers St., Dunfernline
Dundee	Miss N. J. Dawtry (Dawtrey), 35 Perth Rd., Dundee
Edinburgh	Rev. R. V. Hold, 27 Woodburn Terrace, Edinburgh
Falkirk	Mrs. Jesse M. Munro, 17 Cochran St., Falkirk
Glasgow	A. M. Davidson c/o James Marshall, 19 Montrose St., Glasgow
Kilmarnock	A. K. Stitt, 26 Fleming St., Riscarton, Kilmarnock
Motherwell	James Johnstone c/o Rankin, 3 Melville Crescent, M'well
Paisley	A. Maxwell, 8 Johnson St., Paisley
Saltcoats	Thes Maxwell, Townhead St., Stevenson Nr., Saltcoats
Stirling	W. G. Gordon c/o Speedie, 31 Friars Croft, Stirling
West Calder	Adam Linn, North View West, Calder Nr., Edinburgh

*Copy of a list found in Friends Service Committee Files, Friends House Library, London.

Division 2	Divisional Secretary Miss Crutchley, Brook Houses, Little Mayfield, Derbyshire
Barrow and Furness	B. Longstaff, J. L. P. Rooms 8, DaDuke St.
Blackburn	W. Grimshaw, 32 Walt St., Blackburn
Bolton	G. Thompson, 8 Corporation Chambers, Corporation St., B'n
Burnley	R. Wilkington c/o Wesley Hartley, 3 Ness St., Brierfield, Burnley
Kendal	Miss E. Tayler, Horncop Cottage, Kendal
Carlisle	Hugh Dudley, 44 Sheffield St., Carlisle
Lancaster	Wm. Bruce, 5 Rose Cottage, Low Bentham Nr., Lancaster
Leich	T. Brundy, 12 Victoria St., Leich
Liverpool	Lonis A. Fenn, 147 Grove St., Liverpool
Manchester	Miss Kate Wallwork, 41 Oxford St., Manchester
Nelson	R. Bland, 203 Barkerhous Rd., Nelson
Oldham	S. M. Slater, 30 Harper St., Oldham
Penrith	Miss Mary Waid, 23 Graham St., Penrith
Preston	A. Bamber, ILP Rooms, 252 Church St., Preston
Ramsbottom	J. R. Leonard, 29 St. Paul's St., Ramsbottom
Rochdale	Fred Halliwell, 185 Belfield Rd., Rochdale
Rosendale	John Mudd, 5 Stansfield Rd., Waterfoot Nr., Manchester
Stockport	Miss Annie E. Pimlott, 93 Beech Rd., Gale Green, Stockport
Warrington	Albert Clatworthy, 114 Liverpool Road, Sankey, Warrington
Wigan	J. Tayler, 220 Ormskirk Rd., Newton, Wigan

Division 3	Divisional Sec. Mrs. Jack Lees, G3 Gainsbro Rd., Newcastle on Tyne
Ashington	S. E. Hunter, 10 Whitsun Gardens, Bedlington S.C., N'land
Bishop Auckland	Miss Ruby Stoddard, 12 Hackworth St., Dean Bank
Chopwell	Henry Bolton, 31 Clyde St., Chopwell, Co Durham
Jarrow/Tyne	Mark Simpson, 116 Argyle St., Hebburn/Tyne
Leadgate	J. A. Robinson, 8 Park Terrace, Leadgate, Co. Durham
Newcastle/Tyne	John Morley, 33 St. George Terrace, Desmond
South Shields	R. Macdonald, 131 Westoe Rd., South S.
Stockton on Tees	J. Williams, 23 Buckingham Rd., Stockton
Sunderland	Frank Tait, 27 Swing, Bank Cottages
West Hartlepool	F. Ward, 53 Murray St., West Hartlepool
Division 4	Divisional Sec. Mrs. E. Wray, Strathmore, New Conisboro
Barnsley	H. Booth, 288 Barnsley Rd., Cudworth. Nr., Barnsley
Bradford	J. Grashaw, 1 Norman Drive, Eccleshill, Bradford
Bingley	J. Millard, 18 Clavort St., Bingley
Brighouse	F. A. Bapish, 91 Bightcliffe Rd., Brighouse
Doncaster	Mrs. Katherine King, G. Glyn Ave., Christchurch Rd., Doncaster
Halifax	D. R. Stocker, Boro Market, Halifax
Huddersfield	Albert Johnson, Ravensknowle Rd., Modlgreen, H'field
Hull	S. H. Priestman, Ellerburn North, Ferriby East, Yorks
Keighley	H. G. Shackleton, 9 River Mount, Stockbridge, Keighley

Leeds	Arthur Mandefield, 4a Back Oxford Place, Leeds
Mytholmroyd	Herbert Middleton, 29 Havelock St., Sheffield
Wakefield	J. C. Haigh, 24 Queen St., Horbury, Wakefield
York	H. P. Bell, 62 Thorpe St., Scareroft Rd., York
Division 5	Divisional Sec. J. Austin, 41 Herbert Rd., Bearwood, Birmingham
Birmingham	Miss Mary B. Pumphrey, 9 Linden Rd., Bournville
Burton/Trent	J. Austin Smith, 4 Frederick St., Burton/Trent
Coventry	Dennis Criteph, 19 Clara Street, Coventry
Derby	Miss R. Wheeldon, 12 Peartree Nr., Derby
Kettering	E. A. Wade, CO Connought St., Kettering
Leicester	Miss Ella H. Stevens c/o Cafe Vegetaria, Market Place, Leicester
Lincoln	F. W. Shellbourne, 13 Toronto St., Monks R. Lincoln
Long Eaton	W. H. Jordon, 43 Curzon St., Long Eaton
Northampton	J. F. Oldham, 11 Derngate, Northampton
Peterborough	E. R. Green, 73 Granville St., Peterborough
Stoke/Trent	T. Horwill, 292 Prices Rd., Stoke/Trent
Storbridge	Harold D. Wrigley, 18 Belmont Rd., Wollescote Lye Nr., Storbridge
Walsall	J. H. Taylor, 1 Whitehall, Lane Palfrey, Walsall
West Bronwich	W. Sandall, 10 George St., West B.
Wolverhampton	Miss Annie Delaney, 68 Prossar St., Park Village, Wolverhampton
Division 6	Divisional Sec. Mrs. F. S. Mann, 4

Rolandale Mansions, Holmdale Rd., Hampstead

Bedford	Henry White, 14 Adelaide Square, Bedford
Bournemouth	Mrs. A. Hookey, 17 Spurgeon Rd., Pokesdown, Bournemouth
Brighton on Worthing	A. F. Deller, 17 Prestonville Terrace, Brighton
Cambridge	Mrs. Adams or better to W. E. Johnston, Romsey House, Barton Rd.
Canterbury	Stanley Michell, 22 St., Georges Terrace, Canterbury
Chelmsford	J. Youn, 100 Mildmay Rd., Chelmsford
Dorking	Mr. Aseley, Brendon, Radhill, Surrey
Grays	Mrs. Reid Andrews, Pear Tree Corner, Alyan Nr., Momford, Essex
Guildford	H. C. White, Davonham, Victoria Rd., Guildford
Harrow	Leonard Steele, Reshesay, 43 Bedford Rd., Harrow
High Wycombe	Mrs. Parker, Temple Orchard, High Wycombe
Ipswich	J. F. Brome, 26 Nararne St., Ipswich
Letchworth	Peter Mylles, 128 Nilbury Rd., Letchworth
Luton	Horace V. Hall, 35 Vernon Rd., Luton
Norwich	Miss Mary Churchward (Churchyard), 47 Connaught Rd., Norwich
Oxford	W. Chadwick, Wadham College, Oxford
Portsmouth	Miss H. Hatrill, 48 Telepone Rd., Southsea
Reading	G. Coppack, 62 Northumberland Avenue, Reading
Rochester	G. F. Osborne, 6 Morden St., Rochester
Sandown	Frank W. Brown, the Lodge Sandown I of W.

Sheerness	J. J. Williams, 80 Winstanley Rd., Sheerness
Southhampton	A. V. Price, Morris Hall, Commercial Rd., Southhampton
Southend	C. V. Hovett, 55 Beufort St., Southend/Sea
Tunbridge Wells	P. Douglas, 14 Dunstan Rd., Tunbridge Wells
Division 6a	Divisional Sec. Miss Sime Seraya, Little Orchard, Ashstead, Surrey
Barnsbury	W. J. Young, 38 Richmond Rd., Barnsbury
Battersea	Sydney C. Howes, 102 Mysore Rd., Lavender Hill S.W.
Bermondsey	A. T. Lewis, 92 Soughwork Park Rd., S.E.
Central London	Philip Millwood, 34 Tankerville Rd., Streatham S.W.
Chelsea	W. A. Duke, 46 Clancarty Rd., Fulham S.W.
Croydon	Francis Lawley, 1 Fernbank, Lakahall Rd., Thornton Heath
Dulwich	Mrs. E. Cahill, 60 Limas Grove, Lewisham S.E.
Ealing	C. H. Pratt, 1 Mervyn Rd., W. Ealing
Enfield	Harry Adams, 11 Abbey Rd., Bush Hill Park, Enfield
Erith	Miss Edith Hampton, 2 Hurst Rd., Northumberland Heath, Erith, Kent
Forest Gate	Miss K. Read, G. Torrells Sq., The Green Stratford
Golders Green	Miss F. Graham, 73 Wentworth Rd., Golders Gn to July 23
Hackney	Miss A. Stevens, 60 Kenninghall Rd., Clapton
Hampstead	F. A. Durrant, 15 Bathelomew Villas, Kentish Town
Highbury	G. W. Riley, 95 Benwell Rd., Drayton Park, Holloway

Ilford	H. W. Steele, Upton House, Brisbane Rd., Ilford, Essex
Kennington	Miss A. E. Jones, S. Kennington Oval, S.E.
Kentish Town	W. Hastman, 98 Rathcool Gardens, Hornsey N.
Kingston	F. J. Tritton, 65 Bond Rd., Subiton
Leyton	Miss Mary Serpell, 37 Selvorne Rd., Walthamstow
Loughton	E. P. Lovell, Homecroft, Chelmsford Rd., S. Woodford
Poplar	T. S. Attlee, 41 Ottwa Buildings, Poplar
Sutton	T. H. Baldwin, 1 Woodcote Green, Wallington, Sutton
Streatham	J. F. Wilkinson, 38 Thurlow Hill, West Dulwich
Tottenham	J. J. Ford, 128 Russell Avenue, Noel Park, Wood Green N.
Watford	W. Southwood, 96 Kings Avenue, Watford
West Central	Miss Marian Peppercorn, 67 Romney St., Westminster S.W.
Walthamstow	Miss Harvey c/o N.C.W., 8 Merton House, Salisbury Court
Wandsworth	Miss D. Ward, 72 Bermouth Rd., Wandsworth Common
Willesden	F. J. Ballard, 14 Wrentham Avenue, Willesden
Woolwich	S. French, 8 Bastion Rd., Plumstead
Division 7	Divisional Sec. Mrs. Harrison, 332 Whitechurch Rd., Cardiff
Aberdare	P. B. Williams, 118 Brynmair Rd., Cawnaman Glam.
Abercynon	J. R. Taylor, 38 Mountain Ash Rd., Abercynon S., Wales
Abertillery	Hy Gale, 10 Castle St., Abertillery
Bargoed	Moses Price, Fern Lea, Civerthones Rd., Pengarm Glam.
Blaenavon	F. Marchant, 67 High St., Blaenavon

Briton Ferry	H. Armstrong, 9 Tucker Street, Briton Ferry
Cardiff	E. F. Williams, 19 Lon Isa Rhubina, Cardiff
Cardiganshire	Rev. T. R. Nicholas, Llangybi, Cardiganshire
Cwmavon	J. Morris, D. London Terrace
West Glamorgan	W. J. Robetto (Roberts), 10 Weste St., Gorseinon Glam.
Maestag	A. Jones, 54 King St., Nantyglo
Newport	R. M. Ley, 2 Caerau Rd., Newport
Nanty Glo	J. F. Jones, 54 King St., Nantyglo
Pembrokeshire	B. T. L. Jones Penrhiw Tentelly, Boncath Pem.
Pontypridd	E. J. Williams, 37 Llantrisant Rd., Craig, Pontypridd
Port Talbot	Country Davies, 7 North St., Taibach, Port Talbot
Risca	Ken Burris, 22 Hine Mile, Point Rd., Watsville, Cross Keys
Swansea	Miss M. A. Harris c/o Swansea Socialist Centre, the Bomb Shop, Sidehall Building, Alexandra Rd., Swansea
Swansea Valley	T. Evans Dol'y'coed Ynismidw, Swansea Valley
Tonyrefail	T. J. Williams, 8 Pritchard St., Tonyrefail

Appendix B

COIB Reports on Conscientious Objectors July 1916–June 1917

Report No.	Date	Pages	In Army	In Civil Custody	2 Court-Martials	3 Court-Martials	4 Court-Martials
30	28 July 1916	116–19	1,715				
38	25 August 1916	145–47	1,945				
39	29 August 1916	148–50	1,987				
41	5 September 1916	154–55	2,085				
43	12 September 1916	160–62	2,192				
44	15 September 1916	163–65	2,220				
45	19 September 1916	166–68	2,260				
46	22 September 1916	169–70	2,295				
47	26 September 1916	171–73	2,331				
48	29 September 1916	174–76	2,369				
49	3 October 1916	177–78	2,426				
50	6 October 1916	179–82	2,459	521			
51	13 October 1916	183–85	2,514	553			
52	20 October 1916	186–89	2,576	640			
53	27 October 1916	190–93	2,656	770			
54	3 November 1916	194–97	2,734	806			
55	10 November 1916	198–201	2,806	856			
56	17 November 1916	202–5	2,878	921			
57	24 November 1916	206–8	2,961	937			
58	1 December 1916	209–11	3,050	1,070			
59	8 December 1916	212–14	3,126	1,129			
60	15 December 1916	215–17	3,196	1,165			
61	29 December 1916	218–20	3,249	1,172			
62	5 January 1917	221–23	3,361	1,195			
64	19 January 1917	227–29	3,411	1,216			
65	26 January 1917	230–32	3,487	1,232			
66	9 February 1917	233	3,512		408		
67	23 February 1917	234	3,591	1,146	437		
68	9 March 1917	235	3,641	1,200	454		
69	23 March 1917	236	3,715	1,281	478		
71	20 April 1917	238	3,935	1,422	536		
72	4 May 1917	239	4,003	1,471	543		
73	18 May 1917	240	4,111	1,493	563		
75	15 June 1917	242–43	4,284	1,564	596	157	8

Essay on Sources

What follows is not intended to be a complete catalogue of the sources that were consulted in the preparation of this study. This essay includes only those that were particularly valuable to me or that might be especially useful to other scholars pursuing other aspects of the resistance to the First World War and conscription.

I. Private Papers and Other Unpublished Sources

Army Museums Ogilvy Trust, Whitehall, London
    Spencer Wilkinson Papers

Beaverbrook Library (now transferred to the House of Lords Record Office), London
    Bonar Law Papers
    Lloyd George Papers
    J. St. Loe Strachey Papers

Bodleian Library, Oxford
    Asquith Papers (courtesy of Mark Bonham Carter)
    Gilbert Murray Papers
    Milner Papers (courtesy of New College, Oxford)

British Library, British Museum, London
    Balfour Papers
    Marker Papers

Cumberland County Record Office, the Castle, Carlisle
    Catherine E. Marshall Papers (microfilm copies of material on the No-Conscription Fellowship in possession of Jo Vellacott, Acadia University, Wolfville, Nova Scotia

    Friends Library, Friends House, London
    Friends Service Committee: *Minutes, Records of Work and Documents Issued.* 3 vols. June 1915–May 1920
    Friends Service Committee, Correspondence, 1915–1919
    Friends Service Committee Files including Edith Ellis, R. O. Mennell, and Hubert W. Peet Correspondence (sixteen unsorted boxes)
    Minutes of the Meeting for Sufferings, 1915–1917
    T. E. Harvey Papers

Imperial War Museum
    Henry Wilson Papers (courtesy of Maj. Cyril Wilson)

McKissick Library, University of South Carolina, Columbia, S.C.
    Clifford Allen (Lord Allen of Hurtwood) Papers

Mills Memorial Library, McMaster University, Hamilton, Ontario
    Bertrand Russell Archives

National Army Museum, London
    Lord Roberts Papers

National Library of Scotland, Edinburgh
    Lord Haldane of Cloan Papers

Public Record Office, London
    Cabinet Papers
    Cromer Papers
    Home Office Papers, Class 45
    Kitchener Papers
    Ministry of Health Papers, Classes 10 and 47
    Roberts Papers
    War Office Papers, Class 32

Swarthmore College Peace Collection, Swarthmore, Pa.
    Miscellaneous material on the No-Conscription Fellowship
    Sydney R. Turner Papers

Of these sources, the Allen Papers, Marshall Papers, Russell Archives, and Friends Library Collection are indispensable for any study of the No-Conscription Fellowship—or for any study of the pacifist left in Britain during the first World War. In addition to extensive private letters and other papers, the Allen collection contains an invaluable unpublished manuscript by Clifford Allen that presents his reflections on conscription and on conscientious objection in light of his wartime experiences. There is also a fascinating short memoir by Arthur Maxwell Sanders, a rank-and-file member of the NCF and the ILP, which provides a rather different perspective than that found in the autobiographies and memoirs of more famous conscientious objectors. Catherine E. Marshall was an inveterate collector who seems to have saved, though in a loose and haphazard fashion, every piece of paper in her possession, including a great mass of material on the NCF. Jo Vellacott generously allowed me to use microfilm copies of this material. The Bertrand Russell Archives consist, first and foremost, of Russell's immense personal correspondence, but they also contain a considerable number of unpublished manuscripts from the period of the Great War. Taken altogether, this extremely well-organized collection provides an excellent picture of the NCF's internal organization and activity during 1916 and 1917 and is a gold mine for anyone studying dissenting opinion during the First World War (or at almost any other time in the twentieth century). The Friends Library is easily the best source on religious pacifism and much of its material has not been previously consulted. In 1920 the COIB entrusted its records and files to the Friends Library. These were apparently stored in unsorted boxes that remained virtually untouched even after the library moved from Devonshire House to its present location in Euston Road. While this collection mainly consists of routine correspondence, there is much valuable material on the relationship between religious and other pacifists, especially on the disputes that so troubled the peace movement.

All these collections contain circular letters, leaflets, pamphlets, and books printed by the NCF and other pacifist groups, as does the Swarthmore College Peace Collection.

II. Published Sources

A. *Official Publications*

Command Papers

1916 Cd. 8149 Report of Recruiting by the Earl of Derby, K.G., Director General of Recruiting

1917 Cd. 8527 Committee on Employment of Conscientious Objectors: Rules

Cd. 8884 Committee on Employment of Conscientious Objectors: Additional Rules

1919 Cmd. 131 Inquiry Held into the Allegations Made against the Acting Governor of Wandsworth Prison

1921 Cmd. 1193 General Annual Reports of the British Army for the Period from 1st October 1913 to 30th September 1919

Other Government Publications

Manual of Military Law, The War Office, 1919
Military Operations in France and Belgium, 1916, His Majesty's Stationery Office, 1919
Parliamentary Debates, 1900–1919
Registration and Recruiting, The War Office, August 1916
Report from the Select Committee on the Civil Service (Employment of Conscientious Objectors), April 1922
Rules for Military Detention Barracks and Military Prisons, 1912
Statistics of the Military Effort of the British Empire during the Great War, The War Office, 1922

The best guide to official sources on the reaction to and on the treatment of conscientious objectors is John Rae's *Conscience and Politics: The British Government and the Conscientious Objector to Military Service, 1916–1919* (London, 1970), pp. 260–63.

B. *Reference Material*

Useful information on the various Military Service Acts and on the general public's reaction to conscientious objectors can be found in the *Annual Register*. The best contemporary guide to the acts is William Grist Hawtin, *The Law and Practice of Military Conscription under the Military Service Acts*. 2 vols. (London, 1917–1918), which gives a thorough explanation of various provisions and also summarizes some of the more important exemption appeals argued before the central tribunal.

Some of the NCF's official publications are also valuable works of reference. Probably the single most important reference source is the Kraus reprint edition (1970) of *The Tribunal,* with an introduction by John G. Slater. Published in 182 numbers between 8 March 1916 and 8 January 1920, *The Tribunal* was absolutely indispensable to the completion of this work as a cursory glance at the footnotes will indicate. The Kraus edition has no index but is much easier to work with than the incomplete collections of *The Tribunal* in the Allen Papers, the Russell Archives, and the Swarthmore College Peace Collection. Another NCF publication, *C.O.'s Hansard,* is a compilation of debates on the C.O. question in both houses of Parliament running to 97 numbers between 5 January 1916 and 10 April 1919. It is a most convenient means of keeping up with changing policies and especially with parliamentary questions on conscientious objectors. There is, however, no cross-reference with the official *Debates* and the researcher must check both sources to ensure the accuracy of the NCF version. The Allen Papers contain the most complete available set of *C.O.'s Hansard.*

Extracts from the Minutes and Proceedings of the London Yearly Meeting of Friends (London, 1923) is helpful in discovering the "official" position of the Society of Friends on various aspects of the conscription question as is the *Proceedings of the Meeting for Sufferings, Summary, 1917-18* (London, 1921). Biographical information on most major and some minor figures can be found by consulting the *Dictionary of National Biography, Palmer's Index to "The Times," Who's Who,* and *Who Was Who.* Also useful are *Dod's Parliamentary Companion* and J. Vincent and M. Stenton, eds., *McCalmont's Parliamentary Poll Book, 1832-1918* (Brighton, 1971).

C. Autobiographies, Biographies, Diaries, and Memoirs

Most of the leading figures in the NCF have left some personal account of their activities with the fellowship. The most detailed is Allen's unpublished manuscript in the Allen Papers in which he discusses various aspects of the conscientious objectors' stand and the difficulties that arose between factions within the peace movement. He says little, however, about the internal organization of the fellowship. This work can be supplemented by chapters 1-4 of Arthur Marwick's brief but competent biography, *Clifford Allen: The Open Conspirator* (Edinburgh, 1964), and through the documents and letters from the Allen Papers reprinted in Martin Gilbert, ed., *Plough My Own Furrow: The Story of Lord Allen of Hurtwood as Told through His Writings and Correspondence* (London, 1965). A. Fenner Brockway's *Inside the Left* (London, 1942) enthusiastically provides inside information on the movement and is excellent on his prison experiences, but since Brockway has some nice words to say about nearly everyone, the NCF's internal feuds do not emerge too clearly. *The Autobiography of Bertrand Russell,* vol. 2, *1914-1944* (London, 1968), is surprisingly brief regarding his association with the NCF, though Russell does reprint some important and informative letters from this period. Ronald W. Clark's biography, *The*

Life of Bertrand Russell (New York, 1976), makes good use of the Russell–Ottoline Morrell correspondence and offers some new material on Russell's relations with the authorities; Clark is also revealing in his treatment of Russell's complicated personal life during this time. More of that personal life will probably be revealed when the "Letters to Bertrand Russell from Constance Malleson, 1916–1919" are published; the typescript of these letters in the BRA is, unfortunately, still not available to researchers. The most complete published account of Russell's wartime activities is Jo Vellacott Newberry's excellent essay, "Russell and the Pacifists in World War I," in *Russell in Review,* edited by J. E. Thomas and Kenneth Blackwell (Toronto, 1976). A revised version of her doctoral thesis, "Bertrand Russell and the Pacifists in the First World War" (McMaster University, 1975), which promises to be the definitive work on this phase of Russell's career, will be published by Harvester Press. In the meantime one can read Constance Malleson, *After Ten Years* (London, 1931). Marshall left no memoirs, but Vellacott Newberry is now writing a much-needed biography of this remarkable woman.

Other useful autobiographical and biographical material by or about prominent war resisters includes:

Bell, Julian, ed., *We Did Not Fight* (London, 1935). A collection of essays written in the mid-1930s by a variety of war resisters including Allen and Edward Grubb.

Brockway, A. Fenner. *Bermondsey Story* (London, 1949). A biography of Dr. Alfred Salter that includes a brief description of his work for the NCF.

Catchpool, T. Corder. *On Two Fronts* (London, 1918). A saintly Quaker's account of his service in the Friends Ambulance Unit and in the fight against conscription.

Chamberlain, William J. *Fighting for Peace* (London, [1928]). A former NCF leader establishes the link between the NCF and later pacifist movements; distinctly an insider's view.

Dudley, James. *The Life of Edward Grubb, 1854–1939: A Spiritual Pilgrimage* (London, 1946). Some information on Grubb's role as NCF treasurer.

Grubb, Edward. *The True Way of Life* (London, [1909]). Outlines the pacifist philosophy that Grubb put into practice as treasurer of the NCF; good for religious pacifism.

Hobhouse, Stephen. *Autobiography* (Boston, 1952). Good on prisons and prison reform.

Norman, C. H. *A Searchlight on the European War* (London, 1924). The NCF's perpetual malcontent is still highly critical of the policy followed by the fellowship, which, in his view, played into the hands of the government.

Members or friends of the NCF were responsible for a number of books on the prison system. Scott Duckers, *Handed Over* (London, [1917]), relates the experiences of one liberal pacifist with special emphasis on conditions in military and civil prisons. *I Appeal unto Caesar* (London, [1917]), by far the most widely read of wartime exposés on prison life, was credited to Mrs. Henry (Margaret) Hobhouse, but, as Jo Vellacott Newberry has shown in "Russell as Ghost Writer, a New Discovery," *Russell* 15 (Autumn 1974):19–23, the piece was largely written by Russell. The man who inspired Mrs. Hobhouse's secret collaboration with Russell on behalf of conscientious objectors, her son Stephen, also wrote extensively on the prison system including *An English Prison from Within* (London, [1919]) and, with Brockway, *English Prisons Today* (London, 1922). Even though it is, at times, somewhat ponderous, the latter study provides a wealth of information, much of it given by ex-C.O.s, on the repressive atmosphere and harsh practices in English penal institutions. The book is still used as a reference work for contemporary writings on the prison system such as Giles Playfair, *The Punitive Obsession* (London, 1971). Another interesting though somewhat pretentious account of a C.O.'s prison experience is Edward Williamson Mason, *Made Free in Prison* (London, [1918]).

There are several chronicles of the war years by individuals who were not directly involved with the NCF but who were well acquainted with its leaders and methods. These outsiders looking in view the fellowship's work from a different perspective, whether or not they entirely agree with its methods and aims. The best of these is Mary Agnes Hamilton, *Remembering My Good Friends* (London, 1944), which provides charming and incisive portraits of NCF leaders such as Allen, Russell, and Ernest E. Hunter. She also contrasts the passive, comfortable criticism of the Garsington circle with the difficulties and sacrifices of NCF activists. Beatrice Webb was generally critical of the NCF and its activities, but her *Diaries, 1912–1924*, edited by Margaret I. Cole (London, 1952), are extremely perceptive and valuable in showing the place of the NCF on the British left. Other accounts that briefly deal with some aspect of war resistance in the First World War include:

Graves, Robert. *Good-bye to All That,* 2d rev. ed. (Garden City, N.Y., 1957). Dispassionate but moving account of a soldier–poet's journey to disillusionment; presents the Sassoon affair from the soldier's view, which is not at all flattering to pacifists.

Pankhurst, Sylvia. *The Home Front* (London, 1931). Some informative commentary on various war resisters and on public reaction to them.

Sassoon, Siegfried. *Memoirs of an Infantry Officer* (New York, 1920). Slightly fictionalized account of Sassoon's wartime experiences with sketches of various pacifists including Bertrand Russell.

Shaw, George Bernard. *What I Really Wrote about the War* (London, 1931). Includes Shaw's letters and articles attacking government treatment of conscientious objectors with typical Shavian abandon.

Snowden, Philip. *Autobiography.* 2 vols. (London, 1934). The "M.P. for the No-Conscription Fellowship" gloats a bit over his courageous and provocative defense of conscientious objectors in Parliament.

The entire question of conscription and conscientious objection caused immense problems for many politicians and government officials, as well as considerable public ill-will. In *Episodes and Reflections* (London, 1930) Gen. Sir Wyndham Childs recounts some of the difficulties he encountered in attempting to deal with querulous C.O.s. Understandably he is somewhat hostile but also—as his wartime opponents were always forced to admit—unflinchingly honest and fair. Michael MacDonagh, *In London during the Great War* (London, 1935), contains some reflections on conscientious objectors by a journalist who is more puzzled than angered by their behavior. Stephen McKenna's *While I Remember* (New York, 1922) gives the thoughts of a Liberal civil servant who was disgusted and horrified by the war though he never openly dissented. The most useful "inside" accounts on the development of government policy on conscription and conscientious objection are Christopher Addison's two memoirs of the wartime period, *Politics from Within, 1911–1918*. 2 vols. (London, 1924), and *Four and a Half Years: A Personal Diary from June 1914 to January 1919*. 2 vols. (London, 1934), which provide insights into personal attitudes and opinions and also reveal the details of some cabinet deliberations. Randolph Churchill's *Lord Derby: King of Lancashire* (New York, 1960) is good on the Derby scheme, while Lord Riddell's *War Diary, 1914–1918* (London, 1933) reports the unguarded comments of major figures, especially Lloyd George. Also useful is A. J. P. Taylor's edition of *Lloyd George: A Diary by Frances Stevenson* (New York, 1971); Stevenson was the great Welshman's secretary, mistress, and finally his second wife. The most informative and detailed attempt to deal with conscription as a political question is Alfred Gollin, *Proconsul in Politics: A Study of Lord Milner in Opposition and in Power* (New York, 1964). Gollin's emphasis on the importance of the conscription issue before May 1915 has been challenged by Cameron Hazlehurst in *Politicians at War* (New York, 1971). The promised later volumes of this study should add depth to Hazlehurst's impressive arguments even if they do not settle the controversy. Additional information on the conscription question can be found in:

Amery, L. S. *My Political Life*, vol. 2, *War and Peace, 1914–1929* (London, 1953). Presents a strong proconscription bias.

Beaverbrook, Lord. *Politicians and the War, 1914–16* (London, 1928). Deals with some aspects of the conscription question.

Blake, Robert. *The Unknown Prime Minister: The Life and Times of Andrew Bonar Law, 1859–1923* (London, 1955).

George, David Lloyd. *War Memoirs*. 6 vols. (London, 1933). Reveals surprisingly little about the problems over conscription.

James, David. *Lord Roberts* (London, 1954).

Jenkins, Roy. *Asquith: Portrait of a Man and an Era* (London, 1965). Good on Asquith's resistance to conscription and on his method of playing off the opposition.

Wilson, Trevor, ed. *The Political Diaries of C. P. Scott, 1911–28* (Ithaca, N.Y., 1970). Scott was a reluctant supporter of the war and an opponent—up to a point—of conscription, but under his editorship the *Manchester Guardian* consistently advocated decency and common sense in the treatment of conscientious objectors.

D. Pamphlets, Tracts, and Articles by Anticonscriptionists and War Resisters

Each of the private collections listed earlier contains a wealth of pamphlet literature as well as clippings and offprints of various articles about the NCF and its members. Nearly everything published by the NCF—well over a hundred separate titles—seems to have been preserved in one or the other of these archives. Some of the NCF's basic documents include its "Statement of Principles" and "Manifesto," both issued in 1915, as well as the pamphlet *Why We Object* (London, n.d.). Also important are Allen's address to the first national convention in November 1915, reprinted as *Conscription and Conscience* (London, 1916), and his article in the *Labour Leader,* 20 June 1916, "The Conscientious Objector's Struggle: A History of the No-Conscription Fellowship." A postwar summary of the fellowship's activities and achievements is *The No-Conscription Fellowship: A Souvenir of Its Work during the Years, 1914-1919,* edited by A. Fenner Brockway (London, 1919), and later reprinted as *Troublesome People* (London, 1940). This "souvenir" is a useful compendium of reflections and stories but is not too revealing on the NCF's organizational structure or on the various disputes within the group.

Pamphlets and articles that discuss the fellowship or some of its leaders include:

Grubb, Edward. "A Fruitful Furrow and One Who Is Ploughing It," *Ploughshare* 1 (September 1916):236-37. Brief essay praising the ideals and leadership of Clifford Allen.

Meyer, Frederick B. *The Majesty of Conscience* (London, [1917]). A Congregational minister and supporter of the war asks that justice be accorded conscientious objectors.

"The NCF," *Ploughshare* 1 (November 1916):323-24.

The No-Conscription Fellowship: A Record of Its Activities (London, [1917]).

The No-Conscription Fellowship: A Summary of Its Activities (London, n.d.).

The Position of the Conscientious Objector (London, n.d.).

Repeal the Act (London, [1916]). Leaflet for which most of the NCF's national committee was fined and imprisoned under DORA.

Rex v. Bertrand Russell (London, 1916). Largely verbatim transcript of Russell's first trial that also includes the speech that the magistrate would not allow Russell to finish.

Some examples of the attacks on the tribunal system are G. K. Chesterton, "Nonsense, Conscience and the Law," *Sunday Chronicle,* 16 April 1916, which ridicules the idea of attempting to judge the genuineness of any man's conscience, and *Not Genuine* (London, n.d.), chiefly an attack on the central tribunal. Also see Philip

Snowden's two pamphlets, *The Military Service Act* (London, 1916), which explains the workings of the system, and *British Prussianism* (London, 1916), the combining of two parliamentary speeches in which Snowden vigorously assaulted the operation of the tribunals. Literature concerned with the absolutist–alternativist dispute includes two important pieces by Clifford Allen, "Alternative Service," *Ploughshare* 1 (May 1916):101–4, and *Why I Still Resist* (London, [1917]), in which he sets forth his reasons for maintaining an absolutist position. Also useful are Miles Malleson, *The Out-and-Outer* (London, [1916]); Hubert W. Peet, "Alternative and 'National' Service," *Ploughshare* 2 (June 1917):142–43; and an NCF pamphlet, *Compulsory Military Service and Alternative Service and the Conscientious Objector* (London, [1916]). Two highly critical attacks on the operation of the Home Office scheme are C. G. Ammon, *Waste of National Resources* (London, [1917]), and Ernest E. Hunter, *The Home Office Compounds: A Statement as to How Conscientious Objectors Are Penalized* (London, n.d.).

In addition to the books listed earlier, the NCF, its members, and friends also published a sizable body of pamphlet literature on the English prison system.

A. Fenner Brockway's *The C.O. Clink Chronicle* (London, n.d.) is a somewhat jocular look at the means used by C.O.s and other prisoners to circumvent the prison rules, especially by publishing clandestine newspapers, but *Prisons as Crime Factories* (London, 1919) by the same author is a deadly serious socialist attack on the entire basis of the prison system. William J. Chamberlain's *A C.O. in Prison* (London, [1916]) is an occasionally informative but generally silly piece that may have misled some C.O.s into thinking that prison might not be so terrible after all. No one, however, who read Stephen Hobhouse, *The Silence System in British Prisons* (London, n.d.), or Hubert W. Peet, "112 Days' Hard Labour," published as a supplement to *Ploughshare* (April 1917), was likely to be amused. Two other NCF publications—*The Court-Martial Friend and Prison Guide* (London, [1918]) and a mimeographed booklet, *The Visitation of Conscientious Objectors in Detention or Prison*—are filled with useful and enlightening material on English civil and military prisons.

E. Studies on Pacifists, Conscientious Objectors, and Other War Resisters

The standard work on pacifism and conscientious objectors during the First World War is John W. Graham, *Conscription and Conscience* (London, 1922; reprinted 1971). Graham's book, which is written from the viewpoint of the religious pacifist, contains valuable information garnered from firsthand sources. It suffers, however, from a self-declared bias on behalf of conscientious objectors and thus is often embarrassingly partisan. The best corrective to Graham's one-sided view is Rae's *Conscience and Politics,* which presents the story largely from the viewpoint of the government rather than from that of the C.O. Rae's study follows the development of official policy toward conscientious objectors in its legal, political, and moral aspects, and, to a large extent, he succeeds in clarifying the reasons why the government acted as it did. While Graham ascribes government policies injurious to C.O.s to secret conspiracy or personal malice, Rae believes that such policy generally arose from bureaucratic incompetence, the pressure of public opinion, or well-meaning misunderstanding. A weakness in Rae's work is the tendency to identify with government officials, and, like them, to give the NCF too little credit for sincerity of purpose. Keith Robbins, *The Abolition of War: The "Peace Movement" in Britain, 1914–1919* (Cardiff, 1976), follows Rae in pointing up the shortcomings and inconsistencies of wartime peace advocates but is far more strident in questioning the genuineness of their motives. Unfortunately, Robbins's seeming distaste for war resisters is accompanied by numerous errors and distortions, especially in his treatment of the NCF. On the other hand, David Boulton, *Objection Overruled* (London, 1967), is obviously sympathetic to conscientious objectors but the result is, to a considerable extent, an up-to-date rendering of Graham with the addition of a socialist (rather than religious) bias. The finished product is marred by sensationalism and by the assumption that government officials and soldiers were out to get conscientious objectors. More straightforward but less-detailed with regard to the NCF is Denis Hayes, *Conscription Conflict* (London, 1949), which covers the dispute over military conscription from the early years of the twentieth century to the outbreak of the Second World War. It is an excellent reference work for bibliography, though somewhat outdated by now. Hayes continued the story of British conscientious objectors up to 1949 in *Challenge of Conscience* (London, 1949). Another useful work on war resistance is Robert Donington and Barbara Donington, *The Citizen Faces War* (London, 1936); Robert Donington was Allen's private secretary in the 1930s. The best brief account of British C.O.s in the First World War is chapter 2 of Peter Brock, *Twentieth-Century Pacifism* (New York, 1970). Brock has made excellent use of memoirs and secondary works. An important book that was published too late to be incorporated into this study but is an outstanding contribution to literature in this field is Martin Ceadel, *Pacifism in Britain, 1914–1945: The Defining of a Faith* (Oxford, 1980).

There are a number of other works that indirectly or partly deal with the NCF or with conscientious objectors:

Dowse, Robert E. *Left in the Centre: The Independent Labour Party, 1893–1940* (London, 1966). Shows the importance of the "conchie" faction in shaping the postwar constitution and programs of the ILP.

Marwick, Arthur. *The Deluge: British Society and the First World War* (Boston, 1965). Contains a brief section on the NCF and on the problems arising from conscription.

Playne, Caroline E. *Society at War, 1914–1916* (London, 1931).
———. *Britain Holds on, 1916–1918* (London, 1933).

Pollard, Robert S. W. *Conscience and Liberty* (London, 1940). Briefly discusses the NCF as part of an essay on the necessity of maintaining liberty of conscience, even in wartime.

Swartz, Marvin. *The Union of Democratic Control in British Politics during the First World War* (Oxford, 1971). Excellent not only in putting the UDC in proper perspective but also in using cabinet papers to reveal the extent of government concern over all antiwar groups.

F. Studies on British Politics and Society

Clarke, I. F. *Voices Prophesying War, 1763-1914* (London, 1966). The standard work on invasion literature, very good on the period immediately prior to the Great War.

Cole, G. H. D. *History of the Labour Party from 1914* (London, 1948). Useful in dealing with Labour's ambiguous position on conscription and war.

Cunningham, Hugh. *The Volunteer Force: A Social and Political History, 1859-1908* (Hamden, Conn., 1975). An excellent study of the development, composition, and political influence of the volunteers.

d'Ombrain, Nicholas. *War Machinery and High Policy: Defense Administration in Peacetime Britain, 1902-1914* (London, 1973). The best study to date of the ideas, organization, and political importance of the British army before the Great War.

Foot, M. R. D., ed. *War and Society: Historical Essays in Honour and Memory of J. R. Western, 1928-1971* (New York, 1973). Useful essays on conscription both before and during the war.

Fraser, Peter. *Lord Esher* (London, 1973). Useful for wartime politics.

Halévy, Elie. *The Rule of Democracy, 1905-1914* (New York, 1961). Provides considerable information on the prewar influence of militarism and on the debate over the need for conscription.

Howard, Michael. *Studies in War and Peace* (New York, 1971). Contains an excellent essay on Haldane and the territorial army.

Playne, Caroline E. *The Pre-War Mind in Britain* (London, 1929). Deals with the influence of racialism, imperialism, and militarism in preparing the public mind for enthusiastic support of the war.

Semmel, Bernard. *Imperialism and Social Reform: English Social-Imperial Thought, 1895-1914* (London, 1960). Includes an interesting discussion of the influence of Lord Roberts and the National Service League.

Springhall, John. *Youth, Empire and Society: British Youth Movements, 1883-1940* (London, 1977). This book, a carefully researched study of the influence of youth movements before and after the Great War, has the unusual distinction of being too short for its own good; much more could and probably should have been said.

Steiner, Zara S. *Britain and the Origins of the First World War* (New York, 1977). The section on "The Domestic Contest" in prewar British society is an outstanding synthesis; this book is an invaluable contribution to the historical literature of the period.

Taylor, A. J. P. *English History, 1914-1945* (Oxford, 1965). The section on British society in the First World War is provocatively brilliant.

————. *Politics in Wartime and Other Essays* (London, 1964). His essay on wartime politics is an extremely valuable contribution to the issue.

————. *The Troublemakers: Dissent over Foreign Policy, 1792–1939* (Bloomington, Ind., 1958). Contains a long section on the ideas and influence of E. D. Morel and on the Union of Democratic Control.

Wilson, Trevor. *The Downfall of the Liberal Party* (Ithaca, N.Y., 1966). Most informative on debate within the Liberal party over the conscription question.

Wrigley, Chris. *David Lloyd George and the British Labour Movement: Peace and War* (Hassocks, 1976). A convenient and well-written summary, though it offers few new interpretations.

G. Selected Articles and Essays

Boulton, David. "Rebels in Uniform," *Observer Weekend Review*, 7 August 1966. Rather sensational presentation of the story of the thirty-four conscientious objectors sentenced to be shot in 1916.

Clarke, I. F. "The Battle of Dorking, 1871–1914," *Victorian Studies* 8 (June 1965):307–27. Discussion of invasion literature and its influence.

Douglas, Ray. "Voluntary Enlistment in the First World War and the Work of the Parliamentary Recruiting Committee," *Journal of Modern History* 42 (December 1970):564–85. Excellent on background to and working out of the Derby scheme.

French, David. "Spy Fever in Britain, 1900–1915," *Historical Journal* 21/2(1978):355–70. An interesting and sometimes amusing discussion of the sort of public credulity that aided the anti-German campaigns of groups like the National Service League.

Gollin, Alfred. "Freedom or Control in the First World War (the Great Crisis of May 1915)," *Historical Reflections* 2 (Winter 1975):133–55. A continuation of the debate over the importance of compulsory service and other government controls in the wartime political contest.

Kennedy, Thomas C. "Fighting about Peace: The No-Conscription Fellowship and the British Friends Service Committee, 1915–1919," *Quaker History* 69/1 (Spring 1980):3–22. A study of the disputes between two factions of the peace movement largely based on previously unused material from the Friends Library.

————. "Public Opinion and the Conscientious Objector, 1915–1919," *Journal of British Studies* 12 (May 1973):105–19. Attempts to determine the influence of public opinion on government policy toward C.O.s.

————. "Philosopher as Father-Confessor: Bertrand Russell and the No-Conscription Fellowship," *Russell: Journal of the Bertrand Russell Archives* 5 (Spring 1972):11–13. Brief discussion of Russell's importance to the NCF.

Nevinson, Henry W. "The Conscientious Objector," *Atlantic*

Monthly 118 (November 1916):686–94. A British friend of the NCF paints a heroic picture of suffering conscientious objectors for American readers.

Newberry, Jo Vellacott. "Anti-War Suffragists," *History* 62 (October 1977):411–25. An effective refutation of the widely accepted myths that proponents of female suffrage nearly all followed the Pankhursts into the prowar camp and that the militants' support for the war (rather than the constitutionists' careful spadework) was chiefly responsible for female inclusion in the Representation of the People Act (1917).

———. "Russell in 1916," *Russell* 2 (Summer 1971):9–10. Describes Russell's earliest work for the NCF.

Satre, Lowell J. "St. John Brodrick and Army Reform, 1901–1902," *Journal of British Studies* 15/2 (Spring 1976):117–39. Best discussion to date of Brodrick's abortive proposals for army reform.

Slater, John G. "What Happened at Leeds?," *Russell* 4 (Winter 1971–1972):9–10. Brief but informative piece on the Leeds conference of 1917 and on Russell's part in it.

Springhall, J. O. "The Boy Scouts, Class and Militarism in Relation to British Youth Movements, 1908–1930," *International Review of Social History* 16 (1971–pt. 2):125–58. Ground-breaking study of the relationship between youth movements and the growth of the military spirit and influence before and after the Great War.

Stearns, Stephen J. "Conscription and English Society in the 1620s," *Journal of British Studies* 11 (May 1972):1–23. Indicates the widespread practice of enforced military service in the early seventeenth century.

Stubbs, J. O. "Lord Milner and Patriotic Labour, 1914–1918," *English Historical Review* 87 (October 1972):717–54. A fascinating account of Milner's oddly disjointed attempts to form a kind of national socialist organization in order to capture labor from the socialists and the pacifists.

Summers, Anne. "Militarism in Britain before the Great War," *History Workshop* 2 (Autumn 1976):104–23. Incisive discussion of the importance of groups such as the National Service League.

Weinroth, Howard. "Norman Angell and *The Great Illusion:* An Episode in Pre-War Pacifism," *Historical Journal* 27/3 (1974):551–74. The best brief discussion of the influence of Norman Angellism on the British peace movement.

White, Stephen. "Soviets in Britain: The Leeds Convention of 1917," *International Review of Social History* 19/2 (1974):167–93. Supersedes all previous studies.

H. Novels

The best fictionalized account of working-class attitudes toward the war is provided by Walter Allen's *All in a Lifetime* (London, 1959), a superb and sensitive chronicle of the twentieth-century workingman. The "Nightmare" section of D. H. Lawrence's *Kan-*

garoo (London, 1935) gives a frightening though perhaps over-drawn picture of the pressures applied to people suspected of less-than-enthusiastic support for the war. A. J. Cronin, *The Stars Look Down* (New York, 1935), contains a most unflattering picture of a local tribunal in action as well as a rather sensational view of a C.O.'s suffering in prison.

III. Newspapers and Journals

The Daily Express, 1914-1919
The Friend, 1914-1919
The Granite Echo: Organ of the Dyce C.O.s 1 (October 1916):1
The Herald, 1915-1919
The Labour Leader, 1914-1917
Manchester C.O.'s Journal, July-November 1918, January-March 1919
Manchester Guardian, 1902-1919
The Nation in Arms, 1907-1914
The National Service Journal, 1903-1907
NCF News, March 1918
The Ploughshare, 1916-1919
Punch, 1914-1916
The Times, 1902-1919
The Tribunal, 1916-1920

Index